D1567884

NORTHERN PRAIRIE WETLANDS

NORTHERN

IOWA STATE UNIVERSITY PRESS / AMES

PRAIRIE WETLANDS

EDITED BY **ARNOLD VAN DER VALK**

Arnold van der Valk is Professor, Department of Botany, Iowa State University, Ames, Iowa 50010.

Although the compilation of information into this document has been funded wholly or in part by the U.S. Environmental Protection Agency agreement 6B0984NAWX to Dr. Arnold van der Valk of Iowa State University's Department of Botany, it has not been subjected to the Agency's review and therefore does not necessarily reflect the views of the Agency, and no official endorsement should be inferred.

Composed by Iowa State University Press from author-provided disks.
Printed in the United States of America.

First edition, 1989

Library of Congress Cataloging-in-Publication Data

Northern prairie wetlands.

    Papers presented at a regional symposium held in Nov. 1985 at the Northern Prairie Wildlife Research Center, Jamestown, N.D. and sponsored by the National Wetlands Technical Council.
    Includes index.
    Contents: Politicoeconomic overview of prairie potholes / Jay A. Leitch—Hydrologic studies of wetlands in the northern prairie / Thomas C. Winter—Chemical characteristics of water in northern prairie wetlands / James W. LaBaugh—[etc.]
    1. Wetland ecology—Great Plains—Congresses.   2. Wetlands—Great Plains—Congresses.
I. van der Valk, Arnold.   II. National Wetlands Technical Council (U.S.)
QH104.5.G73N67   1989   574.5'26325'0978   88–9266
ISBN 0–8138–0037–4

CONTENTS

PREFACE

THIS book is primarily a review of the ecology of palustrine and lacustrine wetlands in the northern prairie region, although a number of the chapters contain previously unpublished information. It developed out of a symposium held at the Northern Prairie Wildlife Research Center of the United States Fish and Wildlife Service in Jamestown, North Dakota, in November 1985. This region was defined for the purposes of the symposium as the prairie pothole region in the United States and Canada plus the Nebraska sandhills. It was one of a series of symposia held around the country under the auspices of the National Wetlands Technical Council. These regional symposia were held to review what was known about the ecology of each region's wetlands and to identify their unique features. It was the Council's belief that differences in regional climate and topography made the wetlands in each region unique and that this had to be taken into account when a region's wetlands were evaluated.

Currently, ideas about why wetlands are valuable (e.g., for flood storage, production of economically important crops of plants or animals, nutrient retention, etc.) that are derived from studies in one region often are applied uncritically to wetlands in other regions. For example, wetlands that export organic matter are considered more valuable than those that do not in the wetland evaluation scheme of Adamus (1983) that has been adopted by the U.S. Department of Transportation and many other federal and state agencies. This evaluation criterion is based primarily on studies of salt marshes along the Atlantic coast. Salt marshes are valued along this coast because dissolved and particulate carbon exported from them is believed to be an important energy source for estuarine food chains that produce commercially important fish and shellfish.

The concept that export of carbon enhances the value of a wetland is nonsense, however, when applied to prairie potholes. Prairie potholes mostly are closed basins that receive irregular inputs of water from their surroundings and usually only export to groundwater. On the basis of this criterion, prairie potholes would not be considered valuable for "food chain support" in the Adamus system. Nevertheless, prairie potholes are responsible for a significant percentage of the annual production of many species of economically important waterfowl in North America. In coastal wetlands, carbon exported from salt marshes may directly or indirectly provide energy to animals in the adjacent estuary; in prairie potholes, the animals have to go to the wetlands to get this energy. What is important when evaluating both is that each produces economically important crops of animals. Whether or not organic matter is exported from a wetland is only a meaningful criterion for evaluating the overall secondary production of coastal wetlands (i.e., in a specific regional context).

Although the best way to establish criteria to evaluate wetlands is within a regional context, this is only possible if enough information about their composition, structure, primary and secondary production, mineral cycling, and the like exists and is accessible in the form of books, monographs, or review articles. Sufficient information is often available, but it is rarely in an accessible form. This is the case for the wetlands of the northern prairie region. The regional symposia sponsored by the National Wetlands Technical Council were designed to rectify this situation.

In this volume, what is known about the ecology of wetlands of the northern prairie region is reviewed for people with a professional interest in them, but who may have a limited background in wetland ecology. Anyone with a university degree should be able to read and comprehend all of the chapters without undue difficulty. Nevertheless, some of the chapters are more technical than others, and depending on their backgrounds, readers may find some chapters more challenging than others. It is not the purpose of this book to develop or even suggest criteria for evaluating the wetlands of the northern prairie region.

Not only did the authors of all papers participate in the Jamestown symposium, but so did many other people from around the region who deal with its wetlands as researchers, managers, and administrators. Through their comments and suggestions at the symposium and as reviewers of the papers, these people have made a significant contribution to this volume. I would particularly like to thank George Swanson, who helped to organize the symposium; the rest of the staff of the Northern Prairie Wildlife Research Center for their hospitality and assistance; and Dr. Joseph S. Larson of the National Wetlands Technical Council, who was responsible for overseeing the regional symposia and who obtained funding for them from the William H. Donner Foundation, Inc., the

U.S. Fish and Wildlife Service, the Environmental Protection Agency, and the U.S. Army Corps of Engineers. The publication of this book was underwritten by a grant from the U.S. Environmental Protection Agency.

Editorial work on this book was performed while I was on leave from the Department of Botany, Iowa State University, at the Department of Plant Ecology, University of Utrecht, the Netherlands. I would like to thank Professor Peter van der Aart for allowing me to spend my leave in his department and the Nederlandse Organisatie voor Zuiverwetenscappenlijk Onderzoek (ZWO) who provided a grant (B 84-249) to support me while I was there. I would like to thank particularly Jos Verhoeven who did much to make my stay in the Netherlands productive, interesting and enjoyable. Additional support for my leave was provided by the Delta Waterfowl and Wetlands Research Station. Bruce Batt and Henry Murkin deserve special thanks for their patience and tolerance while I worked on this book and neglected my responsibilities to MERP. This is publication number 44 of the Marsh Ecology Research Program, a joint project of the Delta Waterfowl and Wetlands Research Station and Ducks Unlimited Canada.

I have dedicated this book to four people: J. Henry Sather, Jennifer Walker Shay, Peter Ward, and Milton Weller. They have had, each in their own very different way, a profound influence on my development as a wetland ecologist. I hope they will find some merit in it.

REFERENCES

Adamus, P. R. 1983. A method for wetland functional assessment. Vol. 2. FHWA assessment method. FHA Report No. FHWA-IP-82-24. Washington, D.C.: DOT.

INTRODUCTION

THE northern prairie region includes the prairie pothole region and the Nebraska sandhills. Here agriculture is the dominant economic and social force that determines how land is used. Since the region began to be settled by Europeans, beginning generally less than 100 years ago, most of the prairies and many of their associated wetlands have been ploughed up and put under cultivation. Where prairie survives, as in the Nebraska sandhills, it is used as rangeland. The wetlands that were a prominent feature of the prairie landscape have fared better than the prairies themselves. They were more difficult and costly to bring under cultivation. Nevertheless, after settlement, each year more and more wetlands were drained, often with the encouragement and aid of local, state or provincial, and federal government agencies. Today, there are parts of the region where most of the wetlands are gone. Where they remain, almost all of them are affected directly or indirectly by agricultural activities within their watersheds or basins.

Exploitation of the region's natural resources allowed its economic development, and initially there was little opposition to it. The wetlands of the prairie pothole region, however, were very early recognized as a major breeding area for waterfowl in North America. They are often cited as producing between 50 and 75% of the continent's waterfowl (see Batt et al. Chap. 7). As losses in wetland habitat became more and more widespread, this began to have a noticeable impact on fur bearer and waterfowl populations. Eventually significant objections to the loss of wetlands came from trappers within the region and waterfowl hunters both within and outside the region.

But not just hunters and trappers decried the drainage of wetlands. An early commentator on the economic and social significance of wetland drainage in Iowa, W. J. Berry, believed that it was as disastrous for farmers because it put too much land into production. And too much

Prairie wetlands in central North America.

land in production meant crop surpluses and low prices. In 1927, he wrote:

But notwithstanding the additions to cereal production and the increased prosperity that it has brought to north-central Iowa, there is some question as to whether or not the State and the United States as a whole have yet received any real benefits from this drainage. It has, indeed, enabled farmers to produce more corn, but more than the markets could absorb could have been produced on the corn lands already in use. With the exception of a few war-time years drainage has merely contributed to a surplus that has so upset farming conditions as to threaten the very foundations of agriculture. . . . It [drainage] has lowered the ground-water table throughout much of the State and it has destroyed the most valuable breeding grounds of migratory birds in [the] central United States. It would have been better to have left the swamp lands in their original state until, even when the most careful farming methods were employed, the older lands of the corn belt were being taxed to produce the crops demanded by the markets.

It is one of the great tragedies of the region, for not only its farmers, but also waterfowl hunters, trappers, conservationists, and taxpayers all over the United States and Canada, that no one paid any attention to the economic message in Berry's paper.

In the United States, pressure from waterfowl hunting interests did begin eventually to try to reverse the loss of wetland habitat. In response to this pressure, the federal government issued Duck Stamps to fund a program of wetland acquisition and purchase of conservation easements that is administered by the U.S. Fish and Wildlife Service.

Waterfowl populations, however, were not only being affected by habitat loss, but also by fluctuations in the amount of wetland habitat in the region from year to year caused by fluctuations in annual precipitation. The drought during the 1930s caused a significant decline in waterfowl populations, and this, combined with losses of habitat due to drainage, stimulated the formation by concerned waterfowl hunters of Ducks Unlimited. The sole purpose of this first international organization concerned with wetlands was to preserve and improve wetland habitat in the prairies of western Canada. A second institution that started during this same period as a result of the similar concerns was the Delta Waterfowl Research Station in Delta, Manitoba. It began as a duck hatchery but soon became an influential research organization concerned with waterfowl biology and wetland ecology and management.

This conflict between agricultural and wildlife interests is the most important and longstanding conservation issue in the region in both the United States and Canada. It has profoundly affected the type of wetland research that has been done and the types of institutions concerned with wetlands in the region. Not surprisingly the majority of it has been concerned with the ecology of breeding waterfowl, and most of the remainder with wetlands as waterfowl habitat.

The Northern Prairie Wildlife Research Center of the U.S. Fish and Wildlife Service in Jamestown, North Dakota, has been a major center for work on waterfowl, vegetation, mammals, and invertebrates. A great deal of wetland research done by graduate students has been funded through this institution. Manitoba has the distinction of having two wetland research stations located within the same marsh. The University of Manitoba's Delta Marsh Field Station is best known for the work on wetland vegetation carried out by former director Dr. Jennifer Walker Shay and her students. The nearby Delta Waterfowl and Wetlands Research Station is internationally renowned for its work on waterfowl biology. This private station for many years has funded the research of graduate students from all over Canada and the United States. Much of what we know about prairie wetlands comes from work done at or through one of these three institutions. The remainder comes from work done by the Canadian Wildlife Service, primarily the Saskatoon office, and at a handful of universities in the region, most notably Iowa State University, North Dakota State University, the University of Nebraska, and the University of Saskatchewan. Another important institution in the region is Ducks Unlimited Canada, headquartered in Winnipeg. Although it has not been involved in research directly, it has sponsored many important wetland research projects, primarily through the University of Manitoba and the Delta Waterfowl and Wetland Research Station.

As would be expected, the coverage of different aspects of the ecology of northern prairie wetlands in the literature is highly uneven, and reflects the concerns of wetland ecologists and their employers. The topics that have received most attention include the biology of waterfowl breeding in the region, the impact of agriculture on wetlands and water-fowl, and the impacts of periodic droughts (wet-dry cycles) and decreasing annual precipitation from east to west (salinity gradient) on the region's wetlands and waterfowl. This bias is reflected in the topics covered in this volume. There are two chapters on waterfowl; agricultural impacts are dealt with in several chapters; and the myriad impacts of wet-dry cycles are examined in many chapters. There are no chapters, however, on invertebrates, reptiles, amphibians, non-game birds, etc. Little is known yet about the ecology of these species in northern prairie wetlands.

The first chapter by Jay Leitch deals with the social and economic conditions in the prairie pothole region and their impacts on the perception that farmers, business executives, and politicians in the region have of its wetlands. This is an important topic since these perceptions must be understood and appreciated if any headway is to be made in preserving the region's remaining wetlands. As Berry pointed out 60 years ago, wetland drainage occurred in spite of the fact that it was not in the economic interest of farmers.

The next three chapters deal with hydrology and water chemistry. They describe the physical and chemical environment of northern prairie wetlands. Tom Winter reviews what is known about the hydrology of prairie potholes and the wetlands of the Nebraska sandhills. The chapter emphasizes the importance of groundwater flows at different scales for these wetlands. Jim LaBaugh's chapter deals with wetlands water chemistry in general, with an emphasis on the relationship between groundwater movement and salinity. The nature of agricultural runoff and what happens to it when it passes through a wetland are reviewed by Bob Neely and Jim Baker.

The flora and fauna are covered in seven chapters. The composition, classification, and dynamics of vegetation of wetlands in the prairie pothole region are reviewed by Kantrud et al. while Bill Crumpton covers the role of algae in these wetlands. There are two chapters on waterfowl. Batt et al. examine the historic importance of the prairie pothole region for 12 species of ducks by analyzing data collected each spring along a series of transects flown across the region. How ducks exploit different kinds of wetlands as habitat (nesting, feeding, shelter, etc.) is reviewed by Swanson and Duebbert. Information on fur-bearing mammals and fish found in prairie potholes is found in chapters by Erik Fritzell and John Peterka, respectively. Fritzell's chapter also covers the impact of predation on waterfowl recruitment. The final chapter dealing with the flora and fauna of northern prairie wetlands by Henry Murkin examines what is known about their food chains and the relative importance of herbivory and detritivory.

An overview of the ecology of the wetlands of the Nebraska sand-hills is provided by Jean Novacek in the last chapter. Although the Nebraska sandhills are just south of the prairie pothole region, very few ecologists working in one area have worked in the other. Two notable exceptions are Tom Winter and Jim LaBaugh and their chapters on hydrology and water chemistry, respectively, also cover the Nebraska sandhills. The remaining chapters in this book cover primarily or exclusively the prairie pothole region.

REFERENCES

Berry, W. J. 1927. The influence of natural environment in north-central Iowa. Iowa Journal of History and Politics 25:227–98.

NORTHERN PRAIRIE WETLANDS

JAY A. LEITCH

1 POLITICOECONOMIC

ABSTRACT

GLACIAL GEOLOGY, midcontinent temperature extremes, and low annual precipitation together have influenced land form in the prairie lands of the upper Midwest. Settlement of the prairies by northern Europeans little more than 100 years ago began a history of agricultural land development that continues today. Agriculture is the economic backbone and predominant mindset of the people and governments of the area. Prairie wetland issues of concern to government decision makers include economic development, proper land management, maintaining local autonomy, and maintaining a property tax base. Economic and attitudinal factors surrounding prairie wetland use important to prairie farmers include cropland expansion alternatives, farm machinery technology, a strong agricultural heritage, real estate taxes on wetlands, and the nuisance of farming around wetlands.

KEY WORDS: prairie potholes, policy, government, economics, attitudes, history.

OVERVIEW OF PRAIRIE POTHOLES

INTRODUCTION

G LACIERS that covered and then retreated from the central North American landscape over 12,000 years ago left behind millions of depressions in the glacial drift that held rainfall and snowmelt (Wills 1972). The semiarid, midcontinent climate turned this Swiss cheese landscape into a biogeographical system now known to many as the prairie pothole region (See Fig. 2.1). The region encompasses some 300,000 square miles in five states and three provinces (Luoma 1985). The high density of prairie potholes, their transitory nature, and their politicoeconomic setting set them apart from all other North American wetland types (Leitch 1984).

Climate

The climate of the prairie pothole region, which straddles the north 49th parallel, is characterized by midcontinent temperature and precipitation extremes. Jamestown, North Dakota, for example, experiences summer highs of over 38°C (100°F) and winter lows below minus 40°C (−40°F). The east-west, wet-dry dividing line, the 100th meridian, passes through the region just east of Minot, North Dakota. Average annual precipitation ranges from over 56 cm (22 in.) in the southeast to barely 25 cm (10 in.) along the western perimeter. The most critical climatic factor, at least for agriculture, is precipitation that comes mostly as erratic summer rains falling in scattered, isolated cloudbursts. Wetlands, however, usually fill in the spring when snowmelt runs off the frozen soil. These variable weather conditions cause subsequent varia-

JAY A. LEITCH, Department of Agricultural Economics, North Dakota State University, Fargo, North Dakota 58105.

tion in the extent of prairie wetlands basins holding water from year to year (Nelson et al. 1984; Tiner 1984).

Settlement

Settlement of the region began around 1878 with the end of the Indian wars, following a period of fur trade in the early 1800s, a military period through the 1860s, and the coming of the railroad in the 1870s (Hudson 1985). The region remains sparsely populated with descendants of European settlers, particularly Scandinavians. Swedes, Norwegians, Poles, Germans, and Irish were among the first to come, followed by the French, Italians, and Ukrainians. Many were first-time immigrants, while others were following the frontier westward.

Settlers came to farm the glacial drift prairie that was sometimes hilly or rocky, and often too wet for farming. The prairies did not need to be cleared of timber or stumps, but once the streamside timber was gone, settlers imported lumber from Minnesota and points east. Settlement was accelerated by the Homestead Act of 1862, extensions of railroads and stage lines, road building, and improved river transportation. The U.S. Swamp Lands Acts of 1849, 1850, and 1860 promoted drainage of wetlands that were seen as a menace and a hindrance to land development. Approximately 65 million acres of wetlands were given to 15 states for reclamation to lessen destruction caused by inundations and to eliminate mosquito-breeding swamps (Shaw and Fredine 1956).

Taming of the prairie landscape continued through the 1960s and into the 1970s when environmental interests succeeded in stopping most overt government support of wetland drainage (Leitch and Danielson 1979). However, the long-held notion that wetlands are obstacles to economic development continues in the minds of many prairie farmers and others promoting economic development (Leitch and Scott 1984). "Agriculture still remains top priority with Iowa. Wetland alterations are generally accepted by public as well as elected officials" (U.S. Congress 1984, 192).

Agriculture remains the economic base of the prairie pothole region. Variations in growing season and rainfall across the region bring about a different mix of crops, from corn and beans in southern Minnesota to canola and barley in Alberta. Except for these differences in crops grown, the prairie landscape, with its numerous potholes and drainage ditches, is essentially homogeneous across the pothole region. A casual observer transversing the region from northcentral Iowa to central Alberta would notice little if any difference in the landscape.

While energy development (e.g., coal and oil) has occurred during the past few decades in the region, its impact on prairie wetlands has not been significant. The infrastructure associated with agricultural development – urban service areas and transportation/utility networks – represents the only significant influence on wetlands other than farming itself. For instance, drainage of nearly 100,000 acres of prairie wetland in western Minnesota has been facilitated by outlet ditches provided by roads and highways (Tiner 1984).

The region's population has always been sparse, with a peak in the early 1900s when most of the region was covered with small farms (Wills 1972). Population declined until recently because of a general upward trend in the country and energy development in the region. While farm size continues to increase, increases in urban populations more than replaced displaced farm labor.

Drainage

Before the white man began to settle the prairie pothole region, there were an estimated 8 million hectares (20 million acres) of potholes in the region (Frayer et al. 1983). In spite of difficulties in inventorying potholes (Nelson et al. 1984), well over half may have been converted to other uses, primarily agriculture (U.S. Congress 1984). For example, North Dakota's potholes are being drained at a rate of 20,000 acres each year (Luoma 1985) while Iowa's wetlands have all but disappeared due to drainage.

Drainage methods change, from subsurface tiles to surface drains, as one moves northwestward across the region. Drainage in the Dakotas and on the Canadian prairies is accomplished mostly through surface ditching. Much of the ongoing drainage is done in the fall after crops have been harvested and the fields are dry using farmer-owned equipment. Today's high-horsepower, four-wheel-drive tractors enable prairie farmers to do most of the drainage they previously could not do themselves.

GOVERNMENT SETTING

State, provincial, and local governments in the region are primarily interested in the social and economic well-being of their constituencies. The predominantly agricultural economic base has led to an underlying foundation of both de facto and de jure regulations, programs, and institutions that are favorable to agricultural development, yet are no longer explicitly prodrainage. North Dakota drainage laws, for example, were enacted to protect downstream landowners, rather than to protect wetlands from drainage (North Dakota Legislative Council 1985). Among those in the line of drainage permit approval in North Dakota are county water management boards, formerly known as county drain boards.

Local Governments

Local governments include hundreds of townships, cities, counties, municipalities, and special districts. Specifics of government structure in the region have been discussed elsewhere. (See, for example, Leitch and Danielson 1979; U.S. Congress 1984; or Saxowsky and Leitch 1981.) To understand the prairie pothole issue fully, one needs to be familiar with the land survey system that defines township boundaries and the method of recording land ownership. This system has led to considerable controversy in the U.S. portion of the region relative to U.S. Fish and Wildlife Service wetland easements (Sagsveen 1985).

Land in the region (both U.S. and Canada) was surveyed using the township/range system. This is a north/south grid in six-mile intervals with occasional corrections to account for the earth's curvature. Townships are the north/south delineation in six-mile intervals. Ranges are the east/west delineation in approximately six-mile intervals. While the baselines for the township/range system vary depending on location, the system looks generally like a checkerboard of six-mile by six-mile (36 square miles) squares. Each square is called a township. Most U.S. townships are government jurisdictions, with powers granted in state constitutions. Within each township, there are 36 sections (one-mile by one-mile) of 640 acres each. Each section can be further subdivided into halves, quarters, and so forth depending on how many different owners there might be within a section. Prior to 1976, easements purchased by the U.S. Fish and Wildlife Service on lands described by the township/range system did not specify the extent or identify the location of wetlands within blocks of land put under easement. This has led to a considerable number of legal problems and to a less than desirable reputation for the U.S. Fish and Wildlife Service.

By their very nature, local governments are provincial; focusing on local, not national, concerns. Water management has traditionally been the bailiwick of local governments, with the exception of interstate or contested issues, which may be elevated to higher authority (i.e., state or provincial governments). Those elected to represent residents of local jurisdictions (county commissioners, town board members, municipal boards, etc.) generally represent majority opinions and interests. That almost always means agriculture or agribusiness in the prairie pothole region. Local politicians are often only one or two generations removed from their parents or grandparents who settled the region. Their mindset is one of developing the land for agriculture, rather than of preserving it for wildlife or other environmental values. Local politicians have referred, tongue in cheek, to cattails (*Typha latifolia*) as Canadian thistle (*Cirsium arvense*), suggesting how they feel about wetlands! Four issues are especially important to locally elected decision makers concerning prairie wetlands.

Maintenance or enhancement of a property tax base. The major source
of revenue for local governments is real estate taxes. Local decision
makers perceive wetlands as wastelands that contribute little or nothing
to property tax revenues. Real property taxes on wetlands in the range of
$0.25 to $1.00 per acre are a small fraction of the tax on developed
agricultural land. Payments in lieu of taxes (PILOT) by the U.S. Fish
and Wildlife Service do little to appease this problem due to the mechanisms through which they are paid and subsequently distributed to local
jurisdictions (Dorf et al., 1979). Payments to counties in lieu of taxes on
federal lands have only once been made at the 100% level. In most years
the payment is about 50% of the authorized level (National Water Resources Association 1985).

Economic development. Rural economies whose infrastructures are built
around production and export of agricultural commodities are fa-
vorably impacted by intensifying use of existing cropland and developing additional agricultural land. More lands brought into production
lead to increased levels of business activity for the grain elevator, implement dealer, bank, grocery store, hardware store, shoe store, and others
(Leitch and Scott 1984).

Control of noxious weeds. A major responsibility of upper midwest
town boards (township governments) is weed control. Local decision makers, as well as landowners, frequently complain about inadequate weed control on public lands managed for wetland preservation
(Smutko et al. 1984).

Disdain for Big Brother. Revenue sharing, intergovernmental transfers
of funds, and farm programs notwithstanding, local governments in
the region prefer local control over their jurisdictions. Every acre of land
managed or owned by the federal government is viewed as a reduction in
local autonomy.
　These concerns, combined with the provincialism inherent in government, have created a local political atmosphere that is at best neutral
toward wetlands, but often overtly hostile. This, however, is no more or
less than one would expect, and should not be construed as berating their
logical positions.

State Governments
　The apparent postures of state governments in the region toward
wetlands vary (Saxowsky and Leitch 1981). Minnesota, represented by a
strongly urban legislature, has enacted pro-wetland legislation, though
largely without adequate funding or enforcement.
　North Dakota, on the other hand, represented by predominantly

rural, agriculturally minded legislators, is de facto against wetland preservation. The U.S. Supreme Court recently ruled that a state law halting wetland acquisition in North Dakota was improper. While the prohibition was tied to another issue (the Garrison Diversion Project), it represented the state's lack of concern for this resource.

South Dakota has all but ignored the issue of wetland preservation at the state level.

These three dissimilar state postures stem from internal influences and are not at all unlike what one would expect — up-front, well-intentioned representation of the body politic. The mood of the states toward wetlands, while more broadly construed, is of a nature similar to local governments, with two issues being paramount.

States' rights. State governments, like local governments, want to maintain as much autonomy over their lands and peoples as possible. They feel water management, especially of such nondescript waters as wetlands, is their prerogative as states.

Economic and tax base. States are concerned about maintaining and enhancing their tax and economic bases, the primary base being agriculture. Income and sales taxes comprise the main state-level sources of revenue in the region. Thus, state-level decision makers see wetland preservation programs as threatening to their traditional livelihood.

Provincial Government

This chapter focuses on issues in the United States' pothole region primarily because those issues are of longer duration, are more sharply focused, and attract more attention. This is not to imply that there are not similar problems on the Canadian prairies, but they pale in significance when compared to the United States.

There are at least three explanations for this marked difference. First, provincial governments assert more authority in Canada than do state governments in the United States, thus the Canadian national government is less of a presence in rural areas. People tend to be more receptive to programs of governments closer to them. Also, while the United States prairie region was only recently settled, much of the Canadian prairie is even younger in terms of settlement and subsequent agricultural development. Finally, many potholes on the Canadian prairie have been protected by the private sector (i.e., Ducks Unlimited Canada) working *with* prairie farm operators.

SOCIOECONOMIC SETTING

The socioeconomic setting is the least understood and most difficult to describe of all prairie pothole environments. Wetland scientists have studied and described the physical, biological, chemical, and hydrological functions of wetlands in detail, although still not enough is known in some areas for effective policy-making. But, policy-making involves the *choices people make,* direct as well as indirect, regarding uses of wetland resources. Socioeconomic issues contributing to the ongoing controversy surrounding prairie wetlands are generally conceptual, attitudinal, or economic.

Conceptual Issues

Property rights. Effective, equitable natural resource policy cannot be developed without first deciding who has property rights relative to wetland resources. Do landowners have an unlimited right to convert wetlands, or does society have some rights to the flow of wetland benefits (Leitch 1981)? The nature of effective policy is a function of the answer.

The taking issue. A legal issue surrounding wetlands is whether wetland regulatory programs take away from individuals any rights to use their property without due process. This is related to the issue of who has what property rights, but extends to the broader issue of potential redistribution of wealth from landowners to users of wetland products and services. Notwithstanding that the courts have generally ruled that it is not a taking but an exercise of police powers, the issue has not abated.

Public versus private goods. The theoretical foundation of the wetland controversy lies in the classic case of private versus public goods. Generally, by definition, public goods and common property resources do not provide revenue to private individuals who may contribute to their production. For example, who would pay for sediment trapping, food-chain support, flood storage, or the heritage values of wetlands? On the other hand, there are established markets for sunflower oil, hard red spring wheat, and T-bone steaks.

Attitudinal Issues

Nuisance. Potholes in cropland are a nuisance that often require several separate tillage practices (Leitch and Scott 1977). They attract nuisance wildlife and hunters, are a haven for noxious weeds, and catch snow in winter.

Recreational drainage. Because wetlands have been traditionally treated, in practice as well as in law, as impediments to farming, "good" farmers drain them. Being a good farmer means having clean fields. Neighbors look down on those who allow potholes to remain in their cropland. Just as some feel that wetlands have a heritage value, so do others feel that cropland has aesthetic and heritage values (Halstead 1984; Manning 1973; Bergstrom et al. 1985). It is the prairie farmers' heritage to tame the land. When the rest of us are putting on the storm windows, winterizing the car, and raking leaves, prairie farmers are doing their fall work — draining nuisance wetlands.

Dislike of U.S. Fish and Wildlife Service. Wildlife and the environment are not high priority items with many prairie farmers, and the federal agencies charged with protecting these resources receive even less praise (Luoma 1985; Gebert 1985; The Forum 1985). Because of some problems in the past, the U.S. Fish and Wildlife Service is one of the least liked, if not *the* least liked government agency on the prairies. Since many prairie farmers pay little federal income tax, even the Internal Revenue Service is held in higher esteem than the Fish and Wildlife Service. In at least one instance in North Dakota, several local landowners cooperated to outbid the Fish and Wildlife Service on a parcel of land, just to prevent federal acquisition.

Frontier attitude. The prairie pothole region is young and a frontier attitude remains. It is but an infant when compared to New England or the Southeast. Individualism has yielded very little to the increasing pressures of society.

Tyranny of small decisions. A common attitude toward prairie potholes in cases such as this is: "There are plenty of them, why should I save mine?" It is difficult to explain to an individual landowner why their one-half acre wetland should not be converted to agricultural use.

Economic Issues
Expand cropland. Due to both scale economies and wanting to increase individual well-being, wetlands are being converted to cropland. If drainage of already owned land is cheaper than buying new land, then drainage is a rational option for farm operators wishing to expand their operation.

Swampbuster provisions of the Food Security Act of 1985 (United States P.L. 99-198) eliminate indirect federal incentives to drain by denying eligibility for all U.S. farm program benefits on all land operated by the landowner who converts wetland to cropland (Heimlich and Langer

1986). While hotly contested in the prairie pothole region, landowners and government officials are recognizing this social mandate as something they must deal with in the future.

Lender pressure. Agricultural loan officers often encouraged farmers to increase their cash flow by "developing" their wetland acreage.

Wetlands are taxed. Prairie farmers pay property taxes on their wetlands, so they feel they should drain them to realize a positive monetary return (Smutko et al. 1984).

Irrigation. Since much of the region is west of the 100th meridian, supplemental irrigation is often used to ensure crop stability. The advent of center pivot irrigation systems accentuates the nuisance factor of wetlands (Nelson et al. 1984).

Livestock water. Wetlands are often attractive, low-lying areas for blasting or excavating dugouts for stock water (Tiner 1984).

Farm machine technology. Farm machinery technology has led to more powerful tractors and wider implements. Wider implements make it more of a nuisance to circumvent potholes (Nelson et al. 1984). More powerful tractors provide on-farm equipment for drainage.

This web of conceptual, attitudinal, and economic issues intertwined with the institutions of state and local governments has led to an extremely complex socioeconomic setting. Yet, policy choices need to be made if we are to have an efficient, equitable allocation of these natural resources. As evidenced by these issues, choices cannot be made based solely on functional assessments of prairie wetlands.

SUMMARY

Prairie potholes are neither physically nor biologically like Mississippi bottomland hardwood swamps, Florida mangrove swamps, New England tidal flats, or southern California coastal salt marshes. Neither is the politicoeconomic setting like that of these other wetlands types. The region is young geologically, demographically, and politically. It was frontier not long ago and many frontier characteristics and attitudes remain. Prairie farmers convert potholes to cropland for a variety of valid reasons from their perspectives, and they are not easily impressed with one-sided accounts of the social or functional values of their sloughs.

OUTLOOK

Prairie wetlands are being converted for two very basic reasons —
economics and attitudes. Yet social, economic, and political aspects of
wetlands allocation and management continue to be of lowest priority in
stated research needs and funding priority. More evidence on the functional values of wetlands, which currently far outweighs socioeconomic
value data, does little good without both an understanding of the institutional setting and an ability to use this knowledge in making effective,
accepted policy. We do not need to spend much more time plotting the
course of a sinking ship; we need to stop it from sinking. Drainage of
prairie wetlands continues, even on lands under U.S. Fish and Wildlife
Service easement (Silde 1983; Higgens and Woodward 1986). Unfortunately, perhaps, the "other side" (wetland developers) and most of the
rest of the world are not so pedantic. They are developing wetlands
because of the economics of conversion, with an understandably deaf
ear toward functional value assessments.

Much valuable scientific work has been accomplished toward understanding and quantifying the nonhuman aspects of prairie wetlands.
The work of Adamus and Stockwell (1983) and Adamus (1983) and
others helps to catalog and technically quantify the range of functional
benefits attributable to undeveloped wetlands. While it is important to
separate these scientific concerns from socioeconomic issues, prairie
farmers make decisions based on changes in their well-being, very often
measuring these changes in dollars.

There is some light at the end of the tunnel. The U.S. Food Security
Act's swampbuster provisions deny federal farm program benefits to
farmers who plow certain lands or convert wetland to cropland. Prairie
wetlands were given special attention in the Emergency Wetlands Resources Act of 1986. The official federal policy seems to have turned
about-face in less than 50 years, from the Swamp Land Acts and subsequent incentives to drain, to today's coordinated federal policies.
Perhaps with adequate scientifically based support, wetland allocation
decisions will soon be made in closer harmony with society's well-being.

REFERENCES

Adamus, P. R. 1983. A method for wetland functional assessment. Volume 2.
    FHA Rep. No. FHWA-1P-82-24. Washington, D.C.: DOT.
Adamus, P. R., and L. T. Stockwell. 1983. A method for wetland functional
    assessment. Vol. 1. FHA Rep. No. FHWA-1P-82-23. Washington, D.C.:
    DOT.

Bergstrom, J. C., B. L. Dillman, and J. R. Stoll. 1985. Public environmental amenity benefits of private land: The case of prime agricultural land. South. J. of Agric. Econ. 17:139–50.

Dorf, R., T. P. Jorgens, and G. D. Rose. 1979. The fiscal impact of federal and state waterfowl production areas on local units of government in west central Minnesota. Minn. Agric. Exp. St. Spec. Rep. 73. St. Paul: Univ. of Minn.

Fargo Forum. 1985. Wetlands enforcement spurs dispute. May 16: A6, Fargo, N. Dak.

Frayer, W. E., T. J. Monahan, D. C. Bowden, and F. A. Grayhill. 1983. Status and trends of wetlands and deepwater habitats in the coterminous United States, 1950s to 1970s. Fort Collins: Dept. For. Wood Serv., Colo. State Univ.

Gebert, C. 1985. Mahnomen farmer expects to lose easement battle. *Fargo Forum,* June 2: B6, Fargo, N. Dak.

Halstead, J. M. 1984. Measuring the nonmarket value of Massachusetts agricultural land: A case study. J. Northeast Agric. Econ. Counc. 14(1):12–19.

Heimlich, R. E., and L. L. Langer. 1986. Swampbusting in perspective. J. Soil Water Conserv. 41:219–24.

Higgens, K. F., and R. O. Woodward. 1986. Comparison of wetland drainage during and after protection by 20-year easements. Prairie Nat. 18(4):229–33.

Hudson, J. C. 1985. Plains country towns. Minneapolis: Univ. Minn. Press.

Leitch, J. A. 1981. Valuation of prairie wetlands. Ph.D. diss., Dept. Agric. Appl. Econ., Univ. Minn., St. Paul.

_____. 1984. Viewpoint: Tailoring wetland protection policies. Nat. Wetlands Newsl. 6(1):6–8.

Leitch, J. A., and L. E. Danielson. 1979. Social, economic, and institutional incentives to drain or preserve prairie wetlands. Dept. Agric. and Appl. Econ. Rep. ER79-6. St. Paul: Univ. Minn.

Leitch, J. A., and D. F. Scott. 1977. Economic impact of flooding on agricultural production in northeast central North Dakota. Agric. Econ. Rep. No. 120. Fargo: N. Dak. State Univ.

_____. 1984. Improving wetland policy through amelioration of adverse effects on local economies. Water Resour. Bull. 20:687–93.

Luoma, J. R. 1985. Twilight in pothole country. Audubon 87(5):67–85.

Manning, W. J., ed. 1973. The impact of environmental stresses on agriculture. Amherst: Environ. Qual. Exec. Coun., College of Food and Nat. Resour., Univ. Mass.

National Water Resources Association. 1985. Resolutions. Fifty-fourth Annu. Meet., November 3–7, 1985, Honolulu, Hawaii.

Nelson, W. C., D. M. Saxowsky, D. E. Kerestes, and J. A. Leitch. 1984. Trends and issues pertaining to wetlands of the Prairie Pothole Region of Minnesota, North Dakota, and South Dakota. Fargo: Dept. Agric. Econ., N. Dak. State Univ.

North Dakota Legislative Council. 1985. Minutes of the Agriculture Committee Meeting, Friday, June 28, Bismarck.

Sagsveen, M. G. 1985. Waterfowl production areas: A state perspective. N. Dak. Law Rev. 60:659–92.

Saxowsky, D. W., and J. A. Leitch. 1981. Prairie wetland drainage regulations:

Discussion and annotated bibliography. Agric. Exp. St. Res. Rep. No. 83. Fargo: N. Dak. State Univ.

Shaw, S. P., and C. G. Fredine. 1956. Wetlands of the United States: Their extent and their value to waterfowl and other wildlife. U.S. Fish and Wildl. Serv. Circ. 39. Washington, D.C.: U.S. Dept. Inter.

Silde, J. G. 1983. Patrolling prairie potholes. N. Dak. Outdoors 45(11):2–6.

Smutko, L. S., J. A. Leitch, L. E. Danielson, and R. K. Stroh. 1984. Landowner attitudes toward wetland preservation policies in the Prairie Pothole Region. Dept. Agric. Econ. Misc. Rep. No. 78, Fargo: N. Dak. State Univ.

Tiner, R. W. Jr. 1984. Wetlands of the United States: Current status and recent trends. Washington, D.C.: U.S. Fish and Wildl. Serv.

U.S. Congress. Office of Technology Assessment. 1984. Wetlands: Their use and regulation. Washington, D.C.: GPO.

Wills, B. L. 1972. North Dakota: The Northern Prairie State. Ann Arbor, Mich.: Edwards Brothers.

THOMAS C. WINTER

2 HYDROLOGIC STUDIES

ABSTRACT

MOST STUDIES of the effect of wetlands on flood storage in the northern prairie use statistical analysis of existing data, and they usually compare basins that have many ditches with those that do not. Many studies also compare flooding from basins that contain many lakes and wetlands with those that do not. Studies of these types commonly are inconclusive because of the many factors that actually affect runoff from an area, many of which are difficult or impossible to quantify. In addition, antecedent moisture conditions commonly are not adequately accounted for.

The general framework for relating surface water to groundwater flow systems has been studied on a regional, steady-state basis, but only a few studies have concentrated on detailed study of specific sites over a long period of time. Studies by Canadian hydrologists showed the dynamic nature of groundwater and wetland water level changes and the resulting complexities of seasonally changing directions of seepage in beds of lakes and wetlands. Present and ongoing studies in the Cottonwood Lake area of North Dakota indicate that reversals of seepage related to local reversals in direction of groundwater flow are even more complex than indicated by previous studies.

Few studies have been done on evapotranspiration in northern prairie wetlands, even though it is the major water loss in the water balance of these wetlands. Virtually no studies of evapotranspiration have been done on a long-term basis using the most accurate methods available.

KEY WORDS: climate, evapotranspiration, geology, glacial till, groundwater, Nebraska sandhills, prairie pothole, soils, surface runoff, water balance.

INTRODUCTION

FOR decades there has been an increasing need for knowledge of hydrologic processes within the northern prairie region of North America. The need for understanding the hydrology of this region was created largely by the desire to farm the fertile soils developed on the glacial deposits. Water is partly responsible for the fertility of soils here, and yet, drainage of water was necessary to use the soils for agriculture. As the need for more developed land increased, the density of drainage ditches also increased. The need for better understanding of hydrology increased along with drainage because it soon became apparent that drainage and other land-use practices related to agriculture were in conflict with other water-resource concerns in this region, such as flooding, erosion, water quality, recharge to groundwater, and fish and wildlife habitat.

Wetlands are at the core of the conflicting interests regarding water management in the northern prairie region. Wetlands exist because of water; therefore, nearly any comprehensive water-management program or extensive land-use practice in this region eventually affects wetlands. The need to understand the hydrology of northern prairie wetlands is critical, not only so they can be managed to maintain their own integrity, but also for effective management of the other water resources they affect. In spite of this critical need, the hydrology of northern prairie wetlands is known only superficially, based more on hydrologic judgment than on adequate data. To appreciate what is known of the hydrology of northern prairie wetlands, it is important to understand the en-

THOMAS C. WINTER, U.S. Geological Survey, Denver, Colorado 80225.

vironmental framework of the northern prairie and the hydrologic processes that operate within that framework.

The purpose of this chapter is to (1) present information on the geology and climate of the northern prairie, as they relate to wetlands, and (2) discuss the hydrologic interaction between northern prairie wetlands and atmospheric water, surface water, and groundwater. The information presented is based on published reports, unpublished data from current studies, and discussions with hydrologists who have worked in the northern prairie region.

ENVIRONMENTAL FRAMEWORK OF CONCERN TO WETLAND HYDROLOGY

The majority of wetlands considered in this chapter are located in the glaciated prairie region of North America, which extends northward from central Iowa through western Minnesota, eastern South Dakota and North Dakota, southwestern Manitoba, and southern Saskatchewan to southeastern Alberta. A small area of wetlands of this type occurs in extreme northern Montana (Fig. 2.1). Another group of wetlands discussed in this chapter are those in the Nebraska sandhills. These wetlands are not in glacial terrane, most are located within an extensive area of sand dunes. Wetlands in the glaciated prairie commonly are referred to as prairie potholes, wetlands associated with large lakes are lacustrine wetlands, and wetlands in the Nebraska sandhills are referred to as sandhills wetlands. Most lakes less than 2 m deep are referred to as wetlands by Cowardin et al. (1979).

The boundary defining the region of wetlands in the northern prairie of North America is based partly on geology. The general region that includes the northern prairie wetlands lies within depositional glacial deposits (Winter and Woo 1988) that are bounded by the Canadian Shield to the northeast, the Cordilleran to the west, and the limit of Wisconsin glacial advance to the south (Fig. 2.1)

The specific region of northern prairie wetlands is further restricted by climate and vegetation. For example, the wetland region does not extend to the Canadian Shield, but is separated from the Shield by a narrow forested region. Except for the northern extent, the wetland region occurs largely in the area of Wisconsin glacial deposits where evaporation exceeds precipitation by greater than 20 cm (Fig. 2.2).

Geology

In the part of the glaciated North American prairie where wetlands are concentrated, a thin mantle of glacial drift overlies stratified sedi-

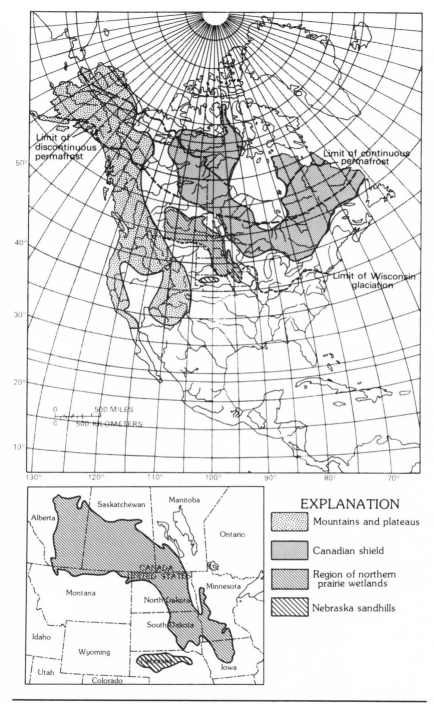

FIG. 2.1. Generalized physiography of the United States and Canada, relative to the region of northern prairie wetlands and to the Nebraska sandhills.

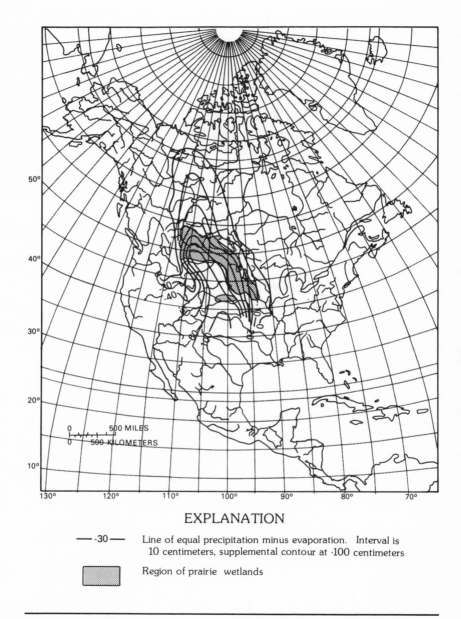

EXPLANATION

—-30— Line of equal precipitation minus evaporation. Interval is
10 centimeters, supplemental contour at -100 centimeters

Region of prairie wetlands

FIG. 2.2. Precipitation minus evaporation in the northern prairie region.

mentary rocks of Mesozoic and Cenozoic age. The rocks consist largely of limestones, sandstones, siltstones, and shales. Much of the area overlies the Williston Basin in Canada and the Dakotas. Total thickness of rocks in the Williston Basin is as much as 5,200 m (Downey 1986). In many areas of the northern prairies, highly mineralized groundwater discharges upward from these sedimentary rocks into the glacial drift (Winter et al. 1984).

The morphology of the glacial drift overlying this bedrock generally consists of end moraines, stagnation moraines, ground moraines, outwash plains, and lake plains. Drift also fills an extensive network of valleys that were eroded into the preglacial bedrock surface. The drift is thickest in areas of end and stagnation moraines, generally 60 to 120 m, but it is as much as 180-m thick locally. Drift commonly is as much as 100-m thick in the bedrock valleys. In areas of ground moraines and lake plains, the drift generally is less than 30-m thick (Bluemle 1971).

Texture of glacial till in the northern prairie region is generally fine-grained. Although the centers of glacial ice were in the mountains to the west and the Canadian Shield to the east, glacial drift at any given locality consists mostly of local bedrock. Therefore, the tills in the prairies are characterized as silty and clayey. In general, the siltier tills occur in Canada and western North Dakota, overlying Tertiary siltstones and sandstones (Scott 1976). Tills that are more clayey overlie shale bedrock in eastern North and South Dakota, Minnesota, and Iowa.

The widespread fine-grained texture of till in the prairie region of North America is somewhat unusual compared to other parts of the continent, where tills are generally more sandy and bouldery. This characteristic of glacial till in the prairie has a significant effect on the surface-water and groundwater hydrology of this region.

In the sandhills area of Nebraska, the dunes commonly are 30- to 90-m high. They overlie sand and gravel, sand, and silt of Pliocene and Pleistocene age, which overlies sandstones and siltstones, largely of Tertiary age. These underlying sandy fluvial and bedrock materials, much of which are poorly consolidated, were the source for the dune sand; therefore, from the standpoint of groundwater hydrology, the sand dunes, fluvial sediments, and bedrock together constitute a single hydrogeologic unit. Because of this, thickness of the groundwater system interacting with lakes and wetlands in the sandhills could be as much as 300 m in western Nebraska.

The most striking physiographic features of the glaciated prairie are the relatively rugged end and stagnation moraines that trend northwestward for hundreds of kilometers through the area. These moraines are characterized by steep slopes at their edges that rise from 10 to greater than 100 m above the surrounding flatter plains. Within the end moraines, local relief along steep land slopes from hilltop to adjacent lowland commonly is 15 to 45 m. Other small, isolated, nonlinear topographic features, such as the Turtle Mountains along the International Boundary, have characteristics of end moraines.

Outside the areas of end moraines, ground moraines also are hummocky, but land slopes are slight, and local relief from hilltop to adjacent depressions are only a few meters. Most northern prairie palustrine wetlands, or prairie potholes, occur within depressions in end moraines, and ground moraines.

Other topographic features of glacial terrane are lake plains and outwash plains. Lake plains are characterized by very flat land slopes and absence of depressions. The deposits largely are clays and silts, but sandy beach ridges are common along the margins of lake plains. Outwash plains also are relatively flat, but they commonly contain lakes and wetlands. Outwash deposits generally consist of stratified sand and gravel.

Overall, the topography of the northern prairie is flat. Where it is not extremely flat, such as in morainal areas, a natural drainage network has not developed, and the many depressions are not connected by an integrated drainage system.

Climate

The northern prairie of North America is characterized by a continental climate. Air masses move into the northern prairie from the Pacific Ocean and from the Arctic. Because much moisture in the Pacific air masses is removed by the mountains to the west, the northern prairie region is relatively dry.

As indicated by Hare and Hay (1974), the small quantities of precipitation in the Canadian Prairie reflect the weakness of atmospheric disturbances and their associated uplift. Eastward moving airstreams fall steadily from the Rocky Mountains to the low ground of Manitoba, a descent of more than 1 km in 1,000 km and at a rate of descent of about 1 cm/sec. This is enough to reduce cyclonic precipitation appreciably, except when the surface airstream runs upslope. There is usually ample moisture in the atmosphere but precipitating mechanisms are not effective. In contrast, the southern tip of the northern prairie region, in Iowa and southern Minnesota, has moisture-laden air masses from the Gulf of Mexico pass over during the summer months, resulting in appreciably greater precipitation in this area.

To compare climatic characteristics across the northern prairie region, Table 2.1 lists temperature and precipitation data for ten locations. The data for all stations are summaries of a common 30 years of record, 1931 to 1960. The large quantities of precipitation in the southern part of the northern prairie region is indicated by comparing the average annual precipitation at Omaha, Nebraska, and Minneapolis-St. Paul, Minnesota, with the other eight locations.

The generally cold character of the northern prairie region also can be seen from Table 2.1. Mean daily temperatures for each month indicate that most of the region has five months in which this temperature characteristic is less than 0°C, the only exceptions are Omaha, Nebraska, and Huron, South Dakota. Extremes in temperature are also characteristic of the continental climate of the northern prairie. Minimum temperatures of less than −40°C occur across Canada and at the North Dakota locations (Table 2.1). Conversely, maximum temperatures of 40°C, or more, occur throughout the region, the exceptions being Edmonton and Calgary, Alberta. Because of the extreme winter cold, northern prairie wetlands are commonly frozen for six months and many are frozen solid for part of this time.

Because of the generally cold and dry climate, wetlands in the northern prairie have a negative water balance with respect to the atmosphere. Precipitation minus evaporation ranges from −10 cm in Iowa to −60 cm in southwestern Saskatchewan and eastern Montana (Fig. 2.2). In the Nebraska sandhills, precipitation minus evaporation ranges from −55 cm to −75 cm.

Soils and Vegetation

Most of the soils in the northern prairie region are developed on silty, clayey till and on lake clays. Therefore, the soils are dense and they do not permit rapid infiltration of water. However, because of the general deficiency of atmospheric water and the high clay content, the soils commonly crack during drying. This secondary permeability allows a greater volume of water to infiltrate. Further, the high moisture-retention capacity of the soils allows a lush and diverse prairie vegetation to develop, especially on the denser soils. Soils developed on outwash plains have rapid infiltration rates. Therefore, vegetation in these areas consists largely of drought-resistant plants.

Vegetation within the wetlands is highly diverse between wetlands, and in some cases, within wetlands. An extensive discussion of the vegetation in prairie potholes and its relation to water chemistry and water depth is presented by Stewart and Kantrud (1972).

In the Nebraska sandhills, nearly all soils have rapid infiltration rates (Dugan 1984). Therefore, vegetation on the sand dunes is sparse and it consists of small, drought-resistant plants. In the lowlands between the dunes, however, the shallow depth to the water table allows the growth of tall, lush prairie vegetation.

TABLE 2.1. Climatic data for ten selected locations throughout the region of northern prairie wetlands

A. Climatic Data for Edmonton, Alberta
(latitude 53°34′N, longitude 113°31′W, elevation 206 m)

Month	Daily mean °C	Temperature Extremes Maximum °C	Minimum °C	Precipitation Mean (mm)	Snowfall (mm)
Jan	−14.1	13	−47	24	239
Feb	−11.6	14	−46	20	193
Mar	− 5.5	21	−36	21	198
Apr	4.2	32	−25	28	152
May	11.2	34	−12	46	30
June	14.3	37	− 2	80	0
July	17.3	34	1	85	0
Aug	15.6	36	− 2	65	0
Sept	10.8	32	−12	34	23
Oct	5.1	28	−25	23	104
Nov	− 4.2	24	−34	22	188
Dec	−10.4	15	−48	25	239
Annual	2.7	37	−48	473	1,366

B. Climatic Data for Calgary, Alberta
(latitude 51°06′N, longitude 114°01′W, elevation 329 m)

Month	Daily mean °C	Temperature Extremes Maximum °C	Minimum °C	Precipitation Mean (mm)	Snowfall (mm)
Jan	− 9.9	16	−43	17	170
Feb	− 8.8	19	−41	20	198
Mar	− 4.4	19	−37	26	249
Apr	3.6	28	−30	35	251
May	9.8	31	−17	52	84
June	13.0	34	− 2	88	20
July	16.7	36	0	58	0
Aug	15.1	34	0	59	tr.
Sept	10.9	31	−12	35	66
Oct.	5.4	29	−22	23	140
Nov	− 2.2	22	−32	16	155
Dec	− 6.6	19	−36	15	152
Annual	3.6	36	−43	444	1,485

C. Climatic Data for Saskatoon, Saskatchewan
(latitude 52°08'N, longitude 106°38'W, elevation 157 m)

Month	Temperature Daily mean °C	Extremes Maximum °C	Extremes Minimum °C	Precipitation Mean (mm)	Snowfall (mm)
Jan	−17.6	9	−46	15	147
Feb	−14.9	13	−44	16	160
Mar	−7.9	19	−35	15	140
Apr	3.6	33	−27	21	97
May	11.2	37	−8	34	25
June	15.4	40	−2	58	tr.
July	19.3	40	2	60	0
Aug	17.6	38	−1	45	0
Sept	11.6	35	−11	34	18
Oct	4.9	32	−22	19	69
Nov	−5.8	20	−34	18	142
Dec	−13.2	13	−40	17	168
Annual	2.0	40	−46	352	966

D. Climatic Data for Regina, Saskatchewan
(latitude 50°26'N, longitude 104°40'W, elevation 175 m)

Month	Temperature Daily mean °C	Extremes Maximum °C	Extremes Minimum °C	Precipitation Mean (mm)	Snowfall (mm)
Jan	−16.9	7	−46	19	188
Feb	−14.8	9	−43	17	165
Mar	−8.1	21	−41	21	183
Apr	3.4	33	−24	21	89
May	11.2	37	−12	40	23
June	15.3	38	−3	83	tr.
July	19.3	40	−2	55	0
Aug	17.8	41	−3	49	0
Sept	11.9	37	−12	34	28
Oct	5.1	31	−19	18	74
Nov	−5.4	21	−33	20	180
Dec	−12.3	15	−40	17	163
Annual	2.2	41	−46	394	1,093

TABLE 2.1. *(continued)*

E. Climatic Data for Winnipeg, Manitoba
(latitude 49°54′N, longitude 97°15′W, elevation 254 m)

Month	Temperature Daily mean °C	Extremes Maximum °C	Extremes Minimum °C	Precipitation Mean (mm)	Snowfall (mm)
Jan	−17.7	8	−44	26	259
Feb	−15.5	12	−45	21	201
Mar	−7.9	23	−39	27	206
Apr	3.3	34	−30	30	99
May	11.3	38	−12	50	25
June	16.5	38	−6	81	0
July	20.2	42	2	69	0
Aug	18.9	40	−1	70	0
Sept	12.8	37	−8	55	5
Oct	6.2	30	−21	37	69
Nov	−4.8	22	−37	29	224
Dec	−12.9	11	−48	22	216
Annual	2.5	42	−48	517	1,303

F. Climatic Data for Williston, North Dakota
(latitude 48°09′N, longitude 103°37′W, elevation 579 m)

Month	Temperature Daily mean °C	Extremes Maximum °C	Extremes Minimum °C	Precipitation Mean (mm)	Snowfall (mm)
Jan	−12.3	13	−40	14	140
Feb	−10.3	19	−46	12	130
Mar	−3.7	26	−34	18	160
Apr	6.0	33	−19	24	80
May	12.9	37	−9	36	20
June	17.3	42	−1	84	tr.
July	21.8	43	3	48	0
Aug	20.4	42	2	38	0
Sept	14.3	38	−8	28	10
Oct	7.8	33	−19	19	60
Nov	−1.9	21	−29	15	110
Dec	−7.9	17	−36	13	130

G. Climatic Data for Bismarck, North Dakota
(latitude 46°46′N, longitude 100°45′W, elevation 502 m[511m])

Month	Temperature Daily mean °C	Extremes Maximum °C	Minimum °C	Precipitation Mean (mm)	Snowfall (mm)
Jan	− 12.8	12	− 42	11	170
Feb	− 10.8	20	− 37	11	150
Mar	− 3.8	27	− 35	20	220
Apr	6.1	33	− 19	31	70
May	13.0	37	− 7	50	20
June	18.1	38	1	86	tr.
July	22.3	42	4	56	0
Aug	21.0	43	3	44	0
Sept	14.8	41	− 9	30	10
Oct	7.9	35	− 15	22	40
Nov	− 2.0	23	− 28	15	140
Dec	− 8.4	16	− 38	9	130
Annual	5.4	43	− 42	385	950

H. Climatic Data for Huron, South Dakota
(latitude 44°23′N, longitude 98°13′W, elevation 391 m[393m])

Month	Temperature Daily mean °C	Extremes Maximum °C	Minimum °C	Precipitation Mean (mm)	Snowfall (mm)
Jan	− 10.3	17	− 37	12	160
Feb	− 8.3	22	− 34	15	210
Mar	− 1.3	32	− 31	28	220
Apr	7.8	33	− 12	47	60
May	14.4	37	− 7	60	10
June	20.1	41	0	80	0
July	24.2	43	4	46	0
Aug	22.9	43	2	53	0
Sept	16.9	39	− 7	39	tr.
Oct	9.9	36	− 12	29	10
Nov	0.1	24	− 28	17	130
Dec	− 6.5	22	− 31	14	130
Annual	7.5	43	− 37	440	930

TABLE 2.1. *(continued)*

I. Climatic Data for Omaha, Nebraska
(latitude 41°18′N, longitude 95°54′W, elevation 298 m[337m])

Month	Temperature Daily mean °C	Extremes Maximum °C	Extremes Minimum °C	Precipitation Mean (mm)	Snowfall (mm)
Jan	− 5.4	21	−29	21	220
Feb	− 3.1	21	−28	24	190
Mar	2.7	31	−27	37	190
Apr	10.9	33	−12	65	30
May	17.2	37	− 2	88	*
June	22.8	41	4	115	0
July	25.8	46	11	86	0
Aug	24.6	43	6	101	0
Sept	19.4	40	− 1	67	0
Oct	13.2	36	− 7	44	10
Nov	3.8	27	−19	32	60
Dec	− 2.1	22	−24	20	130
Annual	10.8	46	−29	700	830

J. Climatic Data for Minneapolis-St. Paul, Minnesota
(latitude 44°53′N, longitude 93°13′W, elevation 254 m[255m])

Month	Temperature Daily mean °C	Extremes Maximum °C	Extremes Minimum °C	Precipitation Mean (mm)	Snowfall (mm)
Jan	−10.9	14	−35	18	160
Feb	− 8.9	15	−33	20	190
Mar	− 2.4	26	−33	39	250
Apr	7.1	33	−13	47	50
May	14.2	35	− 3	81	10
June	19.6	38	1	102	0
July	22.8	40	9	83	0
Aug	21.4	39	4	81	0
Sept	15.8	37	− 3	62	*
Oct	9.1	32	− 8	40	10
Nov	− 0.8	24	−23	36	170
Dec	− 7.9	17	−30	22	180

INTERACTIONS WITHIN THE HYDROLOGIC SYSTEM

Surface Runoff and Geology

The environmental characteristics of the northern prairie affect natural surface runoff in a unique and complex manner. The extremely low regional gradient of the land surface generally results in low runoff velocities. In addition, the numerous small depressions in morainal areas that are not part of an integrated drainage system form large areas that only rarely contribute to stream flow. Furthermore, because the geologic materials have low permeability, infiltration also is minimal.

Climatic characteristics of the northern prairie also have a major effect on surface runoff. In general, soil frost is deep, usually 1 to 1.3 m, so spring snowmelt and some spring rainfall does not readily infiltrate. This water runs into depressions and infiltrates only after soil frost melts. Before extensive drainage was done, much of the prairie region did not contribute to stream flow until the depressions were full of water and they would overflow from one to the next.

The great variability of this process from season to season and year to year was discussed several decades ago by Stichling and Blackwell (1957). They point out, and use the Assiniboine River watershed above Sturgis, Saskatchewan, as an example, that the amount of runoff required to fill the available depressional storage each year is a function of previous runoff and climatic conditions. Areas that contribute runoff to a downstream point one year may not contribute in another, because of changing drainage boundaries. The extremely variable water volume in prairie wetland depressions is indicated by data gathered by Ducks Unlimited of Canada and presented by Stichling and Blackwell (1957). By determining the ratio of water area in lakes and wetlands in eastern Saskatchewan in late summer to water area in the same water bodies in May, they showed the ratio varied from 35 to 95 for the period 1952 to 1956.

Extensive drainage has changed the situation described above, because many depressions no longer hold water. However, overall, the regional land-surface gradients, as well as runoff velocities, remain low. Therefore, the central concerns that have plagued investigators of surface-water hydrology in the northern prairie are related to the volume of water that can actually be stored in the numerous small depressions and the effect of artificial drainage on downstream flooding.

Studies of the Devils Lake basin, North Dakota, have indicated that depressions in the basin have a maximum storage capacity of nearly 8×10^8 m^3, and they can store about 72% of total runoff from a 2-year-frequency flood and about 41% of total runoff from a 100-year-frequency flood (Ludden et al. 1983). In an undrained control block in the

J. Clark Salyer National Wildlife Refuge, all local runoff plus 58% of the inflow was reported to have been retained in wetlands (Malcolm 1979). Undrained wetlands in northern North Dakota have been reported to store 30 cm of water per surface acre of wetland (Kloet 1971). Depressions in north-central Iowa have been reported to store more than 1 cm of surface water over an area of a few square kilometers (Haan and Johnson 1968). In a small (648 ha) area of the Coteau des Prairie in eastern South Dakota, Hubbard and Linder (1986) made a one-time measurement (April 1982) of water held in 213 small wetlands. The wetlands represented 50% the total surface-water area, and they held about 20 ha-m of water. Although Hubbard and Linder (1986) do not put this volume of water into perspective with respect to total potential water storage in these wetlands, they maintain that an enormous quantity of water can be stored in small prairie depressions.

The Agassiz National Wildlife Refuge is reported to have decreased flood peaks in Grand Forks by about 15 cm during a flood in 1979 (Jahn 1981). Brun et al. (1981) indicated that increased streamflows in the southern Red River of the North Valley were significantly correlated to the increase in drainage areas (due to drainage modification) in each subbasin, and the wetlands in this river basin substantially decreased flood levels in downstream major metropolitan areas (Jahn 1981).

Data from several small experimental watersheds in Saskatchewan were used to develop equations describing runoff characteristics of the watersheds. A dimensionless parameter incorporating the physical characteristics of the drainage basin was developed and used as an indicator of "hydrologic similarity" between watersheds. It was determined that watersheds with large amounts of depression storage (high wetland densities) had similar runoff characteristics (Laksham 1976).

A considerable amount of work has been done in Canada with respect to drainage of regions containing wetlands. Unfortunately, most of the work is unpublished or appears in provincial publications that have limited distribution. However, an overview of land drainage in Canada has been published (Province of Manitoba 1984) that summarizes agricultural drainage in each western province. The proceedings also included papers on special topics, such as vertical drainage of prairie potholes, impact of drainage on wildlife, and an overall summary of drainage impacts.

Moore and Larson (1979) used multiple-regression analysis to evaluate factors affecting the mean annual floods from 73 watersheds in four states of the prairie pothole region in the United States. The multiple-regression equation explained 47.5% of the variation in mean annual floods. However, a subset of the data (23 watersheds in Minnesota) produced an equation that explained 82.1% of the variation in mean annual floods. The equation from the Minnesota subset indicated that the mean annual flood increases in proportion to watershed area and inversely with the percentage of lakes and wetlands within the watershed.

A watershed model also was developed and calibrated using available data for two Minnesota watersheds (Moore and Larson 1979). Results of modeling indicate that drainage of depressions substantially increases annual runoff volumes. For individual storms, increased depression drainage increased peak flow for long duration, low-intensity storms. For short duration, intense storms, peak flow was affected to a much lesser degree by depression drainage. Channelizing the main channel increased peak discharge by a much larger percentage than did draining the depressions. In a later report Larson (1981) indicated there is a general lack of data on the effects of drainage on flood flows.

A watershed model also was used by Campbell and Johnson (1975) to evaluate the effect of artificial drainage on discharge characteristics from a landscape characterized by surface depressions. The area of study, East Fork Hardin Creek in central Iowa, is underlain by tile drains. Two of the principal results of the study indicated that (1) an increase in lateral spacing of tiles resulted in lower discharge for the first few days following precipitation, but that the discharge was maintained for a longer period compared to closer-spaced drains, and (2) complete surface drainage of depressions resulted in a greatly increased peak discharge, for the conditions assumed in the study.

In general, studies of runoff in the northern prairie have been studies of flooding in main-stem river valleys. Statistical analyses of existing data have been used to compare basins that have numerous depressions with those that do not, or the comparison is made of areas with and without extensive ditching. Results commonly are a function of study design. Study approach can have a substantial effect on results, and it is not uncommon to find comparisons of results that are fundamentally not comparable. In addition, results of studies commonly are highly dependent on antecedent conditions, and these are not always adequately considered in purely statistical studies. For example, a landscape of totally dry depressions will hold more water than one that has depressions already full of water. Until research on fundamental hydraulic and hydrologic processes unique to the northern prairie landscape, including the full range of flow conditions, is done, controversy on the effect of drainage on runoff will continue.

Surface Water and Groundwater

Just as the landscape and climate of the northern prairie control surface runoff, these factors also control the interaction of surface water and groundwater in this region. The flat and depressional topography, while inhibiting efficient runoff, provides maximum opportunity for infiltration of water. However, the dominance of soils developed on clayey and silty till in the glacial prairie tend to retard infiltration, except for water flow through the fractures. Furthermore, the presence of soil frost at the time of year that recharge is most favorable (i.e., prior to the emergence of vegetation) also tends to inhibit infiltration.

Given these conditions, research on groundwater interaction with lakes and wetlands in the northern prairie has shown the close interaction of groundwater with these surface-water features. Some of the hydrologic processes occurring in the prairie are not unique to this region, but they are far more common here than in other geologic and climatic settings.

Some of the early studies of groundwater flow systems were done in the Canadian prairie. These studies indicated not only how complex flow systems could be, but they also provided a great deal of insight into how and where groundwater is recharged and discharged.

Toth (1963), working in the prairie of Alberta, used theoretical analysis to develop a concept of groundwater flow systems. His analyses indicated that flow systems of different magnitudes could overlie one another and that they have different characteristics. A local flow system is recharged at water-table highs and discharges to adjacent lowlands; most shallow groundwater is part of local flow systems (Fig. 2.3). Intermediate flow systems can underlie local flow systems, and regional flow systems can underlie both. Intermediate and regional flow systems are recharged at major topographic highs and discharge at major lowlands such as rivers, lakes, and wetlands. Toth (1966, 1971) also provided techniques for identifying field evidence of groundwater recharge and discharge, some of which are related to wetlands. Miller et al. (1985) also discuss the effect of groundwater on development of upland and wetland soils in a morainal area of Saskatchewan.

Field studies of groundwater flow systems, also in the Canadian prairies, by Meyboom led to his concept of the "prairie profile," a concept that also integrates recharge, different-magnitude flow systems, and discharge into a continuum (Meyboom 1963).

Using these concepts of integrated flow systems, Canadian hydrologists studied a number of areas in the prairie, many of which involved lakes and wetlands. The studies by Meyboom were largely field studies, and they commonly focused on lakes and wetlands. Studies in the Assiniboine River drainage basin included study of the effect of transpiration on groundwater flow near wetlands (Meyboom 1966a, 1966b) and streams (Meyboom 1964).

Meyboom made extensive use of piezometer nests (small diameter

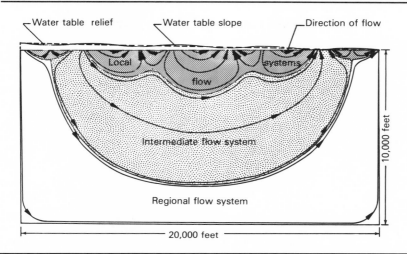

FIG. 2.3.   Hydrologic section showing local, intermediate, and regional flow systems in a hypothetical groundwater basin (*Adapted Toth 1963*).

wells open only at the bottom, and each completed at different depths) to determine vertical flow directions within the groundwater system. By placing piezometer nests at different locations along a transect, the entire cross-sectional profile of flow could be determined. This led to considerable insight into where groundwater is recharged and discharged. This study approach was particularly effective in determining the hydrologic functions of wetlands with respect to groundwater. For example, Meyboom et al. (1966) determined patterns of groundwater flow and discharge characteristics for a wide range of scales, from individual wetlands to large river systems. Intensive study of groundwater movement near individual wetlands indicated seasonal reversal of groundwater flow directions, depending on the magnitude of groundwater recharge relative to water levels in wetlands (Fig. 2.4) (Meyboom 1966b, 1967b). Integrating considerable field experience, Meyboom (1967a) discussed methods of estimating groundwater recharge on the prairies, and he also presented conceptualized flow systems of different magnitudes for the Moose Mountain area, Saskatchewan (Fig. 2.5) (Meyboom 1967c).

The U.S. Geological Survey conducted a ten-year study of the hydrology of prairie wetlands in North Dakota (Eisenlohr et al. 1972). The purpose of those studies primarily was to evaluate methods of determining evaporation from small water bodies. After discovering that prairie wetlands did not have impermeable basins, an assumption required for the evaporation studies, the Survey conducted groundwater studies near

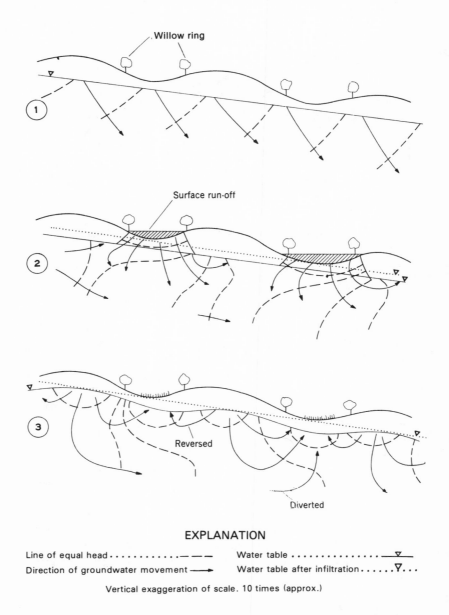

Willow ring

Surface run-off

1

2

3

Reversed

Diverted

EXPLANATION

Line of equal head . . . .— — —   Water table . . . . ▽

Direction of groundwater movement ——►   Water table after infiltration . . . . . .▽. . .

Vertical exaggeration of scale. 10 times (approx.)

FIG. 2.4. Generalized sequence of flow conditions near a willow ring in Saskatchewan (1) a condition of "normal" downward flow; (2) a condition of groundwater mounds produced by infiltrating melt water; and (3) a condition of inverted water-table relief resulting from a cone of depression around the phreatophytic willows (*Meyboom 1966b*).

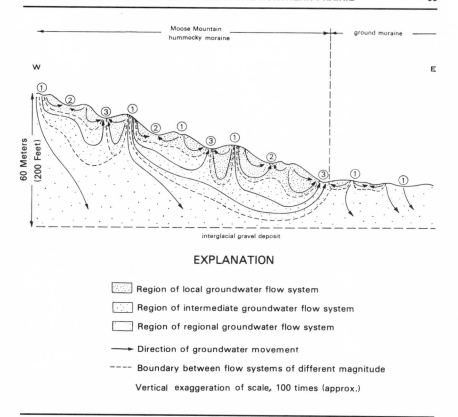

EXPLANATION

░░░ Region of local groundwater flow system

▒▒▒ Region of intermediate groundwater flow system

☐ Region of regional groundwater flow system

———► Direction of groundwater movement

– – – – Boundary between flow systems of different magnitude

Vertical exaggeration of scale, 100 times (approx.)

FIG. 2.5. Diagrammatic section of the flow systems of Moose Mountain, Saskatchewan (1) recharge areas, (2) discharge area of local flow system, (3) discharge area of local and intermediate flow systems (*Meyboom 1967c*).

some of the wetlands. Results of the groundwater studies are summarized in Sloan (1972). According to that report, groundwater flow in poorly permeable glacial till is extremely slow. Weathering increases the permeability at and near the surface, and, as a result, the highest flow rates and the most effective flow systems occur locally in the shallow zones marginal to wetlands. The water table is a shallow surface that is continuous with the water surface in prairie wetlands. The configuration of the water table surrounding the wetland is quite important in determining the seepage conditions at a wetland. If the water table slopes into a wetland, groundwater discharge prevails, and the water is relatively saline and permanent. If the water table slopes away from the wetland, groundwater recharge occurs, and the water in the wetland is relatively fresh and temporary. In most wetlands, the water table slopes into some parts and away from the remainder, resulting in a condition called through flow. Where through flow exists, brackish conditions prevail, and wetlands are semipermanent.

With the development of numerical modeling. Freeze (1969b) used numerical simulation to greatly expand and generalize the concepts of groundwater flow systems. As part of these studies, the computer models also were used to calculate recharge and discharge rates along the entire profile. Freeze used the numerical analysis approach to evaluate groundwater flow patterns, including the relation of groundwater to lakes and wetlands, in the Good Spirit Lake (Freeze n.d.) and Old Wives Lake (Freeze 1969a) drainage basins in Saskatchewan. The study of the Good Spirit Lake drainage basin was part of the International Hydrologic Decade; therefore, the basin was extensively instrumented for hydrologic research.

Studies by Lissey (1971), also in the Canadian prairie, resulted in a modification of Meyboom's concepts of recharge in uplands. Lissey indicated that groundwater recharge and discharge occurred largely in depressions in the prairie, many of which contain lakes and wetlands (Fig. 2.6). Therefore, wetlands could serve both functions of recharge and discharge.

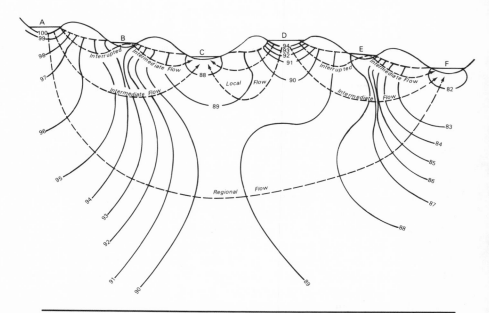

FIG. 2.6.   Depression-focused groundwater recharge and discharge, and development of intermediate groundwater flow systems (*Lissey 1971*).

As more detailed studies were done on smaller and smaller areas, it became clear that some of the assumptions made about the geology of specific sites were inadequate. In many studies the glacial till is treated as homogeneous porous media, when, in fact, studies have shown that the till contains numerous fractures. Because of this, the basic question arose as to whether groundwater flow in the tills is principally fracture flow, and if the fractures are numerous enough and integrated enough to function as a porous medium.

Grisak (1975) presented a general discussion of the fracture porosity of glacial till. Grisak et al. (1976) studied the hydrologic and solute-transport characteristics of fractured till in Canada. Hendry (1982) discussed the hydraulic conductivity of glacial till in Manitoba, and also groundwater recharge through those fractured tills (Hendry 1983). Results of the fractured-till studies indicate that groundwater flow is largely through the fractures, and that the fractures commonly are numerous, are closely spaced, and have a very small opening. Therefore, the movement of water through them is still characterized by that of a low-permeability media, although the permeability may be an order of magnitude, or more, greater than that of the till itself. Study of fracture flow in glacial till is relatively recent and considerably more work needs to be done.

Study of the interaction of wetlands and groundwater in the northern prairie recently received increased impetus in the United States. The studies are a joint effort by the U.S. Fish and Wildlife Service and the U.S. Geological Survey. The overall purpose of these studies is to conduct research on all aspects of the hydrology of a few selected prairie wetlands, with emphasis on groundwater flow and evaporation. The study site, the Cottonwood Lake area of North Dakota, includes a group of wetlands at different altitudes along a valley side. Water-level gauges were placed in wetlands, and about 50 water-table wells and piezometers were drilled in the adjacent uplands. Water-table wells are screened at the top of the groundwater system, whereas, piezometers have screens isolated within the groundwater system. The site also includes extensive climatic instrumentation (Winter and Carr 1980).

Results of a four-year study of the Cottonwood Lake area indicate that the configuration of the water table between wetlands is more complex and dynamic than earlier studies indicated. The wetlands selected for intensive study lie within a groundwater flow system that includes recharge and discharge areas (Fig. 2.7). Wetland T8 is an area of recharge to the groundwater flow system. Between wetlands T8 and T3, configuration of the water table does not follow the topography of the land surface. Wetlands P1 and P8 are in areas of groundwater discharge. In the low areas between wetlands T3, P1, and P8, configuration of the

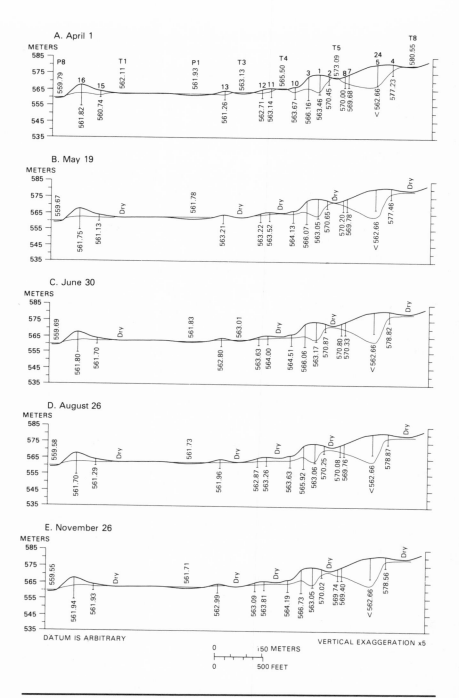

FIG. 2.7. Altitudes of water levels of wetlands and of the water table in a section through the Cottonwood Lake area, North Dakota, for five days in 1980 (*LaBaugh et al. 1987*).

water table is dynamic. Reversals of groundwater flow are common between wetlands T3 and P1 in the vicinity of well 13. Timing and duration of these reversals are affected by seasonal and annual fluctuations in recharge by snowmelt and by rainfall. Less pronounced and less frequent reversals of flow occur between wetlands P1 and P8. Reversals in flow rarely occur higher in the groundwater flow system (LaBaugh et al. 1987).

Results similar to those in the topographically higher part of the Cottonwood Lake area have been reported for a wetland area near Hamiota, Manitoba (Mills and Zwarich 1984). The local relief at this site is about 2 m, and the area is underlain by till. Two lines of wells and piezometers were installed from the wetland to surrounding uplands. Water levels from the piezometers indicated that the general configuration and seasonal pattern of water-level changes at the Hamiota site are much like the area near wetlands T8 and T5 at Cottonwood Lake. That is, water-table highs form beneath the wetlands because recharge is focused there, and water-table lows remain throughout the year beneath the land-surface highs.

Mills and Zwarich (1984) also document seasonal reversals of groundwater flow at the Hamiota site. Water seeps from the wetland to groundwater during high wetland water levels in spring, then reverses and flows toward the wetland as evapotranspiration creates a sink for groundwater during the summer. Mills and Zwarich (1984) conclude that nearly all water that recharges groundwater in the spring does not move very far in the groundwater system before evapotranspiration becomes dominant and discharges most of that groundwater. This would explain the water-table low beneath the land-surface high, and it leads them to further conclude that recharge to regional groundwater is minimal. This conclusion was also reached by LaBaugh et al. (1987) for the Cottonwood Lake area of North Dakota, and by Meyboom (1967c) for the Moose Mountain area of Saskatchewan. Nevertheless, however minimal recharge to regional flow systems is, it is still the source of water in the deeper groundwater flow systems.

The reversals of groundwater flow adjacent to wetlands can result from two processes. In one case, the infiltration to groundwater caused by high wetland water levels in spring, followed by a reversal of flow when the water levels decline because of evapotranspiration is nothing more than a bank storage phenomenon. Bank storage is a term commonly used by surface water hydrologists to refer to surface water that seeps into river banks at high stream stages and seeps back to the river at lower stream stages. In general, the seasonal dynamics of groundwater flow discussed by Meyboom (1966b) and Mills and Zwarich (1984) are of this type. The reversals of groundwater flow discussed by Winter (1983) are of another type, where the flow is reversed because of infiltration and recharge in the adjacent upland (Fig. 2.8). Mills and Zwarich (1984) also discuss this process. Both phenomena occur, and studies are underway to determine the relative importance of each process.

In another study recently completed, the hydrogeologic setting of about 180 lakes and wetlands were examined with respect to regional

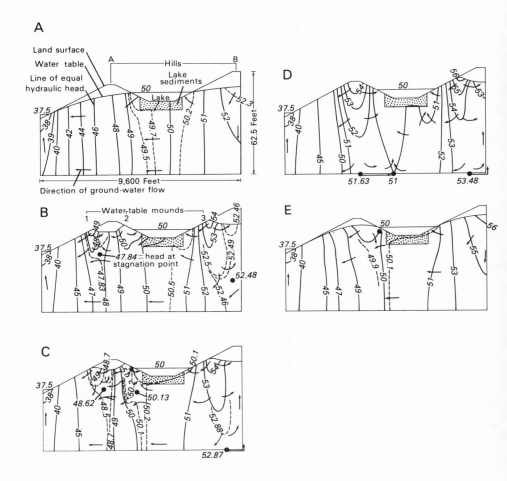

FIG. 2.8. Distribution of hydraulic head and direction of groundwater flow for variably saturated porous media near a lake in a hypothetical basin. Anisotropy of the porous media is 500. Beginning with a steady-state water table (A), results are of conditions following 5 (B), 10 (C), and 15 days (D) of infiltration from snowmelt and its effect on growth of water-table mounds and local groundwater flow systems. The final part (E) shows conditions after 7 months of redistribution. Note that seepage from the lake is about to resume at this time (*Winter 1983*).

groundwater flow systems in Kidder and Stutsman Counties, North Dakota (Swanson et al. in press). The study includes determination and numerical modeling of groundwater flow systems relative to lakes and wetlands along two 80-km transects across the Coteau du Missouri.

Results of this two-county study indicate that, on a regional scale, groundwater is recharged at topographic highs and discharges to regional lowlands, such as lakes and wetlands in the Kidder County outwash plain (Fig. 2.9). Lakes and wetlands in the Crystal Springs area receive discharge from large groundwater flow systems in the drift, and the hydrologic section indicates that some of the lakes and wetlands here might even be receiving some discharge from bedrock water, which moves through the drift before entering the surface water.

Most of the field studies discussed here were designed and instrumented to study one or only a few lines of section radiating from a wetland or lake. Results of the one or two sides of a wetland or lake that is extensively instrumented commonly are generalized for all sides of the wetland and its basin. The drawback of simplifying systems in this manner can be demonstrated by the Cottonwood Lake area. The absence of water-table highs beneath land surface highs between wetlands T8, T5, and T3, as shown in Fig. 2.7, is not the case for the area north and southwest of wetland P1 where the water table has a completely different configuration. Therefore, the discussion of the flow directions and reversals of flow shown apply only to that particular line of section.

Although hydrologic sections are useful to develop concepts of how groundwater can interact with lakes and wetlands on a regional scale, local flow systems can have a significant effect on some lakes and wetlands throughout the landscape. Groundwater recharge occurs in numerous locations throughout the landscape, regardless of regional topographic position. In general, most groundwater recharged locally near any body of surface water will discharge into the surface water nearest the shore (Pfannkuch and Winter 1984). Furthermore, constantly changing recharge conditions adjacent to surface water can cause complex groundwater flow and seepage patterns (Fig. 2.8) (Winter 1983). Therefore, it is not unusual to observe freshwater springs discharging into saline lakes. For example, groundwater discharging into Chase Lake, North Dakota, was consistently more dilute than the lake proper (Swanson et al. 1988). In addition, the relative contribution of groundwater discharge from local groundwater flow systems and that from regional systems can vary considerably between lakes, which causes the overall chemistry of the lakes and wetlands to vary considerably.

Differences in topographic position, even though small, present different opportunities for seepage from lakes and wetlands within any regional topographic position. For example, within a regional topographic low a lake or wetland that is slightly higher than an adjacent lake

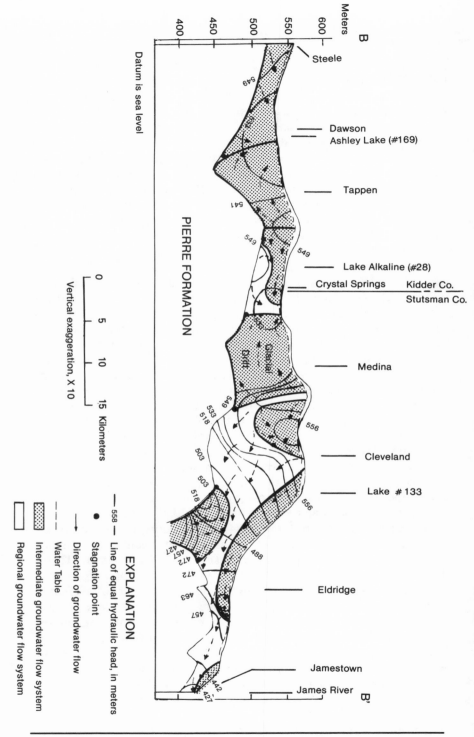

FIG. 2.9. Hydrologic sections showing regional groundwater movement in Kidder and Stutsman counties, North Dakota (*Swanson et al. 1988*).

or wetland could have seepage from it part of the year, whereas the lower lake or wetland might not. This opportunity to discharge water from one of the lakes or wetlands and not the other, together with different relative mixes of groundwater from local and regional flow systems, as previously pointed out, could explain greatly different water chemistry between adjacent lakes or wetlands.

In the Nebraska sandhills, less is known of the relationship of lakes and wetlands and groundwater than in the glacial prairie. In the Crescent Lake National Wildlife Refuge, about 30 water table wells and piezometers and 5 lake-level gauges were installed by the U.S. Geological Survey in 1981 and 1982 (Winter 1986).

Analysis of water-level fluctuations in those wells and lakes indicates water-table configuration beneath sand dunes in this area varies considerably, depending on the topographic configuration of the dunes (Fig. 2.10). If the topography of an interlake dunal area is hummocky (Fig. 2.10A), groundwater recharge is focused at topographic lows causing formation of water-table mounds beneath the surface depressions. These mounds, because of their high hydraulic head relative to adjacent lakes, prevent groundwater movement from topographically high lakes to adjacent lower lakes. If a dune ridge is sharp (Fig. 2.10B), the opportunity for focused recharge does not exist because there are no depressions, resulting in water-table troughs between lakes. Lakes aligned in descending altitude, parallel to the principal direction of regional groundwater movement, generally have seepage from higher lakes toward lower lakes. Other studies of the sandhills have recently been initiated (Ginsberg 1985) but no information has been published yet from those studies.

Surface Water and Atmospheric Water

Gains and losses of water from and to the atmosphere are the dominant components of the water balance of northern prairie wetlands. Precipitation can be measured accurately, given enough rain gauges properly placed. However, evaporation and transpiration are the least-studied components of the hydrology of northern prairie wetlands.

In a seven-year study of small wetlands at Melfort and Swift Current, Saskatchewan, Millar (1971) indicated that the rate of water loss from individual wetlands varied directly with the length of shoreline per unit area. He interpreted the cause to be related partly to transpiration of water by vegetation along the margins of the wetlands. For example, Millar calculated that during the growing season as much as 60 to 80% of water loss from the wetlands can be attributed to transpiration by marginal vegetation and soil-water evaporation.

The study of evaporation conducted by the U.S. Geological Survey

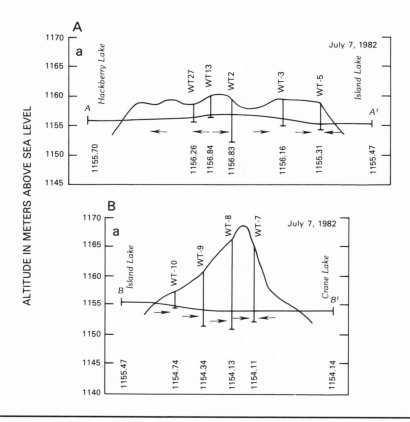

FIG. 2.10. Water-table configuration on opposite sides of Island Lake, Crescent Lake National Wildlife Refuge, Nebraska. Water-table mounds form beneath hummocky sand dunes (A) and water-table troughs form beneath sharp-crested dunes (B) (*Winter 1986*).

(Eisenlohr et al. 1972) is the most comprehensive study of evaporation from northern prairie wetlands. Yet, this study was made primarily to evaluate the mass-transfer method of determining evaporative water loss. The mass-transfer method was developed on large reservoirs in the western United States, and, to be used most effectively, the surface-water body should have minimal to no seepage. The Survey decided to study small lakes in glacial till because these lakes appeared to provide an ideal setting to evaluate the mass-transfer method; they were assumed to have no seepage through their beds.

The mass-transfer method is not the most accurate method of determining evaporation (Winter 1981). This is particularly true if the mass-transfer coefficient, an empirical coefficient unique to each lake, is not determined in the most accurate way. To determine the mass-transfer coefficient, wind speed multiplied by vapor pressure gradient over a water body is related to an independent measure of evaporation for that water boy. Because evaporation determined by the energy budget commonly is accepted as one of the most accurate measures of evaporation, it is among the best methods to use for calibrating a mass-transfer coefficient.

An alternative method of calibrating a mass-transfer coefficient, which is much less expensive but also less accurate than calibration against an energy-budget value, is to relate wind speed multiplied by vapor pressure gradient to change in stage of the water body. The adequacy of the stage change approach is dependent on having minimal seepage or having an accurate measure of seepage volume. Because the studies by the U.S. Geological Survey (Eisenlohr et al. 1972) did not include energy-budget studies, the mass-transfer coefficient was determined by the change-in-stage calibration.

Studies of evaporation of northern prairie lakes patterned after those of Eisenlohr et al. (1972) were conducted by Allred et al. (1971) in Minnesota. Meyboom (1967c) also used the mass-transfer method to determine evapotranspiration in the Moose Mountain area of Saskatchewan. Both of these studies used the change-in-stage method to calibrate the mass-transfer coefficient.

Eisenlohr (1966), and Meyboom (1967c) noted a further complication in determining the mass-transfer coefficient for small prairie lakes. Although the mass-transfer coefficient is considered to be a constant for a given lake (Harbeck 1962), both studies (Eisenlohr 1966; Meyboom 1967c) indicated considerable seasonal variation in the coefficient. Meyboom indicated a general decrease of the coefficient throughout the summer; whereas, Eisenlohr indicated a general increase of the coefficient throughout the summer.

Eisenlohr (1966) indicated that the changing mass-transfer coefficient could be related to the effect of transpiration by hydrophytes. He developed a method using the mass-transfer data to calculate transpiration separately from open-water evaporation. Results of those calculations indicated that the presence of hydrophytes reduces water loss to the atmosphere compared to open-water evaporation.

It is apparent from these few studies of evaporation from northern prairie wetlands that the best possible method of determining mass-transfer coefficients, such as calibration by the energy-budget method, has not been used, and, therefore, that the most accurate determination of evaporation has not yet been made. Knowing this, it is interesting to note that the estimates of groundwater recharge in the studies done by

Eisenlohr et al. (1972) and by Allred et al. (1971) were based on studies of evaporation. Although some groundwater work was part of each of these two studies, the actual volumes of groundwater seepage were based on mass-transfer plots, using the method of Langbein et al. (1951) to calculate seepage.

The present study of the hydrology of lakes and wetlands in the Cottonwood Lake area, North Dakota, includes instrumentation for energy-budget studies, as well as for mass-transfer studies. The energy budget studies have been ongoing since 1981; their primary purpose is to calibrate the best possible mass-transfer coefficient. In addition, it is intended that a thorough analysis of errors associated with a number of empirical methods of determining evaporation will be made at the Cottonwood Lake site.

Detailed studies of evaporation have not been made for Nebraska's sandhills lakes. The present study in the Crescent Lake area has had instruments for mass-transfer studies since 1982, and energy-budget studies are scheduled to begin in 1987.

The Water Balance of Northern Prairie Wetlands

Despite the difficulties in studying the hydrology of northern prairie wetlands, a number of attempts have been made to calculate water budgets for them. The budgets provide an approximate measure of the relative importance of water gains and losses of the hydrologic components that interact with northern prairie wetlands.

Shjeflo (1968) determined the average water sources and sinks for ten prairie wetlands in North Dakota. He indicated that precipitation and runoff from snowmelt were the principal water sources and that evapotranspiration was the principal water loss (Table 2.2). Variations from these averages for the ten wetlands were large, but Shjeflo indicated that the averages remained nearly constant for both wet and dry years. Shjeflo (1968) indicated further that evapotranspiration from vegetated wetlands was about 12% less than from wetlands with open water, and that seepage losses were greater from vegetated wetlands compared to wetlands with open water. The average net seepage losses were about 18 cm or 22% of the total water loss.

Allred et al. (1971) determined the water balance of four prairie lakes in Minnesota, for the open-water periods of 1966 and 1967. The budgets indicate the dominance of precipitation as the principal water gain (Table 2.2) and evaporation as the principal water loss for these four water bodies. Allred et al. (1971) indicated that net seepage losses from the four lakes averaged about 35.6 cm, or 12 to 20% of the total water loss; although they calculated a net seepage out of Ria Lake of 40% of the water loss in 1967. It should be noted that Ria Lake has a particu-

TABLE 2.2. Hydrologic budgets for selected wetlands and lakes in North Dakota and Minnesota

Site	Year	Inflow		Outflow		Change in stage (cm)
		Precipitation (cm)	Surface runoff (cm)	Evapotranspiration (cm)	Groundwater (net) (cm)	
Average of 10 wetlands[a]	1960–64	36.9(48)[d]	40.2(52)[c]	64.3(78)	18.3(22)	NA
Pitcher Lake[b]	1967	39.2(96)	1.7(4)	67.2(84)	12.3(16)	−38.7
Booster Club Lake[b]	1967	49.1(97)	1.6(3)	62.3(84)	11.8(16)	−17.5
Mud Lake[b]	1967	46.0(90)	4.9(10)	55.4(89)	6.5(11)	−12.5
Ria Lake[b]	1967	44.2(81)	10.5(19)	66.4(60)	43.7(40)	−49.3

Note:

Site	Geology
Pitcher	Sandy, silty till; St. Croix lobe
Booster Club	Anoka Sand Plain
Mud	Silty, clayey till; Des Moines lobe
Ria	Sandy, silty till; St. Croix lobe, on bluff over Mississippi River

[a]Adapted from Shjeflo (1968).
[b]Adapted from Allred et al. (1971).
[c]24 cm is snowmelt.
[d]Numbers in parentheses are percent.

larly steep water-table gradient away from it because it is located on a bluff adjacent to a major river valley. Both studies cited used a mass-transfer plot to calculate net seepage; they did not separately measure actual quantities of groundwater discharging to and from the surface water.

The only other readily available published water budgets for prairie lakes are those presented by Crowe and Schwartz (1981b, 1985). Unlike the study approach discussed previously, Crowe and Schwartz (1981a) developed a lumped-parameter, lake-watershed response model to assess water balances of lakes, especially the groundwater component. They applied the model to Baptiste Lake, Alberta, (Crowe and Schwartz 1981b) for the six-year period 1972 to 1977. They determined that groundwater inflow to and outflow from the lake each averaged about 13% of the inflow and outflow for the six-year period. These quantities were similar in magnitude to precipitation and evaporation (Table 2.3). The lake is dominated by surface water inflow and outflow.

Crowe and Schwartz (1985) later applied the model to Wabamun Lake, near Edmonton, Alberta, for the five-year period 1977 to 1981. They determined that groundwater contributed an average of 4.7% of

TABLE 2.3.   Hydrologic budgets of Baptiste Lake and Wabamun Lake, Alberta

A. Baptiste Lake

Year	Percent inflow			Percent outflow		
	Ground-water	Surface water	Precipi-tation	Ground-water	Surface water	Evaporation
1972	22	68	10	13	72	15
1973	13	68	19	14	70	16
1974	18	74	8	8	83	9
1975	9	74	17	14	69	17
1976	7	76	17	18	60	22
1977	9	75	16	13	72	15
Average	13.0	72.5	14.5	13.3	71.0	15.7

Source: Adapted from Crowe and Schwartz (1981b).

B. Wabamun Lake

Year	Percent inflow			Percent outflow		
	Ground-water	Surface water	Precipi-tation	Ground-water	Surface water	Evaporation
1977	1.3	38.9	59.8	43.5	0.0	56.5
1978	4.7	36.8	58.5	39.3	8.8	51.9
1979	8.6	48.3	43.1	35.0	18.5	46.5
1980	2.7	38.2	59.1	42.5	0.0	57.5
1981	5.5	41.7	52.8	39.1	7.1	53.7
Average	4.7	40.7	54.5	39.6	7.5	52.9

Source: Adapted from Crowe and Schwartz (1985).

the inflow during the study period and 39.6% of the water loss from the lake (Table 2.3). The remainder of the water-balance components are given in Table 2.3. Surface water contributed an average of 40.7% of the inflow, but only 7.5% of the outflow from Wabamun Lake.

SUMMARY AND NEEDED RESEARCH

Research on the hydrology of northern prairie wetlands generally has consisted of short-term studies of a relatively small number of wetlands. In some cases, groundwater studies included analysis of evaporation, or evaporation studies led to some work on groundwater. If a large number of wetlands were studied in a given area, the studies commonly were not long-term or comprehensive.

Research has indicated that the greatest advances in understanding wetland hydrology have been made when wetland complexes are studied as interconnected hydrologic units. Furthermore, the most comprehensive results are obtained when a number of scientific disciplines are concentrated in common study areas.

All hydrologic processes are interconnected to some extent. Runoff processes are dependent on geology, topography, the interaction of groundwater and surface water, and the atmospheric water fluxes. The interaction of groundwater and surface water depends on geology, topography, and atmospheric water fluxes. Review of the literature indicates that past studies have provided useful information for water management in the northern prairie region. However, considerably more work is needed before the hydrology of northern prairie wetlands will be understood well enough to manage them within decreasing limits of uncertainty, which will be required as stress on natural resources increases in the future.

Surface Runoff

Concern over the effect of ditching and draining on surface runoff in the northern prairie has led to studies largely concerned with flooding in main-stem valleys. Most of these studies use statistical analysis of existing data, and they usually compare basins that have extensive ditching with those that do not. Many studies also compare flooding from basins that contain lakes and wetlands with those that do not. Rainfall-runoff modeling approaches also have been used to make similar types of comparisons. Although modeling studies offer much potential for increasing understanding of runoff, they usually are calibrated for individual study sites, and their utility for a wide variety of watershed settings commonly are not demonstrated. Studies of these types usually are inconclusive because of the many factors that actually affect runoff from an area, many of which are difficult or impossible to quantify. In addition, antecedent conditions commonly are not adequately accounted for.

Because of the lack of understanding of runoff processes unique to the topography and geology of the northern prairie region, it is presently not possible to evaluate the effects on downstream flooding of draining individual wetlands. In addition, ditching does more than integrate a drainage network for more efficient removal of surface water from the landscape. If a wetland that recharges groundwater is drained, the recharge function of the wetland will no longer exist. In contrast, if a wetland is receiving groundwater discharge, draining the wetland will not take away the groundwater discharge function. By lowering the wetland level, groundwater discharge to the depression will actually increase initially because of the increased groundwater gradients toward the depression. Over a long period this could eventually result in a lower water table near the wetland.

To make a thorough evaluation of artificial drainage on runoff characteristics of the northern prairie, integrated studies of groundwater and surface-water interaction, open-channel hydraulics, overland runoff, network systems analysis, and seasonal and annual changes in climatic characteristics are needed.

Interaction of Surface Water and Groundwater

Studies in the Canadian prairie and theoretical analysis of groundwater flow systems conducted more than 20 years ago presented the conceptual framework for nearly all ensuing studies. Even though the general framework for relating surface water to groundwater flow systems is adequate on a regional basis, only a few studies have concentrated on detailed study of transient flow processes of specific sites. Furthermore, there has never been a long-term, detailed study of an extensively instrumented northern prairie wetland watershed.

The detailed studies that were done, principally by Canadian hydrologists, made effective use of proper placement and construction of piezometers. These studies, which were of only a few sites, indicated the dynamic nature of groundwater and wetland water-level changes and the resulting complexities of seasonally changing directions of seepage in beds of lakes and wetlands. Present and ongoing studies in the Cottonwood Lake area of North Dakota indicate these reversals of seepage related to local reversals in direction of groundwater flow are even more complex than indicated by the previous studies.

To adequately understand groundwater movement near wetlands in the northern prairies for scientific and water management purposes, it will be necessary to conduct long-term studies using well-instrumented wetland watersheds. Such studies are needed to evaluate seepage to and from wetlands for a considerable range of climatic conditions, the effect of antecedent conditions, and timing of snowmelt and frost thaw. Furthermore, studies of this type need to be done for a variety of physiographic, hydrogeologic, and climatic settings.

Evapotranspiration

Water loss to the atmosphere is one of the major components of the water balance of wetlands in the northern prairie. Furthermore, it has a significant effect on water chemistry on a seasonal basis because of the concentration of solutes by evaporation. Few studies have been done on evapotranspiration in northern prairie wetlands, and virtually no long-term studies have been done using the most accurate methods available. As with other aspects of the hydrology of prairie wetlands, long-term, detailed studies using the best methods and instruments need to be done in a variety of climatic environments.

REFERENCES

Allred, E. R., P. W. Manson, G. M. Schwartz, P. Golany, and J. W. Reinke. 1971. Continuation of studies on the hydrology of ponds and small lakes. Univ. Minn. Agric. Exp. St. Tech. Bull. 274.

Bluemle, J. P. 1971. Depth to bedrock in North Dakota. N. Dak. Geol. Surv. Misc. Map 13.

Brun, L. T., J. L. Richardson, J. W. Enz, and J. K. Larson. 1981. Stream flow changes in the southern Red River Valley. N. Dak. Farm Res. 38:1–14.

Campbell, K. L., and H. P. Johnson. 1975. Hydrologic simulation of watersheds with artificial drainage. Water Resour. Res. 11:120–26.

Court, Arnold. 1974. The climate of the conterminous United States. In Climates of North America, ed. R. A. Bryson and F. K. Hare, 193–343. Amsterdam: Elsevier.

Cowardin, L. M., V. Carter, F. C. Golet, and E. T. LaRoe. 1979. Classification of wetlands and deepwater habitats of the United States. U.S. Fish and Wildl. Office of Biol. Serv. Rep. 31. Washington, D.C.: Dept. Inter.

Crowe, A. S., and F. W. Schwartz. 1981a. Simulation of lake-watershed systems. I: Description and sensitivity analysis of the model. J. Hydrol. 52:71–105.

———. 1981b. Simulation of lake-watershed systems. II: Application to Baptiste Lake, Alberta, Canada. J. Hydrol. 52:107–25.

———. 1985. Application of a lake-watershed model for the determination of water balance. J. Hydrol. 81:1–26.

Downey, J. S. 1986. Geohydrology of the bedrock aquifers in the northern Great Plains in parts of Montana, Wyoming, North Dakota and South Dakota. U.S. Geol. Surv. Prof. Paper 1402-E.

Dugan, J. T. 1984. Hydrologic characteristics of Nebraska soils. U.S. Geol. Surv. Water-Supply Paper 2222.

Eisenlohr, W. S., Jr. 1966. Water loss from a natural pond through transpiration by hydrophytes. Water Resour. Res. 2:443–53.

_____. 1972. Hydrologic investigations of prairie potholes in North Dakota, 1959–68. U.S. Geol. Surv. Prof. Paper 585-A.

Ficke, J. F. 1972. Comparison of evaporation computation methods, Pretty Lake, Lagrange County, Indiana. U.S. Geol. Surv. Prof. Paper 686-A.

Freeze, R. A. 1969a. Regional groundwater flow Old Wives Lake drainage basin, Saskatchewan. Can. Dept. Dept. Energy, Mines, Resour., Inland Waters Branch, Sci. Ser. No. 5.

_____. 1969b. Theoretical analysis of regional ground-water flow. Can. Dept. Energy, Mines, and Resour., Inland Waters Branch, Sci. Ser. No. 3.

_____. n.d. Hydrology of the Good Spirit Lake drainage basin, Saskatchewan. Can. Energy, Mines, and Resour., Inland Waters Branch, Tech. Bull. 14.

Ginsberg, M. 1985. Nebraska's sandhills lakes – A hydrogeologic overview. Water Resour. Bull. 21:573–78.

Grisak, G. E. 1975. The fracture porosity of glacial till. Can. J. Earth Sci. 12:513–15.

Grisak, G. E., J. A. Cherry, J. A. Vanhof, and J. P. Bluemle. 1976. Hydrogeologic and hydrochemical properties of fractured till in the Interior Plains region. In Glacial Till – an interdisciplinary study, ed. R. F. Legget, 304–35. Royal Soc. Can. Spec. Publ. No. 12.

Haan, C. T., and H. P. Johnson. 1968. Hydraulic model of runoff from depressional areas. Part I: General considerations. Trans. Amer. Soc. Agric. Eng. 1:364–67.

Harbeck, G. E., Jr. 1962. A practical field technique to measure reservoir evaporation utilizing mass-transfer theory. U.S. Geol. Surv. Prof. Paper 272-E:101–5.

Hare, F. K., and J. E. Hay. 1974. The climate of Canada and Alaska. In Climates of North America, ed. R. A. Bryson and F. K. Hare, 49–192. Amsterdam: Elsevier.

Hendry, M. J. 1982. Hydraulic conductivity of a glacial till in Alberta. Ground Water 20:162–69.

_____. 1983. Ground water recharge through a heavy-textured soil. J. Hydrol. 63:201–9.

Hubbard, D. E., and R. L. Linder. 1986. Spring runoff retention in prairie pothole wetlands. J. Soil Water Conserv. 41:122–25.

Jahn, L. R. 1981. Resource management: Challenge of the eighties. Water Spectrum 13:1–7.

Kloet, L. 1971. Effects of drainage on runoff and flooding within the Pembina River Basin, North Dakota-Manitoba. U.S. Fish and Wildl. Serv. Unpubl. Rep.

LaBaugh, J. W., T. C. Winter, V. A. Adomaitis, and G. A. Swanson. 1987. Geohydrology and chemistry of prairie wetlands, Stutsman County, North Dakota. U.S. Geol. Surv. Prof. Paper 1431.

Laksham, G. 1976. Drainage basin study, progress report no. 9. Saskatchewan Res. Coun., Eng. Div. Rep. E 76-2.

Langbein, W. B., C. H. Hains, and R. C. Culler. 1951. Hydrology of stockwater reservoirs in Arizona. U.S. Geol. Surv. Circ. 110.

Larson, C. L. 1981. Effects of wetland drainage on surface runoff. In Selected Proc. of Midwest Conf. on Wetland Values and Manage., ed. B. Richardson, 117–20, June 17–19, St. Paul, Minn. Navarre, Minn.: Minn. Freshwater Soc.

Lissey, A. 1971. Depression-focused transient groundwater flow patterns in Manitoba. Geol. Assoc. Can. Spec. Paper 9.

Ludden, A. P., D. L. Frink, and D. H. Johnson. 1983. Water storage capacity of natural wetland depressions in the Devils Lake basin of North Dakota. Soil Water Conserv. 38:45–48.

Malcolm, J. M. 1979. The relationship of wetland drainage to flooding and water problems and its impacts on the J. Clark Salyer National Wildlife Refuge. U.S. Fish and Wildl. Serv. Unpubl. Rep.

Meyboom, P. 1963. Patterns of ground-water flow in the prairie profile. Proc. of Hydrol. Symp. No. 3, Groundwater. Ottawa: Queen's Printer.

_____. 1964. Three observations on streamflow depletion by phreatophytes. J. Hydrol. 2:248–61.

_____. 1966a. Ground water studies in the Assiniboine River drainage basin. Part I: The evaluation of a flow system in south-central Saskatchewan. Geol. Surv. Can. Bull. 139.

_____. 1966b. Unsteady groundwater flow near a willow ring in hummocky moraine. J. Hydrol. 4:38–62.

_____. 1967a. Estimates of ground water recharge on the prairies. In Water Resources of Canada, ed. C. E. Dolman, 128–53. Toronto: Univ. Toronto Press.

_____. 1967b. Ground water studies in the Assiniboine River drainage basin. Part II: Hydrologic characteristics of phreatophytic vegetation in south-central Saskatchewan. Geol. Surv. Can. Bull. 139.

_____. 1967c. Mass-transfer studies to determine the ground-water regime of permanent lakes in hummocky moraine of western Canada. J. Hydrol. 5:117–42.

Meyboom, P., R. O. van Everdingen, and R. A. Freeze. 1966. Patterns of ground water flow in seven discharge areas in Saskatchewan and Manitoba. Geol. Surv. Can. Bull. 147.

Millar, J. B. 1971. Shoreline-area ratio as a factor in rate of water loss from small sloughs. J. Hydrol. 14:259–84.

Miller, J. J., D. F. Acton, and R. J. St. Arnaud. 1985. The effect of groundwater on soil formation in a morainal landscape in Saskatchewan. Can. J. Soil Sci. 65:293–307.

Mills, J. G., and M. A. Zwarich. 1984. Transient ground water flow surrounding a recharge slough in a till plain. Proc. Third Annu. West. Prov. Conf., Rationalization of Water and Soil Res. and Manage. Winnipeg, Manitoba.

Moore, I. D., and C. L. Larson. 1979. Effects of drainage projects on surface runoff from small depressional watersheds in the north-central region. Univ. Minn., Water Resour. Res. Cent. Bull. 99.

Pfannkuch, H. O., and T. C. Winter. 1984. Effect of anisotropy and groundwater system geometry on seepage through lakebeds. 1: Analog and dimensional analysis. J. Hydrol. 75:213–37.

Province of Manitoba. 1984. Agricultural land drainage. Proc. Third Annu. West. Prov. Conf., Rationalization of Water and Soil Res. and Manage., Winnipeg, Manitoba.

Scott, J. S. 1976. Geology of Canadian tills. In Glacial till—an interdisciplinary study, ed. R. F. Leggett, 50–66. Royal Soc. of Can. Spec. Publ. No. 12.

Shjeflo, J. B. 1968. Evapotranspiration and the water budget of prairie potholes in North Dakota. U.S. Geol. Surv. Prof. Paper 585-B.

Sloan, C. E. 1972. Ground-water hydrology of prairie potholes in North Dakota. U.S. Geol. Surv. Prof. Paper 585-C.

Stewart, R. E., and H. A. Kantrud. 1972. Vegetation of prairie potholes, North Dakota, in relation to quality of water and other environmental factors. U.S. Geol. Surv. Prof. Paper 585-D.

Stichling, W., and S. R. Blackwell. 1957. Drainage area as a hydrologic factor on the glaciated Canadian prairies. Internatl. Assoc. Sci. Hydrol. Publ. 45.

Swanson, G. A., T. C. Winter, V. A. Adomaitis, and J. W. LaBaugh. 1988. Chemical characteristics of prairie lakes in south-central North Dakota—their potential for impacting fish and wildlife. U.S. Fish and Wildl. Serv. Techn. Rep.

Toth, J. 1963. A theoretical analysis of groundwater flow in small drainage basins. Proc. Hydrol. Symp. No. 3, Groundwater, 75–96. Ottawa: Queen's Printer.

_____. 1966. Mapping and interpretation of field phenomena for ground water reconnaissance in a prairie environment, Alberta, Canada. Bull. Intern. Assoc. of Sci. Hydrol. 11:1–49.

_____. 1971. Ground water discharge—A common generator of diverse geologic and morphologic phenomena. Bull. Int. Assoc. Sci. Hydrol. 16:7–24.

Winter, T. C. 1976. The hydrologic setting of lakes in Minnesota and adjacent states with emphasis on the interaction of lakes and ground water, U.S. Geol. Surv. Open-File Rep. 76–81.

_____. 1981. Uncertainties in estimating the water balance of lakes. Water Resour. Bull. 17:82–115.

_____. 1983. The interaction of lakes with variably saturated porous media. Water Resour. Res. 19:1203–18.

_____. 1986. Effect of ground-water recharge on configuration of the water table beneath sand dunes and on seepage in lakes in the sandhills of Nebraska. J. Hydrol. 86:221–37.

Winter, T. C., and M. R. Carr. 1980. Hydrologic setting of wetlands in the Cottonwood Lake area, Stutsman County, North Dakota. U.S. Geol. Surv. Water-Resour. Invest. WRI 80-99.

Winter, T. C., R. D. Benson, R. A. Engberg, G. J. Wiche, D. G. Emerson, O. A. Crosby, and J. E. Miller. 1984. Synopsis of ground-water and surface-water resources of North Dakota. U.S. Geol. Surv. Open-File Rep. 84-732.

Winter, T. C., and M-K Woo. 1988. Hydrology of lakes and wetlands. *In* Surface Water Hydrology, ed. M. L. Moss, M. G. Wolman, and H. C. Riggs. Boulder, Colorado: Geological Society of America.

JAMES W. LaBAUGH

③ CHEMICAL
IN NORTHERN

ABSTRACT

MOST of the wetlands and lakes in the northern prairie of North America contain water that is alkaline (pH >7.4) and pH values as large as 10.8 have been reported. The concentration of dissolved solids in these waters spans the gradient of salinity from fresh to extremely saline; the most saline water is almost ten times more concentrated than sea water on the basis of specific conductance. Values of specific conductance of water in wetlands and lakes of this region are within the range of 42 to 472,000 $\mu S/cm$.

Diverse types of water occur in the prairie wetlands and lakes within the extreme differences in salinity. Calcium, magnesium, sodium, and potassium have each been determined to be the most abundant cation in water of prairie wetlands and lakes. Bicarbonate, sulfate, and chloride have each been determined to be the most abundant anion in these waters. The least saline waters commonly are a calcium bicarbonate type and the most saline waters commonly are a sodium sulfate type. However, water type and salinity are independent. On the basis of phosphorus supply and concentration of phosphorus, many of these prairie wetlands and lakes are eutrophic.

Chemical characteristic of water in prairie wetlands and lakes vary both seasonally and annually. Seasonal variation in major ions is affected by: concentration under ice cover, dilution due to snowmelt and runoff, concentration by evaporation, dilution from rainfall, and interaction with groundwater. Seasonal variation in phosphorus and nitrogen is affected by phytoplankton uptake and mineralization, as well as by decomposition of macrophyte litter. Annual variation in salinity and concentration of major ions is affected by climatic variation and groundwater.

There was no significant relation between specific conductance and topographic position; relative altitude alone does not determine salinity or water type within a common geographic area. On a local scale, differences in salinity and water type between adjacent wetlands or lakes is a function of the location of the wetlands or lakes in the groundwater flow system: either recharging groundwater, receiving groundwater discharge, or receiving water from the groundwater system on one side and losing water to the groundwater system on the other side.

CHARACTERISTICS OF WATER
PRAIRIE WETLANDS

KEY WORDS: anion, cation, ionic proportions, Nebraska sandhills, pH, phosphorus, prairie potholes, salinity, specific conductance, topography, and water chemistry.

INTRODUCTION

THE northern prairie of North America contains numerous wetlands and lakes. These wetlands and lakes are located in a variety of geological settings, including both glaciated and unglaciated terrane. The area in which these wetlands and lakes are located is spanned by a climatic gradient of evaporation and precipitation; rainfall is nearly equal to evaporation in the extreme eastern part of the region, but decreases relative to evaporation so that in the extreme western part of the region annual average evaporation exceeds rainfall by more than one meter (See Winter, Chap. 2). Considerable differences exist between wetlands and lakes in the northern prairie because of their hydrogeologic setting.

Differences also exist among wetlands and lakes in the northern prairie based on the chemical composition of water in the wetlands and lakes. Evidence of these differences comes from studies of the water chemistry of several wetlands and lakes within different geographic areas of the northern prairie (Rawson and Moore 1944; Moyle 1945; Barica 1975; McCarraher 1977). Differences in chemical characteristics of lakes in one of these areas have been statistically related to hydrogeologic setting (Barr 1978).

Details of the interaction of hydrogeologic setting and chemical

JAMES W. LaBAUGH, U.S. Geological Survey, Denver, Colorado 80225.

characteristics of water within prairie wetlands or lakes are not readily obtained from existing areal data sets (Gorham et al. 1983). Instead, these details can be obtained from studies of the interaction of groundwater and wetlands and lakes at specific sites within those areas (Rozkowski 1969; LaBaugh et al. 1987).

Hydrogeologic setting and chemical characteristics of water in prairie lakes and wetlands result in aquatic plant communities that are very diverse (Kantrud et al., Chap. 5). Plant communities change in response to changes in water level (van der Valk 1981). The length of time a prairie pothole contains water and the salinity of the water affects the type and composition of vegetation in prairie potholes (Stewart and Kantrud 1972).

Changes in water level can affect nitrogen and phosphorus concentrations in prairie lakes and wetlands due to decomposition of macrophyte vegetation (Kadlec 1986a, 1986b). Although nitrogen and phosphorus are relatively abundant in prairie lakes and wetlands, the amount of algal biomass present can be much smaller than expected from nitrogen and phosphorus concentration due to the major ion composition of lake and wetland water (Bierhuizen and Prepas 1985; Campbell and Prepas 1986).

The purpose of this chapter is (1) to summarize the chemical characteristics of water in prairie wetlands and lakes in the northern prairie of North America, in relation to commonly used classification criteria, and in relation to seasonal and annual variation (2) to examine the relation between hydrogeologic setting and chemical characteristics of water in prairie wetlands and lakes, and (3) to identify gaps in current understanding of the relation of hydrogeologic setting to chemical characteristics of prairie wetlands and lakes. Information presented in this chapter is from unpublished data available to the author and published reports about the chemical characteristics of wetlands and lakes in the northern prairie of North America.

CHEMICAL CHARACTERISTICS OF WETLANDS AND LAKES

pH

Most of the wetlands and lakes in the northern prairie of North America are alkaline as defined by Cowardin et al. (1979) (i.e., the pH commonly is larger than 7.4). Representative ranges of pH values reported for wetlands and lakes in this area are given in Table 3.1.

Values of pH larger than pH 7 result from a variety of processes, such as chemical reactions involved in weathering of carbonates, and

TABLE 3.1. Range in values of pH, from selected regional studies, for water in prairie wetlands and lakes in the northern prairie of North America

Geographic location	Number of wetlands or lakes	Range in values of pH	Reference
Alberta, Canada	20	8.3–10.1	Bierhuizen and Prepas (1985)
Saskatchewan, Canada	97	7.1–9.45	Rozkowski (1969)
Saskatchewan, Canada	60	7.8–9.8	Hammer (1978)
Manitoba, Canada	79	7.4–9.65	Barica (1975)
North Dakota, United States	178	7.4–10.3	Swanson et al. (1988)
South Dakota, United States	44	7.9–9.2	Petri and Larson (1973)
South Dakota and Minnesota, United States	14	7.95–9.25	Bright (1968)
Nebraska, United States	262	6.8–10.8	McCarraher (1977)

photosynthetic uptake of dissolved carbon dioxide (Hem 1970). Factors controlling pH in very saline waters are discussed by Hammer (1986).

Salinity

A variety of classification schemes with associated terminology exists in the literature with respect to salinity. Because the literature on prairie wetlands includes such variety, and salinity categories are mentioned in other chapters of this book, an overview of these classification criteria are presented here.

The concentration of dissolved solids in water is used to define salinity, and it is reported in units of milligrams per liter (mg/l), parts per million (ppm), or parts per thousand ‰ (ppt). An approximation of the concentration of dissolved solids commonly is made by the measurement of specific conductance. Specific conductance commonly is reported in units of microsiemens per centimeter at 25°C (μS/cm). Electrical conductance of water increases as charged ion concentrations increase, so that larger values of specific conductance generally indicate larger concentrations of dissolved solids (Hem 1970).

One of the criteria used to distinguish one water body from another on the basis of salinity for prairie systems was suggested by Rawson and Moore (1944). They considered water bodies as fresh if the concentration of dissolved solids in the water was less than 300 ppm. Waters that were not fresh were divided into four categories: moderately saline (300–1,000 ppm), saline (1,000–10,000 ppm), very saline (10,000–30,000 ppm) and extremely saline (>30,000 ppm).

Further definition of gradation in salinity for prairie wetlands and lakes was proposed by Stewart and Kantrud (1972). They used correlation between distinctly different plant communities and relative concentration of dissolved solids, indicated by specific conductance, to define six categories of salinity: fresh (<500 μS/cm), slightly brackish (500–2,000 μS/cm), moderately brackish (2,000–5,000 μS/cm), brackish (5,000–15,000 μS/cm), subsaline (15,000–45,000 μS/cm), and saline (>45,000 μS/cm).

A classification similar to that of Stewart and Kantrud (1972) has been proposed by Millar (1976) for the prairie wetlands of western Canada. This classification also was based on plant communities. Millar considered water to be fresh if the salinity was less than 1,400 ppm or 2,000 μS/cm. Instead of six categories spanning the range of salinity, Millar used only four: fresh (<1,400 ppm), moderately saline (1,400–10,500 ppm), saline (10,500–31,500 ppm), and hypersaline (>31,500 ppm).

The gradient of salinity also has been divided into categories using a geochemical approach for the purpose of classification of prairie lakes by Robinove et al. (1958). Using this classification, waters are considered fresh if the dissolved-solids concentration is less than 1‰ or if the value of specific conductance is less than 1,400 μS/cm. Division of the salinity range in Robinove et al. (1958) used various terms, including three categories of saline water with dissolved-solids concentrations between 1 and 35‰ or with specific-conductance values between 1,400 and 50,000 μS/cm. Water with dissolved-solids concentration greater than 35‰ was considered "briny" because the dissolved-solids concentration of sea water is approximately 35‰. Numerous wetlands and lakes in the northern prairie of North America are more saline than the ocean.

In contrast to the definitions of freshwater proposed by investigators of prairie wetlands and lakes (Rawson and Moore 1944; Robinove et al. 1958; Stewart and Kantrud 1972; Millar 1976), when all inland waters (waters not connected to the sea) are considered, a dissolved-solids concentration of less than 3‰ has been used to define freshwater (Williams 1981). Williams noted the difference between fresh and saline water could logically be defined by biologists on the basis of a distinct change in the biota. Changes in the biota were used by Stewart and Kantrud (1972) and Millar (1976), indicating that within a particular region, such changes can correspond to changes in salinity. However, Williams (1981) noted when all inland waters are examined, well-defined changes in plant communities do not occur between fresh and saline waters because salinity tolerance by the biota occurs over a continuous gradient.

In an attempt to provide a classification of wetlands and lakes within the United States, Cowardin et al. (1979) suggested wetlands and lakes be defined as fresh if the dissolved-solids concentration was less than 0.5‰ or the specific conductance value was less than 800 μS/cm. Cowardin et al. (1979) proposed the following categories for their classification: fresh (< 800 μS/cm) oligosaline (800–8,000 μS/cm), mesosaline (8,000–30,000 μS/cm), polysaline (30,000–45,000 μS/cm), eusaline (45,000–60,000 μS/cm) and hypersaline (>60,000 μS/cm). The classification of Cowardin et al. (1979) included categories that were not defined by the same values as used to define the six categories proposed for prairie wetlands by Stewart and Kantrud (1972).

Cowardin et al. (1979) noted diversity in chemical characteristics of surface water makes meaningful subdivision of the salinity range extremely difficult. Also, as Lieffers and Shay (1983) noted, seasonal and annual changes in salinity can occur such that a single lake could be classified in different salinity categories within a single season or from year to year. Consequently, no attempt will be made here to categorize the water in Table 3.2 according to any of the salinity classifications.

Examination of data provided in regional studies of numerous wetlands and lakes indicates that salinity of these waters ranges from

TABLE 3.2. Summary of the range in concentration of dissolved solids, or value of specific conductance, from water in prairie wetlands and lakes, northern prairie of North America, in selected regional studies

Geographic location	Number of wetlands or lakes	Range in concentration of total dissolved solids or *specific conductance*	Reference
Alberta, Canada	20	979–90,728 mg/l *1,311–57,812 µS/cm*	Bierhuizen and Prepas (1985)
Saskatchewan, Canada	53	126–120,000 ppm	Rawson and Moore (1944)
Saskatchewan, Canada	60	2.23–342 ‰ *3.0–195.1 mS/cm*	Hammer (1978)
Manitoba, Canada	79	268–9,720 mg/l *305–7,837 µS/cm*	Barica (1975)
North Dakota, United States	134	*220–12,070 µS/cm*	Barica (1978)
North Dakota, United States	178	*365–70,300 µS/cm*	Swanson et al. (1988)
North Dakota, United States	160	*230–70,000 µS/cm*	Sloan (1972)
South Dakota, United States	44	31–83,700 mg/l *42–48,000 µS/cm*	Petri and Larson (1973)
South Dakota and Minnesota, United States	14	169–15,254 mg/l *246–14,080 µS/cm*	Bright (1968)
Nebraska, United States	262	95–86,200 mg/l	McCarraher (1977)
Nebraska, United States	18	4,893–123,792 mg/l *6,500–472,000 µS/cm*	Nash (1978)

fresh to very saline (Table 3.2). Of all the wetlands and lakes mentioned in these studies, the most dilute water (42 μS/cm) was measured in Cherry Lake, Clark and Kingsbury counties, South Dakota, by Petri and Larson (1973). The most saline water (472,000 μS/cm) was measured in an unnamed lake in Sheridan County, Nebraska, by Nash (1978).

A summary of the frequency distribution of salinity from selected regional studies is presented in Figure 3.1. Data in this figure indicate

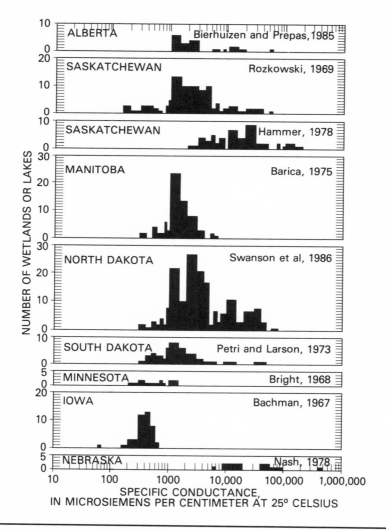

FIG. 3.1.   Frequency distribution of specific conductance for prairie wetlands and lakes in the northern prairie of North America from selected regional studies.

there is a general trend of larger values of specific conductance in regions of increased aridity. However, even in more arid regions values of specific conductance span a large range. Thus, the location of an individual prairie lake or wetland within the regional climate gradient of precipitation-evaporation does not solely account for the specific conductance of water in an individual lake or wetland.

Specific Conductance and Concentration of Major Ions

Rodhe (1949) determined that specific conductance and concentration of individual cations and anions were correlated for lakes in Sweden that had bicarbonate as the most abundant anion. In a study of lakes in the north-central United States, including data from the northern prairie, Gorham et al. (1983) also determined there was a good correlation between specific conductance and concentration of individual major ions. However, the relation among the major ions, and consequently ionic proportions and water type, changed considerably within the large range of specific conductance of their data.

Although Gorham et al. (1983) determined that there was a statistically significant relation between specific conductance and concentration of calcium in their data, considerable variation in concentration of calcium relative to specific conductance occurred when specific conductance values were greater than 1,000 μS/cm. Gorham et al. (1983) noted precipitation of calcium carbonate can occur when specific conductance is larger than 190 μS/cm. Part of the considerable change in the relation among major ions, coincident with large values of specific conductance, is due to geochemical processes, such as precipitation of calcium carbonate (Gorham et al. 1983). Last and Schweyen (1983) indicated most lakes in the region are saturated or supersaturated for calcium and magnesium bicarbonate minerals.

Results of the study by Swanson et al. (1988) indicated there was no statistically significant relation between specific conductance and concentration of calcium for prairie lakes in south-central North Dakota. Most of the lakes in their investigation had values of specific conductance greater than 1,000 μS/cm. The absence of a significant statistical relation between specific conductance and calcium indicates calcium-carbonate precipitation probably is an important mechanism controlling ionic proportions in the lakes.

The fact that calcium carbonate precipitation can be common in the south-central part of North Dakota is supported by chemical equilibrium analyses of water from wetlands in the Cottonwood Lake area, North Dakota (LaBaugh et al. 1987). These wetlands are representative of the most dilute waters used in the regional analysis of Swanson et al. (1987). WATEQ analysis, a computer program for calculating chemical equilibrium of natural waters (Truesdall and Jones 1974), indicates calcite supersaturation occurred in wetlands of four different water types within a range in specific conductance between 200–7,000 μS/cm. Calcite supersaturation has also been determined in prairie potholes in North Dakota by Mitten (1965).

In an analysis of data for all major ions, Barica (1975) found the most variation in concentration versus specific conductance for calcium, bicarbonate, and carbonate occurred for lakes in Manitoba. This variation in the data was assumed to be a function of biological processes in addition to geochemical processes. Regression analysis of Bright's (1968) data for prairie lakes in Minnesota and South Dakota was done for this report and indicated there was no significant relation between specific conductance and concentration of calcium (Figure 3.2A). Statistical analysis of Nash's (1978) data for prairie lakes in Nebraska also indicated no significant relation existed between specific conductance and calcium (Figure 3.2B). Fluctuations in calcium independent of specific conductance due to geochemical or biological processes apparently are a common feature in prairie wetlands and lakes.

Available results of regression analysis for studies of prairie wetlands and lakes in the northern prairie of North America indicate that only sodium, potassium, and sulfate consistently have been significantly related to specific conductance. There was no statistically significant relation between specific conductance and concentrations of magnesium or chloride for lakes in Nebraska (Nash 1978). In contrast, data presented by Barica (1975), Swanson et al. (1988), and analysis of Bright's (1968) data indicate specific conductance is significantly related to concentrations of magnesium and chloride in wetlands and lakes of the glaciated prairie.

The difference in the relation of specific conductance to concentrations of magnesium or of chloride between wetlands and lakes in glaciated and nonglaciated parts of the northern prairie indicates regression analysis is useful in defining differences between concentration of chemical elements in surface water of different geologic terrane. Differences in salinity of lakes in glacial outwash and lakes in glacial till in North Dakota had been noted by Sloan (1972); lakes in outwash commonly were more saline than those in till. Swanson et al. (1988) found differences between lakes in glacial till and lakes in glacial outwash when regression analysis was used to determine the relation of specific conductance to concentration of major ions. Considerably more variation existed in concentration of magnesium, sodium, chloride, and sulfate in relation to specific conductance for lakes in outwash than for lakes in till. Thus, concentration of these elements might be approximated from specific conductance for lakes in till but not in outwash.

The potential of using specific conductance to approximate the concentration of major ions for northern prairie wetlands and lakes within a

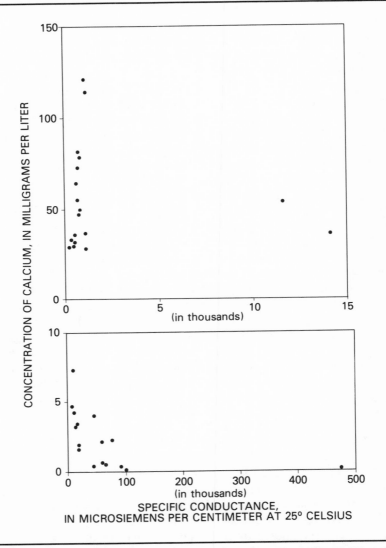

FIG. 3.2. Concentration of calcium in relation to specific conductance for (A) prairie lakes in South Dakota and Minnesota (*Bright 1968*) and (B) prairie lakes in Nebraska (*Nash 1978*).

specific area has been suggested by Barica (1978) and by results of the analysis of lakes in glacial till of North Dakota by Swanson et al. (1988). Yet, waters that have the same most abundant cation and the same most abundant anion can have a considerable range in specific conductance (Tables 3.3 and 3.4).

TABLE 3.3. Examples of prairie lakes in which calcium and bicarbonate are the most abundant cation and anion

Lake	Concentration of individual ions in milligrams per liter and milliequivalents per liter							Dissolved solids or specific conductance	Reference
	Ca	Mg	Na	K	Cl	SO$_4$	HCO$_3$+CO$_3$		
Loch Lomond, Saskatchewan	28.7	8.4	1.4	...	1.0	2.1	118	126 ppm	Rawson and Moore (1944)
	1.4	*0.69*	*0.0*	...	*0.02*	*0.04*	*1.93*		
Lake 306, Manitoba	27.5	9.0	1.58	11.2	2	12	204	305 µS/cm	Barica (1975)
	1.37	*.74*	*.06*	*.28*	*.05*	*.24*	*3.44*		
Lake 175, North Dakota	59.0	24.8	8.4	4.1	15.0	32	300	590 µS/cm	Swanson et al. (1988)
	1.69	*1.23*	*.13*	*.47*	*.35*	*.37*	*2.62*		
Cherry Lake, South Dakota	44	20	15	2.4	7.8	64	200	357 µS/cm	Petri and Larson (1973)
	2.19	*1.64*	*.65*	*.61*	*.21*	*1.33*	*3.27*		
Budd Lake, Minnesota	57.6	21.3	8	3.8	14.2	49.1	102	400 µS/cm	Bright (1968)
	2.88	*1.75*	*.35*	*.10*	*.39*	*1.02*	*3.40*		
Crane Lake, Nebraska	35	10	25	18	5.6	5.7	189	360 µS/cm	LaBaugh (unpublished data)
	1.74	*.82*	*1.08*	*.46*	*.15*	*.11*	*32.7*		

TABLE 3.4. Examples of prairie wetlands or lakes indicating the variety in the identity of the most abundant anion and the most abundant cation

Wetland or lake	Concentration of individual ions in milligrams per liter and milliequivalents per liter								Specific conductance	Reference
	Ca	Mg	Na	K	Cl	SO$_4$	HCO$_3$	CO$_3$		
Lake 306, Manitoba	30.1	165	69.8	44.9	51	392	573	54	1,394 µS/cm	Barica (1975)
	1.50	*13.56*	*3.03*	*1.14*	*1.43*	*8.16*	*9.39*	*1.79*		
Jesse Lake, Nebraska	<0.3	0.4	9,430	10,120	1,482	7,330	20,292	6,605	85,000 µS/cm	Nash (1978)
	<.01	*.03*	*410*	*258*	*41.*	*152*	*332*	*220*		
Wetland T8, North Dakota	7.0	3.4	.4	33	4.6	17	59	...	140 µS/cm	LaBaugh (unpublished data)
	.34	*.28*	*.01*	*.84*	*.13*	*.35*	*.97*			
Traverse Lake, Minnesota	121	39.1	51.5	14	11.8	340	...	97.8	1,050 µS/cm	Bright (1968)
	6.03	*3.21*	*2.24*	*0.35*	*0.33*	*7.08*	...	*3.25*		
Little Manitou Lake, Saskatchewan	497	9,518	12,300	890	18,000	39,600	776	209	72,500 µS/cm	Hammer (1978)
	24	*782*	*535*	*22*	*507*	*824*	*12*	*6.96*		
Lake 150, North Dakota	115.9	390	1,432	180	555	3,500	580	...	7,000 µS/cm	Swanson et al. (1988)
	5.78	*32.09*	*62.31*	*4.60*	*15.65*	*72.91*	*9.50*			
Birchbark Lake, Saskatchewan	177	93	930	20	1,990	0	90	0	5,800 µS/cm	Hammer (1978c)
	8.68	*7.64*	*40.45*	*.51*	*56.1*	*0*	*1.47*	*0*		
Lake 117, North Dakota	18	4.3	1,110	32.8	940	350	530	0	3,330 µS/cm	Swanson et al. (1988)
	.94	*.36*	*30.46*	*.76*	*16.50*	*6.25*	*6.71*	*0*		

Gorham et al. (1983) noted a change in the most abundant cation and anion as specific conductance increased for the set of lakes they examined in the north-central United States. A shift from calcium to magnesium to sodium and a shift from bicarbonate water to sulfate water was indicated by their data. These shifts were attributed to increased aridity and a change from noncalcareous glacial drift to calcareous glacial drift with abundant sulfur minerals towards the western part of their study area. Gorham et al. (1983) did not examine data from the sandhill lakes of Nebraska or lakes in Alberta; data included in this chapter indicate carbonate waters are common in the most arid part of the northern prairie that contain natural wetlands and lakes, all of which, except the most dilute, have sodium as the most abundant cation (McCarraher 1977; Nash 1978; Bierhuizen and Prepas 1985).

Even within an area considered to be quite arid and fairly uniform in geology, such as the Nebraska sandhills, a shift in water type from bicarbonate to sulfate as specific conductance increases is indicated by Nash's (1978) data. These data indicate differences in water types within an area may be related to regional heterogeneity of geologic and hydrologic setting, including interaction with groundwater. Barr (1978) found such a relation between water chemistry and hydrogeologic setting for lakes in the north-central United States. Gorham et al. (1983) also noted some of the differences among lakes in their study was due to the interaction of geologic terrane and the effect of groundwater flow systems, but definition of the interaction was not yet available.

Cation and Anion

One of the common methods of classifying water type on the basis of chemical characteristics is done by examining data for major cations and anions. Using this type of classification with data from lakes in Minnesota and the Dakotas, Tarapchak (1973) identified four water types: calcium bicarbonate, calcium magnesium bicarbonate, magnesium sulfate, and sodium sulfate.

Using only the most abundant cation and anion, eight different types of water can be identified from the studies of prairie wetlands and lakes listed in Table 3.2. Calcium, magnesium, sodium, and potassium, individually have been found to be the most abundant cation, and bicarbonate, sulfate, and chloride individually have been found to be the most abundant anion in the wetlands and lakes.

To provide a ready means of comparing both concentration and water type, data will also be presented in this report in the form of modified Schoeller diagrams (Schoeller 1959). Because of the importance of potassium in some prairie wetlands and lakes, it will be plotted separately from sodium, unlike the format of Schoeller's (1959) diagrams. These diagrams provide a means of comparing waters that differ in the relative abundance of major cations and anions as well as in overall concentration. Concentrations of the individual major cations and anions are plotted on a semilogarithmic scale and values for a particular water are connected. The shape of the resulting curve is characteristic of a particular type of water in relation to the identity of the most abundant cation and anion.

The most dilute wetlands and lakes in the northern prairie commonly have calcium and bicarbonate as the most abundant major ions. These wetlands and lakes have been found throughout the northern prairie of North America (Table 3.3). For the purpose of comparison with other bicarbonate waters in which either magnesium, sodium, or potassium is the most abundant major cation, an example of one of the prairie lakes (Budd Lake, Minnesota) from Table 3.3, in which calcium is the most abundant major cation, is presented in Fig. 3.3.

The combination of magnesium and bicarbonate as the most abundant major ion is very common in comparison to the combination of calcium and bicarbonate. Water in which magnesium and bicarbonate were the most abundant major ions occurs in wetlands and lakes in Saskatchewan (Rawson and Moore 1944), Manitoba (Barica 1975), North Dakota (Sloan 1972; Swanson et al. 1988), South Dakota (Petri and Larson 1973), Minnesota (Bright 1968) and Iowa (Bachmann 1965). An example of water (Lake 306, Manitoba) in which magnesium and bicarbonate are the most abundant cation and anion is presented in Figure 3.3. Waters with this chemical characteristic were rare (McCarraher 1977) or absent in Nebraska (Nash 1978).

Lakes in the sandhills of Nebraska commonly have sodium and bicarbonate as the most abundant cation and anion (McCarraher 1977). One of the more saline lakes with this chemical characteristic is Jesse Lake, Nebraska (Fig. 3.3). Waters with sodium and bicarbonate as the most abundant cation and anion combination also occur in North Dakota (Swanson et al. 1987). This chemical characteristic is not common in the Canadian part of the northern prairie, absent in the studies of Rozkowski (1969), Barica (1975) and Hammer (1978), present in only a few lakes in the investigation of Rawson and Moore (1944), and present in most of the lakes in Alberta studied by Bierhuizen and Prepas (1985). Published studies of prairie wetlands or lakes in South Dakota (Petri and Larson 1973), Minnesota (Bright 1968), and Iowa (Bachmann 1965) indicate the combination of sodium and bicarbonate as the most abundant major ions was not present in those areas.

Potassium and bicarbonate have been identified as the most abundant cation and anion combination in only seasonal wetlands on the Coteau du Missouri in North Dakota (LaBaugh et al. 1987), for exam-

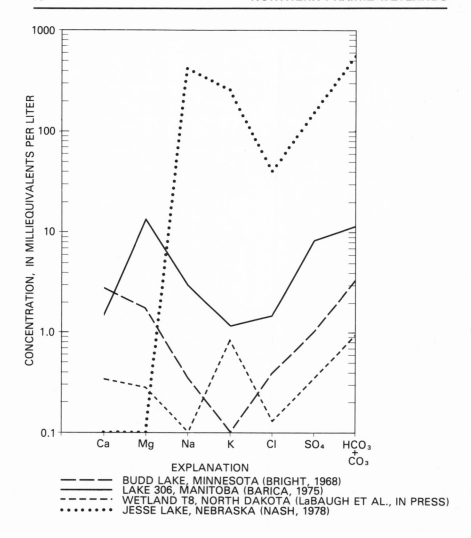

FIG. 3.3. Examples of prairie wetlands or lakes in which bicarbonate is the most abundant anion and either calcium, magnesium, or sodium is the most abundant cation.

ple, wetland T8 in the Cottonwood Lake area (Fig. 3.3). This water type occurs in wetlands containing "freshwater," with values of specific conductance similar to other bicarbonate waters with calcium as the most abundant cation (Table 3.3).

Wetlands and lakes in which sulfate is the major anion are common in the northern prairie of North America. Examples of sulfate waters in this region are presented in Figure 3.4. Sulfate was found to be the most abundant anion in the majority of wetlands and lakes in Saskatchewan (Rawson and Moore 1944; Rozkowski 1969; Hammer 1978), Manitoba (Barica 1975), North Dakota (Sloan 1972; Swanson et al. 1988), and South Dakota (Petri and Larson 1973). Half of the prairie lakes studied

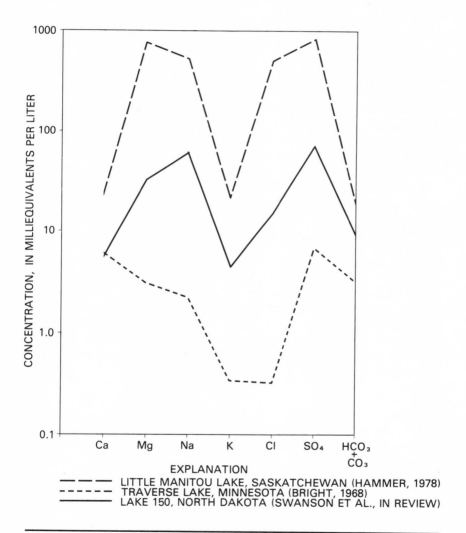

EXPLANATION
— — — LITTLE MANITOU LAKE, SASKATCHEWAN (HAMMER, 1978)
- - - - - TRAVERSE LAKE, MINNESOTA (BRIGHT, 1968)
———— LAKE 150, NORTH DAKOTA (SWANSON ET AL., IN REVIEW)

FIG. 3.4. Examples of prairie wetlands or lakes in which sulfate is the most abundant anion and either calcium, magnesium, or sodium is the most abundant cation.

by Bright (1968) had sulfate as the most abundant anion. In contrast, sulfate rarely is the dominant anion in the lakes of Nebraska; occurring in only 5 of the 18 lakes in Nash's (1978) investigation. None of the lakes or reservoirs in the glaciated prairie of Iowa studied by Bachmann (1965) had sulfate as the dominant anion.

Sulfate waters in which calcium is the most abundant cation occur in wetlands and lakes in the prairie of Minnesota (Bright 1968), North Dakota (LaBaugh et al. 1987), and Saskatchewan (Rozkowski 1969), but are rare in the latter two places. Magnesium was the most abundant cation in the majority of lakes containing sulfate waters in Saskatchewan (Rawson and Moore 1944; Hammer 1978), Manitoba (Barica 1975), and South Dakota (Petri and Larson 1973). Although sulfate waters with magnesium as the most abundant cation occur in wetlands and lakes in North Dakota (Sloan 1972; Swanson et al. 1988), more sulfate waters in North Dakota have sodium as the most abundant cation. Wetlands and lakes in the Canadian part of the prairie include sulfate waters in which sodium is the major cation (Rawson and Moore 1944; Barica 1975; Hammer 1978; Bierhuizen and Prepas 1985). This combination is the only one to occur in lakes containing sulfate waters in Nebraska (Nash 1978), and has been found in a few lakes in South Dakota (Petri and Larson 1973), but not in Minnesota (Bright 1968) or Iowa (Bachmann 1965).

Wetlands and lakes in which chloride was the most abundant anion are rare in the northern prairie of North American, based on the results of studies referenced in Tables 3.1 and 3.2. Swanson et al. (1988) reported finding wetlands with water of a chloride type in North Dakota, but this type was found in only 8 of the 178 wetlands and lakes examined by them. Sodium was the most abundant cation in these chloride waters. Hammer (1978) identified four lakes in Saskatchewan in which the water was a sodium chloride type. Examples from both of these studies are presented in Figure 3.5.

Ionic Proportions

Classification of water type on the basis of just the identity of the most abundant cation and anion groups together waters that can be very different in the relative proportion of the most abundant cation or anion to the other cations or anions. A classification based on ionic proportions has been presented for prairie lakes by Barica (1975). The ratio of the most abundant anion to the next two most abundant anions defined "true," "intermediate," and "mixed" water types. Subclasses within each anion water type were similarly defined by the ratio of the most abundant cation to the next two most abundant cations. These ratios classified as water as being a "true" type if the ratio was greater than 1.9, as

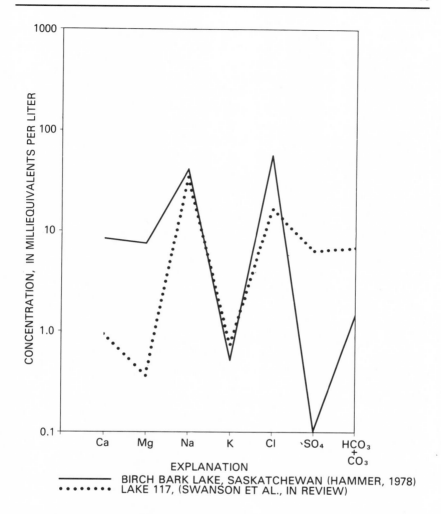

FIG. 3.5. Examples of prairie wetlands or lakes in which chloride is the most abundant anion and sodium is the most abundant cation.

being an "intermediate" type if the ratio was between 1.0 and 1.9, and as being a "mixed" type if the ratio was less than 1.

Barica (1975) only identified subclasses, based on cation proportions, for waters in which calcium, magnesium, or sodium were the most abundant cations. Water in which potassium was the most abundant cation did not occur in Barica's study. However, because potassium has been found as the most abundant cation in some prairie wetlands (La-

Baugh et al. 1987; Swanson unpublished data), it also is possible to include a potassium subclass using ionic proportions similar to the ones defined by Barica (1975).

Studies of prairie wetlands or lakes using ionic proportions indicate there is considerable variety in water types (Barica 1975; Swanson et al. 1987). In these studies "true," "intermediate," and "mixed" water types were found, including a variety of subclasses.

The difference in classification based on most abundant cation and anion and classification based on ionic proportions is apparent from examination of data in Table 3.3. All the lakes in the table are considered to be calcium bicarbonate waters using the simple classification. Differences in water type between these lakes do exist using the ionic-proportion classification. Water in Loch Lomond, Saskatchewan, is a true bicarbonate calcium type. Water in Budd Lake, Minnesota, is a true bicarbonate calcium magnesium type. Water in Crane Lake, Nebraska, is a true bicarbonate calcium sodium type. Increased concentrations of the second most abundant cation, and difference in the identity of the second most abundant cation among these lakes, are made apparent by use of ionic ratios.

Data in Table 3.3 indicate there can be a change in the identity of the second most abundant cation within a small range in specific conductance. However, it is possible for the identity of the second most abundant cation to remain the same within a large range in specific conductance.

In Nebraska sandhills lakes, waters of the true bicarbonate sodium type have a range of specific conductance between 6,500 μS/cm and 85,000 μS/cm (Nash 1978). Figure 3.6 indicates the variety in individual major ion concentration that occur for waters of the true bicarbonate sodium type in the sandhills. Potassium commonly is the second most abundant cation in lakes of the sandhills unlike true bicarbonate sodium waters in North Dakota, where magnesium is more abundant. Swanson et al. (1988) found waters of the true sulfate magnesium sodium type in prairie lakes of North Dakota had specific conductance values of a range of 2,575–70,300 μS/cm (Fig. 3.7).

Phosphorus

The quantity of total phosphorus entering a lake in relation to mean depth has been used to define the trophic status of lakes by Vollenweider (1968). The relation between trophic condition and the amount of phosphorus entering a lake was defined by Vollenweider (1968) such that lakes were classified as eutrophic when the interaction of supply and mean depth produced an in-lake concentration of total phosphorus greater than 0.020 mg/l. Within the classification of eutrophic lakes, a

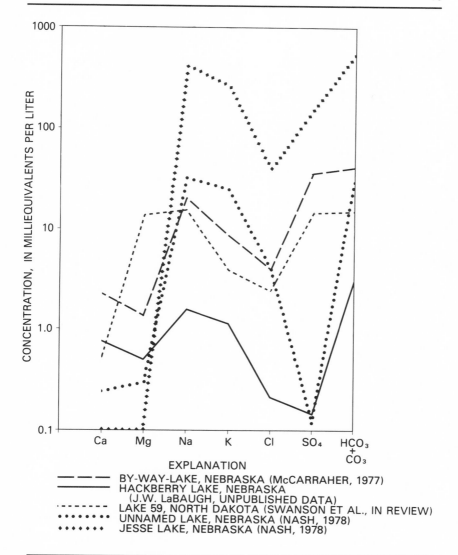

FIG. 3.6.   Examples of prairie wetlands or lakes with waters of the true bicarbonate-sodium type occurring over a large range in specific conductance.

set termed hypereutrophic also has been defined; lakes in this set have concentrations of total phosphorus in the range of 0.030 to greater than 5 mg/l according to Likens (1975).

Data on phosphorus supply to northern prairie lakes in Canada and concentrations of total phosphorus in prairie lakes of Canada indicate

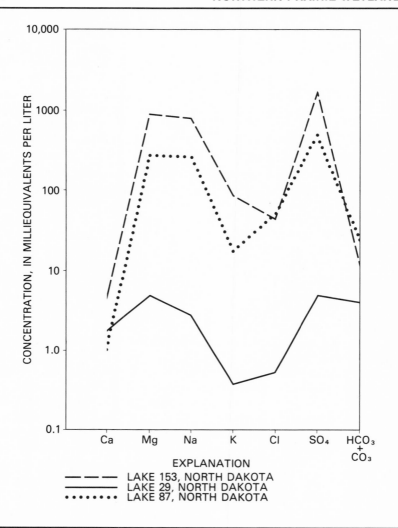

FIG. 3.7. Examples of prairie wetlands or lakes with waters of the true sulfate-magnesium-sodium type occurring over a large range in specific conductance (*Adapted from Swanson et al. 1987*).

these lakes are eutrophic (Barica 1980a; Hammer 1978). Data on the phosphorus supply to wetlands and lakes within the prairie of the United States are rare. Most of the phosphorus data reported for the northern prairie of the United States is for concentrations of soluble reactive phosphorus. Barica (1975) determined that soluble reactive phosphorus fluctuates considerably on a seasonal basis in prairie lakes. Soluble reactive phosphorus usually is some fraction of the value for total phosphorus (Rigler 1973). Consequently, data from studies in the United States would be expected to underestimate trophic conditions based on concentration of phosphorus. Even with this consideration, data for soluble reactive phosphorus from the studies in the United States indicate many of the prairie wetlands and lakes in South Dakota (Petri and Larson 1973) and Nebraska (McCarraher 1977; Nash 1978) are eutrophic. In these studies, the concentration of soluble reactive phosphorus commonly was greater than 0.020 mg/l (Table 3.5).

Few of the prairie lakes in Minnesota investigated by Bright (1968) can be defined as being eutrophic on the basis of phosphorus, probably because only soluble reactive phosphorus data were reported. The small values in most of those lakes probably reflect use by the biota, as noted for lakes in Manitoba by Barica (1975), rather than the actual trophic condition, which should be defined based on concentration of total phosphorus. Phosphorus data were not available from the regional studies in North Dakota (Sloan 1972; Swanson et al. 1988). However, in a study of prairie wetlands in North Dakota, concentration of total phosphorus indicated the wetlands were eutrophic (LaBaugh et al. 1987).

The term hypertrophic also has been applied to lakes with large concentrations of total phosphorus (Barica 1980b). These lakes have additional characteristics defining the condition of hypertrophic: they are shallow lakes with occasional resuspension of sediments due to wind action, large diurnal and seasonal fluctuations in concentrations of nutrients and oxygen, external nutrient loadings greatly exceeding the minimum defining a eutrophic condition, significant internal regeneration of nutrients, small nitrogen to phosphorus ratios, large values of primary production, and large fluctuations in algal biomass (Barica 1980b). Because many of the prairie wetlands and lakes included in the studies referred to in Table 3.1 are shallow and have large concentrations of phosphorus, hypertrophic conditions may be a common characteristic of these prairie wetlands and lakes. Additional information on phosphorus and nitrogen are presented by Neely and Baker (Chap. 4).

TEMPORAL VARIATION IN CHEMICAL CHARACTERISTICS

Seasonal Variation

Analysis of the chemical characteristics of prairie wetlands and lakes presented here enables comparisons of salinity and water types among different areas of the northern prairie. However, as noted by Gorham et al. (1983), there can be enough seasonal fluctuations in chemical characteristics of lakes used in regional analyses so that a single

TABLE 3.5.   Summary of the range in concentration of phosphorus in selected regional studies of prairie wetlands and lakes

Geographic location	Number of wetlands (or lakes)	Range in concentrations of phosphorus	Phosphorus form	Reference
Saskatchewan, Canada	41	0.0–3.5 mg/l	Ortho	Rutherford (1970)
Manitoba, Canada	51	3–2,670 µg/l	Soluble reactive	Barica (1975)
North Dakota, United States	4	0.00–3.06 mg/l	Total	LaBaugh et al. (1987)
South Dakota, United States	44	<.01–7.8 mg/l	Total dissolved	Petri and Larson (1973)
South Dakota, Minnesota, United States	14	.5–250.5 µg/l	Total dissolved	Bright (1978)
Nebraska, United States	124	0.0–23.2 mg/l	Ortho	McCarraher (1977)
Nebraska, United States	18	.3–21.4 mg/l	Soluble reactive	Nash (1978)

water body could change considerably in salinity or water type. Studies of prairie wetlands and lakes indicate considerable seasonal variation in chemical characteristics is common within the northern prairie of North America.

The general pattern of seasonal change in salinity for lakes in the semiarid part of the northern prairie initially was described by Rawson and Moore (1944). These lakes receive considerable water in the spring and then are subject to rapid evaporation in the summer, prior to becoming frozen in the fall, with ice cover persisting for four to six months until spring. Consequently, salinity of the waters is least in the spring, then increases through the summer (e.g., Rozkowska and Rozkowski 1969). In winter, salinity can be maximum because of concentration due to formation of ice (Ficken 1967; Barica 1977b; Schwartz and Gallup 1978; Last and Schweyen 1983; Arndt and Richardson 1985). This general pattern is presented in Figure 3.8.

Seasonal changes in salinity or specific conductance similar to the general pattern described by Rawson and Moore (1944) have been found throughout the northern prairie. In Saskatchewan, Hammer (1978) reported a seasonal increase in salinity from spring to midsummer of as much as 80‰. In Manitoba, Barica (1978) indicated specific conductance doubled between spring and midsummer. LaBaugh et al. (1987) found a four-fold seasonal increase in specific conductance in a shallow

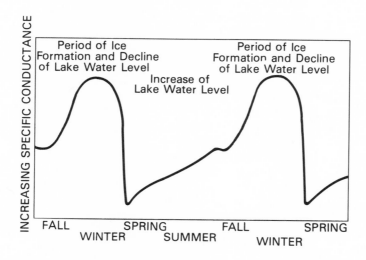

FIG. 3.8.   General pattern of seasonal change in salinity for lakes in the northern prairie of North America.

prairie wetland when the wetland was not ice covered. One of the lakes in South Dakota studied by Petri and Larson (1973) had as much as a six-fold increase in specific conductance between late April and August.

The pronounced seasonal increase in specific conductance between spring and midsummer can be affected by rainfall. Intense June rains caused specific conductance to remain at a steady value in Big Quill Lake, Saskatchewan (Hammer 1978). Barica (1978) found a consistent decrease in specific conductance occurred in October among prairie lakes in Manitoba. This decrease was attributed to rainfall and groundwater input in conjunction with decreased evaporation. The general trend of an increase in specific conductance between spring and midsummer also was interrupted by rainfall.

Concentration under ice cover due to freeze-out (Ficken 1967; Barica 1977b) also is common in the northern prairie. The largest value of specific conductance for many of the lakes in South Dakota mentioned in the study of Petri and Larson (1973) occurred in winter, under ice cover. Other investigations have reported largest values of salinity or specific conductance under ice cover in Saskatchewan (Hammer 1978), Manitoba (Barica 1975), North Dakota (LaBaugh et al. 1987), and Nebraska (McCarraher 1977).

Some investigators of prairie wetlands and lakes have measured relatively small values of specific conductance immediately after loss of ice cover; the subsequent increases in these values have not been attributable to evaporation alone. Ficken (1967) suggested temporary storage of dissolved solids in sediments of prairie potholes could explain this phenomena. Small values of specific conductance in prairie lakes followed by distinct increases have been attributed to freshwater overlying saline water, which then is mixed by the wind (Hammer 1978). Unpublished data from the Cottonwood Lake area wetlands in North Dakota indicate bottom sediments can stay frozen when the water in the wetland is not, and the subsequent increase in dissolved solids in water of the wetland occurs when the sediment-water mixture, containing relatively large concentrations of dissolved solids, thaws.

Details of seasonal changes in concentrations of nutrients have been reported in fewer studies than those reporting seasonal changes in salinity or major ions. Barica (1974, 1975, 1977a, 1977b) found substantial seasonal fluctuations in soluble reactive phosphorus, particulate phosphorus, dissolved organic phosphorus, and total phosphorus, nitrate, ammonia, particulate nitrogen, dissolved organic nitrogen, and total nitrogen, as well as silica in saline eutrophic lakes of Manitoba. Data presented by McCarraher (1977) for Nebraska, and by Petri and Larson (1973) for South Dakota are not as comprehensive as Barica's investigations. However, these studies also indicate soluble reactive phosphorus, nitrate, and silica have considerable seasonal fluctuation in concentrations. Investigation of the biological processes affecting seasonal changes in concentration of nutrients in prairie wetlands and lakes are rare (Barica 1977a, 1977b; van der Valk et al. 1979; Davis and van der Valk 1983).

Processes affecting fluctuations in nitrogen and phosphorus are of interest because there is conflicting evidence about the ability of wetlands to act as sinks for nitrogen and phosphorus (van der Valk et al. 1979; Richardson 1985). Fluctuations of phosphorus and nitrogen in prairie lakes in Manitoba were related to ice cover, distinct increases in algal biomass (algal blooms), and the sudden decreases in algal biomass (Barica 1974). Under ice cover, decomposition resulted in distinct peaks in concentration of inorganic phosphorus and inorganic nitrogen. After loss of ice cover, algal uptake caused concentrations of nitrate, ammonia, and soluble reactive phosphorus to decrease to less than detection limits, with a concurrent increase in particulate phosphorus and nitrogen. When there was a rapid decrease in algal biomass, inorganic phosphorus and nitrogen concentrations increased due to decomposition of the algae.

The sequence of algae uptake and decay after sudden decrease of the algae population can occur several times within one year (Barica 1974) (Fig. 3.9). The sudden decline in algal biomass commonly is followed by a depletion of oxygen particularly when thermal instability

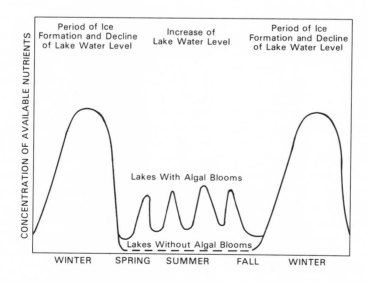

FIG. 3.9. General pattern of seasonal change in dissolved nitrogen and phosphorus of prairie pothole lakes (*Adapted from Barica 1974*).

occurs at the same time or just after the decline in algal biomass (Papst et al. 1980). Barica's (1974) study indicated lakes without algae blooms only had peaks in concentration of dissolved phosphorus and nitrogen during the winter. Similar fluctuations in dissolved phosphorus and nitrogen as related to phytoplankton populations have been described for several lakes in Alberta by Hickman (1978).

Seasonal fluctuations of phosphorus and nitrogen in prairie wetlands also can be affected by macrophytes (Davis and van der Valk 1978; Neely and Davis 1985). In their study of a prairie glacial marsh in Iowa, Davis and van der Valk (1978) noted losses of plant material from standing dead macrophytes occur primarily due to fragmentation of the plants in winter and spring. Additional loss of plant material results from toppling of standing dead material that decomposes when submerged in the spring. This litter material was found to release nitrogen and phosphorus between May and June. Results of the study of decomposition of macrophytes in prairie marshes by Davis and van der Valk (1978) and summarized by Neely and Baker (Chap. 4) indicate this process could add to the concentrations of nitrogen and phosphorus in water of prairie wetlands that contain water in the spring.

Annual Variation

Chemical characteristics of prairie wetlands and lakes also have been found to vary from year to year in response to climatic variation. Hammer (1978) found annual changes in salinity of several Saskatchewan lakes studied by Rawson and Moore (1944) were related to climatic cycles that occurred during 50 years of record. Dry periods coincided with distinct increases in salinity in the lakes. Wet periods coincided with distinct decreases in salinity in the lakes having the largest values of salinity in the area.

Barica (1978) was able to relate annual changes in specific conductance to annual rainfall, such that small values of specific conductance coincided with large values of annual rainfall, and large values of specific conductance coincided with small values of annual rainfall. A climatic cycle of wet and dry years during 1979 to 1982 has been related to annual changes in chemical characteristics of four prairie wetlands in North Dakota by LaBaugh et al. (1987). Considerable annual differences in specific conductance are evident in data presented for some lakes in South Dakota by Petri and Larson (1973), and annual differences in salinity exist for numerous lakes in Nebraska (McCarraher 1977).

Annual variation also occurs in major ion concentrations in prairie wetlands and lakes. This would be expected because it has already been noted that there is year-to-year variation in specific conductance, and that commonly changes in specific conductance are accompanied by corresponding changes in the concentration of at least sodium, potassium, and sulfate in prairie wetlands and lakes.

Although salinity changes between years were large in Barica's (1978) investigation, water types did not change coincident with changes in salinity. Sometimes these annual changes in concentration can result in year-to-year differences in water type. One example of this comes from data published by Petri and Larson (1973). Specific conductance values in Sully Lake near Onida, South Dakota, were within a range of 2,870–5,760 μS/cm in 1959, but only within a range of 155–443 μS/cm in 1960. Water in this lake was a true sulfate sodium calcium type in 1959 and an intermediate bicarbonate sulfate calcium type in 1960.

RELATION OF PHYSICAL SETTING TO CHEMICAL CHARACTERISTICS OF WETLANDS AND LAKES

Topographic Position

One of the common simple assumptions about the interaction between the physical setting of a lake or wetland and specific conductance is that altitude is inversely related to specific conductance (Rozkowski 1969). Although Sloan (1972) provided graphical evidence for this trend, no statistical test of the hypothesis was done. Barica (1978) found no relation between topography and salinity for lakes in southwestern Manitoba. Using regression analysis, Swanson et al. (1988) found no statistically significant relation between altitude and specific conductance in either their entire data set or in data for localized groups of lakes. The absence of a significant relation between altitude and specific conductance indicate more information is needed about the physical setting of a prairie wetland or lake to understand what processes control chemical characteristics of water within those water bodies.

Groundwater

Several studies of prairie wetlands and lakes have included chemical analysis of nearby groundwater. Barica (1975) sampled farm wells in the area of prairie pothole lakes. Nash (1978) sampled wells within 8 meters of one lake. Schnagl (1980) sampled windmill wells, for supplying water to cattle stock tanks, near a group of lakes under investigation. Sloan (1972) sampled nearby springs or springs at lakeshores. Rozkowski (1969) primarily sampled nearby farm wells, some observation wells, and springs. LaBaugh et al. (1987) sampled wells installed during their investigation for the purpose of defining the water table adjacent to a group of prairie wetlands. Schwartz and Gallup (1978) analyzed groundwater samples from different geologic units in a study of groundwater interaction with lakes. These chemical data have been used to examine the relation between chemical characteristics of groundwater and the chemical characteristics of prairie wetlands and lakes.

Rozkowski (1969) based interpretation of the interaction of wetlands ("sloughs") and groundwater on Meyboom's (1966, 1967) concept of recharge under land-surface highs and discharge to adjacent depressions. Barica (1975, 1978) indicated Lissey's (1971) model of depression-focused recharge represented conditions of wetland-groundwater interaction in the Erickson-Elphinstone area of Manitoba. Although both Rozkowski's (1969) study and Barica's (1975) study included chemical analysis of groundwater from nearby wells, Barr (1978) noted nearby wells do not always represent groundwater moving either to or from a lake.

Depending on depth at which the well is open, water samples may be from intermediate or regional groundwater flow systems rather than local groundwater flow systems. Even if the well is completed in local groundwater flow systems, whether it is in an area of flow to the wetland or lake, or out of the wetland or lake, is commonly not known. Consequently, the interpretation of groundwater chemical characteristics in relation to chemical characteristics of water wetlands and lakes may be completely out of the context of the interaction between a wetland or lake and the groundwater flow system. Such interactions have been discussed by Winter (1983, 1984).

One example of the importance of clearly identifying the position of a well sampled for chemical analysis within the groundwater flow system comes from the Nebraska sandhills. Schnagl (1980) used chemical analyses of water from windmills adjacent to one lake, in comparison to chemical composition of water in the lake, to suggest water was moving from the groundwater system to the lake. Subsequent investigations at the site included placement of a network of wells to define the water table within the same group of lakes studied by Schnagl (1980). Using this well network, Winter (1986) determined that groundwater was moving into the lake in some areas, moving out of the lake and into groundwater in other areas, and there were areas where flow reversals occurred. Chemical analyses of water from the water table wells (La-Baugh 1986b) indicated the windmill wells sampled by Schnagl (1980) were not at all representative of the groundwater either moving into or out of the lake.

Schoeller (1959) determined that there will be a general increase in total concentration and a change in water type from bicarbonate to sulfate and finally to chloride as water moves through geologic material. Schoeller (1959) also noted that water present in geologic material that is relatively uniform can differ in type based on quantity of recharge, length of flow path through the aquifer, and climate.

In the study of the relation of groundwater chemistry to wetland water chemistry, Rozkowski (1969) noted chemistry of shallow groundwater is affected by the soluble salt content of soil and glacial deposits and groundwater flow conditions. The evolution of water types in groundwater in Rozkowski's (1969) study area began with calcium bicarbonate, proceeded to magnesium bicarbonate, and ended with magnesium sulfate. Processes resulting in this sequence were: dissolution of calcium and magnesium carbonate minerals because of weathering, precipitation of calcium and magnesium bicarbonate minerals as saturation occurred, and dissolution of readily soluble magnesium sulfate salts.

Rozkowski (1969) found a small concentration of sodium salts in the shallow groundwater system. Only in deeper regional flow systems did the processes of ion exchange take place, coincidentally resulting in groundwater of a sodium sulfate type. Chemical characteristics of water in sloughs and lakes were related to the chemical characteristics of groundwater discharging to those water bodies. This relation of chemical characteristics of lakes to chemical characteristics of groundwater in the Canadian prairie-parkland has also been described by Schwartz and Gallup (1978).

Wallick (1981) studied changes in chemical characteristics of groundwater in glacial drift and bedrock of east-central Alberta. In this study, Wallick was able to define deep regional, intermediate, and shallow local groundwater flow systems. Water in the bedrock of the regional flow system was often a sodium bicarbonate type. Cation exchange and calcite precipitation resulted in sodium-bicarbonate-sulfate water in the intermediate flow system. Wallick indicated calcium magnesium bicarbonate and sulfate water in the shallow flow systems was related to dissolution of calcite and dolomite and leaching of gypsum in the glacial drift, a finding similar to that of Rozkowski's (1969) study in Saskatchewan.

Groundwater movement in the glaciated prairie can occur as fracture flow (Grisak et al. 1976). The properties of fracture flow in glacial till have been studied both in laboratory-column experiments (Grisak and Pickens 1980; Grisak et al. 1980) and in natural systems (Cherry et al. 1971; Grisak et al. 1976). In studies of natural systems, Cherry et al. (1971) found water types and changes in concentration similar to that of Rozkowski (1969). Chemical-equilibria analyses indicated dissolution of calcite and dolomite occurred in areas of recharge and was controlled by the partial pressure of carbon dioxide. As groundwater moved beyond the area of recharge, concentration of all dissolved materials increased.

Similar changes in chemical characteristics of groundwater were found in the Cottonwood Lake area, North Dakota, by LaBaugh et al. (1987). Water of a calcium bicarbonate type was present in areas of recharge and of a magnesium sulfate type in areas of groundwater discharge, some distance along the groundwater flow path from areas of recharge. WATEQ analysis (Truesdall and Jones 1974) indicated all of the groundwater in the area was supersaturated with calcite. Increases in sulfate were attributed to dissolution of calcium sulfate and magnesium sulfate minerals in the glacial till. Also, the increase in magnesium relative to calcium within groundwater occurred because the groundwater was supersaturated for calcite but not magnesium minerals.

In areas of groundwater recharge in the Nebraska sandhills, LaBaugh (1986b) identified water of a calcium bicarbonate type. Nash (1978) identified calcium bicarbonate waters in shallow wells adjacent to Jesse Lake (Table 3.4). Sulfate water types typical of groundwater in the glaciated prairie were not present in the area investigated by LaBaugh (1986b) or Nash (1978). Unlike the glaciated prairie, shallow groundwater in Nebraska sandhills that is some distance along the groundwater flow path typically is a sodium bicarbonate type, with potassium as the second most abundant cation.

Chemical characteristics of prairie lakes also can affect chemical characteristics of adjacent groundwater. Large concentrations of dissolved organic carbon have been reported for prairie lakes in Manitoba 0.4–102 mg/l (Barica 1974, 1975), and Nebraska 139–440 mg/l (Nash 1978), and 20–60 mg/l (LaBaugh 1986b). LaBaugh determined that dissolved organic carbon concentrations were ~1 mg/l in an area of groundwater recharge and values >20 mg/l in areas receiving input to groundwater from lakes.

SUMMARY

Chemical characteristics of prairie wetlands and lakes have been described in several studies. Details of the processes affecting those chemical characteristics were not available from regional sampling programs designed to describe areal variation. Considerable seasonal and annual variation in chemical characteristics occur within these wetlands and lakes so even areal studies might not provide an accurate assessment of salinities and water types within a region depending on the antecedent climatic conditions and time of sampling.

The importance of the interaction of groundwater and these surface waters has been recognized in a few studies and studied in any detail in even fewer studies. Available studies indicate the variety of water types in the glaciated prairies is probably related to the interaction of wetlands and lakes with local, intermediate, and regional groundwater flow systems. Few studies have addressed the impact of biological processes on seasonal variation in chemical characteristics. Further research is needed on the interaction of groundwater, climate, and biological processes as they affect chemical characteristics of these prairie wetlands and lakes.

REFERENCES

Arndt, J. L., and J. L. Richardson. 1985. Winter effects on the salt balance of saline ponds in North Dakota. Proc. N. Dak. Acad. Sci. 39:54.

Bachmann, R. W. 1965. Some chemical characteristics of Iowa lakes and reservoirs. Iowa Acad. Sci. 72:238–43.

Barica, J. 1974. Some observations on internal recycling, regeneration and oscillation of dissolved nitrogen and phosphorus in shallow self-contained lakes. Arch. Hydrobiol. 73:334–60.

_____. 1975. Geochemistry and nutrient regime of saline eutrophic lakes in the Erickson-Elphenstone district of southwestern Manitoba. Fish. Mar. Serv. Techn. Rep. 511.

_____. 1977a. Nitrogen regime of shallow eutrophic lakes on the Canadian prairies. Prog. Water Tech. 8:313–21.

_____. 1977b. Effect of freeze up on major ion and nutrient content of a prairie winterkill lake. J. Fish. Res. Board Can. 34:2210–15.

_____. 1978. Variability in ionic composition and phytoplankton biomass of saline eutrophic prairie lakes within a small geographic area. Arch. Hydrobiol. 81:304–26.

_____. 1980a. Some biological characteristics of plains aquatic ecosystems and their affect on water quality. Proc. 1979 PARC Symp., Can. Plains Res. Cent., Univ. Regina.

_____. 1980b. Why hypertrophic ecosystems? Vol. 2: Developments in Hydrobiology The Hague: Dr. W. Junk Publ.

Barr, K. D. 1978. Estimation of ground water and lake chemistry parameters and their relationship in glaciated terranes. Master's thesis, Univ. Minn., Minneapolis.

Bierhuizen, J. F. H., and E. E. Prepas. 1985. Relationships between nutrients, dominant ions, and phytoplankton standing crop in prairie saline lakes. Can. J. Fish. Aquat. Sci. 4:1588–94.

Bright, R. C. 1968. Surface-water chemistry of some Minnesota lakes, with preliminary notes on diatoms. Minneapolis, Minn.: Limnol. Res. Cent.

Campbell, C. E., and E. E. Prepas. 1986. Evaluation of factors related to unusually low chlorophyll levels in prairie saline lakes. Can. J. Fish. Aquat. Sci. 43:846–54.

Cherry, J. A., B. T. Beswick, W. E. Clister, and M. Lutchman. 1971. Flow patterns and hydrochemistry of two shallow ground water regimes in the Lake Agassiz basin, southern Manitoba. Geol. Assoc. Can. Spec. Paper No. 9.

Cowardin, L. M., V. Carter, F. C. Golet, and E. T. LaRoe. 1979. Classification of wetlands and deepwater habitats of the United States. U.S. Fish and Wildl. Office of Biol. Serv. Rep. 31. Washington, D.C.: Dept. Inter.

Davis, C. B., and A. G. van der Valk. 1978. Litter decomposition in prairie glacial marshes. *In* Freshwater wetlands: Ecological processes and management potential, ed. R. E. Good et al., 99–114. New York: Academic Press.

―――. 1983. Uptake and release of nutrients by living and decomposing *Typha glauca* Godr. tissues at Eagle Lake, Iowa. Aquat. Bot. 16:75–89.

Eisenlohr, W. S., Jr. 1972. Hydrologic investigations of prairie potholes in North Dakota, 1959–68. U.S. Geol. Surv. Prof. Paper 585-A.

Ficken, J. H. 1967. Winter loss and spring recovery of dissolved solids in two prairie pothole ponds in North Dakota. U.S. Geol. Surv. Prof. Paper 575-C.

Gorham, E., W. E. Dean, and J. E. Sanger. 1983. The chemical composition of lakes in the north-central United States. Limnol. and Oceanogr. 28:287–301.

Grisak, G. E., and J. F. Pickens. 1980. Solute transport through fractured media. 1: The effect of matrix diffusion. Water Resour. Res. 16:719–30.

Grisak, G. E., J. A. Cherry, J. A. Vonhof, and J. P. Blumele. 1976. Hydrogeologic and hydrochemical properties of fractured till in the Interior Plains Region. *In* Glacial Till, ed. R. F. Legget, 304–35. Royal Soc. Can. Spec. Publ. No. 12.

Grisak, G. E., J. F. Pickens, and J. A. Cherry. 1980. Solute transport through fractured media. 2: Column study of fractured till. Water Resour. Res. 16:731–39.

Hammer, U.T. 1978. The saline lakes of Saskatchewan. III: Chemical characterization. Internatl. Rev. de gesamten Hydrobiol. 63:311–35.

―――. 1986. Saline lake ecosystems of the world. Monographiae Biologicae Vol. 59. The Hague: Dr. W. Junk Publishers.

Hem, J. D. 1970. Study and interpretation of the chemical characteristics of natural waters. 2d ed. U.S. Geol. Surv. Water Supply Paper 1473. Washington, D.C.: GPO.

Hickman, M. 1978. Ecological studies on the epipelic algal community in five prairie-parkland lakes in central Alberta. Can. J. Bot. 56:991–1009.

Kadlec, J. A. 1986a. Effects of flooding on dissolved and suspended nutrients in small diked marshes. Can. J. Fish. and Aqua. Sci. 43:1999–2008.

―――. 1986b. Input-output nutrient budgets for small diked marshes. Can. J. Fish. and Aquat. Sci. 43:2009–16.

LaBaugh, J. W. 1986a. Wetland ecosystem studies from a hydrologic perspective. Water Resour. Bull. 22:1–10.

―――. 1986b. Limnological characteristics of selected lakes in the Nebraska sandhills and their relation to chemical characteristics of adjacent ground water. J. Hydrol. 86:279–98.

LaBaugh, J. W., T. C. Winter, V. A. Adomaitis, and G. A. Swanson. 1987. Hydrology and chemistry of selected prairie wetlands in the Cottonwood Lake area, Stutsman County, North Dakota. 1979–82. U.S. Geol. Surv. Prof. Paper 1431.

Last, W. M., and T. H. Schweyen, 1983. Sedimentology and geochemistry of saline lakes of the Great Plains. Hydrobiol. 105:245–63.

Lieffers, V. J., and J. M. Shay. 1983. Ephemeral saline lakes on the Canadian prairies: Their classification and management for emergent macrophyte growth. Hydrobiol. 105:85–94.

Likens, G. E. 1975. Primary production of inland aquatic ecosystems. *In* Primary productivity of the biosphere, ed. H. Lieth and R. H. Whittaker, 185–202. New York: Springer-Verlag.

Lissey, A. 1971. Depression-focused transient ground-water flow patterns in Manitoba. Geolog. Assoc. Can. Spec. Paper 9. Ottawa: Queen's Printer.

McCarraher, D. B. 1977. Nebraska sandhills lakes. Lincoln: Nebr. Game and Parks Comm.

Meyboom, P. 1966. Unsteady ground-water flow near a willow ring in hummocky moraine. J. Hydrol. 4:38–62.

_____. 1967. Mass-transfer studies to determine the groundwater regime of permanent lakes in hummocky moraine of western Canada. J. Hydrol. 5:117–42.

Millar, J. B. 1976. Wetland classification in western Canada: A guide to marshes and shallow open water wetlands in the grasslands and parklands of the prairie provinces. Can. Wildl. Serv. Rep. Ser. No. 37.

Mitten, H. T. 1965. Diurnal variations of the chemical quality of water in two prairie potholes in North Dakota. U.S. Geol. Surv. Prof. Paper 525-C.

Moyle, J. B. 1945. Some chemical factors influencing the distribution of aquatic plants in Minnesota. Amer. Midl. Nat. 34:402–20.

Nash, K. G. 1978. Geochemistry of selected closed basin lakes in Sheridan County, Nebraska. Master's thesis, Univ. Nebr., Lincoln.

Neely, R. L., and C. B. Davis. 1985. Nitrogen and phosphorus fertilization of *Sparganium eurycarpum* Enzehn. and *Typha glauca* Godr. stands. II: Emergent plant decomposition. Aquat. Bot. 22:363–75.

Papst, M. H., J. A. Mathias, and J. Barica. 1980. Relationship between thermal stability and summer oxygen depletion in a prairie pothole lake. Can. J. Fish. and Aquat. Sci. 37:1433–38.

Petri, L. R., and L. R. Larson. 1973. Quality of water in selected lakes of eastern South Dakota. S. Dak. Water Resour. Comm. Rep. Invest. No. 1.

Rawson, D. S., and J. E. Moore. 1944. The saline lakes of Saskatchewan. Can. J. Res. 22:141–201.

Richardson, C. J. 1985. Mechanisms controlling phosphorus retention capacity in freshwater wetlands. Sci. 228:1424–26.

Rigler, F. H. 1973. A dynamic view of the phosphorus cycle in lakes. *In* Environmental phosphorus handbook, ed. E. J. Griffith et al., 539–72. New York: John Wiley and Sons.

Rodhe, W. 1949. The ionic composition of lake waters. Verh. Internatl. ver. Limnol. 10:377–86.

Robinove, C. T., R. H. Langford, and J. W. Brookhart. 1958. Saline-water resources of North Dakota. U.S. Geol. Surv. Water Supply Paper 1428.

Rozkowski, A. 1969. Chemistry of ground and surface waters in the Moose Mountain area, southern Saskatchewan. Geol. Surv. Can. Paper 67–9.

Rozkowska, A. D., and A. Rozkowski. 1969. Seasonal changes of slough and lake water chemistry in southern Saskatchewan (Canada). J. Hydrol. 7:1–13.

Rutherford, A. A. 1970. Water quality survey of Saskatchewan surface waters. Saskatchewan Res. Counc. Chem. Div. Rep. C-70-1.

Schnagl, J. A. 1980. Seasonal variations in water chemistry and primary productivity in four alkaline lakes in the sandhills of western Nebraska. Master's thesis, Univ. Nebr., Lincoln.

Schoeller, H. 1959. Arid zone hydrology, recent developments. Paris: UNESCO Press.

Schwartz, F. W., and D. N. Gallup. 1978. Some factors controlling the major ion chemistry of small lakes: Examples from the prairie parkland of Canada. Hydrobiol. 58:65–81.

Sloan, C. E. 1972. Ground-water hydrology of prairie potholes in North Dakota. U.S. Geol. Surv. Prof. Paper 585-C.

Stewart, R. F., and H. A. Kantrud. 1972. Vegetation of prairie potholes, North Dakota, in relation to quality of water and other environmental factors. U.S. Geol. Surv. Prof. Paper 585-D.

Swanson, G. A., T. C. Winter, V. A. Adomaitis, and J. W. LaBaugh. 1988. Chemical characteristics of prairie lakes in south-central North Dakota—their potential for impacting fish and wildlife. U.S. Fish and Wildl. Rep.

Tarapchak, J. J. 1973. Studies of phytoplankton distribution and indicators of trophic state in Minnesota lakes. Ph.D. diss., Univ. Minn., Minneapolis.

Truesdell, A. H., and Jones, B. J. 1974. WATEQ, a computer program for calculating chemical equilibria of natural waters. U.S. Geol. Surv. J. Res. 2:238–48.

van der Valk, A. G. 1981. Succession in wetlands: A Gleasonian approach. Ecol. 62:688–96.

van der Valk, A. G., C. B. Davis, J. L. Baker, and C. E. Beer. 1979. Natural fresh water wetlands as nitrogen and phosphorus traps for land runoff. *In* Wetland function and values: The state of one understanding, ed. P. E. Greeson et al., 457–67. Minneapolis, Minn.: Amer. Water Resour. Assoc.

Vollenweider, R. A. 1968. Scientific fundamentals of the eutrophication of lakes and flowing waters with particular reference to nitrogen and phosphorus as factors in eutrophication. Paris: Organ. for Econ. Coop. and Dev.

Wallick, E. I. 1981. Chemical evolution of groundwater in a drainage basin of Holocene age, east-central Alberta, Canada. J. Hydrol. 54:245–83.

Williams, W. D. 1981. Inland salt lakes: An introduction. Hydrobiol. 81:1–14.

Winter, T. C. 1983. The interaction of lakes with variably saturated porous media. Water Resour. Res. 19:1203–18.

———. 1984. Modeling the interrelationship of ground-water and surface water. *In* Modeling of total and precipitation impacts, ed. J. L. Schnoor, 89–119. Boston: Butterworth.

———. 1988. Hydrologic studies of wetlands and lakes in the northern prairie of North America. *In* Northern Prairie Wetlands, ed. A. G. van der Valk. Ames: Iowa State Univ. Press.

Winter, T. C., and M-K Woo. 1988. Hydrology of lakes and wetlands. *In* Surface Water Hydrology, ed. M. L. Moss, M. G. Wolman, and H. C. Riggs. Boulder, Colorado: Geological Society of America.

ROBERT K. NEELY and JAMES L. BAKER

4 NITROGEN AND
AND THE FATE OF

PRAIRIE WETLANDS often experience significant contamination by agricultural pollutants. Contaminants may be carried from cultivated fields and enter the wetland with sediment, surface runoff, or subsurface drainage. The mode of transport is determined primarily by the properties of the contaminant that influence its infiltration, soil adsorption, and persistence. NH_4-N and pesticides are predominantly carried in surface runoff, PO_4-P is transported mainly by sediment, and NO_3-N is lost predominantly with subsurface drainage.

In the prairie wetland, contaminants can be transferred to or retained in the sediment-interstitial water column, atmosphere, and/or biomass of microbes, plants, and animals. On a net basis, nitrogen is removed more effectively than phosphorus from marsh surface waters, and NO_3-N is removed to a greater extent than NH_4-N. The most important processes of removal seem to be denitrification for NO_3-N, sedimentation and precipitation for PO_4-P, and assimilation of the major nitrogen and phosphorus inorganic forms by emergent vegetation and microbial decomposers.

The effects of excessive nitrogen and phosphorus inputs in wetlands is far from clear, but they seem to include enrichment of emergent plant tissues, stimulation of emergent plant production, and eventual acceleration of emergent plant decomposition. In combination, these factors act to increase nutrient accumulation in living plants, but accelerate nutrient release from decaying plants.

> KEY WORDS: prairie wetland, prairie-glacial marsh, nitrogen, phosphorus, submerged sediments, agricultural pollutants, nutrient cycling

PHOSPHORUS DYNAMICS
AGRICULTURAL RUNOFF

INTRODUCTION

SINCE the turn of the century, prairie pothole wetlands, which
once numbered in the millions, have been drained for agricultural purposes (see Kantrud et al., Chap. 5). Consequently,
many of the remaining prairie pothole wetlands are surrounded by cultivated fields and frequently receive large inputs of sediment, nutrients,
and other agricultural chemicals with the agricultural drainage that re-
plenishes the water that is lost by flow through or evapotranspiration.
For example, the Eagle Lake Marsh in north-central Iowa has an area of
about 360 ha and receives drainage in the forms of snowmelt, rainfall
runoff, and subsurface flow (both natural and through installed subsurface drainage systems) from a 2560 ha watershed. About two-thirds of
the area is intensively farmed in row crops that receive annual fertilizer
and pesticide applications.

Chemicals that contaminate the agricultural drainage feeding into
wetlands are often removed from the water passing through the wetland;
thus, prairie marshes can be important in the preservation of local water
quality. The purpose of this chapter is (1) to summarize the processes
which influence the loss of chemicals from cultivated fields and therefore determine the quality of agricultural drainage that enters wetlands,
and (2) to discuss the role of prairie marshes in the cycling and removal
of nitrogen and phosphorus from agricultural drainage. The two major
subdivisions of this chapter are devoted to these two topics, respectively.

ROBERT K. NEELY, Department of Biology, Eastern Michigan University, Ypsilanti,
Michigan 48197. JAMES L. BAKER, Department of Agricultural Engineering, Iowa State
University, Ames, Iowa 50011.

I. QUALITY OF AGRICULTURAL DRAINAGE

Hydrologic and Soil Adsorption Factors

The sediment and chemical contamination of agricultural drainage (surface runoff as well as subsurface drainage) is dependent on a combination of soil and climatic factors that affect the quantity and route of that drainage. The degree of contamination is also dependent on the chemical's properties that affect its persistence and adsorption to soil. In this section, a discussion of these factors will be presented, followed by examples of representative chemical concentrations and losses in agricultural drainage and consideration of the effects of crop production management practices on them. Effects of soil conservation practices on sediment losses will also be included.

It is obvious that the water infiltration rate into soil relative to the supply rate from rainfall, irrigation, or snowmelt will determine how much surface runoff, if any, occurs. Furthermore, the capacity of the soil to store that water for later evaporation or transpiration by growing plants will determine the magnitude of water removal from the soil profile as percolation or subsurface drainage. Factors that influence infiltration will then influence the relative amounts of surface runoff and subsurface drainage. In particular, tight or fine-textured heavy soils with naturally lower permeabilities generally generate more surface runoff from a given storm event than a lighter soil. Antecedent soil moisture content will also affect the infiltration rate, and the storm intensity will affect the supply rate.

For sediment, surface runoff is essentially the only carrier; however, for chemical transport there are three carriers: sediment, surface runoff, and subsurface drainage. In fact, for purposes of considering how to control chemical losses, classification of chemicals into those lost mainly with sediment, mainly in surface runoff, or mainly with subsurface drainage is helpful. The key factor in determining to which category a chemical belongs is its affinity for soil. An equilibrium is usually approached between existence in the solution phase and adsorption to soil particles for soil-applied chemicals. A distribution coefficient, K, can be defined as a ratio of the concentration of a chemical adsorbed to soil to the concentration dissolved in water. Therefore, chemicals with high K values are strongly adsorbed and are transported mainly with sediment. In a first appraisal, it might seem logical that with lower K values more of the chemical would be transported in surface runoff. However, the schematic in Fig. 4.1 shows that there is a thin soil "runoff mixing zone" (10 mm in this illustration) from which a chemical can be released to water either running off the surface or infiltrating into deeper soil that does not interact with precipitation that produces runoff (Ahuja and

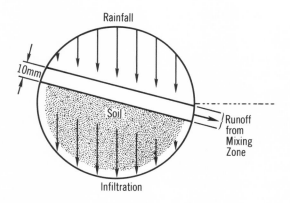

FIG. 4.1.   Schematic of soil-air interface during precipitation.

Lehman 1983; Donigian et al. 1977). Chemicals with high K values (e.g., >100) in the "runoff mixing zone" are not significantly released to either infiltrating or runoff water and, as stated earlier, are transported mainly with sediment.

Soluble chemicals with low K values (e.g., <0.1) are not held back by the soil; however, in instances where soil properties and moisture contents allow significant infiltration to occur before (and during) runoff, much of the chemical is removed from the "runoff mixing zone" and concentrations in surface runoff are low by the time runoff begins. These less strongly adsorbed chemicals are then the ones lost predominantly in subsurface drainage.

Chemicals with intermediate K values are lost mostly with surface runoff water, depending to some degree on the ratio of infiltration to runoff. Their adsorption is weak to the extent that some release to surface runoff water occurs (remember in most cases, unless there is very severe erosion, total runoff water lost weighs at least 100 times the sediment lost per unit area), but not so weak that significant leaching occurs.

Chemicals that fall into the first category of being transported mainly with sediment include many of the now-banned chlorinated hydrocarbon insecticides, herbicides such as trifluralin, profluralin, and paraquat, and total organic N and total P including PO_4-P. NO_3-N is the most important chemical in the third category of loss (i.e., with subsurface drainage). Losses of NO_3-N in surface runoff are usually low unless tight or wet soils prevent significant initial infiltration, which would remove much of the NO_3-N from the "runoff mixing zone" before runoff begins. NH_4-N and a majority of the pesticides used in the Midwest today would fall into the second category of chemicals lost mostly with surface runoff water.

In addition to adsorption, the location, amount, and persistence of a chemical in the soil profile affect its concentration in sediment and water. The location of a chemical below the "runoff mixing zone" should nearly eliminate any losses associated with surface runoff or sediment, but closer proximity to the water table might enhance losses with subsurface drainage. The amount of chemical present in the soil profile is a summation of the amount naturally present (in the case of nutrients), the amount possibly carried over from previous years' applications (for both pesticides and nutrients), and the amount currently applied. Experiments have shown that concentrations of a chemical in drainage are correlated with the quantity of the chemical in the soil profile. Persistence, as affected by chemical transformations, physical losses, and plant uptake, affects the amount of chemical present. Pesticides tend to degrade or decompose with time, usually within a growing season for most currently used pesticides.

Representative Chemical Concentrations and Losses in Drainage

Table 4.1 presents flow and nutrient concentration data for surface runoff from areas under different crop management. Because concentrations are averaged on a flow-weighted basis, losses (in kg/ha) are easy to calculate and are equal to the flow volume (in cm of water depth) times concentration (in mg/l or ppm) divided by 10. Similarly, Table 4.2 presents data for nutrients in subsurface flow. Table 4.3 presents data for flow in a stream or river, which includes both surface flow and some subsurface drainage. These tables illustrate that concentrations (and losses) vary greatly between studies, with weather, soils, crops, and chemical management all having effects. Table 4.4 summarizes flow and pesticide concentration data for both streamflow and surface runoff from several studies. Table 4.5 presents only concentration data for pesticides in subsurface flow because flow volume data were not available. Despite the degree of variability, chemicals with K values or distribution coefficients greater than 1 have higher to much higher concentrations in surface runoff compared to subsurface drainage. This includes the nutrients NH_4-N and PO_4-P and all the pesticides with the possible exception of 2,4-D.

Normally, N is applied at rates in the range of 125 to 200 kg/ha, P at 25 to 100 kg/ha, and pesticides at 0.5 to 4 kg/ha in midwestern corn production. The amounts lost with agricultural drainage can range from an equivalent of 10 to 50% of the N applied, usually less than 5% of the P applied, and usually less than 2% of the pesticide applied. Partially

TABLE 4.1. Flow and nutrient concentrations in surface runoff

Land use	Location of studies	Flow (cm)	NH$_4$-N	NO$_3$-N (mg/l) [a]	PO$_4$-P	Reference
Corn (rot. w/beans)	Iowa	3.1	0.8	4.5	0.16	Baker et al. (1978)
Soybeans (rot. w/corn)		2.9	0.1	3.5	0.03	
Pasture (grazed)		1.1	0.4	0.7	1.06	
Cont. corn (448 kg N/ha-yr)		5.6	1.0	2.4	0.20	Alberts et al. (1978)
Cont. corn (168 kg N/ha-yr)		4.9	1.1	1.3	0.18	
Corn (terraced)		3.6	0.6	3.0	0.26	
Pasture-corn		2.2	0.8	2.6	...	Burwell et al. (1976)
Row crop (corn and soybeans)		4.4	...[b]	5.2[b]	0.06	Hanway and Laflen (1974)
Cont. corn (no-till)		3.2[c]	0.2	0.6	0.73	Johnson et al. (1979)
Cont. corn (conventional tillage)		5.4[c]	0.2	0.7	0.18	
Fallow	Minnesota	14.0	0.3	1.3	0.05	Burwell et al. (1975)
Cont. corn		8.0	0.5	1.5	0.22	
Corn (in rotation)		4.6	0.4	1.0	0.24	
Oats (in rotation)		6.9	0.4	2.3	0.12	
Hay (in rotation)		14.2	1.0	0.4	0.21	
Native Prairie		3.0	0.5	0.4	0.07	Timmons and Holt (1977)
Fallow	South Dakota	1.0	1.6	0.4	0.1	White and Williamson (1973)
Corn		1.3	1.0	0.6	0.2	
Oats		0.5	1.0	0.7	0.2	
Alfalfa		0.3	1.7	0.2	0.1	
Cont. corn	Missouri	18.2	...[b]	5.3[b]	0.41	Smith et al. (1974)
Cont. soybeans		17.4	...[b]	4.1[b]	0.74	
Meadow		8.7	...[b]	1.8[b]	0.55	
Corn	Ohio	10.7	...[b]	16.3[b]	...	Schwab et al. (1973)
Pasture (summer grazed)		1.0	...[b]	1.5[b]	0.80[d]	van Keuren et al. (1979); and
Pasture (winter grazed)		12.9	...[b]	4.4[b]	1.12[d]	Chichester et al. (1979)

[a] Flow-weighted average concentrations (if flow was measured); kg/ha losses = mg/l × cm/10.

[b] NH$_4$-N is included with NO$_3$-N.

[c] Growing season runoff (late April–October).

[d] Total P.

[e] Organic N is included with NH$_4$-N.

TABLE 4.1. *(continued)*

Land use	Location of studies	Flow (cm)	NH₄-N	NO₃-N (mg/l) [a]	PO₄-P	Reference
Wheat stubble (snowmelt runoff)	Saskatchewan	4.6	0.9e	0.2	0.22	Nickoliachuk and Read (1978)
Summer fallow (snowmelt runoff)		3.7	6.8e	0.8	0.54	
Fall-fert. summer fallow (snowmelt runoff)		2.8	14.6e	1.1	4.29	
Cotton (irrigated and dryland)	Oklahoma	22	0.1	0.8	0.55	Olness et al. (1975)
Wheat (dryland)		18	0.1	0.5	0.20	
Alfalfa		16	0.6	1.4	0.81	
Pasture (grazed)		25	0.1	0.4	0.01	
Corn (high, mod. fert.)	New York	8.9	0.5	1.3	0.24	Klausener et al. (1974)
Soybeans-wheat (high, mod. fert.)		10.3	0.4	8.6	0.17	
Wheat (high, mod. fert.)		10.7	0.5	0.7	0.19	
Corn	Vermont	...	...	2.3	0.7	Benoit (1973)
Alfalfa		...	...	0.3	0.8	
Hay-pasture		...	...	0.6	0.9	
Corn	Georgia	9.1	...	0.3	...	Jackson et al. (1973)
Corn		16.1	1.1	0.8	...	Langdale et al. (1979)
Pasture (control plots)	Alabama	36.4	0.3	0.8	...	Long et al. (1979)
Pasture (manure-treated plots)		34.4	0.9	4.1	...	

Land use	Location of studies	Flow (cm)	NH$_4$-N	NO$_3$-N (mg/l) [a]	PO$_4$-P	Reference
Mixed cover watersheds	Iowa	..	0.1	12.1	0.12	Baker et al. (1978)
Cont. corn (448 kg N/ha-yr)		9.9	0.2	21.0	...	Burwell et al. (1976)
Cont. corn (168 kg N/ha-yr)		11.8	0.2	5.8	...	
Corn (terraced, 448 kg N/ha-yr)		17.6	0.3	20.0	...	
Pasture-corn		15.5	0.2	7.2	...	Baker et al. (1975)
Corn, oats, corn, soybeans rotation		14.6	0.3	21.0	0.005	Hanway and Laflen (1974)
Corn and soybeans		7.3	..[b]	13.0[b]	0.01	Willrich (1979)
Mixed cover watersheds	Minnesota			19	...	Gast et al. (1978)
Corn (20 kg N/ha-yr)		7.8		17.5	...	
Corn (112 kg N/ha-yr)		8.2		21.5	...	
Corn (224 kg N/ha-yr)		8.3		37.3	...	
Corn (448 kg N/ha-yr)		9.3		61.2	...	
Corn	Ohio	13.6		12.2	...	Schwab et al. (1973)
Corn				15.7[b]	0.16	Logan and Schwab (1976)
Alfalfa			..[b]	1.5[b]	0.20	
Pasture (summer grazed)		41.3	..[b]	5.1[b]	0.10[c]	van Keuren et al. (1979); and Chichester et al. (1979)
Pasture (winter grazed)		38.8	..[b]	2.3[b]	0.10[c]	
Mixed cover watersheds	Illinois	..		5–22	...	Harmeson et al. (1971)
Corn, oats, alfalfa, grass (no fert.)	Ontario	7.0		6.4[d]	0.18	Bolton et al. (1970)
Corn, oats, alfalfa (fert.)		9.3		8.1[d]	0.21	
Corn, soybeans, small grain, vegetables (mineral soil)		24.4	1.2[e]	10.6	0.03	Miller (1979)
Vegetables (organic soil)		40.2		31.0	4.65	
Intensively cropped	England		0.02	17.7	0.18	Cooke and Williams (1970)
Grassland			0.07	5.6	0.08	
Corn	New York		0.03	15.6	0.006	Zwerman et al. (1972)
Soybeans			0.02	32.0	0.004	
Wheat			0.03	3.4	0.010	
Cultivated muckland	Vermont	37.9	0.4	17.2	2.74	Duxbary and Peverly (1978)
Corn				9.2	<0.02	Benoit (1973)
Alfalfa				2.2	<0.02	
Hay-pasture				0.6	<0.02	
Cotton, alfalfa, rice	California			25.1[d]	0.08	Johnson et al. (1965)
Citrus (high rainfall period)	Florida			3.7	0.36	Calvert (1975)
Citrus (low rainfall period)				1.1	0.17	
Row crops	South Carolina			4.8	...	Peele and Gilliangham (1972)
Corn	Georgia	39.1		8.9	...	Jackson et al. (1973)

[a] Flow-weighted average concentrations (if flow was measured); kg/ha losses = mg/l × cm/10.
[b] NH$_4$-N is included with NO$_3$-N.
[c] Total P.
[d] NH$_4$-N and organic N are included with NO$_3$-N; NO$_3$-N would dominate.
[e] Organic N is included with NH$_4$-N.

99

TABLE 4.3. Soluble nutrients in streamflow draining Iowa agricultural watersheds

Location	Year	Precip (cm)	Flow	NH$_4$-N	NO$_3$-N (mg/L) [a]	PO$_4$-P	Reference
East Central Iowa	1976	55.4	12.3	0.2	7.9	0.07	Johnson and Baker (1982, 1984)
	1977	82.8	4.4	0.2	10.0	0.11	
	1978	87.8	19.7	0.4	11.0	0.11	
	1979	100.9	44.5	0.5	8.0	0.16	
	1980	74.4	18.2	0.5	6.3	0.14	
Central Iowa [b]	1972	...	...	0.4	9.1	0.31	Johnson and Baker (1973)
Central Iowa [b]	1981	...	...	0.3	6.1	0.12	Bauman et al. (1982, 1983)
	1982	...	...	0.2	9.4	...	
Northeast Iowa	1982	86.4	33.0	...	9.3	...	Hallberg et al. (1983, 1984, 1985)
	1983	114.3	55.9	...	8.7	...	
	1984	83.8	35.6	...	8.6	...	
North Central Iowa	1976	57.5	0.3	0.4	16.9	0.08	Davis et al. (1981)
	1977	96.3	0.2	1.8	8.0	0.60	
	1978	70.9	1.5	0.3	17.3	0.40	
	1979	94.4	14.6	0.1	11.0	0.24	

[a]Flow-weighted average concentrations.
[b]Arithmetic averages.

TABLE 4.4. Pesticide concentrations in surface runoff and streamflow

Pesticide 1		Pesticide 2		Flow (cm)	Note	Reference
Name	ug/l	Name	ug/l			
Atrazine	38.9	Alachlor	24.6	4.3	Average, 1973 growing season, conv.	Baker and Johnson (1979)
Atrazine	52.2	Alachlor	33.8	2.0	Average, 1973 growing season, till-plant	
Cyanazine	186.5	Alachlor	89.0	8.4	Average, 1974 growing season, conv.	
Cyanazine	157.7	Alachlor	58.6	5.7	Average, 1974 growing season, till-plant	
Cyanazine	109.7	Alachlor	26.9	3.9	Average, 1974 growing season, no-till	
Fonofos	0.6	Alachlor	7.6	3.4	Average, 1975 growing season, conv.	
Fonofos	0.7	Alachlor	3.6	2.8	Average, 1975 growing season, till-plant	
Fonofos	0.3	Alachlor	1.0	3.1	Average, 1975 growing season, no-till	
Carbofuran	580.3	...	...	0.8	Average, 1971 growing season	Caro et al. (1973)
Carbofuran	103.0	...	...	4.1	Average, 1972 growing season	
Carbaryl	21.8	...	...	2.5	Average, 1973 growing season	
Atrazine	103.0	...	...	4.8	Average, 1967 growing season	Caro et al. (1974)
Atrazine	236.1	...	...	4.1	Average, 1970 growing season	Ritter et al. (1974)
Alachlor	4.8	Metribuzin	0.4	31.4	2-yr avg., Four-mile creek	Johnson and Baker (1984)
Alachlor	27.8	Metribuzin	12.6	14.4	2-yr avg., treated soybean field	
Propachlor	0.1	Cyanazine	1.6	31.4	2-yr avg., Four-mile creek	
Propachlor	6.7	Cyanazine	35.3	18.6	2-yr avg., treated corn field	

TABLE 4.5. Pesticide concentrations in subsurface drainage

Pesticide 1		Pesticide 2		Note	Reference
Name	µg/l	Name	µg/l		
Atrazine	0.3	· · ·	· · ·	3-yr average (max. 10.0 µg/l)	Hallberg et al. (1985)
Alachlor	4.0	Cyanazine	1.7	3-yr maximum	Baker and Austin (1984)
Atrazine	0.1	Dicamba	0.2	arithmetic average	
Alachlor	0.2	Cyanazine	0.5	arithmetic average	
Atrazine	1.5	Cyanazine	0.6	maximum value	Muir and Baker (1976)
Metribuzin	1.6	Cyanazine	0.7	maximum value	

because of their limited persistence, pesticide losses are usually lower. Therefore, the timing of runoff-producing storms, relative to the time of application, is particularly important in determining the magnitude of pesticide losses.

Table 4.6 summarizes the relevant studies cited in Tables 4.1, 4.3, and 4.4 regarding amounts of chemicals transported with sediment. One of the undetermined factors, relative to the potential impact of sediment-carried chemicals, is what fraction and how quickly are these chemicals released to the water phase. There are some data for herbicides that indicate the equilibrium concentration in the water phase in contact with soil or sediment containing herbicides is reached fairly quickly, possibly in a matter of minutes (Wauchope and Myers 1985). The same would be expected to be true for NH_4-N adsorbed on soil surfaces. For total N and P where chemical or biological transformations to inorganic forms are necessary to solubilize the nutrients, there is some potential through burial by later sediment deposits to decrease the release.

Effects of Management Practices

Agricultural chemical losses associated with sediment losses equal chemical concentrations in sediment times the volume or mass of sediment lost. Similarly chemical losses associated with water losses equal chemical concentrations in water times the volume or mass of water lost. Obviously any practice that decreases the volume of carrier will reduce chemical losses; likewise any practice that reduces chemical concentrations in sediment or water will also reduce losses. In planning a strategy to reduce chemical loss, knowledge of the chemical's major means of transport is important, (i.e., is it transported mainly with sediment, surface runoff, or subsurface drainage). For sediment itself, and for those chemicals transported mainly with sediment, there are several soil conservation practices available to the producer to limit losses. Currently the most notable practice is conservation tillage, where an effort is made usually through zero or reduced tillage to maintain a soil cover of crop residue. It should be emphasized that the term "conservation tillage" is not necessarily tied to an implement or tillage tool, but instead to surface crop residue.

Data in Table 4.7 show the effects of conservation tillage on soil loss and chemical losses with sediment and runoff water. The data shown are relative to losses from the conventional plow-disk-plant tillage system. Conservation tillage is obviously effective in controlling erosion (and sediment-carried chemicals), and the degree of erosion control has been shown to be an exponential function of percent residue cover (Laflen and Colvin 1981). Normally the reduction in sediment-carried chemicals

TABLE 4.6. Chemical concentrations in suspended sediment

Chemical 1		Chemical 2		Erosion	Note	Reference
name	ppm	name	ppm	(T/ha)		
Atrazine	1.38	Alachlor	1.34	83.0	Average, 1973 growing season, conv.	Baker and Johnson (1979)
Atrazine	0.34	Alachlor	0.74	32.1	Average, 1973 growing season, till-plant	
Cyanazine	0.43	Alachlor	0.33	56.9	Average, 1974 growing season, conv.	
Cyanazine	0.53	Alachlor	0.32	24.5	Average, 1974 growing season, till-plant	
Cyanazine	0.62	Alachlor	0.24	3.4	Average, 1974 growing season, no-till	
Fonofos	0.03	Alachlor	0.04	19.1	Average, 1975 growing season, conv.	
Fonofos	0.03	Alachlor	0.03	7.6	Average, 1975 growing season, till-plant	
Fonofos	0.02	Alachlor	<0.01	5.6	Average, 1975 growing season, no-till	
Carbofuran	0.76	...	...	4.1	Average, 1971 growing season	Caro et al. (1973)
Carbofuran	0.96	...	...	18.2	Average, 1972 growing season	
Carbaryl	0.47	...	...	3.8	Average, 1973 growing season	Caro et al. (1974)
Atrazine	0.24	...	...	18.2	Average, 1967 growing season	Ritter et al. (1974)
Atrazine	1.22	...	...	10.0	Average, 1970 growing season	
Total N	2990	Total P	1080	2.8	5-yr average, Four-mile creek	Johnson and Baker (1982, 1984)
Total N	2040	Total P	710	15.2	5-yr average, corn field	
Total N	1980	Total P	620	16.3	5-yr average, soybean field	
Total N	930	Total P	2090	31.5	3-yr average, conventional	Johnson et al. (1979)
Total N	1330	Total P	2910	12.0	3-yr average, till-plant	
Total N	1630	Total P	2030	3.5	3-yr average, no-till	

TABLE 4.7. Effects of conservation tillage on surface runoff, erosion, and chemical losses

Practice	Runoff (%)[a]	Erosion (%)[a]	Chemical 1	Solution	Sediment (%)[a]	Total	Chemical 2	Solution	Sediment (%)[b]	Total	Reference
Till-plant	65	38	N	68	54	55	P	180	112[b]	130	Johnson et al. (1979)
No-till ridge	58	11	N	44	19	20	P	230	36[b]	58	McDowell and McGregor (1980)
No-till flat[c]	106	12	N	180	40	52	P	450	36	39	
	80	3	N	410	14	47	P	1650	13	25	
Till-plant	86	33	N	2100	41	92	P	2250	46	47	Romkens et al. (1973)
Chisel-plow	49	5	N	1900	9	52	P	1950	10	11	
Disk	85	15	N	1050	18	42	P	1850	16	17	
No-till flat	74	8	N	3950	10	99	P	100,000	24	55	
Chisel-plow	70	39	N	140	40	41	P	83	42	42	Siemens and Oschwald (1978)
Disk	70	20	N	240	26	29	P	75	26	27	
No-till flat	90	17	N	120	21	22	P	100	21	22	
Till-plant	83	77	ala[d]	96	77	91	fon[d]	115	131	127	Barisas et al. (1978); and Laflen et al. (1978)
Chisel-plow	96	62	ala	150	62	125	fon	163	64	90	
Disk	84	31	ala	115	31	92	fon	127	49	70	
No-till ridge	77	15	ala	116	15	87	fon	137	71	88	
No-till flat	75	8	ala	127	8	93	fon	145	19	52	

[a] Amounts are expressed as % of conventional (plow-disk-plant).
[b] P lost with sediment expressed as available P, for other studies as Total P.
[c] First line soybeans-corn rotation; second line corn-soybeans rotation.
[d] Ala is alachlor, and fon is fonofos.

is somewhat less than the reduction in soil loss, because the coarser, less chemically active sediment is conserved first (Baker and Laflen 1983b). Table 4.7 also illustrates that although runoff volumes are often reduced with conservation tillage, soluble chemical losses can be increased, particularly for nutrients. This means that concentrations are increased more than runoff is reduced. The source of these increased concentrations is believed to be due to increased chemical amounts in the runoff mixing zone because of reduced fertilizer incorporation and crop residue on the soil surface (Barisas et al. 1978; McDowell and McGregor 1980; Alberts and Spomer 1985). For the herbicides studied, it has been shown they wash off with corn residue quickly when precipitation falls shortly after broadcast spraying (Martin et al. 1978; Baker and Shiers 1985). Hence, if this washoff becomes part of runoff, herbicide concentrations in runoff could be increased.

Studies involving soil incorporation of nutrients (Timmons et al. 1973; Baker and Laflen 1983a) and herbicides (Baker and Laflen 1979) have shown that runoff losses can be significantly reduced by soil incorporation that reduces the amount of chemical in the runoff mixing zone. Because surface-protecting residue is destroyed by tillage (Colvin et al. 1981), the use of tillage to incorporate chemicals is less desirable. Other means of incorporation are being developed (Solie et al. 1981; Baker et al. 1985). Data in Table 4.8 show that terraces, contouring, and the use of grassed waterways, filter strips, and close-grown crops are also effective in controlling erosion and losses of sediment-carried chemicals.

For chemicals transported mainly with subsurface drainage, principally NO_3-N, timing and rate of application relative to crop needs seem to hold the most promise for reduction of leaching losses, especially since control or reduction of the volume of water passing through the soil profile is nearly impossible. Table 4.9 presents some of the limited data available showing that the concentrations of NO_3-N found in leachate water increase almost linearly with application rates.

Data in Table 4.9 also show that delayed timing resulting from four N applications with irrigation water during the growing season decreased leaching losses relative to a single early N application. For corn growth, Baker and Timmons (1984) found that plant uptake and yields were improved if the N was applied three times postplant as opposed to once preplant.

SUMMARY

The concept of the runoff mixing zone and consideration of the factors of infiltration, soil adsorption, and persistence help in under-

TABLE 4.8. Effects of terraces, contouring, grassed waterways, filter strips, and close-grown crops on runoff, erosion, and chemical losses

Practice	Runoff (%)[a]	Erosion (%)[a]	Chemical 1	Solution	Sediment (%)[a]	Total	Chemical 2	Solution	Sediment (%)[a]	Total	Reference
Terrace	27	5	N	50	13	16	P	158	27	44	Burwell et al. (1974)
Terrace	12	5	N	14	7	8	P	29	8	11	Schuman et al. (1973a,b)
Contour	46	26	...[b]	...	...	...	...	...	...	...	Onstad (1972)
Grassed waterways	98	6	2,4-D	31	1	31	...	...	...	76	Asmussen et al. (1977)
Filter strip	90	75	N	...	...	48	P	204	11	40	Aull et al. (1980)
Pasture[c]	45	4	N	61	5	9	P	230	...	...	Schuman et al. (1973a,b)
Pasture[c]	34	1	N	15	...	...	P	27	26	26	Baker et al. (1978)
Wheat[d]	89	30	N	51	41	45	P	68	14	22	Olness et al. (1975)
Alfalfa[d]	50	7	N	81	24	42	P	2	12	11	
Range[d]	73	13	N	19	15	16	P	...	...	...	

[a] Amounts are expressed as % of those without practice.
[b] An ... indicates no measurement made.
[c] Pasture relative to corn.
[d] Relative to cotton.

TABLE 4.9.   Effects of timing and rate of N fertilization of corn on NO$_3$-N concen-
              trations in subsurface drainage

Practice	NO$_3$-N (%)	Explanation	Reference
Timing	84	Four applications relative to one (full irrigation)	Timmons and Dylla (1981)
	79	Four applications relative to one (partial irrigation)	
Rate	230	240 relative to 0 kg N/ha	Timmons and Dylla (1981)
Rate	370	448 relative to 168 kg N/ha	Burwell et al. (1976)
Rate	200	116 relative to 56 kg N/ha	Baker and Johnson (1981)
Rate	121	112 relative to 20 kg N/ha	Gast et al. (1978)
	225	224 relative to 20 kg N/ha	
	425	448 relative to 20 kg N/ha	
Rate	200	129 relative to 0 kg N/ha	Bolton et al. (1970)

standing the trends in chemical concentrations among modes of transport as a function of time during and between storm events, and as
affected by the properties of the chemical of interest. Chemicals can be
classified as being transported mainly in sediment, in surface runoff, or
in subsurface flow. Total N and P and insoluble or strongly adsorbed
pesticides are in the first category. Most pesticides and NH$_4$-N are moderately adsorbed and are transported mainly in surface runoff. The non-
adsorbed NO$_3$-N anion is lost mainly through leaching. Because of
physical removal from the runoff mixing zone with runoff and infiltrating water, chemical concentrations in runoff steadily decrease during a
storm event. Between storm events, chemical or biological removal can
result in ever decreasing chemical concentrations throughout the growing season. On the other hand, surface chemical applications can increase amounts available to runoff.

Concentrations of NO$_3$-N in surface runoff are usually less than 5
mg/l and lower than the 10 to 20 mg/l usually found in subsurface
drainage. However, because of soil adsorption and precipitation, concentrations of NH$_4$-N and PO$_4$-P in subsurface drainage are usually
lower than in surface runoff. Unless recent fertilization has occurred,
NH$_4$-N and PO$_4$-P concentrations in surface runoff are typically less
than 1 and 0.5 mg/l, respectively. Pesticide concentrations in surface
runoff can be in the mg/l range, particularly for a runoff event immediately after pesticide application, but they are generally less than 1 mg/
l. Pesticide concentrations in subsurface drainage are usually in the μ/l
or lower range. Loss of inorganic N with total agricultural drainage can
represent 10 to 50% of the N applied; whereas, inorganic P and pesticide
losses are usually less than 5 and 2%, respectively.

Best management practices to control erosion and sediment-carried
chemicals include conservation tillage, terraces, and grass used in filter
strips or waterways. To control chemical losses with surface runoff, an

attempt can be made to reduce the volume of runoff and/or to reduce concentrations in runoff. Chemical incorporation into the soil is an excellent practice to reduce concentrations. Improved timing and reduced N application rates seem logical ways to reduce NO_3-N leaching.

II. NITROGEN AND PHOSPHORUS IN PRAIRIE WETLANDS

Agricultural Drainage in Prairie Wetlands: Removal and Processes

Literature regarding the fate and impact of agricultural contaminants is limited (particularly for pesticides and sediments) for marshes of the northern prairie region; thus, the purpose of this section is to examine the role of prairie marshes in the cycling and removal of nitrogen (N) and phosphorus (P) from agricultural drainage. Literature from other wetlands types will also be presented when relevant to the understanding of N and P cycling in the prairie pothole marsh. More comprehensive reviews of N and P cycling in other sediment-water systems can be found in Hutchison (1957), Ponnamperuma (1972), Keeney (1973), Syers et al. (1973), van der Valk et al. (1979), Kadlec (1979) and Wetzel (1983). Additionally, information on the rates and impacts of sedimentation in wetland types from other regions can be found in Walker (1970), van der Valk and Bliss (1971), Boto and Patrick (1978), Mudie and Byrne (1980), and van der Valk et al. (1983).

Much of our understanding of N and P cycling in wetlands of the northern prairie region has come from studies of wetlands as potential nutrient traps. Studies of wetlands in this region and from other areas of the United States have generally demonstrated that natural and artificial wetlands can function, at least on a seasonal basis, as N and/or P sinks (Lee et al. 1975; Kitchens et al. 1975; Steward and Ornes 1975; Spangler et al. 1976; Tilton et al. 1976; Tourbier and Pierson 1976; Fetter et al. 1978; van der Valk et al. 1979; Davis et al. 1981, 1983; Davis and van der Valk 1983; Gersberg et al. 1983; and others). The main compartments to which N and P can be transferred from wetland surface waters are the atmosphere, sediment-interstitial water, and living and dead biomass (Figs. 4.2 and 4.3). Each of these compartments, however, can also be sources of N and P for surface water.

Because land-use in the prairie pothole region is dominated by intensive agriculture, prairie marshes frequently experience high nutrient loadings and may be important in preserving local water quality by removing N and P from nutrient-rich agricultural runoff. Davis et al. (1981) reported that Eagle Lake Marsh (a prairie marsh with a drainage basin dedicated to row-crop cultivation of corn and soybeans) received annual N and P inputs of 210 kg NO_3-N/ha, 9.1 kg NH_4-N/ha, and 3.1 kg PO_4-P/ha in 1979, a year of near normal rainfall. Of these amounts, approximately 86%, 78%, and 20% of these compounds, respectively, were removed within Eagle Lake Marsh. In the three years prior to 1979, the lack of any outflow from Eagle Lake prevented any incoming nutrients from exiting the marsh via surface water; thus, the marsh seemed a perfect nutrient sink for N and P in those years. However, this can only be stated with certainty for surface water since the possibility for groundwater export does exist.

Prairie marshes are dynamic ecosystems with short- and long-term vegetation cycles that are associated with wet and dry phases of prairie marshes (van der Valk and Davis 1978a, 1979, 1981); thus, the status of a marsh as a nutrient sink can vary substantially between years (Davis et al. 1981; Kadlec 1986b). Studies within the Marsh Ecology Research Program, Delta Marsh, Manitoba are currently being carried out to determine the influence of long-term cycles on the major components of wetland ecosystems, including nutrient concentrations and cycling (Murkin et al. 1985; Kadlec 1986a, 1986b).

Numerous factors influence the internal dynamics of N and P cycling in wetlands and the capacity of a wetland to trap these elements (Figs. 4.2 and 4.3). The most important of these factors include the hydrologic balance between inflows and outflows and the retention time of surface waters, timing of precipitation events and litter fall patterns, plant uptake and production, numerous physical and chemical processes, and rates of microbial processes (van der Valk et al. 1979; Kadlec 1979, 1986b). With the possible exception of emergent plant production and decomposition dynamics for above-ground tissues (Davis and van der Valk 1978a, 1978b, 1978c; Davis et al. 1983; van der Valk and Davis 1978b; Davis and Neely 1982; Neely 1982; Neely and Davis 1985a, 1985b), detailed information on any of these processes in prairie marshes is generally lacking.

Inasmuch as both N and P are removed from marsh waters or sediments through assimilation by living organisms and later released from these organisms (excretion, leaching, and decomposition), internal N and P cycles of prairie wetlands are similar. However, some distinct differences between these cycles exist. First, phosphorus occurs in wetlands in basically two forms, inorganic (as PO_4-P and its polymers, i.e., polyphophates) and organic. These P forms can be either dissolved or a portion of total particulate matter. Nitrogen occurs in organic forms and as inorganic N that can potentially exist in seven different oxidation states, five of which are gaseous (Soderlund and Rosswall 1982). The important inorganic forms of nitrogen in biological processes are nitrogen gas (N_2), nitrite (NO_2), nitrate (NO_3), and ammonia (NH_3). Second, several microbe-mediated transformations are unique to the N cycle and may affect the N budget of a wetland (i.e., N-fixation, denitrification, and nitrification). No analogous processes are evident for the P cycle. Third, P availability and solubility in the surface or interstitial water column is determined by the oxygen status of the local environment (Stumm and Morgan 1981). Oxygen regimes do not affect the solubility of N, but various N transformations are dependent on the presence or absence of oxygen, (e.g., denitrification and nitrification).

In the following sections, the literature regarding internal N and P movements and transformations between the water, sediment, atmosphere, and biota will be discussed for prairie pothole wetlands. Much of the discussion will focus on Eagle Lake Marsh, one of the few prairie wetlands in which N and P dynamics have been intensively studied.

Atmospheric — Wetland Fluxes

Basic Processes. Neither organic P nor PO_4-P are volatile, thus P loss to the atmosphere is minimal. Perhaps the only potential for gaseous P movement to the atmosphere is through the production of phosphine (PH_3), which is formed in small quantities during the putrification of organic matter containing phosphorus. Golley (1983) has cited the potential for such losses in tropical systems. Phosphine losses are unreported in prairie wetlands, but are probably insignificant.

Exchange of gaseous nitrogen forms between the atmosphere and wetland waters may be considerable. The basic processes are N-fixation, NH_3 volatilization, denitrification, and possibly nitrification. N-fixation and denitrification result in additions or losses of nitrogen from wetlands and therefore have a direct impact on the N budget of a wetland (van der Valk et al. 1978). Similarly, NH_3 volatilization can represent a significant N loss at basic pH values. Nitrification, the oxidation of NH_3 to NO_2 and NO_3, has generally been assumed to have little impact on the N budget of a wetland. Evidence from other ecosystems, however, suggests that N may escape as nitrous oxide (N_2O) during nitrification (Bremner and Blackmer 1981; Soderlund and Rosswall 1982). Smith et al. (1982) have also suggested that losses of N_2O during nitrification in a Louisiana *Spartina alterniflora* marsh may be important.

N-fixation. Rates of N-fixation are unknown for prairie pothole wetlands. In other wetland types, estimates of the contribution of N fixation to N budgets have ranged from inconsequential to significant. Lee et al. (1975) suggested that N-fixation was important in wetlands and Bristow (1974) estimated that as much as 60 kg N/ha/yr was fixed in the rhizosphere of *Glyceria borealis*. Bristow (1974) also estimated that N-fixation provided as much as 10 to 20% of the N requirement for

Typha stands. In contrast, Isirimah and Keeney (1973) unsuccessfully attempted to detect N-fixation in Lake Wingra Marsh, Wisconsin.

Denitrification. While the magnitude of N-fixation in prairie pothole marshes is certainly questionable, denitrification is assumed to be a dominant process in the removal of nitrogen in many wetland types (Lee et al. 1975; Kadlec 1979; van der Valk et al. 1979; Davis et al. 1981; Gersberg et al. 1983). In the absence of actual measurements, this assumption in prairie wetlands is largely based on circumstantial evidence: (1) suitable conditions exist for denitrification in wetlands (i.e., the presence of anoxic waters due to plant decomposition) (Maystrenko et al. 1969; Jewell 1971; Klopatek 1975; van der Valk et al. 1979) and the presence of a large carbon base because of autotrophic production; and (2) nitrate disappears rapidly from prairie marsh water, thus surface water concentrations are often low. From 1976 to 1979, the concentration of NO_3-N averaged 16 mg/l in the inflow to Eagle Lake Marsh (Davis, et al. 1981), but NO_3-N concentrations in the interior of the marsh are generally low (average values of 0.92 and 1.44 mg/l in 1979 and 1980, respectively [Neely 1982]). Similarly, Neely (1982) reported that NO_3-N concentrations declined by 5–8 mg/l/day after elevation of Eagle Lake surface waters to approximately 20 mg NO_3-N/l.

Although denitrification in prairie marshes may indeed be significant, the variability among estimates of denitrification from other wetland and submersed-soil studies indicates that reliable measurements are needed. For example, Chen et al. (1972a) estimated that as much as 63% of applied $^{15}NO_3$-N was denitrified in Lake Mendota, Wisconsin, sediments; MacRae et al. (1968) observed large losses of $^{15}NO_3$-N from submerged tropical soils; Bartlett et al. (1979) reported 90–95% reductions of added NO_3-N from freshwater wetland soil; and, Kadlec (1979) cited losses of 2–4 mg/l/day from laboratory studies of southern wetlands. But, Prentki et al. (1978), using the data of Isirimah and Keeney (1973), concluded that denitrification in Lake Wingra Marsh, Wisconsin, was insignificant. In shallow Danish lakes, estimates of denitrification ranged from 0–54% of annual N inputs (Andersen 1974).

Volatilization. Rates of NH_3 volatilization in prairie marshes are evidently unreported, but they may be significant in these wetlands because of alkaline pH regimes (pH > 7.4) and NH_3 generation from decomposing plant tissues.

Nitrification. Substantial N losses associated with denitrification in prairie wetlands depend on a ready supply of NO_3-N. In addition to outside inputs of NO_3-N to a marsh, NO_3-N can be formed internally during the nitrification of NH_4-N. Because nitrification is an oxidative process, close proximity of an aerobic zone for nitrification and an anaerobic zone for denitrification is essential for sustained N losses through denitrification (Kadlec 1979). Sequential processes of nitrification and denitrification may also result in large N losses in wetlands experiencing frequent drying and inundation. Increased aeration associated with periodic drying stimulates the oxidation of NH_4-N to NO_3-N during nitrification, which in turn can be denitrified with the return of water and anaerobic conditions (Patrick and Wyatt 1964; Patrick and Tusneem 1972).

The role and magnitude of nitrification in continuously saturated wetlands, however, is unclear. For instance, Neely (1982) noted moderate declines of added NH_4-N in Eagle Lake surface waters, but no corresponding increase in NO_3-N concentration to suggest that nitrification was an important process. Optimal conditions for nitrification are at 30° C, a near neutral pH (Alexander 1965) and a dissolved oxygen concentration greater than 1 to 2 mg/l (Chen et al. 1972b). Keeney (1973) has also indicated that nitrification will occur down to 0.3 mg/l of dissolved oxygen. With the exception of temperature, most prairie wetland surface waters probably meet these criteria.

Exchange between Substrate and Surface Water

When downward water movement because of local hydrologic characteristics is unimportant, the movement of N or P directly from surface water to the sediment-interstitial water column depends on the processes of sedimentation, precipitation, and/or diffusion. In an estuarine system, Correll et al. (1975) have also presented evidence that P can be transferred into sediment by downward migration of microbial cells.

Because the major N ions are soluble and do not form precipitates in wetlands, diffusion seems the main mechanism for N transfer into the substrate, particularly for NO_3-N. For phosphorus, sedimentation and precipitation with metal ions (e.g., Fe and Al) under aerobic conditions (Stumm and Morgan 1981; Emsley 1980) are the significant processes in pothole marshes and have been postulated as the major means of P removal from water passing through wetlands (Kadlec 1979; van der Valk et al. 1978; Davis et al. 1981, 1983) Kadlec (1979) has suggested that chemical precipitation of P could result in enrichment of sediments and interstitial water.

Fertilization studies have clearly demonstrated that surface-applied N and P can move through the sediment profile of some wetland types. At Eagle Lake Marsh, Neely and Davis (1985a) found that seasonal averages of PO_4-P and NH_4-N were elevated 200% and 66%, respectively, in 15-cm deep interstitial water of fertilized plots. In other studies,

Nicholls and MacCrimmon (1974) observed increases in NO_3-N, NH_4-N and soluble reactive phosphorus in interstitial water from cultivated, fertilized plots within Holland Marsh, Ontario, and Savant and De Datta (1980) reported the elevation of NH_4-N in 1- to 4-cm deep interstitial water of a wetland rice soil after addition of urea. Elevation of N and P concentrations in interstitial water after surface water enrichment has also been demonstrated in estuarine systems (Valiela and Teal 1974; Correll et al. 1975). Klopatek (1978) and Davis and van der Valk (1983) have suggested that nutrient assimilation by the roots of emergent vegetation may free exchange sites on sediment particles thereby stimulating the movement of ions from surface water into sediment-interstitial water.

Work at Eagle Lake suggests that the two-way exchange of nutrients between interstitial and surface waters can be affected by (1) emergent plant litter buildup at the soil-water interface and (2) the oxygen status of the surface water (Neely 1982; Davis and Neely 1982; Neely and Davis 1985a). Fallen litter, with its associated populations of microbes, may restrict downward N and P movement through obstruction and immobilization. In contrast, anaerobic surface waters may act to enhance nutrient exchange, particularly from interstitial to surface water. In lakes and ponds, separation of an aerobic surface water column from the anaerobic interstitial water profile can cause accumulation of some nutrients in interstitial waters, particularly PO_4-P. In Lake Mendota, Holdren et al. (1977) reported PO_4-P levels in interstitial water five to twenty times surface water concentrations. At Eagle Lake, however, Neely (1982) found that interstitial and surface water concentrations of NH_4-N and PO_4-P were relatively similar. Because oxygen concentrations inside marsh surface waters are often low, the distinction between an aerated surface water column and an anaerobic interstitial water profile is probably less pronounced in a shallow prairie marsh than in some lakes.

Fluxes during Emergent Plant Production and Decomposition

Production. Emergent plants, submersed plants, and planktonic and epiphytic algae all immobilize N and P from marsh waters or sediments. The N and P demands of emergent plants are presumably met by root uptake alone (Bernatowicz 1969; Klopatek 1978; Davis et al. 1983). Rooted submersed plants are capable of supplementing root uptake with foliar uptake (Bristow and Whitcomb 1971; Nichols and Keeney 1976). Algae, on the other hand, remove N and P only from surface waters, but may have a major impact on water quality (Allen 1971). Because emergent plants are the dominant macro-lifeform in wetlands, only their

N and P fluxes and contribution to N and P removal in prairie pothole systems have been studied in some detail.

Since emergent plant nutritional requirements are met by root uptake alone, growing emergent plants are perceived as having little direct impact on N and P removal from wetland surface waters, and they have been characterized as nutrient pumps that remove nutrients from interstitial water and return them to surface water via leaching and decomposition (Klopatek 1978; Davis and van der Valk 1983). While the removal of N and P by emergent plants directly from surface water may be minimal, studies in Iowa wetlands suggest that enriched surface waters may result in increased production and increased N and P levels in emergent plant tissues. Davis and van der Valk (1978a) referred to the fertility of Eagle Lake Marsh when reporting that N and P concentrations in *Typha glauca* from Eagle Lake Marsh were 1.5 to 2.0 times higher than values for the same species from other wetlands. In the second year of a fertilization study at Eagle Lake, Neely (1982) reported further increases in nitrogen concentration of shoots and roots of *Typha glauca* and *Sparganium eurycarpum* shoots after enrichment of surface waters with ammonia and nitrate. In that study, shoot concentrations eventually increased 14% and 34% and root concentrations increased 40% and 25% for *Typha* and *Sparganium,* respectively, after fertilizer treatments.

Perhaps as a function of high N and P tissue concentrations, the production of *Typha* and *Sparganium* at Eagle Lake is high. Estimates of production for *Typha* at Eagle Lake (1,726–2,106 g/m²) are at the high end of the range of values typical for production in inland freshwater marshes (Table 4.10). While *Sparganium* production at Eagle Lake (637–1,054 g/m²) is substantially below Lindsley's et al. (1976) estimate of 1,950 g/m² in a Wisconsin marsh, this species is clearly very productive at Eagle Lake. Neely and Davis (1985a) suggest that the productivity of Eagle Lake *Typha* and *Sparganium* could be a result of the high input of N and P from field fertilizer runoff and drainage. Increased *Typha* and *Sparganium* biomass in the next growing season after the fertilization of marsh surface waters support this possibility (Table 4.10). Boyd (1978) and Neely and Davis (1985a) cite other studies in which increased productivity and/or positive correlations have been observed relative to site fertility; thus, excessive nutrient input from agricultural activities in prairie wetlands may stimulate the productivity of some plant species.

The extent to which emergent plant productivity and nutrient immobilization affect nutrient retention in wetlands is in part a function of the magnitude of internal nutrient cycling between plant tissues (Figs. 4.2 and 4.3). The internal cycling of N and P between emergent plant

TABLE 4.10. Typha and Sparganium above-ground biomass (g m⁻²) in inland freshwater marshes

Species	Biomass	Site	Reference
Typha sp.	1,527	Oklahoma	Penfound (1956)
	1,360	Minnesota	Bray (1962)
	1,754	Manitoba, Canada	Shay and Shay (1986)
	1,336	Texas	McNaughton (1966)
	730	Oklahoma	
	416	Nebraska	
	378	South Dakota	
	404	North Dakota	
Typha latifolia	686	South Carolina	Boyd (1970)
	530–1,132	South Carolina	Boyd (1971)
	428–2,252	Southeastern USA	Boyd and Hess (1970)
	1,482	South Carolina	Polisini and Boyd (1971)
Typha glauca	1,549	Iowa	Van Dyke (1972)
	2,106	Iowa[a]	van der Valk and Davis (1978b)
	1,726	Iowa[a]	Neely and Davis (1985)
	2,343	Iowa[b]	
Sparganium eurycarpum	1,950	Wisconsin	Lindsley et al. (1976)
	770	Iowa	Van Dyke (1972)
	1,054	Iowa[a]	van der Valk and Davis (1978b)
	637	Iowa[a]	Neely and Davis (1985)
	1,185	Iowa[b]	

Source: Adapted from Neely and Davis (1985).
[a]Values from Eagle Lake Marsh.
[b]Values from fertilized plots at Eagle Lake Marsh.

shoots and roots reduces the amounts of these elements that must be obtained from outside sources. Studies of Eagle Lake species and species in other freshwater wetlands suggest a high degree of internal nutrient cycling (Klopatek 1975; Davis and van der Valk 1983; Davis et al. 1983). The change in concentration of N and P in living shoots and roots of emergent vegetation typically follows a distinct seasonal pattern. Concentrations of both nutrients in shoot tissues decline throughout the growing season because of (1) dilution due to growth, (2) leaching, and (3) translocation to below-ground structures in the latter part of the season. In contrast, initial root concentrations are high at the onset of the growing season, but rapidly decline because of translocation to actively growing shoots. N and P concentrations in root tissues are restored during the late fall and early winter months because of the accumulation of N and P from the shoot tissues.

By coupling nutrient concentrations with biomass estimates, van der Valk and Davis (1983) estimated that approximately 40% of the N and P requirements of *Typha glauca* at Eagle Lake Marsh could be met by internal cycling between roots and shoots alone. Despite this degree of internal cycling, Davis et al. (1983) reported that even when 40% was subtracted from N and P standing crops, emergent macrophytes still accumulated during the growing season more than twice the amount of

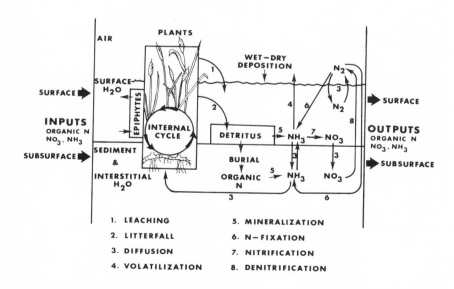

FIG. 4.2.   Generalized diagram of nitrogen transformation, storage compartments, and fluxes in a prairie wetland.

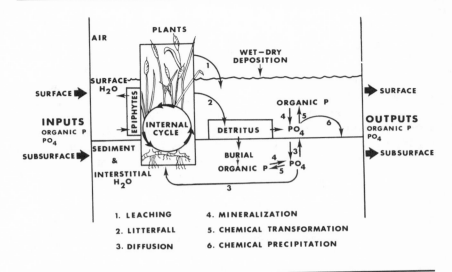

FIG. 4.3.   Generalized diagram of phosphorus transformation, storage compartments, and fluxes in a prairie wetland.

N and ten times the amount of P that entered Eagle Lake Marsh in precipitation, drainage, and runoff combined.

Decomposition.   Because immobilization and accumulation of N and P in above-ground emergent plant tissues during growth is only temporary, the patterns of litter fall, litter decomposition, and nutrient uptake and release are critical to nutrient retention in wetlands. Typically, shoot litter undergoes two phases of decomposition: (1) an initial period of rapid weight loss because of leaching of soluble compounds and (2) a longer period of microbial breakdown (Boyd 1970; Mason and Bryant 1975; Howard-Williams and Howard-Williams 1978; Davis and van der Valk 1978b, 1978c; Puriveth 1980; Rogers and Breen 1982; Davis et al. 1983; Neely and Davis 1985b). The extent to which emergent plant litter functions as a nutrient sink depends on at least three factors: (1) the quantity of N and P leached from the litter, (2) the quantity of nutrients accrued through microbial activity, and (3) the rate of decomposition and mineralization (Neely and Davis 1985b).

Leaching during decomposition begins immediately upon shoot death and is essentially a function of the timing and quantity of precipitation events for standing litter (Davis and van der Valk 1978c). Leaching continues after inundation and can be significant even when litter has been standing for a period of several months (e.g., 16–27% weight loss within 24 hours after submergence of approximately 6-month-old litter) (Neely and Davis 1985b). Although both N and P seem intermediate in their ability to resist leaching (Davis and van der Valk 1978c), data from prairie wetlands show that N is leached in greater amounts than P. During 525 days of decomposition in Goose Lake, Iowa, Davis and van der Valk (1978b, 1978c) observed losses of approximately 1.1 and 1.5 g N/m² from standing litter of *Typha glauca* and *Scirpus fluviatilis,* respectively. In contrast, losses of P from standing litter were 0.1 and 0.5 g P/m² for the two species, respectively. Amounts of N leached from inundated litter ranged from about 40–67% of standing litter losses. Because most of the P had been leached while the litter was standing, only negligible amounts of P were leached after inundation.

After leaching is complete, older litter often functions as a N and P sink during microbial breakdown and may be the major compartment for accumulation of N and P in wetlands (Richardson et al. 1976; Davis and Harris 1978; Davis and van der Valk 1978b, 1978c; Davis et al. 1983; Neely and Davis 1985b). Microbes acting on fallen litter use the litter as a carbon source but may augment the N and P within the litter with N and P from surrounding waters and sediment (Fig. 4.4 [Neely and Davis 1985b]); consequently, nitrogen and phosphorus often accumulate in decaying litter. The quantity of nutrients accrued by microbes seems a function of the C:N and C:P ratios in the fallen litter. A C:N ratio greater than 16–23 and a C:P ratio greater than 200 are presumably

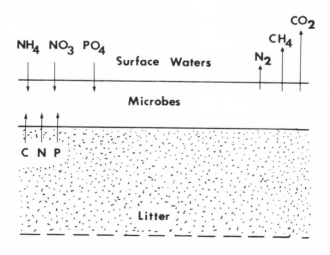

FIG. 4.4. Sources of carbon, nitrogen, and phosphorus for microbial decomposers (*Adapted from Neely and Davis 1985b*).

indicative of a microbial nutrient demand in excess of the N and P content of the litter (Enwezor 1976; Brinson 1977). The absolute ratios presented here, however, are somewhat questionable given that carbon is continually respired by microbes while N and P are not; thus, these ratios may be too low. Nonetheless, Neely and Davis (1985b) estimated initial C:N and C:P ratios to range from 82–94 and 570–1800, respectively, in *Typha glauca* and *Sparganium eurycarpum* from Eagle Lake Marsh thereby suggesting a microbial demand for N and P.

Accumulation of N and P in decomposing emergent plant tissues has been effectively demonstrated in prairie marshes. At various periods during decomposition, absolute quantities of N and/or P remaining in emergent tissues (relative to initial amounts) have been as high as 131% N for *T. glauca* and *S. eurycarpum* in Eagle Lake Marsh, 135% N for *T. glauca* in fertilized Eagle Lake waters, 200% P for *Scirpus fluviatilis* in Goose Lake, Iowa, 125% P for *T. glauca* in Eagle Lake Marsh, and 221% P for *T. glauca* in fertilized Eagle Lake waters (Davis and van der Valk 1978c; Neely and Davis 1985b).

Although N and P are accrued in decomposing plant tissues, the permanence of the litter as an N and P sink depends on the length of time required for complete mineralization and decomposition. Plants with extremely slow decompositional rates are more likely to facilitate nutrient retention within the wetland. Slow N and P release rates from decomposing litter increase the probability that some residual N and P will persist after complete conversion of the litter to organic soil (Davis and van der Valk 1983). Some rates of dry weight loss for prairie marsh species are listed in Table 4.11.

TABLE 4.11.   Standardized rates of decay for fallen emergent plant litter in Eagle Lake and Goose Lake, Iowa

Species	Duration of study (days)	Decay constant (k yr^{-1})	Half-life in days ($0.693/k$ days^{-1})
Scirpus fluviatilis[a]	525	0.34	741
Typha glauca[a]	525	0.52	485
Typha glauca[b]	330	0.79	321
Typha glauca[b]	505	0.36	704
Typha glauca[c]	505	0.36	704
Sparganium eurycarpum[b]	330	1.23	204
Sparganium eurycarpum[b]	505	0.36	704
Sparganium eurycarpum[c]	505	0.36	704
Carex atherodes[b]	330	0.25	1,011
Scirpus validus[b]	330	2.00	128

Note: Decay constants and half-life indices were determined by using the exponential decay equation ($X/X_0 = e^{-kt}$).

  [a]Values from Goose Lake Marsh (adapted from Davis and van der Valk 1978a).
  [b]Values from Eagle Lake Marsh (adapted from Davis and van der Valk 1978a; Neely and Davis 1985b).
  [c]Values from fertilized plots at Eagle Lake Marsh (adapted from Neely and Davis 1985b).

Obviously, factors that affect the rates of emergent plant decomposition will affect the capacity of a marsh to trap nutrients. Brinson et al. (1981) have reviewed rates of decomposition from a range of latitudes and have discussed factors that affect rates of decomposition. But the factors most important to litter decomposition in the prairie pothole region seem relatively few and include: (1) oxygen availability, (2) structural composition of decomposing tissues, and (3) the initial nutrient concentration of the decomposing litter. Anaerobic conditions limit the decomposition rates and are generally considered one main reason for slow decomposition in wetlands (Chamie and Richardson 1978). Similarly, high amounts of structural tissue or structural compounds, (e.g., lignin and total fiber) also result in slower decomposition rates (Crawford and Crawford 1976; Godshalk and Wetzel 1978; Davis and van der Valk 1978a; Polunin 1983). Decomposition has also been positively correlated with initial nutrient contents (Kaushik and Hynes 1971; Almazan and Boyd 1978; Coulson and Butterfield 1978; Neely and Davis 1985b) (i.e., faster decomposition rates are facilitated by higher initial nutrient contents).

The role of the emergent vegetation has been characterized as the "driving force" for the removal of nutrients from marsh waters (Davis and van der Valk 1983). The most important role of emergent production is not nutrient retention as living tissues, but as litter on the marsh bottom. However, because N and P concentrations in surface waters can lead to higher concentrations in the living plants, the nutritional quality of vegetation entering the litter compartment is likely to be significantly improved and its rate of decomposition significantly faster. After presenting data that showed that high-nutrient litter was a poor nutrient sink at Eagle Lake, Neely and Davis (1985b) concluded that the optimal condition for nutrient removal by the litter-microbe association, litter with a low initial nutrient content in nutrient-rich water, was unlikely to exist.

Summary of N and P Dynamics

Prairie marshes can be exposed to unusually high concentrations of N and P from agricultural drainage and runoff. On the basis of research on Eagle Lake Marsh, prairie marshes effectively remove N and less effectively P from surface waters. The major compartments to which N and/or P are removed are the atmosphere, biomass, and sediment-interstitial water.

Only the role of emergent vegetation in nitrogen and phosphorus removal has been studied in any detail in prairie marshes. Surface N and P concentrations influence both the production and decomposition of emergent species, particularly when surface concentrations are extreme.

For growing emergent plants, the effect of high surface concentrations is likely exerted through sequential movement of N and P from surface water to interstitial water and from interstitial water into the plant. Increases in root and shoot nitrogen content, shoot density, and above-ground production have been reported for *Typha* and *Sparganium* at Eagle Lake after elevation of N and P concentrations in surface water.

High surface water concentrations of N and P can affect emergent plant decomposition in two ways. First, high N and P concentrations can have a direct effect on decomposition. This effect is not one of altering the rate of decomposition; rather, only amounts of N and P accrued during microbial decomposition increase with increasing N and P concentrations. Secondly, through enrichment of living emergent plant tissues, high surface N and P concentrations can indirectly affect decomposition by ultimately influencing the nutritional quality of emergent plant debris entering the litter compartment. Fallen litter with a high initial percentage of N and P seems to decompose at a faster rate and is consequently more likely to function as a nutrient exporter.

ACKNOWLEDGMENTS

We would like to thank Gary Hannan, Jeff Allen, Barbara Drake, Jim Hohman, and Brian Lake for their constructive criticisms of this chapter. Gratitude is also expressed to Renee Neely for her secretarial assistance.

REFERENCES

Ahuja, L. R., and O. R. Lehman. 1983. The extent and nature of rainfall-soil interaction in the release of soluble chemicals in runoff. J. Environ. Qual. 12:34–40.
Alberts, E. E., and R. G. Spomer. 1985. Dissolved nitrogen and phosphorus in runoff from watersheds in conservation and conventional tillage. J. Soil Water Conserv. 40:153–57.
Alberts, E. E., G. E. Schuman, and R. E. Burwell. 1978. Seasonal runoff losses of nitrogen and phosphorus from Missouri Valley loess watersheds. J. Environ. Qual. 7:203–8.
Alexander, M. 1965. Nitrification. Agron. 10:307–43.
Allen, H. L. 1971. Primary productivity, chemo-organotrophy, and nutrient interactions of epiphytic algae and bacteria on macrophytes in the littoral of a lake. Ecol. Monogr. 41:97–127.
Almazan, G., and C. E. Boyd. 1978. Effects of nitrogen levels on rates of oxygen consumption during decay of aquatic plants. Aquat. Bot. 5:119–26.

Andersen, V. J. M. 1974. Nitrogen and phosphorus budgets and the role of sediments in six shallow Danish lakes. Archiv. Hydrobiol. 74:528–50.

Asmussen, L. E., A. W. White, Jr., E. W. Hauser, and J. M. Sheridan. 1977. Reduction of 2,4-D load in surface runoff down a grassed waterway. J. Environ. Qual. 6:159–62.

Aull, G. H., T. L. Loudon, and J. B. Gerrish. 1980. Runoff quality enhancement with a vegetated buffer. Amer. Soc. Agric. Eng. Paper No. 80-2538. St. Joseph, Mich.: Amer. Soc. Agric. Eng.

Baker, J. L., and T. A. Austin. 1984. Impact of agricultural drainage wells on groundwater quality. Dept. Agric. Eng. Civil Eng., Completion Report, EPA Grant No. G007228010. Ames, Iowa: Iowa State Univ.

Baker, J. L., and H. P. Johnson. 1979. The effect of tillage systems on pesticides in runoff from soil watersheds. Trans. Amer. Soc. Agric. Eng. 22:554–59.

———. 1981. Nitrate-nitrogen in tile drainage as affected by fertilization. J. Environ. Qual. 10:519–22.

Baker, J. L., and J. M. Laflen. 1979. Runoff losses of surface-applied herbicides as affected by wheel tracks and incorporation. J. Environ. Qual. 8:602–07.

———. 1983a. Runoff losses of nutrients and soil from ground fall-fertilized after soybean harvest. Trans. Amer. Soc. Agric. Eng. 26:1122–27.

———. 1983b. Water quality consequences of conservation tillage. J. Soil Water Conserv. 38:186–93.

Baker, J. L., and L. E. Shiers. 1985. Washoff characteristics of herbicides applied to corn residue. Amer. Soc. Agric. Eng. Paper 85-1519. St. Joseph, Mich.: Amer. Soc. Agric. Eng.

Baker, J. L., and D. R. Timmons. 1984. Effect of method, timing, and number of fertilizer applications on corn yield and nutrient uptake. Agron. Abstr. 197.

Baker, J. L., K. L. Campbell, H. P. Johnson, and J. J. Hanway. 1975. Nitrate, phosphorus and sulfate in subsurface drainage water. J. Environ. Qual. 4:406–12.

Baker, J. L., H. P. Johnson, M. A. Borcherding, and W. R. Payne. 1978a. Nutrient and pesticide movement from field to stream: A field study. In Best Management Practices for Agriculture and Silviculture, ed. R. C. Loehr, et al. Ann Arbor, Mich.: Ann Arbor Sci. Publ. Inc.

Baker, J. L., J. M. Laflen, and H. P. Johnson. 1978b. Effect of tillage systems on runoff losses of pesticides, a rainfall simulation study. Trans. Amer. Soc. Agric. Eng. 21:886–92.

Baker, J. L., T. S. Colvin, S. J. Marley, and M. Dawelbeit. 1985. Improved fertilizer management with a point-injector applicator. Amer. Soc. Agric. Eng. Paper No. 85-1516. St. Joseph, Mich.: Amer. Soc. Agric. Eng.

Barisas, S. G., J. L. Baker, H. P. Johnson, and J. M. Laflen. 1978. Effect of tillage systems on runoff losses of nutrients: A rainfall simulation study. Trans. Amer. Soc. Agric. Eng. 21:893–97.

Barnett, A. P. 1965. Using perennial grasses and legumes to control runoff and erosion. J. Soil Water Conserv. 20:212–15.

Bartlett, M. S., L. C. Brown, N. B. Hanes, and N. H. Nickerson. 1979. Denitrification in freshwater wetland soil. J. Environ. Qual. 8:460–64.

Baumann, E. R., D. L. Schulze, D. P. Bierl, and E. D. Ricci. 1982. Annual Report. Water Quality Studies—Red Rock and Saylorville Reservoirs, Des Moines River, Iowa. Iowa State Univ., ERI Rep. No. 82149. Ames: Iowa State Univ.

Baumann, E. R., D. L. Schulze, D. P. Bierl, and E. A. Harrold. 1983. Annual Report. Water Quality Studies — Red Rock and Saylorville Reservoirs, Des Moines River, Iowa. Iowa State Univ., ERI Rep. No. 83285. Ames: Iowa State Univ.

Benoit, G. R. 1973. Effect of agricultural management of wet sloping soil on nitrate and phosphorus in surface and subsurface water. Water Resour. Res. 9:1296–1303.

Bernatowicz, S. 1969. Macrophytes in the Lake Warniak and their chemical composition. Ekol. Pol. (Ser. A) 17:447–67.

Bolton, E. F., J. W. Aylesworth, and F. R. Hore. 1970. Nutrient losses through tile drains under three cropping systems and two fertility levels on a Brookston clay loam. Can. J. Soil Sci. 50:275–79.

Boto, K. G., and W. H. Patrick. 1978. Role of wetlands in the removal of suspended sediments. *In* Wetland functions and values: The state of our understanding, ed. P. E. Greeson et al. Minneapolis, Minn: Amer. Water Resour. Assoc.

Boyd, C. E. 1970. Losses of mineral nutrients during decomposition of *Typha latifolia*. Arch. Hydrobiol. 66:511–17.

_____. 1971. Further studies on productivity, nutrient and pigment relationships in *Typha latifolia* populations. Bull. Torrey Bot. Club 98:144–50.

_____. 1978. Chemical composition of wetland plants. *In* Freshwater wetlands: Ecological processes and management potential, ed. R. E. Good, et al., 155–67. New York: Academic Press.

Boyd, C. E., and L. W. Hess. 1970. Factors influencing shoot production and mineral nutrient levels in *Typha latifolia*. Ecol. 51:285–90.

Bray, J. R. 1962. Estimates of energy budgets for a *Typha* (cattail) marsh. Sci. 136:1119–20.

Bremner, J. M., and A. M. Blackmer. 1981. Terrestrial nitrification as a source of atmospheric nitrous oxide. *In* Denitrification, nitrification, and atmospheric nitrous oxide, ed. C.C. Delwiche, 151–70. New York: John Wiley and Sons.

Brinson, M. M. 1977. Decomposition and nutrient exchange of litter in an alluvial swamp forest. Ecol. 58:601–09.

Brinson, M. M., A. E. Lugo, and S. Brown. 1981. Primary productivity, decomposition and consumer activity in freshwater wetlands. Annu. Rev. Ecol. System. 12:123–61.

Bristow, J. M. 1974. Nitrogen fixation in the rhizosphere of freshwater angiosperms. Can. J. Bot. 52:217–21.

Bristow, J. M., and Whitcombe, M. 1971. The role of roots in the nutrition of aquatic vascular plants. Amer. J. Bot. 58:8–13.

Burwell, R. E., G. E. Schuman, R. F. Piest, R. G. Spomer, and T. M. McCalla. 1974. Quality of water discharged from two agricultural watersheds in southwestern Iowa. Water Resour. Res. 10:359–65.

Burwell, R. E., D. R. Timmons, and R. F. Holt. 1975. Nutrient transport in surface runoff as influenced by soil cover and seasonal periods. Soil Sci. Soc. Amer. Proc. 39:523–28.

Burwell, R. E., G. E. Schuman, K. E. Saxton, and H. G. Heinemann. 1976. Nitrogen in subsurface discharge from agricultural watersheds. J. Environ. Qual. 5(3):325–29.

Calvert, D. V. 1975. Nitrate, phosphate, and potassium movement into drainage lines under three soil management systems. J. Environ. Qual. 4:183–86.

Caro, J. H., H. P. Freeman, D. E. Glotfelty, B. C. Turner, and W. M. Edwards. 1973. Dissipation of soil-incorporated carbofuran in the field. J. Agric. Food Chem. 21:1010–15.

Caro, J. H., H. P. Freeman, and B. C. Turner. 1974. Persistence in soil and losses in runoff of soil-incorporated carbaryl in a small watershed. J. Agric. Food Chem. 22:860–63.

Chamie, J. P. M., and C. J. Richardson. 1978. Decomposition in northern wetlands. In Freshwater wetlands: Ecological processes and management potential, ed. R.E. Good et al., 115–30. New York: Academic Press.

Chen, R. L., D. R. Keeney, D. A. Graetz, and A. J. Holding. 1972a. Denitrification and nitrate reduction in Wisconsin lake sediments. J. Environ. Qual. 1:158–62.

Chen, R. L., D. R. Keeney, and J. G. Konrad. 1972b. Nitrification in sediments of selected Wisconsin lakes. J. Environ. Qual. 1:151–54.

Chichester, F. W., R. W. van Keuren, and J. L. McGuiness. 1979. Hydrology and chemical quality of flow from small pastured watersheds. II: Chemical quality. J. Environ. Qual. 8:167–71.

Colvin, T. S., J. M. Laflen, and D. C. Erbach. 1981. A review of residue reduction by individual tillage implements. In Crop production with conservation in the 80s. Amer. Soc. Agric. Eng. Publ. 7-81. St. Joseph, Mich.: Amer. Soc. Agric. Eng.

Cooke, G. W., and R. J. B. Williams. 1970. Losses of nitrogen and phosphorus from agricultural land. Water Treat. Exam. 19:253–74.

Correll, D. L., M. A. Faust, and D. J. Severn. 1975. Phosphorus flux and cycling in estuaries. In Estuarine research, vol. 1, ed. L. E. Cronin, 108–36. New York: Academic Press.

Coulson, J. C., and J. Butterfield. 1978. An investigation of the biotic factors determining the rates of plant decomposition on blanket bog. J. Ecol. 66:631–50.

Crawford, D. L., and R. L. Crawford. 1976. Microbial degradation of lignocellulose: The lignin component. Appl. Environ. Microbiol. 31:714–17.

Davis, C. B., and R. K. Neely. 1982. The effects of excessive nitrogen and phosphorus in the surface waters of a prairie marsh. O.W.R.T. Project Completion Report, Iowa State Univ., ERI-83206. Ames: Iowa State Univ.

Davis, C. B., and A. G. van der Valk. 1978a. Litter decomposition in prairie glacial marshes. In Freshwater wetlands: Ecological processes and management potential, ed. R.E. Good et al., 99–113. New York: Academic Press.

_____. 1978b. The decomposition of standing and fallen litter of Typha glauca and Scirpus fluviatilis. Can. J. Bot. 56:662–75.

_____. 1978c. Mineral release from the litter of Bidens cernua L., a mudflat annual at Eagle Lake, Iowa. Proc. Internatl. Assoc. Theor. Appl. Limnol. 20:452–57.

_____. 1983. Uptake and release of nutrients by living and decomposing Typha glauca Godr. tissues at Eagle Lake, Iowa. Aquat. Bot. 16:75–89.

Davis, C. B., J. L. Baker, A. G. van der Valk, and C. E. Beer. 1981. Prairie pothole marshes as traps for nitrogen and phosphorus in agricultural runoff. In Proc. Midwest Conf. on Wetland Values and Manage., ed. B. Richardson, 153–63. Navarre, Minn.: Freshwater Soc.

Davis, C. B., A. G. van der Valk, and J. L. Baker. 1983. The role of four macrophyte species in the removal of nitrogen and phosphorus from nutrient-rich water in a prairie marsh, Iowa. Madrono 30:133–42.

Davis, S. M., and L. A. Harris. 1978. Marsh plant production and phosphorus flux in Everglades conservation area 2. *In* Environmental quality through wetland utilization, ed. M.A. Drew, 105–31. Tallahassee, Fl.: Coord. Counc. on the Restoration of the Kissimmee River Valley and Taylor Creek-Nubbin Slough Basin.

Donigian, A. S., Jr., D. C. Beyerlein, H. H. Davis, and N. H. Crawford. 1977. Agricultural runoff management (ARM) model. Version II: Refinement and testing. EPA 600/3-77-098. Washington, D.C.: EPA.

Duxbury, J. M., and J. H. Peverly. 1978. Nitrogen and phosphorus losses from organic soils. J. Environ. Qual. 7:566–70.

Emsley, J. 1980. The phosphorus cycle. *In* The handbook of environmental chemistry, vol 1, part A: The natural environment and the biogeochemical cycles, ed. O. Hutzinger, 147–67. New York: Springer-Verlag.

Enwezor, W. O. 1976. The mineralization of nitrogen and phosphorus in organic materials of varying C:N and C:P ratios. Plant and Soil 44:237–40.

Fetter, C. W., Jr., W. E. Sloey, and F. L. Spandgler. 1978. Use of a natural marsh for waste-water polishing. J. Water Pollut. Control Fed. 509:290–307.

Gast, R. G., W. W. Nelson, and G. W. Randall. 1978. Nitrate accumulation in soils and loss in tile drainage following nitrogen application to continuous corn. J. Environ. Qual. 7:258–62.

Gersberg, R. M., B. V. Elkins, and C. R. Goldman. 1983. Nitrogen removal in artificial wetlands. Water Res. 17:1009–14.

Godshalk, G. L., and R. G. Wetzel. 1978. Decomposition in the littoral zone of lakes. *In* Freshwater wetlands: Ecological processes and management potential, ed. R.E. Good et al., 131–43. New York: Academic Press.

Golley, F. B. 1983. Decomposition. *In* Tropical rain forest ecosystems, structure and function, ed. F.B. Golley. Amsterdam: Elsevier Science.

Gosz, J. R., G. E. Likens, and F. H. Borman. 1973. Nutrient release from decomposing leaf and branch litter in the Hubbard Brook Forest, New Hampshire. Ecol. Monogr. 43:173–91.

Hall, J. K., K. M. Pawlus, and E. R. Higgins. 1972. Losses of atrazine in runoff and soil sediment. J. Environ. Qual. 1:172–76.

Hallberg, G. R., B. E. Hoyer, E. A. Bettis, and R. D. Libra. 1983. Hydrogeology, water quality, and land management in the Big Spring basin, Clayton County, Iowa. Iowa Geol. Surv. Res. Rep. 83-3.

———. 1984. Hydrogeology, water quality, and land management in the Big Spring basin, Clayton County, Iowa. Iowa Geol. Surv. Res. Rep. 84.

———. 1985. Hydrogeology, water quality, and land management in the Big Spring basin, Clayton County, Iowa. Iowa Geol. Surv. Res. Rep. 85.

Hanway, J. J., and J. M. Laflen. 1974. Plant nutrient losses from tile-outlet terraces. J. Environ. Qual. 3:351–56.

Harmeson, R. H., F. W. Sollo, and T. E. Larson. 1971. The nitrate situation in Illinois. J. Amer. Water Works Assoc. 63:303–10.

Holdren, G. C., D. E. Armstrong, and R. F. Harris. 1977. Interstitial inorganic phosphorus concentrations in Lakes Mendota and Wingra. Water Res. 2:1041–47.

Howard-Williams, C., and W. Howard-Williams. 1978. Nutrient leaching from the swamp vegetation of Lake Chilwa, a shallow African Lake. Aquat. Bot. 4:257–67.

Hutchinson, G. E. 1957. A treatise on limnology. Vol. 1, Part 2: Chemistry of lakes. New York: John Wiley and Sons.

Isirimah, N. O., and D. R. Keeney. 1973. Contribution of developed and natural marshland soils to surface and subsurface water quality. Water Resour. Cent. Tech. Completion Rep. Madison: Univ. Wis.

Jackson, W. A., L. E. Asmussen, E. W. Hauser, and A. W. White. 1973. Nitrate in surface and subsurface flow from a small agricultural watershed. J. Environ. Qual. 2:480–82.

Jewell, W. J. 1971. Aquatic weed decay: Dissolved oxygen utilization and nitrogen and phosphorus regeneration. J. Water Pollut. Control Fed. 43:1457–67.

Johnson, H. P., and J. L. Baker. 1973. Water quality implications of cropland nutrients. Ames Reservoir Environmental Study, ISWRRI Rep. 60-A4. Ames: Iowa State Univ.

_____. 1982. Field-to-stream transport of agricultural chemicals and sediment in an Iowa watershed. Part I. Data base for model testing (1976–1978). Rep. PB 82-254046. Springfield, Va.: NTIS.

_____. 1984. Field-to-stream transport of agricultural chemicals and sediment in an Iowa watershed. Part II: Data base for model testing (1979–1980). Rep. PB 84-177419. Springfield, Va.: NTIS.

Johnson, H. P., J. L. Baker, W. D. Shrader, and J. M. Laflen. 1979. Tillage system effects on sediment and nutrients in runoff from small watersheds. Trans Amer. Soc. Agric. Eng. 22:1110–14.

Johnston, W. R., F. Ittihadieh, R. H. Daum, and A. F. Pillsbury. 1965. Nitrogen and phosphorus in tile drainage effluent. Soil Sci. Soc. Amer. Proc. 29:287–90.

Kadlec, J. A. 1979. Nitrogen and phosphorus in inland freshwater wetlands. In Waterfowl and wetlands—An integrated review, ed. T.A. Bookhout 17–41. LaCrosse, Wis.: LaCrosse Printing.

_____. 1986a. Effects of flooding on dissolved and suspended nutrients in small diked marshes. Can. J. Fish. Aquat. Sci. 43:1999–2006.

_____. 1986b. Input-output nutrient budgets for small diked marshes. Can. J. Fish. Aquat. Sci. 43:2009–16.

Kaushik, N. K., and H. B. N. Hynes. 1971. The fate of the dead leaves that fall into streams. Archiv. Hydrobiol. 68:465–515.

Keeney, D. R. 1973. The nitrogen cycle in sediment-water systems. J. Environ. Qual. 3:151–62.

Kitchens, W. M., J. M. Dean, L. H. Stevenson, and J. H. Hooper. 1975. The Santee Swamp as a nutrient sink. In Symposium on mineral cycling in southeastern ecosystems, ed. F. Howell et al., 349–66. ERDA Symp. Ser. CONF 740513.

Klausner, S. D., P. J. Zwerman, and D. F. Ellis. 1974. Surface runoff losses of soluble nitrogen and phosphorus under two systems of soil management. J. Environ. Qual. 3:42–46.

Klopatek, J. M. 1975. The role of emergents in mineral cycling in a freshwater marsh. In Symposium on mineral cycling in southeastern ecosystems, ed. F. Howell et al., 357–93. ERDA Symp. Ser. (CONF 740513).

_____. 1978. Nutrient dynamics of freshwater riverine marshes and the role of emergent macrophytes. In Freshwater wetlands: Ecological processes and management potential, ed. R.E. Good et al., 195–216. New York: Academic Press.

Laflen, J. M., and T. S. Colvin. 1981. Effect of crop residue on soil loss from continuous row cropping. Trans. Amer. Soc. Agric. Eng. 24:605–09.

Langdale, G. W., R. A. Leonard, W. G. Fleming, and W. A. Jackson. 1979. Nitrogen and chloride movement in small upland Piedmont watersheds. II: Nitrogen and chloride transport in runoff. J. Environ. Qual. 8:57–63.

Lee, G. F., E. Bentley, and R. Amundson. 1975. Effects of marshes on water quality. In Coupling of land and water systems. ed. A. D. Hasler, 105–27. New York: Springer-Verlag.

Lindsley, D., T. Schuck, and F. Stearns. 1976. Productivity and nutrient content of emergent macrophytes in two Wisconsin marshes. In Freshwater wetlands and sewage effluent disposal, ed. D. L. Tilton et al., 51–75. Ann Arbor: Univ. Mich.

Logan, T. J., and G. O. Schwab. 1976. Nutrient and sediment characteristics of tile effluents in Ohio. J. Soil Water Conserv. 31:24–37.

Long, F. L. 1979. Runoff water quality as affected by surface-applied dairy cattle manure. J. Environ. Qual. 8:215–18.

McDowell, L. L., and K. C. McGregor. 1980. Nitrogen and phosphorus losses in runoff from no-till soybeans. Trans. Amer. Soc. Agric. Eng. 23:643–48.

McNaughton, S. J. 1966. Ecotype function in the Typha community-type. Ecol. Monogr. 36:297–325.

MacRae, I. C., R. R. Ancajas, and S. Salandanan. 1968. The fate of nitrate nitrogen in some tropical soils following submergence. Soil Sci. 105:327–34.

Martin, C. D., J. L. Baker, D. C. Erbach, and H. P. Johnson. 1978. Washoff of herbicides applied to corn residue. Trans. Amer. Soc. Agric. Eng. 21:1164–68.

Mason, C. F., and R. J. Bryant. 1975. Production, nutrient content and decomposition of Phragmites communis Trin. and Typha angustifolia L. J. Ecol. 63:71–95.

Maystrenko, Yu, A. I. Denisova, V. M. Bognyuk, and Zh. M. Arymaova. 1969. The role of higher aquatic plants in the accumulation of organic and biogenic substances in water bodies. Hydrobiol. J. 5:20–31.

Miller, M. H. 1979. Contribution of nitrogen and phosphorus to subsurface drainage water from intensively cropped mineral and organic soils in Ontario. J. Environ. Qual. 8:42–48.

Mudie, P. J., and R. Byrne. 1980. Pollen evidence for historic sedimentation rates in California coastal marshes. Estuarine Coastal Mar. Sci. 10:305–16.

Muir, D. C., and B. E. Baker. 1976. Detection of triazine herbicides and their degradation products in tile-drain water from fields under intensive corn (maize) production. J. Agric. Food Chem. 24:122–25.

Murkin, H. R., B. D. J. Batt, P. J. Caldwell, C. B. Davis, J. A. Kadlec, and A. G. van der Valk. 1985. Perpectives on the Delta Waterfowl Station-Ducks Unlimited Canada marsh ecology research program. Trans. N. Amer. Wildl. and Nat. Resour. Conf. 49:253–61.

Neely, R. K. 1982. Nitrogen and phosphorus fertilization of Sparganium eurycarpum and Typha glauca stands, Eagle Lake, Iowa. Ph.D. diss., Iowa State Univ., Ames.

Neely, R. K., and C. B. Davis. 1985a. Nitrogen and phosphorus fertilization of Sparganium eurycarpum Engelm. and Typha glauca Godr. stands. I: Emergent plant production. Aquat. Bot. 22:347–61.

_____. 1985b. Nitrogen and phosphorus fertilization of Sparganium eurycarpum Engelm. and Typha glauca Godr. Stands. II: Emergent plant decomposition. Aquat. Bot. 22:363–75.

Nicholaichuk, W., and D. W. L. Read. 1978. Nutrient runoff from fertilized and unfertilized fields in western Canada. J. Environ. Qual. 7:542–44.

Nicholls, K. H., and H. R. MacCrimmon. 1974. Nutrients in subsurface and runoff waters of the Holland Marsh, Ontario. J. Environ. Qual. 3:31–35.

Nichols, D. S., and Keeney, D. R. 1976. Nitrogen nutrition of *Myriophyllum spicatum:* uptake and translocation of 15N by shoots and roots. Freshwater Biol. 6:145–54.

Olness, A., S. J. Smith, E. D. Rhoades, and R. G. Menzel. 1975. Nutrient and sediment discharge from agricultural watersheds in Oklahoma. J. Environ. Qual. 4:331–36.

Onstad, C. A. 1972. Soil and water losses as affected by tillage practices. Trans. Amer. Soc. Agric. Eng. 15:287–89.

Patrick, W. H., and M. E. Tusneem. 1972. Nitrogen loss from a flooded soil. Ecol. 53:735–37.

Patrick, W. H., and R. Wyatt. 1964. Soil nitrogen loss as a result of alternate submergence and drying. Soil Sci. Soc. Proc. 28:647–53.

Peele, T. C., and J. T. Gillingham. 1972. Influence of fertilization and crops on nitrate content of groundwater and tile drainage effluent. Clemson Univ., Water Resourc. Res. Inst. Report No. 33. Clemson, S. Carolina.

Penfound, W. T. 1956. Primary production of vascular aquatic plants. Limnol. Ocean. 1:92–101.

Polisini, J. M., and Claude E. Boyd. 1972. Relationships between cell-wall fractions, nitrogen, and standing crop in aquatic macrophytes. Ecol. 53:484–88.

Polunin, N. V. C. 1983. The decomposition of emergent macrophytes in freshwater. Adv. Ecol. Res. 14:115–66.

Ponnamperuma, F. N. 1972. The chemistry of submerged soils. Adv. Agron. 22:29–96.

Prentki, R. F., T. D. Gustafson, and H. S. Adams. 1978. Nutrient movements in lakeshore marshes. *In* Freshwater wetlands: Ecological processes and management potential, ed. R.E. Good et al., 169–194. New York: Academic Press.

Puriveth, P. 1980. Decomposition of emergent macrophytes in a Wisconsin marsh. Hydrobiol. 72:231–42.

Richardson, C. J., W. A. Wentz, J. P. M. Chamie, J. A. Kadlec, and D. L. Tilton. 1976. Plant growth, nutrient accumulation and decomposition in a central Michigan peatland used for effluent treatment. *In* Freshwater wetlands and sewage effluent disposal, ed. D.L. Tilton et al., 77–117. Ann Arbor: Univ. Mich.

Ritter, W. F., H. P. Johnson, W. G. Lovely, and M. Molnau. 1974. Atrazine, propachlor, and diazinon residues on small agricultural watersheds. Environ. Sci. Tech. 8:38–42.

Rogers, K. H., and C. M. Breen. 1982. Decomposition of *Potamogeton crispus* L.: The effects of drying on the pattern of mass and nutrient loss. Aquat. Bot. 12:1–12.

Romkens, M. J. M., D. W. Nelson, and J. V. Mannering. 1973. Nitrogen and phosphorus composition of surface runoff as affected by tillage method. J. Environ. Qual. 2:292–95.

Savant, N. K., and S. K. De Datta. 1980. Movement and distribution of ammonium-N following deep placement of urea in a wetland rice soil. Soil Sci. Soc. of Amer. J. 44:559–65.

Schuman, G. E., R. E. Burwell, R. F. Piest, and R. G. Spomer. 1973a. Nitrogen losses in surface runoff from agricultural watersheds on Missouri Valley loess. J. Environ. Qual. 2:299–302.

Schuman, G. E., R. G. Spomer, and R. F. Piest. 1973a. Phosphorus losses from four agricultural watersheds on Missouri Valley loess. Soil Sci. Soc. of Amer. Proc. 37:424–27.

Schwab, G. O., E. O. McLean, A. C. Waldron, R. K. White, and D. W. Michener. 1973. Quality of drainage water from a heavy textured soil. Trans. Amer. Soc. Agric. Eng. 16:1104–07.

Shay, J. M., and C. T. Shay. 1986. Prairie marshes in western Canada, with specific reference to the ecology of five emergent macrophytes. Can. J. Bot. 64:443–54.

Siemens, J. C., and W. R. Oschwald. 1978. Corn-soybean tillage systems: Erosion control, effects on crop production cost. Trans. Amer. Soc. Agric. Eng. 21:293–302.

Smith, C. J., R. D. DeLaune, and W. H. Patrick, Jr. 1982. Carbon and nitrogen cycling in a *Spartina alterniflora* salt marsh. *In* Cycling of carbon, nitrogen, sulfur, and phosphorus in terrestrial and aquatic ecosystems, ed. J.R. Freney and I. E. Galbally, 97–103. New York: Springer-Verlag.

Smith, G. E., F. D. Whittaker, and H. G. Heinemann. 1974. Losses of fertilizers and pesticides from claypan soils. Environ. Prot. Tech. Ser. EPA-660/2-74-068. Washington, D.C.: EPA.

Soderlund, R., and T. Rosswall. 1982. The nitrogen cycles. *In* Environmental chemistry, Vol. 1, Part B, ed. O. Hutzinger, 61–81. New York: Springer-Verlag.

Solie, J. B., H. D. Wittmus, and O. C. Burnside. 1981. Subsurface injection of herbicides for weed control. Amer. Soc. Agric. Eng. Paper No. 81-1011. St. Joseph, Mich.: Amer. Soc. Agric. Eng.

Spangler, F. L., W. E. Sloey, and C. W. Fetter. 1976. Wastewater treatment by natural and artificial marshes. Environ Prot. Tech. Ser. EPA-60012-76-207. Environ. Res. Lab.

Steward, K. K., and W. H. Ornes. 1975. Assessing a marsh environment for wastewater renovation. J. Water Pollut. Control Fed. 47:1880–91.

Stumm, W., and J. J. Morgan. 1981 Aquatic Chemistry. New York: John Wiley and Sons.

Syers, J. K., R. F. Harris, and D. E. Armstrong. 1973. Phosphate chemistry in lake sediments. J. Environ. Qual. 2:1–14.

Tilton, D. L., R. H. Kadlec, and C. J. Richardson. 1976. Freshwater wetlands and sewage effluent disposal. Ann Arbor, Mich.: Univ. Mich.

Timmons, D. R., and A. S. Dylla. 1981. Nitrogen leaching as influenced by nitrogen management and supplemental irrigation level. J. Environ. Qual. 10:421–26.

Timmons, D. R., and R. F. Holt. 1977. Nutrient losses in surface runoff from a natural prairie. J. Environ. Qual. 6:369–73.

Timmons, D. R., R. E. Burwell, and R. F. Holt. 1973. Nitrogen and phosphorus losses in surface runoff from agricultural land as influenced by placement of broadcast fertilizer. Water Resour. Res. 9:658–67.

Tourbier, J., and R. W. Pierson. 1976. Biological Control of Water Pollution. Philadelphia, Pa.: Univ. Pa. Press.

Valiela, I., and J. M. Teal. 1974. Nutrient limitation in salt marsh vegetation. *In* Ecology of Halophytes, ed. R. J. Reimold and W. H. Queen, 547–63. New York: Academic Press.

van der Valk, A. G., and L. C. Bliss. 1971. Hydrarch succession and net primary production of oxbow lakes in central Alberta. Can. J. Bot. 49:1177–99.

van der Valk, A. G., and C. B. Davis. 1978a. The role of the seed bank in the vegetation dynamics of prairie glacial marshes. Ecol. 59:322–35.

———. 1978b. Primary production in prairie glacial marshes. *In* Freshwater wetlands: Ecological processes and management potential, ed. R.E. Good et al., 21–37. New York: Academic Press.

———. 1979. A reconstruction of recent vegetational history of a prairie glacial marsh, Eagle Lake, Iowa, from its seed bank. Aquat. Bot. 5:19–51.

———. 1981. The impact of a natural draw-down on the growth of four emergent species in a prairie glacial marsh. Aquat. Bot. 9:301–22.

van der Valk, A. G., C. B. Davis, J. L. Baker, and C. E. Beer. 1979. Natural freshwater wetlands as nitrogen and phosphorus traps for land runoff. *In* Wetland functions and values: The state of our understanding, ed. P.E. Greeson et al., Minneapolis, Minn.: Amer. Water Resour. Assoc.

van der Valk, A. G., S. D. Swanson, and R. F. Nuss. 1983. The response of plant species to burial in three types of Alaskan wetlands. Can. J. Bot. 61:1150–64.

Van Dyke, G. 1972. Aspects relating to emergent vegetation dynamics in a deep marsh, north central Iowa. Ph.D. diss., Iowa State Univ., Ames.

van Keuren, R. W., J. L. McGuiness, and F. W. Chichester. 1979. Hydrology and chemical quality of flow from small pastured watersheds. I: Hydrology. J. Environ. Qual. 8:162–66.

Walker, D. 1970. Direction and rate in some British post-glacial hydroseres. *In* Studies in the vegetational history of the British Isles, ed. D. Walker and R. G. West, 117–39. Cambridge: Cambridge Univ. Press.

Wauchope, R. D., and R. S. Myers. 1985. Adsorption-desorption kinetics of atrazine and linuron in freshwater-sediment aqueous slurries. J. Environ. Qual. 14:132–36.

Wetzel, R. G. 1983. Limnology. New York: Sauders College Publ.

White, E. M., and E. J. Williamson. 1973. Plant nutrient concentrations in runoff from fertilized cultivated erosion plots and prairie in eastern South Dakota. J. Environ. Qual. 2:453–55.

Zwerman, P. L., T. Greweling, S. D. Klausner, and D. J. Lathwell. 1972. Nitrogen and phosphorus content of water from tile drains at two levels of management and fertilization. Soil Sci. Soc. Amer. Proc. 36:134–37.

HAROLD A. KANTRUD

⑤ VEGETATION OF WETLANDS

ABSTRACT

FIVE THEMES dominate the literature dealing with the vegetation of palustrine and lacustrine wetlands of the prairie pothole region: environmental conditions (water or moisture regime, salinity), agricultural disturbances (draining, grazing, burning, sedimentation, etc.), vegetation dynamics, zonation patterns, and classification of the wetlands.

The flora of a prairie wetland is a function of its water regime, salinity, and disturbance by man. Within a pothole, water depth and duration determines distribution of species. In potholes deep enough to have standing water even during droughts, the central zone will be dominated by submersed species (open water). In wetlands that go dry during periods of drought or annually, the central zone will be dominated by either tall emergent species (deep marsh) or midheight emergents (shallow marsh), respectively. Potholes that are only flooded briefly in the spring are dominated by grasses, sedges, and forbs (wet meadow). Within a pothole, the depth of standing water in the deepest, usually central, part of the basin determines how many zones will be present. Lists of species associated with different water regimes and salinity levels are presented.

Disturbances due to agricultural activities have impacted wetlands throughout the region. Drainage has eliminated many potholes, particularly in the southern and eastern parts of the region. Grazing, mowing, and burning have altered the composition of pothole vegetation. The composition of different vegetation types impacted by grazing, haying, and cultivation is presented in a series of tables. Indirect impacts of agriculture (increased sediment, nutrient, and pesticide inputs) are widespread over the region, but their impacts on the vegetation have never been studied.

Because of the periodic droughts and wet periods, many palustrine and lacustrine wetlands undergo vegetation cycles associated with water-level changes produced by these wet-dry cycles. Periods of above normal precipitation can raise water levels high enough to drown out emergent vegetation or produce "eat outs" due to increases in the size of muskrat populations that accompany periods of high water. The elimination of emergents creates a lake marsh dominated by submersed vegetation. During the next drought when the marsh bottom is exposed by receding water levels (a drawdown), seeds of emergents and mudflat annuals in the soil (the seed bank) germinate (the dry marsh stage). When the marsh refloods, ending the dry marsh stage, the emergents survive and spread vegetatively. This is the regenerating marsh. This stage continues until high water again eliminates the emergents, starting the next degenerating stage.

Zonation patterns are conspicuous because each zone often is dominated by a single species that has a lifeform different from those in adjacent zones. The species composition of each zone is a function of its environment (water or moisture regime, salinity, and disturbance history). Within a zone it may take a year or more for species composition to adjust to a change of environmental conditions. These lags sometimes result in abnormal zonation patterns, particularly after a change in water level.

Classification of prairie wetlands is more difficult than for most other wetland types because of these vegetation cycles. Early attempts to classify prairie wetlands did not take the dynamic nature of their vegetation into account. Stewart and Kantrud (1971) developed a classification system for prairie potholes that recognized different phases of vegetation zones dominated by deep marsh species. It used the composition of the vegetation in the deepest part (zone) of a pothole as an indicator of its water-level regime and water chemistry. The application of the national wetland classification system of Cowardin et al. (1979) to potholes is also discussed, and lists of species that characterize the various dominance types associated with the subclasses in this system are presented.

KEY WORDS: burning, classification, cycles, disturbance, drainage, fire, grazing, haying, lacustrine, palustrine, pothole, prairie, salinity, vegetation dynamics, water regime, wetland, zonation.

INTRODUCTION

PRAIRIE POTHOLES, or sloughs as they are often called in Canada, occur in those parts of the North American prairies that were covered with glacial drift deposits during the Wisconsin glacial advance. (See Fig. 2.1). In Canada, the region is divided into two

HAROLD A. KANTRUD, U.S. Fish and Wildlife Service, Northern Prairie Wildlife Research Center, Jamestown, North Dakota 58401. JOHN B. MILLAR, Canadian Wildlife Service, Environment Canada, 115 Perimeter Road, Saskatoon, Saskatchewan S7N 0X4. A. G. ᴠᴀɴ ᴅᴇʀ VALK, Department of Botany, Iowa State University, Ames, Iowa 50011.

districts (Fig. 5.1), the Grassland Prairie Wetland District and the Aspen Parkland Prairie Wetland District (Zoltai and Pollett 1983). The latter district is distinguished from the former by the presence of a border of willows (*Salix* spp.) or trees (predominantly *Populus tremuloides* Michx.) around the wetlands. These two districts correspond to the grassland and parkland zones of Rowe and Coupland (1984), recognized on the basis of upland vegetation.

On the surface of much of this geologically young landscape are numerous, unconnected depressions, the prairie potholes or sloughs (Fig. 5.2). An early account of the soils of Story County Iowa, which is at the southern edge of the region, describes the general features of the prairie pothole landscape:

Low knolls are separated by saucerlike depressions in which impounded water often stands year round. In many cases these low-lying areas have been reclaimed by artificial drainage, but in the main rainwater which falls upon uplands has to escape by seepage or evaporation. Little ponds and marshes are found in almost innumerable places scattered all over the county. (Marean and Jones 1903)

Each one of these "saucerlike depressions" or potholes contained a wetland. In such a landscape, 40 to 60% of the area often was covered with wetlands (Hewes and Frandson 1952). This brief description of northern prairie landscapes encapsulates most of major physical features of classic pothole country (see also Fig. 5.2). There are many potholes in any given area, and they are thus a major feature of the landscape. They are usually small (mostly less than 1 ha), shallow, and lack a well-developed outlet, although many overflow during wet springs (Cowardin et al. 1981). The amount of water that they contain is dependent usually on the amount of recent precipitation, often primarily on spring runoff in the northern parts of the region. Many have been or are being drained.

Although the classic prairie pothole landscape described above is found throughout much of the region, this is not the only type of landscape found. Across the region, the terrain varies from almost level lacustrine plains to very rough terminal moraines, and wetlands are found in all these situations. Thus in the prairie pothole region are found not only prairie potholes or sloughs (palustrine wetlands), but also a variety of wetlands associated with saline, brackish, and freshwater lakes (lacustrine wetlands) as well as riverine wetlands.

In this chapter, we will review what is known about the composition, dynamics, and classification of the vegetation found in palustrine and lacustrine wetlands of the prairie pothole region, and the influence of various environmental factors on the composition and dynamics of this vegetation. (Information about the wetland vegetation of the Nebraska sandhills can be found in Novacek, Chap. 12.)

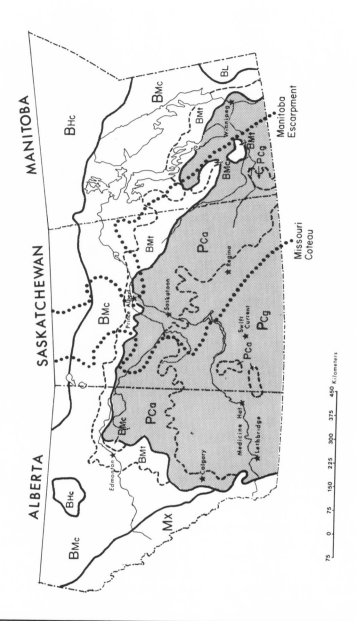

FIG. 5.1. Wetland regions of western Canada. Wetland region and district boundaries after Canada Committee on Ecological Land Classification; physiographic boundaries (dotted lines) after Bostock, Geological Survey of Canada. The prairie wetland region (PCa and PCg) is shaded. **BHc** - High Boreal Wetland Region; **BMc** - Continental Mid-Boreal Wetland District; **BMt** - Transitional Mid-Boreal Wetland District; **BL** - Low Boreal Wetland Region; **PCa** - Aspen Parkland Prairie Wetland Region; **PCg** - Grassland Prairie District; **MX** - Mountain Complex.

FIG. 5.2. An aerial view of some pothole country in North Dakota (*USFWS photograph*).

VEGETATION STUDIES

"The entire face of the country is covered with these shallow lakes, ponds and puddles, many of which are, however, dry or undergoing a process of gradual drying out." These wetlands contained a "central portion" surrounded by "concentric circles of different species of plants" (Froebel 1870). These observations, made in 1865, of the landscape bordering the Cheyenne and James rivers, when Froebel was on an expedition in the Dakota Territory against the hostile Sioux, summarize what was known about northern prairie wetlands prior to the twentieth century. The first detailed surveys of plant species and their distributions within these wetlands were not made until nearly 50 years later. They began with a list of plants found in marshes, streams, and ponds in south-central South Dakota (Visher 1912). A more significant pioneering study, however, was that of Shunk (1917) who described the aquatic and wetland plant associations in southeastern North Dakota. He noted the zonal arrangement of dominant species and the shifting of these zones during drought and flood. Later Metcalf (1931) recorded the abundance of plant species in about 500 wetlands, and proposed associations (assemblages of plant species) typical of the various combinations of salinities, water regimes, and soil textures found in North Dakota. These early studies of Shunk and Metcalf identified the major feature of the wetland vegetation (i.e., one or more easily recognized vegetation zones dominated often by a single species), and the factors that seem to control the composition and distribution of these zones (water depth or duration of flooding, salinity). Most of the subsequent literature has been an elaboration of these themes along with the impact of natural (changes in water levels or salinity) or human disturbance (cultivation, grazing, haying, fire, etc.) on the composition, distribution, and dynamics of the vegetation. Figure 5.3 illustrates zonation in a freshwater and saline pothole. Table 5.1 provides a brief description of the vegetation zones found throughout the region.

Almost all of the early vegetation data was collected in conjunction with waterfowl studies or later for waterfowl management purposes. As interest in waterfowl habitat grew so did the need for more detailed studies that could relate habitat characteristics to waterfowl use. In this context, Nord et al. (1951) recorded the species found in open water (i.e., in areas without emergents), deep water, shallow water, and intermittently flooded shorelines. They, too, noted that species were usually distributed in concentric rings around the basin and that the order of these rings was determined by water depth. They also noted that grazing altered the composition of the vegetation.

In the early 1950s, the first attempt to classify and inventory the wetlands of the United States was made by the U.S. Fish and Wildlife Service. The classification scheme developed for this purpose was quite simple and relied on water regime (primarily water depth) and the dominant species to distinguish different wetland types (Martin et al. 1953). The results of the only national inventory of wetlands that used the scheme were published in 1956 (Shaw and Fredine 1956). Evans and Black (1956) used this classification system in South Dakota and assigned different species to the various wetland types found in their survey. They made the following observations about the vegetation: (1) species tend to be arranged in zones related to water depth (elevation); (2) under intensive grazing whitetop (*Scolochloa festucacea*) and sedges (*Carex* spp.) are replaced by cattail (*Typha* spp) and hardstem bulrush (*Scirpus acutus*); and (3) periodic droughts and cultivation often cause very complex vegetation patterns to develop. Other studies during this

FIG. 5.3. Vegetation zonation in prairie potholes. The upper photograph shows a freshwater, seasonally flooded pothole with a central zone dominated by an aquatic bed, dominance type *Utricularia vulgaris.* It is surrounded by an emergent wetland, dominance type *Scolochloa festucea.* The lower photograph is of an intermittently flooded, saline pothole. The central zone contains an aquatic bed, dominance type *Ruppia maritima.* It is surrounded by an unconsolidated shore much of which is covered with salt crystals.

TABLE 5.1.   Basic stable vegetation zones of prairie pothole wetlands

Common description	Lifeform of dominant vegetation	Normal period of inundation
Wet meadow	Low herbaceous — grasses, fine sedges and forbes (shrubs in parkland)	A few weeks in the spring.
Shallow marsh	Mid-height herbaceous — grasses, coarse sedges	Spring to mid-summer or early fall.
(Emergent) deep marsh	Tall, coarse herbaceous — cattail, bulrushes	Spring through fall and frequently overwinter.
Shallow (permanent) open water	Submergent or floating aquatics	Year-round except in periods of severe drought.
Alkali (open or intermittent)	Either devoid of vegetation or containing the submergent *Ruppia maritima*	Highly variable — from a few weeks in the spring to fall or overwinter, depending on runoff and ground water conditions.

period that made similar observations were those of Bach (1950), Hibbard (1956), Seabloom (1958), and Wilson (1958).

Wetland vegetation began to be described in more detail beginning in the 1960s with a series of long-term studies of individual wetlands. These either focused on vegetation dynamics or on the relations between environmental conditions and the composition and distribution of the vegetation.

In a reclaimed wetland in northwestern Minnesota, Harris and Marshall (1963) described the impact of a drawdown (i.e., the period when the marsh was free of standing water) on the composition of the vegetation. They were among the first to recognize the importance of the drawdown phase for the reestablishment of emergent species that had been eliminated previously during high-water years. In Iowa, Weller and Spatcher (1965) described the impact of water-level changes and muskrats on the vegetation and avifauna of two wetlands. They recognized that the vegetation and associated fauna changed cyclically as a result of cycles of annual precipitation (wet-dry cycles) and muskrat densities. They divided habitat cycles into five stages: dry marsh, dense marsh, hemi-marsh, open marsh, and open water (Table 5.2). The hemi-marsh, when there is a 50:50 ratio of emergent vegetation to open water, is the most important stage in the cycle from a wildlife perspective because that is when animal diversity and density reach their maxima (Table 5.2). From these studies developed the concept that the main purpose of marsh management in the region was to maintain a wetland in a hemi-marsh state as long as possible (Weller 1978, 1981; Kaminski and Prince 1981; Murkin et al. 1982). Other studies by Weller and Fredrickson (1974), Bishop et al. (1979), and van der Valk and Davis (1978b) provide additional descriptions of habitat cycles in Iowa marshes (see section on VEGETATION DYNAMICS).

TABLE 5.2. Stages of the typical habitat cycle in semipermanent marshes

Stage name	Water in relation to basin capacity	Vegetation	Muskrat populations	Bird populations	Conspicuous indicator conditions
Dry marsh	Absent or low; emergents dry or nearly dry at base	Dense revegetation; most species find a suitable seedbed	Low to absent; populations centrally located	Redwings sparse; some use by upland birds	Redwings; few muskrat lodges; low water
Dense marsh; more vegetation than open water	Increasing water levels; emergents flooded	Very dense; rate of opening dependent upon muskrat populations and influence of flooding on certain species	Increasing	Numbers and variety increasing	Redwings increase; first yellowheads adjacent to sparse open pools; few coots and grebes
Hemi-marsh; open water and vegetation are equal	Median to near maximum	Muskrat eat-out; flotation and death; decline in shallow-water species. Veg. propag. by deep-water species	Increasing rapidly; well distributed	Maximum species diversity and production for most species	Many redwings; yellowheads uniformly distributed; coots and pied-billed grebes abundant
Open marsh; more open water than vegetation	Maximum	Submergents and deep-water species persist; others gone or going	Maximum or declining	Most species declining; a few swimming species tolerate as long as some vegetation persists	Sparse bird populations and emergents
Open water marsh (virtually an eutrophic lake)	Maximum or as low as median	Hardstem bulrush may persist in sparse populations	Sparse; bank dense common	Redwings use shoreline vegetation; other species virtually absent except as migrants	Redwings use shoreline shrubs and trees

Source: Adapted from Weller and Spatcher 1965.

In North Dakota, Stewart and Kantrud (1963) studied the relation-ship between the floristic composition of wet-meadow, shallow-marsh, deep-marsh, and open-water zones and water permanence and salinity. The impacts of drawdowns were also emphasized, and the species that became established in these zones during summer drawdowns was also noted. Later publications by Stewart and Kantrud (1969, 1971, 1972) extended this work and, in addition, related vegetation to various land-uses and recognized some other wetland vegetation types (i.e., low prairies and fens). Moyle (1964), Jessen et al. (1964), Dix and Smeins (1967), Hadley and Buccos (1967), Disrud (1968), Burgess and Disrud (1969), Ungar (1970), and Johnson et al. (1982) were other studies done in the United States that related the distribution of plant species to en-vironmental factors. Much of this information has been summarized in Stewart and Kantrud (1971, 1972) and Fulton et al. (1986).

An important source of unpublished vegetation data is the Minne-sota Game Lake Survey (Minnesota Department of Natural Resources, Bureau of Wildlife Development, Pittman-Robertson Project W-24R), which contains much valuable information on wetland vegetation. This survey, which began in 1949, contains data on submersed and emergent plants, water chemistry and other physical factors for nearly 2,500 shal-low waterfowl lakes, many of them prairie wetlands in western Minne-sota. Much of this information is summarized and combined with addi-tional data in the reports and special investigations under Minnesota's Public Law 556 Watershed Survey Program conducted during the 1960s and early 1970s.

On the basis of their own work and that of previous workers, Ste-wart and Kantrud (1971) developed a classification of prairie potholes that used the composition of vegetation zones within a basin as indica-tors of both its hydrologic regime and water chemistry. At the end of the same decade, Cowardin et al. (1979) published a new hierarchical classi-fication for the United States. Table 5.3 outlines the systems, subsystems, classes, and subclasses of the Cowardin et al. classifications that are found in the northern prairie region. Both the Stewart and Kantrud (1971) and Cowardin et al. (1979) classifications are described in more detail in the section on WETLAND CLASSIFICATIONS.

Most of the studies of the floristic composition of the vegetation of Canadian prairie wetlands have dealt with relatively restricted geo-graphic areas. Löve and Löve (1954) produced a brief floristic account of the Delta Marsh, a lacustrine marsh along the south shore of Lake Manitoba, in Manitoba. This same marsh has been described in more detail by Walker (1959, 1965) who studied the impact of a period of high water and the subsequent period of low water on the vegetation. Ander-son and Jones (1976) examined the submersed vegetation of this

TABLE 5.3. Wetland systems, subsystems, classes, and subclasses defined by Cowardin et al. (1979) that may occur in the prairie pothole region and for which dominance types based on vegetation may be described

System	Subsystem	Class	Subclass
Riverine	Lower perennial	Aquatic bed	Algal
			Aquatic moss
			Rooted vascular
			Floating
		Unconsolidated shore	Vegetated
		Emergent wetland	Nonpersistent
	Upper perennial	Aquatic bed	Algal
			Aquatic moss
			Rooted vascular
			Floating
		Unconsolidated shore	Vegetated
	Intermittent	Streambed	Vegetated
Lacustrine	Limnetic	Aquatic bed	Algal
			Aquatic moss
			Rooted vascular
			Floating
	Littoral	Aquatic bed	Algal
			Aquatic moss
			Rooted vascular
			Floating
		Emergent wetland	Nonpersistent
Palustrine	(none)	Aquatic bed	Algal[a]
			Aquatic moss[a]
			Rooted vascular[a]
			Floating[a]
		Unconsolidated shore	Vegetated
		Moss-lichen wetland	Moss
			Lichen
		Emergent wetland	Persistent[a]
			Nonpersistent[a]
		Scrub-shrub wetland	Broad-leaved deciduous
			Needle-leaved deciduous
			Needle-leaved evergreen
		Forested wetland	Broad-leaved deciduous
			Needle-leaved deciduous
			Needle-leaved evergreen

[a]See Tables 5.4–5.9 for common dominance types.

wetland. In Saskatchewan, Dodd and Coupland (1966) studied saline wetlands and Walker and Coupland (1970) studied both saline and non-saline wetlands of the grassland and aspen parkland regions. Wetlands in southeastern Alberta were studied by Keith (1961). Millar (1976) ar-ranged the dominant wetland species into seven vegetation zones primarily on the basis of different life forms. Life form had not been a criterion used in developing earlier groupings of species by either Dodd and Coupland (1966) or Walker and Coupland (1970). Millar also noted the high degree of similarity between wetlands of the Canadian prairies and those in the adjacent United States. Some 80% of the primary species found in North Dakota by Stewart and Kantrud (1971) also occur throughout the grassland and parkland districts of the prairie provinces.

There have been changes in the flora of the region, but these have been poorly documented. *Typha angustifolia* likely spread into the region during the first half of the twentieth century (Kantrud 1986). This species and its putative hybrid with *Typha latifolia, Typha x glauca,* have invaded many wetlands in the eastern and southern parts of the region (Smith 1967, Grace and Harrison 1986). Purple loosestrife (*Lythrum salicaria*) has also invaded many wetlands in the same parts of the region. Other species that have become established in the region's wetlands are reed canary grass (*Phalaris arundinacea*), which has been widely cultivated as a hay or forage crop in wetlands throughout the region, and several woody species, especially Russian olive (*Eleagnus angustifolia*), cottonwood (*Populus deltoides*), peachleaved willow (*Salix amygdaloides*), and sandbar willow (*Salix exigua*), which have become established in wet meadows. The invasion of wetlands by these woody species seems to have been made possible because of fire suppression.

In the 1970s studies of the primary production of prairie wetlands were initiated in response to a general interest in this topic among ecologists. Kollman and Wali (1976) and Wali (1976) investigated the physical and chemical factors that influenced the productivity of *Potamogeton pectinatus* communities in North Dakota. A similar study of this species was done by Anderson (1978) in the East Delta Marsh, Manitoba. Barker and Larson (1976), Barker and Fulton (1979), Fulton et al. (1979), Olson (1979), Fulton and Barker (1981) collected data on the biomass and shoot density of many macrophyte communities. Production studies done in Iowa are summarized in van der Valk and Davis (1978a). Fulton et al. (1986) summarize primary production data from the whole prairie pothole region as well as adjacent regions. Those in Canada are summarized by Shay and Shay (1986). The annual production of individual species (van der Valk and Davis 1980) and of the whole wetland (van der Valk and Davis 1978a) is dependent on water levels. During a wet-dry cycle, the total annual production of a wetland has been estimated to vary twenty-fold (van der Valk and Davis 1978a). A table summarizing primary production data is found in Murkin (Chap. 11).

The fate of the primary production in these wetlands is reviewed in several other chapters in this book. Various aspects of herbivory are discussed by Murkin (Chap. 11), Fritzell (Chap. 9), and Swanson and Duebbert (Chap. 8). Nutrient uptake, litter decomposition and mineral cycling are reviewed in Neely and Baker (Chap. 4).

ENVIRONMENTAL FACTORS

Climatic Factors

Borchert (1950) in his classic study of the climate of North American grasslands noted a number of important features: (1) low precipitation during the winter, (2) periodic major droughts that occur synchronously within the region, and (3) large positive departures from annual temperatures and frequent hot winds during the summer months. The climate of the Canadian prairies is semiarid (around 500 mm in Manitoba to around 300 mm in Alberta and Saskatchewan) with most of the precipitation occurring in the spring and summer). It has cold winters (to −40°C), warm summers (to 40°C) and highly variable temperatures and precipitation (Hare and Thomas 1979). More detailed information on the climate of the region is presented in Winter (Chap. 2). In this region, there are two important environmental gradients that influence the character of the wetlands and their vegetation. First, the climate becomes progressively warmer and drier to the west and south and consequently the proportion of wetlands that are nonpermanent increases in that direction. Second, the frequency of saline wetlands increases from east to west.

Because of its climate, wetlands of the prairie pothole region have annual (Fig. 5.4) and seasonal (Fig. 5.5) fluctuations in water depth. These annual fluctuations (Fig. 5.4) in water depth are cyclical in nature and reflect the 10- to 20-year wet-dry cycles that characterize the region (Duvick and Blasing 1981; Karl and Koscielny 1982; Karl and Riebsame 1984; Diaz 1983, 1986). The seasonal decline in water level (Fig. 5.5) reflects the importance of spring runoff and precipitation for the annual water budget of a shallow pothole.

Hydrologic Factors

Two hydrologic factors determine the composition and distribution of wetland vegetation, namely water regime (water permanence) and water chemistry (concentration of dissolved salts) (Eisenlohr and Sloan 1968; Eisenlohr 1972a, 1972b). A complex of factors determines the nature of the water regime both within a wetland and among wetlands including basin morphometry (Millar 1971), soils (Freeze 1969), the vegetation (Meyboom 1966, 1967), snow accumulation over the winter,

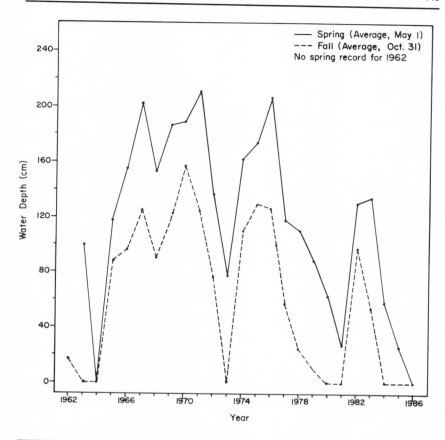

FIG. 5.4.   A 25-year record of spring and fall water depths in a shallow open-water wetland in the grassland district of southwestern Saskatchewan (*Adapted from J. B. Millar*).

groundwater flow (Born et al. 1979, Winter, Chap. 2), and weather conditions (precipitation, wind speed, temperature, etc.). Water chemistry is a function largely of the configuration of the water table surrounding the wetland (Sloan 1972) and subsurface geology (Van Voast and Novitzki 1968). Many types of agricultural activities, particularly drainage, have had a major impact on the hydrologic characteristics of the wetlands of most of this region.

Salinity. There are two chapters in this book on the water chemistry of prairie wetlands. LaBaugh (Chap. 3) reviews what is known about their water chemistry, while Neely and Baker (Chap. 4) review what is

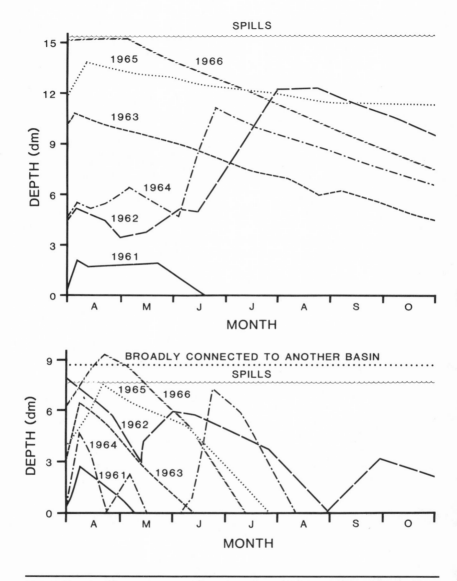

FIG. 5.5. Seasonal water-level changes over a six-year period in a seasonal and semiper-manent wetland in North Dakota (*Adapted from H. A. Kantrud unpubl. data*).

known about the fate of agricultural runoff entering these wetlands. Here we will restrict ourselves to a consideration of the impacts of salinity on the composition of wetland vegetation.

Salinity (concentration of total dissolved solids in the soil or water column) has a profound effect on the composition and distribution of species, and extensive information is available on the impact of increasing salinity. In general, the number of species in a vegetation zone decreases with increasing salinity (see Tables 5.4 to 5.9). This trend was first noted by Bailey (1888) and was commented on also by another early investigator, Visher (1912). For example, in hypersaline lakes the only submersed species is *Ruppia maritima,* while in oligosaline wetlands as many as ten to fifteen submersed aquatics may be found.

Numerous systems for categorizing saline water have been developed and the number of classes or divisions recognized have varied from two to eight (Millar 1976). Since the gradient from freshwater to hypersaline water is a continuum, any divisions are arbitrary. Not surprisingly there has been little agreement about what are ecologically significant divisions along this continuum. Stewart and Kantrud (1971) recognized six salinity classes. These were reduced to four by Millar (1976) who questioned whether there was any ecologically meaningful difference between some of the lower-level classes. The Cowardin et al. (1979) system uses six salinity classes: fresh (<800 μS), oligosaline (800–8,000 μS), mesosaline (8,000–30,000 μS), polysaline (30,000–45,000 μS), eusaline (45,000–60,000 μS) and hypersaline ($>60,000$ μS). The oligosaline, mesosaline, and polysaline classes are grouped as a mixosaline or brackish water class. A table relating the salinity classes in Stewart and Kantrud to those of Cowardin et al. is found in Cowardin et al. (1979).

Metcalf (1931) conducted the first detailed investigation of the impact of salinity on the composition of wetland vegetation. With D. C. Mabbott, he surveyed about 500 North Dakota wetlands in 1917. He listed the abundance and species composition of 75 wetlands varying from 350 to 91,529 ppm. In Minnesota, Moyle (1945) conducted another very influential study, although only part of it covered the prairie pothole region. He surveyed 225 lakes and classified the flora of these lakes into six groups on the basis of water chemistry (total alkalinity, sulphate, and pH). Smeins (1967) placed 119 species found in wetlands of the Red River Valley and adjacent drift plain into five soil salinity classes and gave indicator species for each class. Walker and Coupland (1970) placed species in Saskatchewan into four soil-salinity classes: nonsaline, light saline, moderate saline and very saline. These were not defined in their paper, but were defined in Walker's dissertation (Walker 1968). Millar (1976) also has assigned species in Saskatchewan to one of

TABLE 5.4. Common dominance types of persistent emergent vegetation in temporarily flooded palustrine wetlands in the northern plains and prairies

	Land-use			
Grazed	Idle	Hayed	Farmed
Water chemistry modifier — Fresh			
Hordeum jubatum	Poa palustris	Juncus balticus	Agropyron repens
Juncus balticus	Calamagrostis canadensis	Calamagrostis inexpansa	Echinochloa crusgalli
Spartina pectinata	Spartina pectinata	Carex lanuginosa	Polygonum lapathifolium
Aster simplex	Carex sartwellii	Carex praegracilis	Hordeum jubatum
Water chemistry modifier — Oligosaline			
Hordeum jubatum	Calamagrostis inexpansa	Juncus balticus	Agropyron repens
Juncus balticus	Spartina pectinata	Calamagrostis inexpansa	Hordeum jubatum
Distichlis spicata	Poa palustris		Artemisia biennis
Potentilla anserina			
Water chemistry modifier — Mesosaline			
Distichlis spicata	Distichlis spicata	not seen	not seen
Hordeum jubatum	Triglochin maritima		
	Spartina gracilis		
	Atriplex patula		
	Muhlenbergia asperifolia		

palustrine wetlands in the northern plains and prairies

... (persistent) emergent vegetation in seasonally flooded

	Land-use		
Grazed	Idle	Hayed	Farmed
Water chemistry modifier – Fresh			
Glyceria grandis	Carex atherodes	Carex atherodes	Beckmannia syzigachne
Beckmannia syzigachne	Sparganium eurycarpum	Phalaris arundinacea	Alisma plantago-aquatica
Sparganium eurycarpum	Phalaris arundinacea		Alopecurus aequalis
Sium suave	Polygonum coccineum		Polygonum coccineum
Alisma plantago-aquatica*			
Water chemistry modifier – Oligosaline			
Eleocharis palustris	Scolochloa festucacea	Scolochloa festucacea	Beckmannia syzigachne
Beckmannia syzigachne	Carex atherodes	Carex atherodes	Sium suave
Alisma gramineum*	Polygonum coccineum		Polygonum coccineum
Sium suave	Sagittaria cuneata*		
Water chemistry modifier – Mesosaline			
Salicornia rubra*	Scirpus americanus	not seen	not seen
Suaeda depressa	Puccinellia nuttalliana		
Scirpus americanus			
Eleocharis palustris			

TABLE 5.6. Common dominance types of persistent vegetation in palustrine emergent wetland with semipermanently flooded water regime in the northern plains and prairies

	Land-use		
Grazed	Idle	Hayed	Farmed
Water chemistry modifier – Fresh			
Scirpus heterochaetus	Typha latifolia	not seen	Scirpus fluviatilis
Scirpus validus	Typha angustifolia		Scirpus validus
Scirpus fluviatilis	Typha × glauca		
Water chemistry modifier – Oligosaline			
Scirpus acutus	Typha latifolia	not seen	Scirpus fluviatilis
Scirpus maritimus	Typha angustifolia		
	Typha × glauca		
	Scirpus acutus		
Water chemistry modifier – Mesosaline			
Scirpus maritimus	Scirpus maritimus	not seen	not seen
Scirpus acutus	Scirpus acutus		

149

TABLE 5.7.   Dominance types (D) and proposed indicator species of persistent vegetation in mixosaline palustrine emergent wetland with saturated water regime in the northern plains and prairies[a]

Typha latifolia (D)
Phragmites australis (D)
Scirpus validus (D)
Cicuta maculata
Scirpus atrovirens (D)
Carex aquatilis (D)
Eleocharis calva
Glyceria striata (D)
Asclepias incarnata
Triglochin maritima
Carex rostrata (D)
Eupatorium maculatum
Scutellaria epilobiifolia
Deschampsia caespitosa (D)
Carex aurea
Parnassia palustris
Ranunculus septentrionalis
Lysimachia thrysiflora
Eriophorum angustifolium
Aster junciformis
Juncus torreyi
Calamagrostis inexpansa (D)
Muhlenbergia glomerata
Lobelia kalmii
Carex sartwellii
Carex interior
Carex lanuginosa (D)
Viola nephrophylla
Epilobium glandulosum
Solidago graminifolia
Helianthus nuttallii

[a]Soils are saturated to a greater degree toward the center of these wetlands; plants are listed in approximate order of decreasing saturation of bottom soils.

four surface-water salinity classes. Stewart and Kantrud (1965, 1969, 1971, 1972) present considerable information on the distribution of plants in relation to surface-water salinity. They also note that in some of the more saline wetlands there are gradients of salinity across the wetland caused by groundwater flow patterns.

Most studies dealing only with saline wetlands have been done in western Canada. Saline wetlands are more numerous in this region and the economic implications of salinization have resulted in much interest in them. Rawson and Moore (1944) studied the distribution of submersed aquatics in lakes in Saskatchewan. Keith (1958) examined the impact of increasing salinity on the composition of plant communities around three impoundments in southern Alberta. At the dry end of the water regime spectrum, Dodd and Coupland (1966) surveyed the vegetation of saline soils in Saskatchewan while Hammer et al. (1975) and Hammer and Heseltine (1987) working with saline lakes have examined

TABLE 5.8. Dominance types of vegetation in aquatic bed algal (A), aquatic moss and liverwort (M), rooted vascular (R), and floating vascular (F) vegetation in palustrine wetland with seasonally flooded water regime in the northern plains and prairies

	Land-use		
Grazed	Idle	Hayed	Farmed
Water chemistry modifier – Fresh			
Potamogeton gramineus (R)	Utricularia vulgaris (R)	Lemna trisulca (F)	Ranunculus subrigidus (R)
Utricularia vulgaris (R)	Drepanocladus spp. (M)	Lemna minor (F)	Potamogeton foliosus (R)
Potamogeton foliosus (R)	Callitriche verna (R)	Riccia fluitans (M)	Marsilea vestita (R)
Drepanocladus spp. (M)	Ranunculus sceleratus (R)		Bacopa rotundifolia (R)
Ranunculus cymbalaria (R)	Lemna trisulca (F)		Eleocharis acicularis
Eleocharis acicularis	Lemna minor (F)		(submerged form) (R)
(submerged form) (R)	Riccia fluitans (M)		Ranunculus sceleratus (R)
Riccia fluitans (M)	Ricciocarpus natans (M)		
Ricciocarpus natans (M)			
Lemna trisulca (F)			
Lemna minor (F)			
Ranunculus subrigidus (R)			
Water chemistry modifier – Oligosaline			
Utricularia vulgaris (R)	Utricularia vulgaris (R)	not seen	Ranunculus subrigidus
Lemna minor (F)	Lemna minor (F)		Eleocharis acicularis
Lemna trisulca (F)	Lemna trisulca (F)		(submerged form) (R)
Drepanocladus spp. (M)	Drepanocladus spp. (M)		
Ranunculus subrigidus (R)	Riccia fluitans (M)		
Ricciocarpus natans (M)	Ricciocarpus natans (M)		
Zannichellia palustris (R)	Zannichellia palustris (R)		
	Chara spp. (A)		
Water chemistry modifier – Mesosaline			
no plants in this group	no plants in this group	not seen	not seen

TABLE 5.9. Dominance types of vegetation in aquatic bed algal (A), aquatic moss and liverwort (M), rooted vascular (R), and floating vascular (F) subclasses of palustrine wetland with semipermanently flooded water regime in the northern plains and prairies

Water chemistry modifier—Fresh

Elodea longivaginata (R)	*Ceratophyllum demersum* (R)
Spirodela polyrhiza (F)	*Myriophyllum spicatum* (R)
Riccia fluitans (M)	*Drepanocladus* spp. (M)
Potamogeton gramineus (R)	*Ranunculus subrigidus* (R)
Lemna trisulca (F)	*Lemna minor* (F)
Utricularia vulgaris (R)	*Ranunculus flabellaris* (R)
Ricciocarpus natans (M)	
Potamogeton richardsonii (R)	

Water chemistry modifier—Oligosaline

Hippuris vulgaris (R)	*Drepanocladus* spp. (M)
Ranunculus gmelini (R)	*Ranunculus subrigidus* (R)
Ricciocarpus natans (F)	*Lemna minor* (F)
Callitriche hermaphroditica (R)	*Zannichellia palustris* (R)
Potamogeton zosteriformis (R)	*Chara* supp. (A)
Potamogeton pusillus (R)	*Potamogeton pectinatus* (R)
Lemna trisulca (F)	
Utricularia vulgaris (R)	
Potamogeton richardsonii (R)	
Ceratophyllum demersum (R)	
Myriophyllum spicatum (R)	

Water chemistry modifier—Mesosaline

Zannichellia palustris (R)
Chara spp. (A)
Potamogeton pectinatus (R)
Ruppia maritima (R)

the distribution of submersed plants at the wet end. Other studies of saline prairie wetland vegetation include those of Ungar (1970, 1974). Smeins (1967) suggested that differences in soil moisture regimes rather than salinity controlled the distribution of halophytic species within and among saline wetlands.

Salts in wetlands are brought into them either by overland runoff leaching salts from the surrounding soils or by groundwater. Predictions about the salinity of wetlands can be made from an examination of the location of the wetland in the landscape and the salinity of the adjacent soils. Groundwater discharge wetlands are more likely to occur in topographically low areas. These are more likely to be more saline than wetlands at high points in the landscape. Soils maps showing the location of saline soils in a region, however, should be even more useful in locating areas with saline wetlands. Soil salinity maps have been published for Saskatchewan (Ballantyne 1984a, 1984b) and Alberta (Peters 1981).

Salinity levels can fluctuate widely within and among seasons, particularly in smaller wetlands and those of intermediate and high salinity, due to the amount of water present (Rozkowska and Rozkowski 1969; Stewart and Kantrud 1972). These changes in salinity can be accompanied by changes in the composition of the vegetation (Ungar et al. 1979). Differential recruitment of species from saline wetland seed banks at different salinity levels may be responsible for the observed changes (Ungar and Riehl 1980). High salinities inhibit seed germination, but species vary in their ability to germinate at different salinity levels (Ungar 1978; Galinato and van der Valk 1986).

Both soil salinity and the salinity of the water column have been used to examine the impact of salinity on the distribution of species. Which provides the most reliable and consistent measure of salinity? Both Smeins (1967) and Walker and Coupland (1970) measured surface-water salinities as well as soil salinities, but they did not comment on the relationship between the two.

Lieffers and Shay (1983) point out that salinities vary over a wet-dry cycle and that in classifying these wetlands the water volume-salinity cycle should be used rather than single measurements of water or soil salinities. The complex of factors associated with such fluctuations (the magnitude of the change in salinity, the length of time the change persists, the change in depth of water associated with these changes in salinity) makes it difficult to establish salinity tolerances of a particular species. The approach most often taken is to identify the range of salinities over which a species is found and to try to identify where in this range the species grows best. Since these studies often examine species over a wide geographical range, it is likely that the species ranges actually are composites of the ranges of many ecotypes of these species.

On the basis of published information in Smeins (1967) and Disrud (1968) and unpublished data of Kantrud, we have estimated the salinity tolerances of emergent species found in temporarily, seasonally, and semipermanently flooded and saturated water or moisture regimes in Tables 5.10 and 5.11 and of submersed and floating plants in Table 5.12. These tolerances are crude estimates because specific conductivity measurements of surface water often differ greatly from measurements of soil extracts. We have arranged the plant species in order of observed salt tolerance, but these tables cannot be used to derive dominance types for various ranges of salinity because specific species exhibit a broad range of salinity tolerance. Species that are tolerant of high salinities can survive low salinities (Ungar 1966).

This suggests that competition or other factors may play an important role in determining the composition of vegetation on less saline sites (Ungar 1974). Competition among species in prairie wetlands has never been studied, but it has been demonstrated to occur in other types of wetlands (Buttery and Lambert 1965; Grace and Wetzel 1981).

TABLE 5.10. **Hydrophytes of temporarily flooded moisture regimes in the northern plains and prairies arranged according to increasing maximum observed tolerance of dissolved salts**

Species	Specific conductivity (mS)		
	Mean	Minimum	Maximum
Vernonia fasciculata	0.1[a]	0.1	0.2
Agrostis stolonifera	0.2	—	—
Lycopus americanus	0.3	—	—
Potentilla rivalis	0.3	—	—
Carex stipata	0.4	—	—
Eleocharis compressa	0.4	—	—
Equisetum arvense	0.4	—	—
Juncus interior	0.4	0.3	0.9
Aster sagittifolius	1.0	—	—
Plantago major	1.0	—	—
Potentilla norvegica	0.3	0.1	1.1
Juncus dudleyi	0.4	0.3	1.3
Carex buxbaumii	1.2	1.0	1.4
Lysimachia hybrida	0.1	0.1	1.6
Carex vulpinoidea	1.0	0.1	1.7
Ranunculus macounii	1.1	0.1	2.1
Rumex mexicanus	0.5	0.1	2.2
Juncus bufonius	2.3	—	—
Cirsium arvense	2.5	—	—
Bidens cernua	1.5	0.7	2.5
Helenium autumnale	1.5	0.5	2.5
Carex praegracilis	0.3	0.1	3.0
Echinochloa crusgalli	1.3	0.5	3.2
Carex laeviconica	1.5	0.1	3.2
Rorippa islandica	1.7	0.1	3.2
Poa palustris	1.4	Tr.[b]	3.4
Stachys palustris	1.8	0.1	3.6
Calamagrostis canadensis	1.4	0.4	3.8
Carex sartwellii	1.5	0.4	3.8
Epilobium glandulosum	1.5	0.5	4.7
Mentha arvensis	1.6	0.1	4.9
Apocynum sibiricum	1.8	0.4	5.0
Eleocharis compressa	2.0	0.7	5.0
Carex tetanica	2.0	0.9	5.5
Potentilla anserina	1.6	0.1	6.0
Boltonia asteroides	1.4	0.1	6.8

Source: Adapted from Smeins 1967; Disrud 1968; Sletten and Larson 1984; Kantrud, unpubl. data.

[a]Underlined means (Disrud 1968; Kantrud, unpubl.) are for surface water measurements in wetlands where the species reached peak abundance; underlined ranges (ibid.) are for instances where the species occurred in waters of greater or lesser salinity than that recorded by Smeins (1967).

[b]Indicates measurements <0.05 mS.

TABLE 5.10. *(continued)*

Species	Specific conductivity (mS)		
	Mean	Minimum	Maximum
Teucrium occidentale	3.1	0.2	9.1
Carex stricta	0.9	0.1	9.4
Aster hesperius	2.4	0.4	9.8
Juncus torreyi	1.7	0.2	10.0
Aster simplex	1.8	0.1	16.1
Calamagrostis inexpansa	2.6	Tr.	17.6
Juncus balticus	3.3	0.1	20.1
Spartina gracilis	9.0	0.7	20.1
Plantago eriopoda	9.8	1.0	20.1
Sonchus arvensis	5.2	0.5	20.8
Lycopus asper	1.9	0.1	32.6
Carex lanuginosa	2.0	0.1	32.6
Spartina pectinata	3.0	Tr.	33.5
Muhlenbergia asperifolia	11.0	0.7	38.5
Hordeum jubatum	7.8	Tr.	48.6
Triglochin maritima	12.5	0.7	50.9
Distichlis spicata	17.0	0.5	76.4
Atriplex patula	23.0	6.9	76.4

Water Regime. A number of studies have been conducted into various aspects of the relations between vegetation and water regime. Walker and Coupland (1968) established an association for 24 leading dominant species along a moisture gradient at three sites in Saskatchewan and in a later study (Walker and Coupland 1970), they arranged 174 species into 27 groups whose distribution was controlled by three factors, one of which was water regime (salinity and disturbance were the other two).

Efforts to match vegetation to the overall hydrology of a basin have only been moderately successful because groundwater flow patterns through many prairie wetlands, particularly semipermanently flooded wetlands, are transitional between the two extremes of wetlands acting as recharge areas and as discharge areas. Transitional wetlands are difficult to classify hydrologically as their flow patterns are highly variable (Lissey 1968, 1971; Williams 1968; Winter and Carr 1980; Winter Chap. 2). In the Dakotas, recharge wetlands have plant communities typical of temporarily or seasonally flooded water regimes with oligosaline water (Tables 5.4 and 5.5) whereas discharge wetlands have vegetation typical of semipermanently flooded, intermittently exposed, or permanently flooded regimes with meso- or hypersaline water (Tables 5.6 and 5.7). Many semipermanent prairie wetlands, however, are intermediate between these two types and exhibit various mixed patterns of groundwater flow. Over the year they may be both discharge and recharge areas.

TABLE 5.11. Hydrophytes of seasonally (SE), semipermanently flooded (SP), and saturated (SA) moisture regimes in the northern plains and prairies arranged according to increasing maximum observed tolerance of dissolved salts

Species	Water regime	Specific conductivity (mS)		
		Mean	Minimum	Maximum
Equisetum fluviatile	SE	0.3[a]	—	—
Galium trifidum	SA	0.3	—	—
Scutellaria galericulata	SA	0.3	—	—
Impatiens biflora	SA	0.4	—	—
Scirpus microcarpus	SA	0.5	0.3	0.9
Mimulus ringens	SA	0.6	—	—
Eupatorium maculatum	SA	0.7	—	—
Sagittaria cuneata	SE	0.7	—	—
Glyceria striata	SA	0.8	—	—
Ranunculus gmelini	SA	0.8	—	—
Asclepias incarnata	SA	0.8	0.8	0.9
Parnassia glauca	SA	0.9	—	—
Glyceria borealis	SE	1.0	—	—
Salix interior	SA	0.4	0.3	1.7
Carex lacustris	SA	1.4	0.9	1.7
Solidago graminifolia	SA	0.8	0.1	2.1
Polygonum amphibium	SE	0.6	0.1	2.2
Scirpus atrovirens	SA	1.0	0.5	2.2
Cicuta maculata	SA	1.4	0.5	2.2
Eriophorum angustifolium	SA	1.8	0.5	2.2
Carex rostrata	SA	1.1	0.2	2.6
Polygonum coccineum	SE	1.3	Tr.[b]	3.4
Phalaris arundinacea	SE	1.6	0.1	3.8
Carex aquatilis	SA	1.6	0.3	3.8
Lysimachia thrysiflora	SA	1.7	0.5	3.8
Glyceria grandis	SE	0.7	Tr.	4.0
Sium suave	SE	1.8	0.1	4.0
Scirpus heterochaetus	SP	1.4	0.1	4.2
Alopecurus aequalis	SE	1.1	0.1	4.5
Sparganium eurycarpum	SE	1.8	Tr.	4.6
Eleocharis acicularis	SE	1.5	0.1	5.8
Scirpus validus	SP, SA	1.8	0.2	6.2
Typha × glauca	SP	0.8	0.1	6.6
Sagittaria cuneata	SE	1.8	0.1	6.7
Scirpus fluviatilis	SP	1.9	0.3	6.7
Alisma gramineum	SE	2.0	0.3	6.7

Sources: Adapted from Smeins 1967; Disrud 1968; Sletten and Larson 1984; Kantrud unpubl. data.

[a]Underlined means (Disrud 1968; Kantrud, unpubl.) are for surface water measurements in wetlands where the species reached peak abundance; underlined ranges (ibid.) are for instances where the species occurred in waters of greater or lesser salinity than that recorded by Smeins (1967).

[b]Indicates measurements <0.05 mS.

TABLE 5.11. *(continued)*

Species	Water regime	Specific conductivity (mS)		
		Mean	Minimum	Maximum
Carex atherodes	SE	2.0	Tr.	8.5
Ranunculus sceleratus	SE	3.6	0.1	8.5
Bechmannia syzigachne	SE	1.5	Tr.	9.5
Alisma plantago-aquatica	SE	1.8	Tr.	9.5
Ranunculus cymbalaria	SE	3.5	0.6	9.5
Scolochloa festucacea	SE	3.4	0.1	12.1
Typha latifolia	SP, SA	2.1	0.1	13.6
Typha angustifolia	SP	3.4	0.4	13.6
Scirpus nevadensis	SE	15.7	12.0	20.5
Phragmites australis	SA	3.5	0.1	32.6
Scirpus acutus	SP	4.3	0.2	37.0
Eleocharis macrostachya	SE	2.7	0.1	41.0
Suaeda depressa	SE	24.0	5.0	66.0
Scirpus pungens	SE	4.9	0.1	70.0
Scirpus maritimus	SP	10.3	0.2	76.4
Puccinellia nuttalliana	SE	20.0	0.7	76.4

These wetlands are primarily mixosaline and semipermanently flooded (Table 5.6). Smeins (1967) cautioned about making judgments about the vegetation from the current water regime because previous water regimes and land uses have lingering effects. The broad ecological amplitudes or physiological tolerances of many of the wetland species in this region also make it difficult to relate the composition of vegetation to hydrology (Dix and Smeins 1967).

The impact of water-level changes during wet-dry cycles is discussed in detail in the section on VEGETATION DYNAMICS. The impact of vegetation on hydrology is presented in Chapter 2.

AGRICULTURAL DISTURBANCES

Most prairie wetlands are now imbedded in a matrix of farm land. Before Europeans settled the region, its wetlands were regularly disturbed by fire, water-level fluctuations, and probably grazing, but since settlement, human disturbance has become so widespread that nearly every wetland is affected either directly or indirectly. Before World War II, wetlands were widely exploited for native hay and as pasture, but after the war the expansion of row crops (corn, wheat, soybeans, sunflower, etc.) throughout the region and the advent of more powerful farm machinery resulted in many wetlands being cultivated during dry years or drained permanently by means of drainage tiles or ditches to

TABLE 5.12.   Submerged and floating aquatic plants of the northern plains and prairies arranged according to increasing maximum observed tolerance of dissolved salts

Species	Specific conductivity (mS)		
	Mean or single measurement	Minimum	Maximum
Myriophyllum pinnatum	0.1[a]	—	—
Nuphar variegatum	0.4	—	—
Najas flexilis	0.4	0.3	0.7
Elodea canadensis	0.4	—	—
Potamogeton friesii	0.6	0.3	1.0
Myriophyllum verticillatum	0.6	0.4	1.1
Potamogeton gramineus	0.8	0.1	1.2
Callitriche palustris	0.3	0.1	1.7
Hippuris vulgaris	0.7	0.5	2.3
Callitriche hermaphroditica	1.2	0.5	2.5
Ranunculus flabellaris	2.0	0.4	2.5
Potamogeton zosteriformis	1.0	0.3	2.8
Spirodela polyrhiza	1.5	0.1	3.0
Ricciocarpus natans	2.2	0.3	3.2
Drepanocladus spp.	1.2	0.1	3.3
Potamogeton vaginatus	3.3	—	—
Potamogeton richardsonii	1.7	0.3	4.0
Ranunculus subrigidus	1.4	0.2	4.5
Riccia fluitans	2.1	0.1	4.7
Ceratophyllum demersum	2.1	0.1	5.1
Potamogeton pusillus	2.1	0.1	6.7
Myriophyllum spicatum	2.2	0.2	6.7
Utricularia vulgaris	2.7	0.1	8.1
Lemna minor	3.1	0.1	10.9
Lemna triscula	3.2	0.1	13.9
Ruppia maritima var. *occidentalis*	4.1	0.6	14.2
Zannichellia palustris	4.8	0.3	25.0
Chara spp.	2.2	0.3	42.0
Potamogeton pectinatus	6.5	0.2	60.0
Ruppia maritima var. *rostrata*	36.1	5.5	66.0

Source: Adapted Smeins 1967; Disrud 1968; Sletten and Larson 1984; Kantrud, unpubl. data.

[a]Underlined means (Disrud 1968; Kantrud, unpubl.) are for surface water measurements in wetlands where the species reached peak abundance; underlined ranges (ibid) are for instances where the species occurred in waters of greater or lesser salinity than that recorded by Smeins (1967).

allow annual cultivation. These changes in land-use were accompanied by an increase in the use of inorganic fertilizers and pesticides to increase production. Since wetlands are low points in this agricultural landscape, runoff from surrounding farm fields, particularly after World War II, has carried ever increasing quantities of soil, fertilizer, and pesticides into them.

Drainage

Drainage has reduced wetland acreage throughout the region (Frayer et al. 1983; Tiner 1984; Sugden and Beyersbergen 1984). It has been most extensive in southeastern parts (i.e., Iowa, southern and western Minnesota and parts of the eastern Dakotas). In Iowa, it has been estimated that over 95% of the prairie wetlands have been drained (Bishop 1981). In the Minnedosa region of western Manitoba, wetlands covered 13.2% of the area in 1928, but only 3.8% by 1982 (Anonymous 1986). In all of Western Canada, it is estimated that 1.2×10^6 ha of wetland had been converted to farmland by 1976 (Anonymous 1986). Hewes and Frandson (1952) have documented the impact of drainage on the wetlands of Story County, Iowa. Figure 5.6 presents an example of

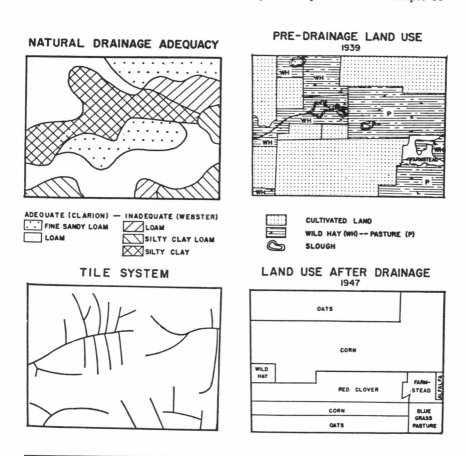

FIG. 5.6. Land-use prior to (upper half of figure) and after (lower half) drainage of the Postgate farm in Story County, Iowa (*Hewes and Frandson 1952*).

land-use on an Iowa farm before and after the wetlands were drained. Before drainage, wetland areas on this farm were often harvested for wild hay, but they could not be cultivated because it was impossible to get equipment into these areas in the spring. After drainage, however, land-use practices changed dramatically. There was a major realignment of field boundaries and the former wetland areas were all put under cultivation (corn, oats, and more recently soybeans).

The drainage of wetlands does not always result in productive farmland as in Iowa. Drainage followed by tillage can result in land salinization in areas where the groundwater is brackish or saline. Wetlands that receive most of their water from groundwater are particularly susceptible to salinization when they are drained. Salinization can quickly prevent the cultivation of row crops, and only hay production is sometimes feasible in these drained basins (Fulton et al. 1986).

Fortunately, many wetland species can become reestablished quickly if a drained and cultivated wetland is reflooded less than 20 years after it was drained (Erlandson 1987). The presence of relict seed banks in former wetland basins seems to be largely responsible for this. Temporary reestablishment of wetland vegetation often occurs in very wet springs because the drainage tiles or ditches cannot carry off water fast enough or because tiles or ditches become plugged up. Several wetland restorations have been initiated in recent years in Minnesota and Iowa by destroying or plugging up drainage systems (Madsen 1986; Erlandson 1987).

Impacts of Agricultural Activities

Information on the impacts of different kinds of agricultural activities on wetland vegetation is not extensive and for the most part consists of incidental observations recorded as part of vegetation surveys or waterfowl studies. Among the most important and widespread of these disturbances are grazing, mowing, burning, and siltation. Both direct and indirect disturbances are so widespread that they are often the most important factors controlling the distribution and composition of contemporary wetland vegetation (Smeins 1967; Walker and Coupland 1970).

Walker and Coupland (1970) recognized three types of disturbances (cultivation, grazing, and mowing) as important in Saskatchewan. The intensity of the disturbance rather than the specific type of disturbance was often more important, and they were able to establish various groupings of species based on their responses to intensity of disturbance. Some forms of disturbance, like mowing, may favor the growth of a particular species. Smeins (1967), Walker and Coupland (1968, 1970), and Stewart and Kantrud (1972) all suggested that *Scolochloa festucacea* was favored by mowing. Unpublished observations by Millar, however, suggest that after 25 years of mowing no detectable change in the dominant emergents occurred in Saskatchewan wetlands.

Grazing. The general impacts of grazing on wetland plant communities are well known from studies done on wetlands in other parts of the world. It is likely, however, that prairie wetlands were grazed regularly by native ungulates, and hence had grazing-resistant species before the introduction of cattle into the region. Unless unusually severe, grazing results in greater species diversity, more complex distribution patterns, and sharper boundaries between zones (Bakker and Ruyter 1981). Livestock trampling, rather than consumption, may have more impact on the height and density of wetland vegetation (Hilliard 1974). Overgrazing may decrease primary production (Reimold et al. 1975), increase water turbidity (Logan 1975), and, in extreme cases, eliminate all vegetation (Bassett 1980).

Several studies have reported that there are wetland species that increase due to or are tolerant of grazing (Evans et al. 1952; Smith 1953; Smeins 1965; Dix and Smeins 1967; Walker and Coupland 1968; Stewart and Kantrud 1972; Millar 1973). Dominance types in wetlands that are grazed are often very different from nongrazed wetlands. These differences seem to be related to differences in the palatability of emergent species, but may also be due to changes in environmental conditions brought about by grazing. In ungrazed wetlands, there are usually only small openings in the canopy; grazing removes much of the wetland canopy and allows species to become established that are not present under closed canopies (Kantrud 1986).

Burning. Based on the accounts of early traders and travelers in the region, fires were common in prairie wetlands in the early nineteenth century. For example, in 1803 Henry and Thompson recorded fires rushing through "low places covered with reeds and rushes" (Henry and Thompson 1965). In 1858 or 1859, Boller (1972) saw a large conflagration spread for many miles after being set by American Indians in "dry rushes in the prairie bottoms." Denig (1961) observed, while he was in the region (1833–1854), that fires even swept through wetlands over the ice.

Wild prairie fires are uncommon now, but burning continues. Today fires are used to improve the quality of wild hay or forage by removing accumulated litter (Kantrud 1986), and burning of wetlands may occur with a frequency much greater than under natural conditions. Early studies of fire impacts by Lewis et al. (1928), Furniss (1938), and Ward (1942) indicated that fire could sometimes alter the composition of wetland vegetation. For example, Ward (1942) found that fire could open up dense beds of *Phragmites australis*. Later studies by Tester and Marshall (1962), Smeins (1965), Schlichtemeier (1967), Ward (1968), Smith (1969), Millar (1973), Thompson (1982), Diiro (1982), and Thompson and Shay (1985) in Minnesota, North Dakota, Nebraska, Alberta, Saskatchewan, and Manitoba have revealed that the impacts of fires are quite variable and depend on the fuel load, time of the year, and species involved. Because of differences among these studies, the results are inconsistent and of minimal predictive value. A more complete review on the impacts of burning on wetlands is found in Kantrud (1986).

The spring and autumn burning of wetlands often has significant impact on the water regime of prairie potholes. Burning removes plant litter, exposing the soil to erosion. More importantly, however, it reduces the trapping of snow during the winter (Diiro 1982). Since snow accumulation during the winter may be the single most important source of water each year for many potholes, the removal of standing litter that traps snow can alter the production and even composition of their vegetation.

Sedimentation. One of the more insidious and widespread forms of disturbance is increased sedimentation. Large inputs of sediment into wetlands due to wind and water erosion are common (Martin and Hartman 1986). Nevertheless, we could find not a single published study that has documented the impacts of increased sedimentation on wetland vegetation. The only published studies that we could find are those of Jackson and Starrett (1959) and Bellrose et al. (1979) in Illinois and van der Valk et al. (1983) in Alaska. Likewise there seems to be nothing known about the impacts of nutrients and pesticides carried into wetlands with the sediment (see Neely and Baker, Chap. 4).

VEGETATION DYNAMICS

Prairie wetlands, because of their fluctuating hydrologic regime, are one of the most dynamic types of wetlands in North America. This dynamism is a direct result of the extreme variability of the prairie climate and parallels in intensity the climatic gradients of the region. In Canada it is most pronounced in the warmer and drier southwestern area and more subdued in the cooler and moister northeast.

Annual variation in spring runoff, summer precipitation, and evapotranspiration produce cyclical fluctuations in the water levels of prairie wetlands (Figs. 5.4 and 5.5). The severe drought of the 1930s was followed by record or near record high water levels in the early 1950s and by the 1960s the prairies were experiencing another drought. Surface water conditions improved again in the late 1960s to be followed by one or two minor dry periods in the 1970s. Beginning in the early 1980s and continuing through 1985 there was a drought in parts of the region, particularly southwestern Saskatchewan and southern Alberta, that was comparable in severity to that of the 1930s. An example of the extent to which water levels in a prairie wetland can be affected over a 25-year period by these cyclical fluctuations in annual precipitation is given in Figure 5.4.

Since hydrologic regime (i.e., the depth and duration of inundation during the growing season) is a principal factor in controlling distribution and composition of the vegetation, it follows that fluctuations in this regime will induce changes in the composition and structure of the vegetation within a wetland. Consequently, any attempt to deal with the composition, classification, or dynamics of the region's wetland vegetation must take into account the impact of wet-dry cycles.

There have been a few studies of wet-dry cycles in Canada. Walker (1959, 1965) did a detailed study of the impact of high water and falling water levels on the vegetation of the Delta Marsh, a lacustrine marsh at the southern end of Lake Manitoba. High water levels killed as much as 25% of the emergent vegetation. During the years that water levels were falling, newly exposed shorelines were colonized by a series of new bands of vegetation that underwent changes in composition and structure from year to year. Walker also did some pioneering work on the seed banks (i.e., the reserve of viable seed stored in the upper few centimeters of soil) of this marsh, and noted the lack of similarity between the composition of the seed bank and the surrounding vegetation. For ten years, Millar (1973) documented the changes in species composition and cover in shallow marshes under an improving moisture regime in Saskatchewan. Many shallow water emergents were eliminated if periods of high water lasted two or more years. Water-level and vegetation data have continued to be collected on these wetlands by Millar and a continuous record now exists for 25 years (Fig. 5.4).

The most detailed studies of wet-dry cycles and their impact on the vegetation and fauna have been conducted in Iowa. Two long-term studies by Weller and Spatcher (1965) and Weller and Fredrickson (1974) have documented the overall changes that occur in Iowa wetlands during such a cycle, particularly changes in their bird populations (Table 5.2). These studies documented that the emergent vegetation in these marshes was largely eliminated as a result of muskrat activity (i.e., "eat outs" during high water periods). (See Fritzell, Chap. 9, for more information about muskrats in prairie potholes.) Their studies stimulated studies by van der Valk and Davis (1976b, 1978b) on how the vegetation responds to water-level changes.

Figure 5.7 outlines the four vegetation stages that occur during a wet-dry cycle. One of the most important features of these wetlands was their seed bank (van der Valk and Davis 1976b, 1978b). It is the presence of seeds of emergent, submersed, free-floating, and mudflat annual species that allows some type of vegetation to develop in these wetlands in response to any change in water depth. During periods of high water, the vegetation is eliminated by a combination of muskrat damage and the direct effects of prolonged flooding. This is the degenerating stage of the cycle during which the marsh loses its emergent vegetation. The first few years of this stage correspond to the hemi-marsh stage (Table 5.2) of Weller and Spatcher (1965). When the emergents are gone, the marsh enters the lake marsh stage during which submersed vegetation predominates. Most emergents are unable to become reestablished during these two phases because their seeds will not germinate under water. The next drought, however, will result in a drawdown that exposes part or all of

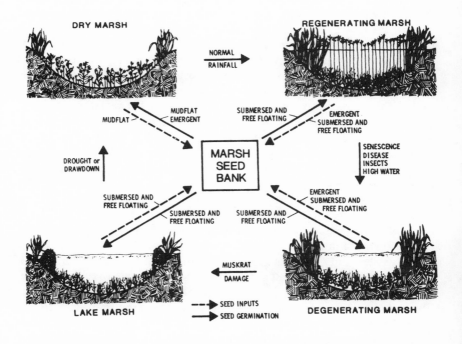

FIG. 5.7. A generalized vegetation cycle in an Iowa prairie pothole (*van der Valk and Davis 1978*).

the marsh bottom (the dry marsh stage). During this drawdown, the seeds of emergent species present in the seed bank germinate as well as the seeds of a large number of mudflat annuals also present in the seed bank. When the drought ends, the marsh refloods. This eliminates all the annuals that cannot tolerate flooding, but leaves the emergents. Submersed species also become reestablished from seed as soon as the marsh refloods. During the next year or two (the regenerating stage), the emergent populations spread by vegetative propagation and the zonation patterns that characterize these wetlands redevelop. The return of high water for a number of years initiates a new cycle as muskrat populations begin to increase again and some emergent species begin to be drowned out.

The cycle outlined in Figure 5.7 is an idealized cycle (see also Table 5.2). In reality, very complex changes in the composition and distribution of vegetation, including inverted or multiple zonation patterns, can occur in the field due to partial drawdowns or several drawdowns over a very short period (see ZONATION). Not all wetlands in this region undergo such cycles. They are a feature of deeper basins. Shallow basins or even the shallow parts of deeper basins may not have them (van der Valk and Davis 1979) unless they have the capacity to store 1 m of flood water during wet years. In western Canada, shallow wetlands that flood during wet years to a depth of 1 m or more develop a form of the lake marsh stage that is locally referred to as a transitional open water zone (Millar 1973).

In more arid parts of the region, muskrats do not play as significant a role in wet-dry cycles. This may be because they are frozen out during the winter. Nevertheless, similar cycles still occur in the deeper wetlands, particularly the lacustrine wetlands, where they seem to be driven solely by hydrologic changes (Walker 1959, 1965).

An examination of wet-dry cycles in a northern lacustrine marsh (the Delta Marsh, Manitoba) and Iowa potholes reveals two major differences between them with respect to their seed banks. First, the seed bank of the lacustrine wetland is most dense at about the elevation of the "normal" shoreline and declines sharply both above and below this zone (i.e., seeds become windrowed along the shoreline in very large quantities) (Pederson 1981, 1983; Pederson and van der Valk 1985). Seed banks of palustrine wetlands have similar densities over the entire basin (van der Valk and Davis 1976b, 1978b, 1979). Second, large quantities of standing and fallen litter are present during drawdowns in lacustrine wetlands. In Iowa potholes, there is almost no litter present on exposed mudflats during drawdowns. The impact of litter on recruitment from the seed bank has been investigated by van der Valk (1986). It reduces the number of individuals of a species recruited from the seed bank, but has no qualitative impact.

Currently these wet-dry cycles in a northern lacustrine wetland, the Delta Marsh, are being examined experimentally in a long-term study at the Delta Waterfowl and Wetland Research Station (Batt et al. 1983; Murkin et al. 1985). As part of this study, Welling (1987) has examined the recruitment of species from the seed bank during one- and two-year drawdowns. He found that most recruitment of emergents occurred during the first couple of months of the drawdown, and differences in soil temperature and moisture from year to year influenced the timing of recruitment and density of species (see also Welling et al. 1988).

Smith (1971) and Stoudt (1971) recorded water-level and vegetation data over a 14-year period from 1952 to 1965 as part of waterfowl production studies in the aspen parkland near Lousana, Alberta, and Redvers, Saskatchewan, respectively. These studies covered a complete wet-dry cycle, but little information on the response of the vegetation to changing water conditions was included in their final reports.

An understanding of the ecology of individual wetland species can be used to predict the response of wetland vegetation to changes in water regime and salinity (see van der Valk 1981; Galinato and van der Valk 1986). Our understanding of the dynamics and composition of wetland vegetation would improve significantly if we had better information (seed germination characteristics, water depth tolerances of seedlings and adults, salinity tolerances of seedlings and adults, rates of vegetative propagation under different conditions, etc.) about the major emergent and submersed species in the region.

Information on the ecology of most species so far has been generated in a piecemeal fashion in the course of general studies of wetland vegetation. Intensive studies of individual species are less common, but are of particular value in that they not only probe the ecology of the species in greater depth and detail, but also serve to draw together much of the fragmentary knowledge of the species reported in earlier studies. Information on studies of individual species is summarized in Table 5.13. The shortness of the list is indicative of how little work of this type has been done. Most of these studies were done in Canada.

ZONATION

Most authors who have examined the vegetation of prairie wetlands noted that the vegetation is composed of a series of concentric rings, each often dominated by a different species (Fig. 5.2). Changes in the dominant species across the elevation gradient usually are accompanied by a change in lifeform. It is these changes in lifeform (size, morphology,

TABLE 5.13.　Major studies or reviews of the autecology of species in the prairie pothole region

Species	Reference/Topic
Distichlis stricta	Tiku (1976)/Salinity, photosynthesis
	L'Hirondelle (1980)/Salinity, growth
Phragmites australis	Walker and Waygood (1968)/Photosynthesis
	Phillips (1976)/Evapotranspiration
	Thompson and Shay (1985)/Effects of fire
	Shay and Shay (1986)/Summary of autecology
	Galinato and van der Valk (1986)/Seed germination
Potamogeton pectinatus	Kollman and Wali (1976)/Production
	Anderson (1978)/Distribution and production
Ruppia occidentalis	Husband (1985)/General ecology
Salicornia rubra	Tiku (1976)/Salinity, photosynthesis
	Ungar (1978)/Review of halophyte seed germination
Scirpus lacustris spp. *glaucus* (*S. acutus*)	Dabbs (1971)/Water regime
	Macauley (1973)/Water regime, salinity tolerance
	Shay and Shay (1986)/Summary of autecology
Scirpus lacustris spp. *validus*	Dabbs (1971)/Water regime
	Macauley (1973)/Water regime, salinity tolerance
	van der Valk and Davis (1980)/Production and growth
	Shay and Shay (1986)/Summary of autecology
Scirpus maritimus	Lieffers and Shay (1981)/Water regime, growth, and re-production
	Lieffers and Shay (1982a)/Growth and standing crop
	Lieffers and Shay (1982b)/Distribution, growth, water regime
	Shay and Shay (1986)/Summary of autecology
Scolochloa festucaea	Smith (1972)/Seed germination
	Smith (1973a)/Production
	Smith (1973b)/Life-cycle
	Diiro (1982)/Effects of burning and mowing
	Neckles (1984)/Water regime
	Neckles et al. (1985)/Review
	Galinato and van der Valk (1986)/Seed germination
Typha × glauca	Weller (1975)/Water depth tolerances of seedlings
	van der Valk and Davis (1980)/Production and growth
	Grace and Harrison (1986)/Review
	Galinato and van der Valk (1986)/Seed germination
Typha latifolia	Sifton (1959)/Seed germination
	Bonnewell et al. (1983)/Seed germination
	Lieffers (1983)/Seasonal growth patterns
	Grace and Harrison (1986)/Review
	Shay and Shay (1986)/Summary of autecology

Note: Nomenclature follows Scoggan (1978–1979).

color, etc.) from one zone to another that make these zones such a prominent feature of the vegetation. These different lifeforms are commonly accepted as indicators of the hydrologic regime within a zone (i.e., they are a function of the duration of flooding or water depth at that elevation) (Stewart and Kantrud 1971; Millar 1976). Most of the subdominant or minor species growing in these wetlands, however, are distributed independently of the dominants along elevation gradients (van der Valk and Davis 1976a); that is, these zones are not assemblages of species with a similar distribution, but simply areas where a particular species is dominant.

Although different authors have varied in the terminology and degree of detail used to describe these zones as well as what constitutes the outer limit of the wetland proper, there is widespread agreement about the more common zones: wet meadow, shallow marsh, deep marsh, and open water in freshwater wetlands. The general features of these zones are outlined in Table 5.1. The only significant variation in the general character of these zones occurs in the parkland region in Canada. In this region wetland margins are usually dominated by willows (*Salix* spp.) instead of wet meadow vegetation. These willow zones, however, often have been removed by brush clearing operations and, as a result, many wetlands in the parkland region now have a peripheral wet meadow zone.

Zonation studies have established a number of basic patterns in these wetlands. First, the complexity of the zonation (i.e., the number of zones) typically increases with the length of time a wetland normally holds water during the growing season. Second, in fresh to moderately saline wetlands, the stature of emergent vegetation increases along the gradient from areas less frequently to areas more frequently inundated. In hypersaline wetlands, however, all the emergent vegetation has a low stature, and in extreme cases disappears. Third, the species richness in a zone tends to decrease as water permanence increases. Fourth, deviations from "normal" zonation patterns occur regularly in the form of zonal inversions or deletions (Smeins 1967; Millar 1976).

These deviant zonation patterns are a result of water-level fluctuations. For example, if a drought is severe enough for the open-water zone of a basin to be reduced to mudflat, shallow marsh species like whitetop (*Scolochloa festucacea*) or manna grass (*Glyceria* spp.) may become established inside the deep marsh zone, which is usually cattail (*Typha* spp.) or bulrush (*Scirpus* spp.). If subsequent water levels are not too high, these zonal inversions (in this case, a shallow marsh zone inside a deep marsh zone) can persist for a few years. Zonal deviations of this sort can be very useful for interpreting the recent hydrologic history of a wetland.

WETLAND CLASSIFICATIONS

During the past 70 years, several wetland classification systems have been used in this region. The first system, although rather crude, may be attributed to Bailey (1916) who differentiated between shallow, grassy "sloughs" and deeper "tule marshes." He also noted that wetlands in North Dakota were normally called lakes if a central, open-water area was present. Vegetation features, water chemistry, and water regime (permanency) were used by a number of subsequent authors to develop more elaborate classifications (Metcalf 1931; Moyle 1945; Bach 1950; Nord et al. 1951).

Hayden (1943) developed a classification for Iowa wetlands, based on the principles of Clementsian succession, that began with a newly formed basin and ended in climax prairie. Later Clambey (1975) developed a classification of wetlands in northwest Iowa along similar lines. Because of cyclical changes in the vegetation resulting from wet-dry cycles and the persistence of these wetlands for thousands of years (Watts and Winter 1966; Watts and Bright 1968), the suitability and adequacy of Clementsian successional models to cope with the vegetation dynamics of Iowa marshes was questioned by Weller and Spatcher (1965). An alternative model has been developed by van der Valk (1981) that uses the life-history features (life expectancy, seed germination requirements, presence or absence in the wetland's permanent seed bank) of each species to predict their behavior during vegetation cycles (van der Valk et al. 1988).

To inventory the wetlands of the United States as habitat for waterfowl, Martin et al. (1953) developed a classification system that could be applied simply and easily to all types of wetlands. Its freshwater and saline wetland types were distinguished on the basis of water depth and permanence, life form of the vegetation, and dominant plant species. This classification was used in the first inventory of the wetlands of the United States (Shaw and Fredine 1956).

Stewart and Kantrud (1963, 1969, 1971) is the definitive classification of prairie potholes in the grassland district. In their scheme, whole wetland basins are assigned to different classes on the basis of the vegetation found in their central or deepest zone. A wetland may have one, two, three, or more zones depending on its depth. The vegetation of the deepest, usually central, part of the basin is a measure of the permanency of water in that zone. In freshwater wetlands, five possible zones are recognized: low prairie, wet meadow, shallow marsh, deep marsh, and permanent open water (see section on ZONATION for details). Five corresponding classes of freshwater wetlands are recognized, each distinguished by a different vegetation zone occupying the central or deepest part of the basin. The five wetland classes are: class I, ephemeral ponds with a central low-prairie zone; class II, temporary ponds with a central wet-meadow zone; class III, seasonal ponds and lakes with a central shallow-marsh zone; class IV, semipermanent ponds and lakes with a central deep-marsh zone, and class V, permanent ponds and lakes with a central permanent open-water zone (Fig. 5.8). Detailed descriptions of the different vegetation zones, including lists of species that characterize each zone, are provided by Stewart and Kantrud (1971, 1972). Provisions are also made in the system for saline wetlands (Fig. 5.8). Because of water-level fluctuations, the vegetation of some zones, particularly shallow- and deep-marsh zones, can be in found in two or more phases (see section on VEGETATION DYNAMICS); it is essential that these alternative phases be recognized for what they are if the classification is to be applied correctly. Four phases are recognized: normal emergent phase, open-water phase, drawdown bare-soil phase, and drawdown emergent phase (Fig. 5.9). These phases roughly correspond to the degenerating, lake marsh, dry marsh and regenerating stages, respectively, of the van der Valk and Davis (1978b) vegetation cycle (Fig. 5.7). Phases are also recognized by Stewart and Kantrud (1971) for tilled wetlands.

Millar (1976) has adapted Stewart and Kantrud (1971) to make it compatible with Canadian conditions and the Canadian national classification of Zoltai et al. (1973). His classification system has recently been expanded and modified and a revised list of his wetland types is presented in Appendix 1. The most significant modifications to Stewart and Kantrud's system include exclusion of the low prairie zone from the definition of the wetland proper, although it is still included in the system, and the recognition of a peripheral zone of woody vegetation around wetlands in the aspen parkland zone. Use of wetland phases has been dropped in favor of classification on the basis of stable vegetation condition and the recognition of a transitional open-water wetland type. Finally, Millar's classification includes the use of physical characteristics of the basin as well as vegetation. This component has particular value in predicting the potential for future vegetation changes in a wetland.

In 1973, a national wetland classification for Canada was proposed by Zoltai et al. that was designed to be compatible with the Bio-Physical Land Classification System prepared by the National Committee on Forest Land (Lacate 1969). To date this classification has not been formally adopted at the national level, but it is being applied in various areas and has been described in its most recent form in Zoltai and Pollett (1983). It involves the following four levels of detail:

1. Wetland Class
   —based on the broad physiognomy of the wetland.
   —categories: bog, fen, swamp, marsh, and shallow open water.
2. Wetland Form
   —based on the surface morphology of the wetland.
   —named by attaching an appropriate wetland class.

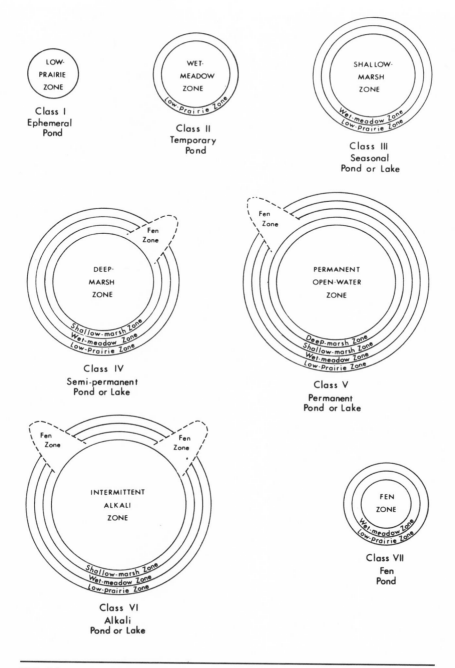

FIG. 5.8. Vegetation zonation patterns in different classes of northern prairie wetlands (*Stewart and Kantrud 1971*).

NORMAL EMERGENT PHASE

OPEN WATER PHASE

NORMAL WATER CONDITIONS

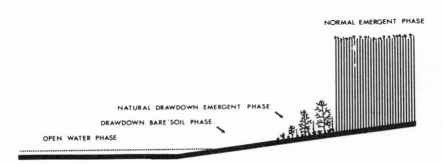

NORMAL EMERGENT PHASE

NATURAL DRAWDOWN EMERGENT PHASE

DRAWDOWN BARE SOIL PHASE

OPEN WATER PHASE

LOW WATER CONDITIONS

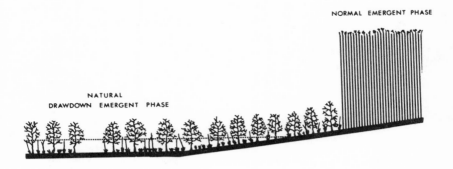

NORMAL EMERGENT PHASE

NATURAL
DRAWDOWN EMERGENT PHASE

REFLOODING OF POND

FIG. 5.9. Wetland phases or stages found under different water conditions in northern prairie wetlands (*Stewart and Kantrud 1971*).

3. Wetland Type
   — based on the physiognomy of the plant cover.
4. Wetland Variety
   — undefined.

The most extensive and detailed attempt to classify wetland plant communities in Canada has been that of Looman (1981, 1982, 1986a, 1986b). Looman (1981) pointed out that Dodd and Coupland (1966) and Walker and Coupland (1970) differentiated groupings of wetland vegetation often on the basis of a single species and suggested that some groups could be combined. He also noted similarities between many prairie-wetland vegetation types recognized in North America and comparable types in Eurasia recognized by the Zurich-Montpellier school of phytosociology. He has applied this scheme to prairie wetlands, but has created new units to accommodate associations unique to the Canadian prairies. This approach deals with wetland communities per se and not with their interrelationships within a particular basin as is the case with Hayden (1943), Stewart and Kantrud (1971) and Millar (1976). Emergent vegetation has been classified in Looman (1981, 1982), submersed communities in Looman (1986a), and shrub dominated communities in Looman (1986b). This is a rare attempt to adapt a widely used European classification system that is largely unknown here to North American vegetation.

The latest wetland classification system to be applied to the region is that of Cowardin et al. (1979). This is a system developed by the U. S. Fish and Wildlife Service for inventorying the wetlands of the United States. It replaces the earlier system by Martin et al. (1953) developed for the same purpose. In the Cowardin et al. system, wetlands are first classified according to the hydrologic system and subsystem to which they belong (Table 5.3). For example, a particular lacustrine system includes all wetlands found in a given basin that is larger than 8 ha or, if less than 8 ha, is deeper than 2 m. It has two subsystems, the limnetic (areas deeper than 2m) and the littoral (to a depth of 2 m or to the maximum extent of nonpersistent emergent vegetation, if such emergents grow in depths of more than 2 m). Each subsystem is divided into classes, subclasses, and dominance types. A class is defined by the general appearance of the habitat in terms of the lifeform of the vegetation or the nature of the substrate. The littoral subsystem has, for example, six classes: rock bottom, unconsolidated bottom, aquatic bed, rocky shore, unconsolidated shore, and emergent wetland. Only two of these classes, aquatic bed and emergent wetland, are dominated by plants. Classes are in turn subdivided into subclasses on the basis of finer lifeform distinctions. For example, the class aquatic bed has four subclasses: algal, aquatic moss, rooted vascular, and floating. Dominance types are defined on the basis of the dominant plant or animal species. Dominance types in this context are based on dominant plant species (i.e., the species that provide most of the biomass, produce most of the shading, or otherwise dominate energy flow). Dominance types vary with water regime (increasing water permanence), water chemistry, grazing intensity, fire frequency, and human disturbances such as cultivation and mowing. For example, dominance types found in the rooted vascular subclass would include *Potamogeton pectinatus* and *Ruppia maritima*. Water regime (permanently flooded, semipermanently flooded, seasonally flooded, etc.), water chemistry (salinity and pH), soil (mineral and organic), and special (excavated, impounded, diked, partly drained, farmed) modifiers are applied at the class and lower levels (Cowardin et al. 1979).

In this system, palustrine and lacustrine systems predominate over the whole northern prairie region. There is little riverine habitat or deepwater habitat. The common species found in different wetland zones in palustrine and lacustrine were summarized by Stewart and Kantrud (1971). These zones were defined on the basis of their water regime and water chemistry (Fig. 5.8). Figure 5.10 illustrates how the water regime modifiers of Cowardin et al. (1979) are applied to palustrine and lacustrine wetlands in the region. Likewise the special modifier "farmed" in the Cowardin et al. system corresponds to the "cropland" phases in Stewart and Kantrud. The drawdown phases recognized by Stewart and Kantrud have no counterpart in the Cowardin et al. system since these occur irregularly and are not present when "normal" hydrologic conditions prevail.

From measurements and field observations in North Dakota, Stewart and Kantrud (1971, 1972) compiled information about 194 wetland species into tables based on water regime, salinity, and land-use. From this data base, the dominance types that characterize the emergent (Tables 5.4 to 5.7) and aquatic bed (Tables 5.8 and 5.9) classes as defined in the Cowardin et al. (1979) were developed. This system classifies each vegetation zone rather than the entire wetland as in the Stewart and Kantrud system. Dominant emergents under various moisture regimes are categorized by land-use practice and salinity (Tables 5.4 to 5.6) or salinity alone (Table 5.7). Dominance types in the seasonally flooded palustrine system of the class aquatic bed (Table 5.8) are categorized for various subclasses and land-uses because wetlands in this water regime are often subject to human disturbance. Land-use categories were omitted for the aquatic bed plants in semipermanently flooded palustrine system (Table 5.9) because of the relatively low frequency of disturbance of bottom soils in this regime. These tables are incomplete because we

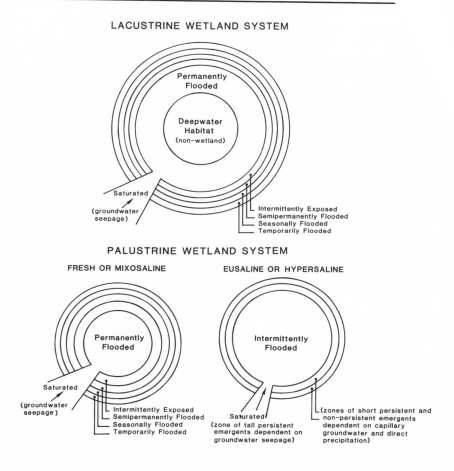

LACUSTRINE WETLAND SYSTEM

PALUSTRINE WETLAND SYSTEM

FIG. 5.10. The arrangement of Cowardin et al. (1979) water regimes in palustrine and lacustrine wetlands of the prairie pothole region.

lack information on the habitat requirements and responses to environmental change for many species. It should be stressed that these are dominance types found in the American portion of the northern prairie region.

As noted, Stewart and Kantrud (1971) and Millar (1976) classify entire wetlands as an entity while Cowardin et al. (1979) classify each area with a different dominance type as a separate entity and call each a wetland (Cowardin 1982). This means that a class IV wetland in Stewart and Kantrud (i.e., a deep marsh or semipermanent pothole) would consist of at least three "wetlands" (deep marsh, shallow marsh and wet meadow) in the Cowardin et al. system rather than a single wetland with three vegetation components or zones. Besides the semantic conundrum created by the Cowardin et al. system when it is applied to these wetlands, there are practical problems in relating the results of surveys done using one system with those using the other. The Stewart and Kantrud (1971) or Millar (1976) systems are more useful and meaningful for many regional applications. These systems are designed to accommodate the dynamic nature of the vegetation. No matter what phase a wetland is in it can be assigned to the correct category. A survey done during a low-water year should give results that can be related to one during a high-water year even though very different vegetation would be present during these two years.

To minimize problems with assigning wetlands to the right class using any classification system, surveys should be conducted in mid- to late summer when the full vegetation character of the wetland has developed. This is particularly advisable during high-water years when most, if not all, wetlands appear as open water in the spring.

SUMMARY

The palustrine and lacustrine wetlands of the prairie pothole region are found on a land surface created by Wisconsin glaciation in the north-central parts of the United States (Iowa, western Minnesota, and the Dakotas) and the southern parts of the Canadian prairie provinces. This area has a continental climate with cyclical fluctuations in annual precipitation and temperature (wet-dry cycles).

Because precipitation decreases from east to west while mean temperature increases, wetlands tend to be more saline in the western parts of the region. Differences in salinity among wetlands are one major factor responsible for differences in their floras. The length of time a basin contains water also influences its flora. Within a wetland, species are distributed along an elevation gradient often forming a series of distinct bands or zones when the wetland is viewed from a distance. These zones are conspicuous because one species normally dominates an elevation range, and the species that dominate higher or lower elevations have a different lifeform.

Agriculture has had a major impact on prairie wetlands. Many wetlands have been drained using tiles and ditches. Wetlands are also exploited for native hay and as pastures. When used in this way, they are sometimes burned regularly. Less permanent wetlands are used extensively for crop production during dry years. Agricultural activities, however, also have affected many wetlands indirectly because they receive runoff from farm fields often containing large quantities of sediment, nutrients, and pesticides.

The wet-dry cycles produce significant changes in the water level in a wetland from year to year. These changes alter the vegetation and fauna of susceptible wetlands. Over an idealized wet-dry cycle, the vegetation goes through four stages: dry marsh, regenerating marsh, degenerating marsh, and lake marsh. It is the presence of a seed bank containing seeds of emergent, submersed, mudflat annuals, and free floating species that enables different kinds of vegetation to develop quickly in response to changing water levels.

Two national classification systems have been developed and used in the region by the U.S. Fish and Wildlife Service. The first of these systems, Martin et al. (1953), has been superseded by that of Cowardin et al. (1979). Stewart and Kantrud (1971) developed a classification system just for prairie potholes. They recognized different classes on the basis of the vegetation in the deepest part of a basin and water chemistry. Millar (1976) has adapted this system for use in Canada. Looman (1981, 1982, 1986a, 1986b) has classified the wetlands of western Canada using the European phytosociological approach.

ACKNOWLEDGMENTS

Support for this work was provided by the Canadian Wildlife Service (JBM), the U.S. Fish and Wildlife Service (HAK), the Science and Humanities Research Institute of Iowa State University (AvdV), and the National Wetlands Technical Council. Parts of this chapter were written and the final draft prepared while one of us (AvdV) was on leave in the Department of Plant Ecology, University of Utrecht, The Netherlands. Funds for this leave were provided by the Nederlandse Organisatie voor Zuiver-Wetenschappelijk Onderzoek (ZWO) in the form of grant B 84-249 and a grant from the Marsh Ecology Research Program of the Delta Waterfowl and Wetlands Research Station.

We would like to thank Jos Verhoeven, Suzanne van der Valk, Chip Welling, and Roger Pederson, who read over various drafts of this chapter, for their suggestions.

APPENDIX Revised classification of depressions, wetlands, and other water-bodies for the Canadian Prairies

Type No.	Type — Description
0.0	Totally drained or filled depression or wetland
0.1	Herbaceous or shrub-filled depression — low Prairie or drier species
0.2	Treed depression — aspen or other species
0.3	Unclassified depression — most commonly applied to cultivated sheetwater depression in cropland
0.8	Low Prairie depression — in abandoned channel or watercourse (oxbow)
0.9	Low Prairie depression — in active, intermittent watercourse
1.1	Wet Meadow — herbaceous vegetation
1.2	Wet Meadow — willow-filled (shrub carr)
1.8	Wet Meadow — in abandoned channel or watercourse (oxbow)
1.9	Wet Meadow — in active, intermittent "beaded" watercourse
2.1	Shallow Marsh
2.8	Shallow Marsh — in abandoned channel or watercourse (oxbow)
2.9	Shallow Marsh — in active, intermittent "beaded" watercourse
3.1	Emergent Deep Marsh
3.8	Emergent Deep Marsh — in abandoned channel or watercourse (oxbow)
3.9	Emergent Deep Marsh — in active, intermittent "beaded" watercourse
4.1	Transitional Open Water Wetland
4.8	Transitional Open Water Wetland — in abandoned channel or watercourse (oxbow)
4.9	Transitional Open Water Wetland — in active, intermittent "beaded" watercourse
5.1	Open Water Marsh — <75% of wetland diameter
5.2	Shallow Open Water Wetland — >75% of wetland diameter
5.3	Artificial Shallow Open Water — a deepened natural wetland in which the excavation extends over 10% of wetland diameter
5.4	Artificial Shallow Open Water — totally man-made excavation (dugout, ditch, etc.) in an upland location
5.5	Artificial Shallow Open Water — shallow man-made dam or impoundment in an upland site
5.6	Artificial Shallow Open Water — man-made excavation or dugout in a watercourse or stream channel
5.7	Artificial Shallow Open Water — man-made or beaver dam or impoundment in a watercourse or stream channel
5.8	Shallow Open Water Wetland — in abandoned channel or watercourse (oxbow)
5.9	Shallow Open Water Wetland — in active, intermittent "beaded" watercourse
6.1	Open Alkali Wetland
8.1	Spring
8.2	Fen
8.3	Bog
8.4	Swamp
9.1	Artificial Stream Channel (drainage or irrigation ditch or stream diversion channel) — dominated by emergent (usually Deep Marsh) wetland vegetation
9.2	Artificial Stream Channel (drainage or irrigation ditch or stream diversion channel) — shallow open water dominated by submergent aquatics
9.3	Natural Perennial or Semi-perennial Stream Channel — dominated by emergent (usually Deep Marsh) wetland vegetation
9.5	Natural Perennial or Semi-perennial Stream Channel — shallow open water dominated by submergent aquatics
9.6	Natural Perennial Stream Channel — unvegetated waterwashed bed
9.8	Artificial Lake — large deep impoundment
9.9	Natural Lake

REFERENCES

Anderson, M. G. 1978. Distribution and production of sago pondweed (*Potamogeton pectinatus*) on a northern prairie marsh. Ecol. 59:154–60.

Anderson, M. G., and R. E. Jones. 1976. Submerged aquatic vascular plants of east Delta Marsh. Winnipeg: Manitoba Dept. Renewable Resour. Trans. Serv.

Anonymous. 1986. Wetlands in Canada: A valuable resource. Land Use Directorate. Fact Sheet 86-4. Ottawa: Environ. Can.

Bach, R. N. 1950. Some general aspects of North Dakota water areas and their study. N. Dak. Game Fish Dept.

Bailey, F. M. 1916. Characteristic birds of the Dakota prairies. III: Among the sloughs and marshes. Condor 18:14–21.

Bailey, V. 1888. Report on some of the results of a trip through parts of Minnesota and Dakota. *In* Report of the Commissioner of Agriculture: 1887, 426–54. Washington, D.C.: GPO.

Bakker, J. P., and J. C. Ruyter. 1981. Effects of five years of grazing on a salt marsh. Vegetatio 44:81–100.

Ballantyne, A. K. 1984a. Salinity map of the agricultural region of Saskatchewan (south half). Regina: Land Resour. Res. Inst., Agric. Can.

———. 1984b. Salinity map of the agricultural region of Saskatchewan (north half). Regina: Land Resour. Res. Inst., Agric. Can.

Barker, W. T., and G. W. Fulton. 1979. Analysis of wetland vegetation on selected areas in southwestern North Dakota. N. Dak. Reg. Environ. Assess. Prog. Rep. No. 79-15. Fargo: N. Dak. State Univ.

Barker, W. T., and G. E. Larson. 1976. Aquatic plant communities. *In* Wildlife biological and vegetation resources of the Dunn County coal gasification project study area, 2.2C1-2.2C96. Fargo: N. Dak. State Univ.

Bassett, P. A. 1980. Some aspects of grazing on vegetation dynamics in the Camargue, France. Vegetatio 43:173–84.

Batt, B. D. J., P. J. Caldwell, C. B. Davis, J. A. Kadlec, R. M. Kaminski, H. R. Murkin, and A. G. van der Valk. 1983. The Delta Waterfowl Research Station-Ducks Unlimited (Canada) marsh ecology research program. *In* First Western Hemisphere Waterfowl and Waterbird Symposium, ed. H. Boyd, 10–23. Ottawa: Can. Wildlife Serv.

Bellrose, F. C., F. L. Paveglio, Jr., and D. W. Steffeck. 1979. Waterfowl populations and the changing environment of the Illinois River Valley. Ill. Nat. Hist. Surv. Bull. 32.

Bishop, R. A. 1981. Iowa's wetlands. Proc. Iowa Acad. Sci. 88:11–16.

Bishop, R. A., R. D. Andrews, and R. J. Bridges. 1979. Marsh management and its relationship to vegetation, waterfowl, and muskrats. Proc. Iowa Acad. Sci. 86:50–56.

Boller, H. A. 1972. Among the Indians: Four years on the upper Missouri, 1858–1862. Ed. M. M. Quaife. Lincoln: Univ. Nebr. Press.

Bonnewell, V., W. L. Koukkari, and D. C. Pratt. 1983. Light, oxygen, and temperature requirements for *Typha latifolia* seed germination. Can. J. Bot. 61:1330–36.

Borchert, J. R. 1950. The climate of the central North American grassland. Ann. Assoc. Amer. Geogr. 40:1–39.

Born, S. M., S. A. Smith, and D. A. Stephenson. 1979. Hydrogeology of glacial-terrain lakes, with management and planning applications. J. Hydrol. 43:7–43.

Burgess, R. L., and D. T. Disrud. 1969. Wetland vegetation of the Turtle Mountains, North Dakota. Prairie Nat. 1:19–30.

Buttery, B. R., and J. M. Lambert. 1965. Competition between *Glyceria maxima*
and *Phragmites communis* in the region of the Surlingham Broad. I: The
competition mechanism. J. Ecol. 53:163–81.

Clambey, G. K. 1975. A survey of wetland vegetation in north-central Iowa.
Ph.D. diss., Iowa State Univ., Ames.

Cowardin, L. M. 1982. Some conceptual and semantic problems in wetland
classification and inventory. Wildl. Soc. Bull. 10:57–60.

Cowardin, L. M., V. Carter, F. C. Golet, and E. T. LaRoe. 1979. Classification
of wetlands and deepwater habitats of the United States. U. S. Fish and
Wildl. Serv., FWS/OBS-79/31. Washington, D.C.

Cowardin, L. M., O. S. Gilmer, and L. M. Mechlin. 1981. Characteristics of
central North Dakota wetlands determined from sample aerial photographs
and ground study. Wildl. Soc. Bull. 9:280–88.

Dabbs, D. L. 1971. A study of *Scirpus acutus* and *Scirpus validus* in the Saskatchewan River delta. Can. J. Bot. 49:143–53.

Denig, E. T. 1961. Five Indian tribes of the upper Missouri. ed. J. C. Ewers.
Norman: Univ. Okla. Press.

Diaz, H. F. 1983. Some aspects of major dry and wet periods in the contiguous
United States, 1895–1981. J. Clim. Appl. Meteorol. 22:3–16.

_____. 1986. An analysis of twentieth century climate fluctuations in northern
North America. J. Clim. Appl. Meteorol. 25:1625–57.

Diiro, B. W. 1982. Effects of burning and mowing on seasonal whitetop ponds in
southern Manitoba. Master's thesis, Iowa State Univ., Ames.

Disrud, D. T. 1968. Wetland vegetation of the Turtle Mountains of North Dakota. Master's thesis, N. Dak. State Univ., Fargo.

Dix, R. L., and F. E. Smeins. 1967. The prairie, meadow, and marsh vegetation
of Nelson County, North Dakota. Can. J. Bot. 45:21–58.

Dodd, J. D., and R. T. Coupland. 1966. Vegetation of saline areas in Saskatchewan. Ecol. 47:958–68.

Duvick, D. N., and T. J. Blasing. 1981. A dendroclimatic reconstruction of
annual precipitation amounts in Iowa since 1680. Water Resourc. Res.
17:1183–89.

Eisenlohr, W. S., Jr. 1972a. Hydrology of marshy ponds on the coteau. *In* Hydrology of marsh-ridden areas, 305–11. Proc. Minsk Symp., June 1972.
Paris: Unesco Press.

_____. 1972b. Hydrologic investigations of prairie pothole in North Dakota,
1959–1968. U. S. Geol. Surv. Prof. Paper 585-A.

Eisenlohr, W. S., and C. E. Sloan. 1968. Generalized hydrology of prairie
potholes on the Coteau du Missouri, North Dakota. U. S. Geol. Surv. Circ.
558.

Erlandson, C. S. 1987. The potential role of seed banks in the restoration of
drained prairie wetlands. Master's thesis, Iowa State Univ., Ames.

Evans, C. D., and K. E. Black. 1956. Duck production studies on the prairie
potholes of South Dakota. U. S. Fish and Wildl. Serv. Spec. Sci. Rep.
Wildlife 32.

Evans, C. D., A. S. Hawkins, and W. H. Marshall. 1952. Movements of waterfowl broods in Manitoba. U. S. Fish and Wildl. Serv. Spec. Sci. Rep.
Wildlife 16.

Frayer, W. E., T. J. Monahan, D. C. Bowden, and F. A. Graybill. 1983. Status and trends of wetlands and deepwater habitats in the coterminous United States, 1950's to 1970's. Fort Collins: Dept. Forest and Wood Sci., Colo. State Univ.

Freeze, R. A. 1969. Hydrology of the Good Spirit Lake drainage basin, Saskatchewan: A preliminary analysis. Inland Waters Branch, Can. Dept. Energy, Mines, Resourc. Tech. Bull. 14.

Froebel, C. 1870. Notes of some observations made in Dakota, during two expeditions under the command of General Alfred Sully against the hostile Sioux, in the years 1864 and 1865. Proc. Lyc. Nat. Hist. New York 1:4–73.

Fulton, G. W., and W. T. Barker. 1981. Above ground biomass of selected wetlands of the Missouri Coteau. Proc. N. Dak. Acad. Sci. 35:6.

Fulton, G. W., R. J. Bigler, W. T. Barker, and J. L. Richardson. 1979. Soil and plant relationships of selected wetlands on the Missouri Coteau. Proc. N. Dak. Acad. Sci. 33:63.

Fulton, G. W., J. L. Richardson, and W. T. Barker. 1986. Wetland soils and vegetation. N. Dak. Res. Rep. 106. Fargo: Agric. Exper. Stat., N. Dak. State Univ.

Furniss, O. C. 1938. The waterfowl season in the Prince Albert District, central Saskatchewan. Wilson Bull. 50:17–27.

Galinato, M. I., and A. G. van der Valk. 1986. Seed germination traits of annuals and emergents recruited during drawdowns in the Delta Marsh, Manitoba, Canada. Aquat. Bot. 26:89–102.

Grace, J. B., and J. S. Harrison. 1986. The biology of Canadian weeds. 73: *Typha latifolia L., Typha angustifolia L.* and *Typha x glauca Godr.* Can. J. Plant Sci. 66:351–79.

Grace, J. B., and R. G. Wetzel. 1981. Habitat partitioning and competitive displacement in cattails (Typha): Experimental field studies. Amer. Nat. 188:453–74.

Hadley, E. B., and R. P. Buccos. 1967. Plant community composition and net primary production within a native eastern North Dakota prairie. Amer. Midl. Nat. 77:116–27.

Hammer, U. T., and J. M. Heseltine. 1987. Aquatic macrophytes in saline lakes of the Canadian provinces. Hydrobiol. (Submitted for publication.)

Hammer, U. T., R. C. Haynes, J. M. Heseltine, and S. M. Swanson. 1975. The saline lakes of Saskatchewan. Verh. Int. Ver. Limnol. 19:589–98.

Hare, F. K., and M. K. Thomas. 1979. Climate Canada. Toronto, Canada: John Wiley and Sons.

Harris, S. W., and W. H. Marshall. 1963. Ecology of water-level manipulations on a northern marsh. Ecol. 44:331–44.

Hayden, A. 1943. A botanical survey in the Iowa lake region of Clay and Palo Alto counties. Iowa State College J. Sci. 17:277–416.

Henry, A., and D. Thompson. 1965. New light on the early history of the greater northwest: The manuscript journals of Alexander Henry and David Thompson, 1799–1814. ed. E. Coues. Minneapolis: Ross and Hains.

Hewes, L., and P. E. Frandson. 1952. Occupying the wet prairie: The role of artificial drainage in Story County, Iowa. Ann. Amer. Assoc. Geogr. 42:24–50.

Hibbard, E. 1956. Waterfowl production, pothole inventory and waterfowl movements in the Cleveland, North Dakota area. N. Dak. Game and Fish Dept., Pittman-Robertson Div., Project No. W-38-R-3.

Hilliard, M. A. 1974. The effects of regulated livestock grazing on waterfowl production. Utah Dept. Nat. Resour. Publ. 74-8.

Husband, B. 1985. Ecology of *Ruppia occidentalis* S. Wats. Master's thesis, Univ. Alberta, Edmonton.

Jackson, H. O., and W. C. Starrett. 1959. Turbidity and sedimentation at Lake Chautaqua, Illinois. J. Wildl. Manage. 23:157–68.

Jessen, R. L., J. P. Lindmeier and R. E. Farmes. 1964. A study of duck nesting and production as related to land use in Mahnomen County, Minnesota. Minn. Dept. Conserv. Tech. Bull. 8.

Johnson, W. C., R. A. Maynes, and T. L. Sharik. 1982. Use of vegetation in delineating wetland borders in the Upper Missouri River Basin of the north-central United States. Tech. Rep. Y-82-1. Blacksburg: Va. Polytech. Inst. State Univ.

Kaminski, R. H., and H. H. Prince. 1981. Dabbling duck and aquatic macroin-vertebrate responses to manipulated wetland habitat. J. Wildl. Manage. 44:1–15.

Kantrud, H. A. 1986. Effects of vegetation manipulation on breeding waterfowl in prairie wetlands – a literature review. U. S. Fish and Wildl. Serv. Tech. Rep. 3.

Karl, T. R., and A. J. Koscielny. 1982. Drought in the United States: 1895–1981. J. Climatol. 2:313–29.

Karl, T. R., and W. E. Riebsame. 1984. The identification of 10- to 20-year temperature and precipitation fluctuations in the contiguous United States. J. Clim. Appl. Meteorol. 23:950–66.

Keith, L. B. 1958. Some effects of increasing soil salinity on plant communities. Can. J. Bot. 36:79–89.

––––––. 1961. A study of waterfowl ecology on small impoundments in south-eastern Alberta. Wildl. Soc., Wildl. Monogr. No. 6.

Kollman, A. L., and M. K. Wali. 1976. Intraseasonal variations in environmen-tal and productivity relations of *Potamogeton pectinatus* communities. Arch. Hydrobiol. Suppl. 50:439–72.

Lacate, D. S. 1969. Guidelines for bio-physical land classification. Dept. Fish. For., Can. For. Serv. Publ. No. 1264.

Lewis, F. J., E. S. Downing, and E. H. Moss. 1928. The vegetation of Alberta. II: The swamp, moor and bog forest vegetation of central Alberta. J. Ecol. 16:19–70.

L'Hirondelle, S. J. 1980. The effect of salt concentrations on ecological and physiological aspects of growth of *Distichlis stricta*. Master's thesis, Univ. Alberta, Edmonton.

Lieffers, V. J. 1983. Growth of *Typha latifolia* in Boreal forest habitats as measured by double sampling. Aquat. Bot. 15:335–48.

Lieffers, V. J., and J. M. Shay. 1981. The effects of water level on the growth and reproduction of *Scirpus maritimus* var. paludosus. Can. J. of Bot. 59:118–25.

––––––. 1982a. Seasonal growth and standing crop of *Scirpus maritimus* var. *paludosus* in Saskatchewan. Can. J. Bot. 60:117–25.

––––––. 1982b. Distribution and variation in growth of *Scirpus maritimus* var. *paludosus* on the Canadian prairies. Can. J. Bot. 60:1938–49.

––––––. 1983. Ephemeral saline lakes on the Canadian prairies: Their classifica-tion and management for emergent macrophyte growth. Hydrobiol. 105:85–94.

Lissey, A. 1968. Surficial mapping of groundwater flow systems with application to the Oak River Basin, Manitoba. Master's thesis, Univ. Saskatchewan, Saskatoon.

_____. 1971. Depression-focused transient groundwater flow patterns in Manitoba. Geol. Assoc. Can. Spec. Paper 9:333–41.

Logan, T. H. 1975. Characteristics of small impoundments in western Oklahoma, their value as waterfowl habitat and potential for management. Master's thesis. Okla. State Univ., Stillwater.

Looman, J. 1981. The vegetation of the Canadian Prairie Provinces. III: Aquatic and semi-aquatic vegetation. Phytocoenologia 9:473–97.

_____. 1982. The vegetation of the Canadian Prairie Provinces. III: Aquatic and semi-aquatic vegetation, Pt. 2: Freshwater marshes and bogs. Phytocoenologia 10:401–23.

_____. 1986a. The vegetation of the Canadian Prairie Provinces. III: Aquatic and semi-aquatic plant communities, Pt. 3: Aquatic plant communities. Phytocoenologia 14:19–54.

_____. 1986b. The vegetation of the Canadian Prairie Provinces. IV: The woody vegetation, Pt. 2: Wetland shrubbery. Phytocoenologia 14:439–66.

Löve, A., and D. Löve. 1954. Vegetation of a prairie marsh. Bull. Torrey Bot. Club 81:16–34.

Macaulay, A. J. 1973. Taxonomic and ecological relationships of *Scirpus acutus* Muhl. and *S. validus* Vahl. (Cyperaceae) in southern Manitoba. Ph.D. diss., Univ. Manitoba, Winnipeg.

Madsen, C. 1986. Wetland restoration: A pilot project. J. Soil Water Conserv. 41:159–60.

Marean, H. W., and G. B. Jones. 1903. Soil survey of Story County, Iowa. Field Operations of the Bureau of Soils. Washington, D.C.: Cited in Hewes and Frandson (1952).

Martin, A. C., N. Hotchkiss, F. M. Uhler, and W. S. Bourn. 1953. Classification of wetlands of the United States. U. S. Fish and Wildl. Serv., Spec. Sci. Rep. Wildl. 20.

Martin, D. B., and W. A. Hartman. 1986. The effect of cultivation on sediment composition and deposition in prairie pothole wetlands. Yankton, S. Dak.: U.S. Fish and Wildl. Serv., Nat. Fish. Contaminant Res. Stn.

Metcalf, F. P. 1931. Wild duck foods of North Dakota lakes. U. S. Dept. Agric. Tech. Bull. 221.

Meyboom, P. 1966. Unsteady groundwater flow near a willow ring in hummocky moraine. J. Hydrol. 4:38–62.

_____. 1967. Groundwater studies in the Assiniboine River drainage basin. II: Hydrologic characteristics of phreatophyte vegetation in south-central Saskatchewan. Geol. Surv. Can. Bull. 139.

Millar, J. B. 1971. Shoreline-area ratio as a factor in the rate of water loss from small sloughs. Hydrol. 14:259–84.

_____. 1973. Vegetation changes in shallow marsh wetlands under improving moisture regime. Can. J. Bot. 51:1443–57.

_____. 1976. Wetland classification in western Canada. Can. Wildl. Serv., Rep. Ser. No. 37.

Moyle, J. B. 1945. Some chemical factors influencing the distribution of aquatic plants in Minnesota. Amer. Midl. Nat. 34:402–20.

_____. 1964. Ducks and land use in Minnesota. Minn. Dept. Conserv. Tech. Bull. 8.

Murkin, H. R., R. M. Kaminski, and R. D. Titman. 1982. Responses by dabbling ducks and aquatic invertebrates to an experimentally manipulated cattail marsh. Can. J. Zool. 60:2234–332.

Murkin, H. R., B. D. J. Batt, P. J. Caldwell, C. B. Davis, J. A. Kadlec, and A. G. van der Valk. 1985. Perspectives on the Delta Waterfowl Research Station-Ducks Unlimited Canada marsh ecology research program. Trans. N. Amer. Wildl. Nat. Resour. Conf. 49:253–61.

Neckles, H. A. 1984. Plant and macroinvertebrate responses to water regime in a whitetop marsh. Master's thesis, Univ. Minn., St. Paul.

Neckles, H. A., J. W. Nelson, and R. L. Pederson. 1985. Management of white-top (*Scolochloa festucacea*) marshes for livestock forage and wildlife. Tech. Bull. 1. Portage La Prairie, Manitoba: Delta Waterfowl and Wetlands Res. Stn.

Nord, W. H., C. D. Evans, and G. E. Mann. 1951. Ducks and drainage: Relationship of drainage to waterfowl in the prairie pothole region. Bureau of River Basin Studies, U. S. Fish and Wildl. Serv. Report. Washington, D.C.: GPO.

Olson, R. A. 1979. Ecology of wetland vegetation on selected strip mine ponds and stockdams in the northern Great Plains. Ph.D. diss., N. Dak. State Univ., Fargo.

Pederson, R. L. 1981. Seed bank characteristics of the Delta Marsh, Manitoba: Applications for wetland management. *In* Selected proc. of the midwest conf. on wetland values and manage., ed. B. Richardson, 61–69. Navarre, Minn.: Freshwater Soc.

——. 1983. Abundance and distribution, and diversity of buried viable seed populations in the Delta Mash, Manitoba. Ph.D. diss., Iowa State Univ., Ames.

Pederson, R. L., and A. G. van der Valk. 1985. Vegetation change and seed banks: Ecological and management implications. Trans. N. Amer. Wildl. Nat. Resour. Conf. 49:271–80.

Peters, T. W. 1981. Solonetzic soils of Alberta. Edmonton, Alberta: Agric. Can. Soil Surv. Alberta Inst. Pedol.

Phillips, S. F. 1976. The relationship between evapotranspiration by *Phragmites communis Trin.* and water table fluctuations in the Delta Marsh, Manitoba. Ph.D. diss., Univ. Manitoba, Winnipeg.

Rawson, D. S., and J. E. Moore. 1944. The saline lakes of Saskatchewan. Can. J. Res. 22:141–201.

Reimold, R. J., R. A. Linthurst, and P. L. Wolf. 1975. Effects of grazing on a salt marsh. Biol. Conserv. 8:105–25.

Rowe, J. S., and R. T. Coupland. 1984. Vegetation of the Canadian Plains. Prairie Forum 9:231–48.

Rozkowska, A. D., and A. Rozkowski. 1969. Seasonal changes of slough and lake water chemistry in southern Saskatchewan (Canada). J. Hydrol. 7:1–13.

Schlichtemeier, G. 1967. Marsh burning for waterfowl. Proc. Annu. Tall Timbers Fire Ecol. Conf. 6:41–46.

Scoggan, H. J. 1978–1979. The flora of Canada, Pt. 1–4. Ottawa, Ont.: Natl. Mus. Nat. Sci.

Seabloom, R. W. 1958. A study of production, survival and movements of the Great Plains muskrat (*Ondatra zibethica cinnamoninus*) in North Dakota. Master's thesis, Univ. Minn., St. Paul.

Shaw, S. P., and C. G. Fredine. 1956. Wetlands of the United States. U. S. Fish and Wildl. Serv. Circ. 39.

Shay, J. M., and C. T. Shay. 1986. Prairie marshes in western Canada, with specific reference to the ecology of five emergent macrophytes. Can. J. Bot. 64:443–54.

Shunk, R. A. 1917. Plant associations of Shenford and Owego Townships, Ransom County, North Dakota. Master's thesis, Univ. N. Dak., Grand Forks.

Sifton, H. B. 1959. The germination of light-sensitive seeds of *Typha latifolia L.* Can. J. Bot. 37:719–39.

Sletten, K. K., and G. E. Larson. 1984. Possible relationships between surface water chemistry and aquatic plants in the northern Great Plains. Proc. S. Dak. Acad. Sci. 63:70–76.

Sloan, C. E. 1972. Groundwater hydrology of prairie potholes in North Dakota. U. S. Geol. Surv. Prof. Paper 585-C.

Smeins, F. E. 1965. The grassland and marshes of Nelson County, North Dakota. Master's thesis, Univ. Saskatchewan, Saskatoon.

———. 1967. The wetland vegetation of the Red River Valley and drift prairie regions of Minnesota, North Dakota and Manitoba. Ph.D. diss., Univ. Saskatchewan, Saskatoon.

Smith, A. G. 1969. Waterfowl-habitat relationships on the Lousana, Alberta, waterfowl study area. Can. Wildl. Serv. Rep. Ser. 6.

———. 1971. Ecological factors affecting waterfowl production in the Alberta parklands. U. S. Bur. Sport Fish. Wildl. Resour. Publ. 98.

———. 1972. Factors influencing germination of *Scolochloa festucacea* caryopses. Can. J. Bot. 50:2085–92.

———. 1973a. Production and nutrient status of whitetop. J. Range Manage. 26:117–20.

———. 1973b. Life cycle of the marsh grass, *Scolochloa festucacea.* Can. J. Bot. 51:1661–68.

Smith, R. H. 1953. A study of waterfowl production on artificial reservoirs in eastern Montana. J. Wildl. Manage. 17:276–91.

Smith, S. G. 1967. Experimental and natural hybrids in North American *Typha* (Typhaceae). Amer. Midl. Nat. 78:257–87.

Stewart, R. E., and H. A. Kantrud. 1963. Long-term investigations of pothole complexes on the Missouri Coteau in Stutsman County, North Dakota. Annu. Prog. Rep. Wildl. Res. Work Unit a-7.1. Denver: Denver Wildl. Res. Cent.

———. 1965. Long-term investigations of pothole complexes on the Missouri Coteau in Stutsman County, North Dakota. Annu. Prog. Rep. Work Unit a-7.1. Jamestown, N. Dak.: North. Prairie Wildl. Res. Cent.

———. 1969. Proposed classification of potholes in the glaciated prairie region. Saskatoon Wetlands Sem., Can. Wildl. Serv. Rep. Ser. 6.

———. 1971. Classification of natural ponds and lakes in the glaciated prairie region. U. S. Fish and Wildl. Serv., Resour. Publ. 92.

———. 1972. Vegetation of prairie potholes, North Dakota, in relation to quality of water and other environmental factors. U. S. Geol. Surv. Prof. Paper 585-D.

Stoudt, J. H. 1971. Ecological factors affecting waterfowl production in the Saskatchewan parkland. U. S. Bur. Sport Fish. Wildl., Resour. Publ. 99.

Sugden, L. G., and G. W. Beyersbergen. 1984. Farming intensity on waterfowl breeding grounds in Saskatchewan parklands. Wildl. Soc. Bull. 12:22–26.

Tester, J. R., and W. H. Marshall. 1962. Minnesota prairie management techniques and their wildlife implications. Trans. N. Amer. Wildl. Conf. 27:267–87.

Thompson, D. J. 1982. Effects of fire on *Phragmites australis (Cav.)* Trin. ex Steudel and associated species at Delta Marsh, Manitoba, Canada. Master's thesis, Univ. Manitoba, Winnipeg.

Thompson, D. J., and J. M. Shay. 1985. The effects of fire on *Phragmites communis* in the Delta Marsh, Manitoba. Can. J. Bot. 63:1864–69.

Tiku, B. L. 1976. Effect of salinity on the photosynthesis of the halophyte *Salicornia rubra* and *Distichlis stricta*. Physiol. Plant. 37:23–28.

Tiner, R. W. 1984. Wetlands of the United States: Current status and recent trends. U. S. Fish and Wildl. Serv., Natl. Wetlands Invent.

Ungar, I. A. 1966. Salt tolerance of plants growing in saline areas of Kansas and Oklahoma. Ecol. 47:154–55.

_____. 1970. Species-soil relationships on sulfate dominated soils in South Dakota. Amer. Midl. Nat. 83:343–57.

_____. 1974. Inland halophytes of the United States. *In* Ecology of Halophytes, ed. R. J. Reimold and W. H. Queen, 235–305. New York: Academic Press.

_____. 1978. Halophyte seed germination. Bot. Rev. 44:233–64.

Ungar, I. A., and T. E. Riehl. 1980. The effect of seed reserves on species composition in zonal halophyte communities. Bot. Gaz. 141:447–52.

Ungar, I. A., D. K. Benner, and D. C. McGraw. 1979. The distribution and growth of *Salicornia europaea* on an inland salt pan. Ecol. 60:329–36.

van der Valk, A. G. 1981. Succession in wetlands: A Gleasonian approach. Ecol. 62:688–96.

_____. 1986. The impact of litter and annual plants on recruitment from the seed bank of a lacustrine wetland. Aquat. Bot. 24:13–26.

van der Valk, A. G., and C. B. Davis. 1976a. Changes in composition, structure, and production of plant communities along a perturbed wetland coenocline. Vegetatio 32:87–96.

_____. 1976b. The seed banks of prairie glacial marshes. Can. J. Bot. 54:1832–38.

_____. 1978a. Primary production of prairie glacial marshes. *In* Freshwater wetlands, ed. R. E. Good et al., 21–37. New York: Academic Press.

_____. 1978b. The role of seed banks in the vegetation dynamics of prairie glacial marshes. Ecol. 59:322–35.

_____. 1979. A reconstruction of the recent vegetation history of a prairie marsh, Eagle Lake, Iowa, from its seed bank. Aquat. Bot. 6:29–51.

_____. 1980. The impact of a natural drawdown on the growth of four emergent species in a prairie glacial marsh. Aquat. Bot. 9:301–22.

van der Valk, A. G., S. D. Swanson, and R. F. Nuss. 1983. The response of plant species to burial in three types of Alaskan wetlands. Can. J. Bot. 61:1150–61.

van der Valk, A. G., C. H. Welling, and R. L. Pederson. 1988. Predicting vegetation change in a freshwater wetland: A test of a priori predictions. Proc. Wetland and Waterfowl Symp., Charleston, S. C.

Van Voast, W. A., and R. P. Novitzki. 1968. Ground-water flow related to streamflow and water quality. Water Resour. Res. 4:769–75.

Visher, S. S. 1912. The biology of south-central South Dakota. S. Dak. Geol. Biol. Surv. Bull. 5:61–130.

Wali, M. K. 1976. Comparative studies of some inland saline aquatic ecosystems in North Dakota. N. Dak. Water Resour. Res. Inst. Rep. No. WI-221-033-76. Fargo.

Walker, B. H. 1968. Ecology of herbaceous wetland vegetation in the aspen grove and grassland regions of Saskatchewan. Ph.D. diss., Univ. Saskatchewan, Saskatoon.

Walker, B. H., and R. T. Coupland. 1968. An analysis of vegetation-environment relationships in Saskatchewan sloughs. Can. J. Bot. 46:509–22.

————. 1970. Herbaceous wetland vegetation in the aspen grove and grassland regions of Saskatchewan. Can. J. Bot. 48:1861–78.

Walker, J. M. 1959. Vegetation studies on the Delta Marsh, Manitoba. Master's thesis, Univ. Manitoba, Winnipeg.

————. 1965. Vegetation changes with falling water levels in the Delta Marsh, Manitoba. Ph.D. diss., Univ. Manitoba, Winnipeg.

Walker, J. M., and E. R. Waygood. 1968. Ecology of *Phragmites communis*. I: Photosynthesis of a single shoot in situ. Can. J. Bot. 46:549–55.

Ward, E. 1942. Phragmites management. Trans. N. Amer. Wildl. Conf. 7:294–98.

Ward, P. 1968. Fire in relation to waterfowl habitat of the Delta Marshes. Proc. Tall Timbers Fire Ecol. Conf. 8:254–67.

Watts, W. A., and R. C. Bright. 1968. Pollen, seed, and mollusk analysis of a sediment core from Pickerel Lake, northeastern South Dakota. Bull. Geol. Soc. Amer. 79:855–76.

Watts, W. A., and T. C. Winter. 1966. Plant macrofossils from Kirchner Marsh, Minnesota—a paleoecological study. Bull. Geol. Soc. Amer. 77:1339–59.

Weller, M. W. 1975. Studies of cattail in relation to management for marsh wildlife. Iowa State J. Res. 49:383–412.

————. 1978. Management of freshwater marshes for wildlife. 267–284. *In* Freshwater wetlands, ed. R. E. Good et al. New York: Academic Press.

————. 1981. Freshwater marshes, ecology and wildlife management. Minneapolis: Univ. Minn. Press.

Weller, M. W., and L. H. Fredrickson. 1974. Avian ecology of a managed glacial marsh. Living Bird 12:269–91.

Weller, M. W., and C. E. Spatcher. 1965. Role of habitat in the distribution and abundance of marsh birds. Iowa State Univ. Agric. Home Econ. Exper. Stn. Spec. Rep. No. 43. Ames.

Welling, C. H. 1987. Reestablishment of perennial emergent macrophytes during a drawdown in a lacustrine marsh. Master's thesis, Iowa State Univ., Ames.

Welling, C. H., R. L. Pederson, and A. G. van der Valk. 1988. Recruitment from the seed bank and the development of emergent zonation during a drawdown in a lacustrine, prairie marsh. J. Ecol. 76:483–96.

Williams, R. E. 1968. Flow of groundwater adjacent to small, closed basins in glacial till. Water Resour. Res. 4:777–83.

Wilson, J. N. 1958. The limnology of certain prairie lakes in Minnesota. Amer. Midl. Nat. 59:418–37.

Winter, T. C., and M. R. Carr. 1980. Hydrologic setting of wetlands in the Cottonwood Lake area, Stutsman County, North Dakota. U. S. Geol. Surv. Water Resour. Invest. 80-99.

Zoltai, S. C., and F. C. Pollett. 1983. Wetlands in Canada: their classification, distribution, and use. *In* Mires: swamp, bog, fen and moor, ed. A. J. P. Gore, 245–68. Amsterdam: Elsevier.

Zoltai, S. C., F. C. Pollett, J. K. Jeglum, and G. D. Adams. 1973. Developing a wetland classification for Canada. Proc. Fourth N. Amer. Forest Soils Conf., Laval Univ., Quebec City, Canada.

WILLIAM G. CRUMPTON

6 ALGAE IN NORTHER

ABSTRACT

FOUR ALGAL ASSEMBLAGES are of likely significance in northern prairie wetlands: phytoplankton, metaphyton, epiphytic algae, and epipelic algae. All may display striking and complex patterns that are difficult to generalize. In more productive systems, summer blooms of any or all assemblages are likely, but not predictable. These blooms can be extensive and severe. Particularly in more fertile systems, algae are expected to contribute a major portion of the total primary production, in cases surpassing that of the macrophytes. Research is needed concerning the production of different autotrophic components in wetlands and factors controlling the balance between these components.

KEY WORDS: algae, periphyton, epiphyton, phytoplankton, metaphyton, wetlands, marshes.

PRAIRIE WETLANDS

INTRODUCTION

A LGAE are a major component of most aquatic communities and are undoubtedly important in wetlands. However, there has been very little research on the role of algae in freshwater wetlands and almost none on the role of algae in northern prairie wetlands. This chapter considers the role of algae in wetlands in the prairie pothole region in the United States and Canada and the aspen parkland zone in Canada (see Figure 2.1). Most of what we know or surmise about the role of algae in wetlands is derived from our somewhat better but still limited knowledge of algae in the littoral zone of lakes. In contrast to the tremendous amount of literature on planktonic algae in lakes, there is relatively little information concerning the taxonomy, physiology, and ecology of littoral and marsh algae. Much of the reason for this lack of information stems from the extreme heterogeneity of littoral and wetland habitats, especially on the scale relevant to microorganisms (Allanson 1973). A related problem concerns the methodological difficulties in dealing with these exceptionally complex microbial communities (Austin et al. 1981; Robinson 1983; Wetzel 1983a).

COMMUNITY STRUCTURE

The algae comprise a diverse assemblage of organisms occupying a wide variety of aquatic habitats. As a result, the terminology applied to algae is complex (Hutchinson 1975; Round 1981; Wetzel 1983a, 1983b). Four algal assemblages are of particular significance in prairie wetlands:

WILLIAM G. CRUMPTON, Department of Botany, Iowa State University, Ames, Iowa 50011.

planktonic algae suspended in the open-water zone; metaphyton, which
are unattached but loosely associated with substrata; and two assemblages of periphytic or attached algae, epiphytic algae attached to
plants and epipelic algae growing in or on sediments.

Those algae that grow suspended in the open-water or pelagic zone
of lakes and ponds are referred to as planktonic algae or phytoplankton
and include euplankton and pseudoplankton. The euplankton comprise
those algae that are truly adapted to a planktonic existence. These especially include centric and pseudoraphidean diatoms, a number of unicel-
lular and colonial as well as some filamentous chlorophytes, cyanobacteria, and diverse flagellates (Fig. 6.1). In addition, planktonic communities often include a number of forms more characteristic of attached communities, such as algae that commonly grow and reproduce
in littoral or benthic communities but are occasionally found in suspension. These organisms are referred to as pseudoplankton or tycho-
plankton.

The metaphyton are an assemblage of unattached algae that are
found loosely associated with substrata (Round 1981). These commonly
include filamentous chlorophytes and cyanbacteria, with their associated
epiphytes. This assemblage may also include a variety of normally
planktonic or attached algae that become entangled in the filamentous

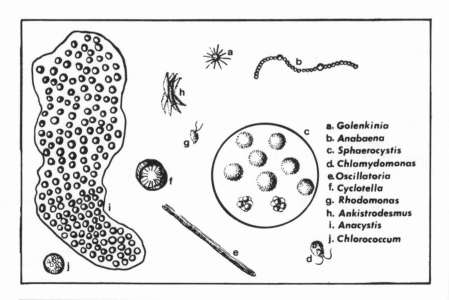

a. *Golenkinia*
b. *Anabaena*
c. *Sphaerocystis*
d. *Chlamydomonas*
e. *Oscillatoria*
f. *Cyclotella*
g. *Rhodomonas*
h. *Ankistrodesmus*
i. *Anacystis*
j. *Chlorococcum*

FIG. 6.1.   Some common, freshwater phytoplankton.

mass. As a result, the origin of the metaphyton is often unclear without detailed studies of all algal communities within a system. However, the metaphyton are not simply the ensnared products of planktonic and periphytic communities but rather a dynamic and productive assemblage (Gurney and Robinson 1987). Metaphyton can form a quite extensive community in prairie wetlands, significant both in terms of production and as food and habitat for invertebrates and waterfowl (Hosseini 1986; Gurney and Robinson 1987; Murkin, Chap. 11).

Those algae that grow attached to substrata are very broadly termed periphytic algae. Sometimes the term periphyton is applied to these algae but this term is widely understood to include a complex community of algae, bacteria, and animals. Periphyton is essentially synonymous with the German *Aufwuchs* and thus analogous to the term plankton, which designates the pelagic community. Benthos has been suggested instead of periphyton, but it is a term widely taken to refer to the animals associated with substrates. There is sufficient confusion over the application of these terms that various authorities advocate revising the terminology, although the specific recommendations of these authorities differ (Hutchinson 1975; Round 1981; Wetzel 1983a, 1983b). In any event, the term periphyton and the less ambiguous term periphytic algae are firmly ingrained in the literature and allow useful categorization (Wetzel 1983b).

Periphytic algae (or the algal benthos of Hutchinson 1975), can be separated into two broad categories, those algae that grow on a solid substratum such as a plant or rock and those algae that grow either in or upon sediments. This distinction is significant as it separates two distinct types of association and two relatively distinct floras, although some evidence suggests these distinctions become blurred in more productive systems (Moss 1981). Those algae that grow attached to solid substrates are referred to as the haptobenthos and include the epiphytic algae, those attached to plants or to other algae, and the epilithic algae, those attached to rocks. Algae that grow in or upon sediments are referred to as the herpobenthos, which is essentially equivalent to epipelic algae in the broadest context of the latter term.

Although the sediments of wetlands may seem to be rather sterile environments, they host a rich microbial flora. The epipelic flora is often evidenced by a greenish brown to black film on the sediment surface and is usually dominated by chlorophytes, cyanobacteria, and especially diatoms (Fig. 6.2). By most accounts, the algae in sediments are considerably more diverse than in planktonic communities and comprise an assemblage very distinct from either the epiphytic or planktonic algae (Round 1981; Wetzel 1983a). Nearly all of the epipelic diatoms are biraphidean and highly motile, mostly Naviculales and Nitzschiales although a few species of Achnanthales are important (Hutchinson 1975; Round 1981).

Naviculales and Nitzschiales are also well represented in epiphytic communities, which is not surprising considering the large number of biraphidean genera and species. However, monoraphidean Achnanthales, pseudoraphidean Fragilariales, and weakly motile Eunotiales assume proportionately greater significance in epiphytic communities, as do the stalked and tube dwelling Naviculales (Fig. 6.3). Chlorophytes and cyanobacteria are also common components of epiphytic communities, often forming massive growths. Outside the diatoms, mucilaginous attachment is common among the epiphytic algae and some have special attachment mechanisms. Epiphytic algae exhibit two distinct types of habit. Some live appressed to the epidermis of the host and are thus firmly attached, while others have only a basal cell or attachment in contact with the host and are thus loosely attached. These latter include what are often termed the overstory species and are very susceptible to grazing (Higashi et al. 1981; Sumner and McIntyre 1982).

PRODUCTION AND DYNAMICS

Wetlands are among the most productive ecosystems in the world, and emergent macrophytes dramatically illustrate the fertility of north-

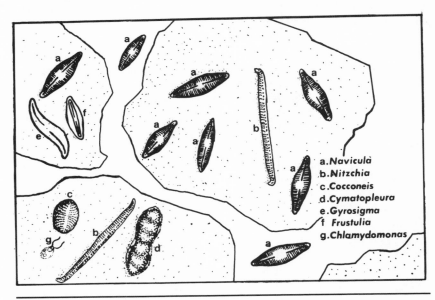

FIG. 6.2.   Examples of epipelic algae from surface sediment.

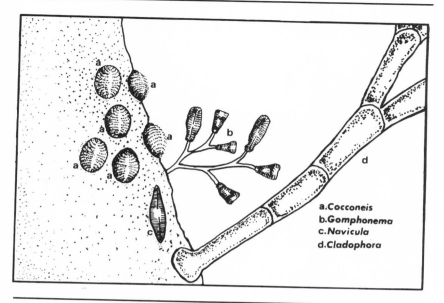

FIG. 6.3.   Epiphytic algae growing on *Cladophora*.

ern prairie wetlands (Murkin, Chap. 11). Patterns in lake morphometry and productivity suggest that algal production should also be very high in such shallow, fertile systems (Fee 1980). Although there is little quantitative information concerning algal production in prairie wetlands, substantial growths of planktonic and periphytic algae are often found in these systems (Hosseini 1986; Murkin, Chap. 11). Algal production may be especially significant because of the potentially high nutritional value of algae. Studies in lake littoral zones show that algal production in such habitats may be quite substantial. Algal production in lake littoral zones varies widely between and within lakes but generally comprises a major portion of littoral zone production, especially in more fertile systems. Per area of lake surface, algal production in littoral zones often approaches and at times surpasses that of macrophytes, especially in shallow, fertile systems (Table 6.1) (Allen 1971; Kowalczewski 1975; Cattaneo and Kalff 1980; Kairesalo 1980; Howard-Williams and Allanson 1981; Wetzel 1983a; Jones 1984). The combined production of phytoplankton, metaphyton, epiphytic algae, and epipelic algae in northern prairie wetlands probably ranges near a few hundred g C/m^{-2}/year, which is comparable to the above ground production of emergent macrophytes in these systems (Murkin Chap. 11). However, while algal production in northern prairie wetlands is clearly high, published data are as yet insufficient to make specific comparisons with

TABLE 6.1. Percent of total littoral zone production by algae and macrophytes in selected systems

Lake	Algae (%)	Macrophyte (%)
Marion Lake, British Columbia	69	31
Lawrence Lake, Michigan	89	11
Laca, USSR	43	57
Kalgaard, Denmark	2	98
Mikolajskie Lake, Poland		
Eulittoral	72	28
Emergent stands	43	57
Fishponds, Bohemia	22	78

Source: Adapted from Wetzel 1983a.

macrophyte production in these systems (Hooper and Robinson 1976; Shamess et al. 1985; Hosseini 1986; Murkin Chap. 11). In addition, the relative significance of algal and macrophyte production in prairie wetlands can be expected to vary in relation to vegetation cycles in these systems.

Prairie wetlands undergo cyclic changes in vegetation related to water-level fluctuations, ranging from dry marsh through regenerating and degenerating stages to an open-water or lake stage (van der Valk and Davis 1978; Kantrud et al., Chap. 5). The dry marsh stage occurs during periods of drought, when much of the marsh is exposed and mudflat annuals and emergent plants establish from seed. This is followed by a regenerating stage when the marsh refloods. Mudflat species are eliminated, emergent perennials spread rapidly, and submersed and free-floating species become established. Macrophyte production is very high during the regenerating stage but algal production may be suppressed. Although substrata for epiphytic algae are most available during the regenerating stage, several studies have documented phytoplankton and periphyton depression by submergent and emergent macrophytes, apparently due to shading (Goulder 1969; Brandl et al. 1970; Straskraba and Pieczynska 1970; Nichols 1973). With continued high water, macrophyte production eventually declines, marking the degenerating stage. Algal production can be expected to increase during the degenerating marsh stage. Shading by macrophytes is reduced and substrata are still available for epiphytic algae. In addition, nutrients released from decomposing vegetation could contribute to increased algal production (cf. Landers 1982). Continued reduction of emergent vegetation produces the lake stage during which submersed plants are suppressed and blooms of planktonic algae are common.

In exceptionally wet years, high water levels may kill much of the emergent vegetation in a prairie wetland. Hosseini (1986) considered the effects of prolonged high water (1 m above normal) on the production of planktonic and epiphytic algae in sections of a prairie lacustrine wetland.

Per area of colonizable substrata, epiphytic algal production was comparable in flooded and unflooded marshes, and on a volumetric basis, phytoplankton production was actually lower in flooded marshes. However, on a marshwide basis, production of epiphytic algae was significantly higher in flooded marshes because of increased substrata for colonization. Likewise, marshwide phytoplankton production was significantly higher in flooded marshes because of the greatly increased volume of water and increased coverage of standing water.

There is considerable evidence that algae are more sensitive than macrophytes to levels of dissolved nutrients (Eminson and Phillips 1978; Phillips et al. 1978; Cattaneo and Kalff 1980; Howard-Williams 1981; Moss 1981; Sand-Jensen and Sondergaard 1981). This is not surprising since even epiphytic algae must largely derive their nutrients from surrounding waters, having no direct access to nutrients available to macrophytes rooted in the sediments. This response has significant implications regarding the relative importance of algal production and macrophyte production as nutrient loads increase. Studies have shown that if algae are sufficiently stimulated, submersed macrophytes can be suppressed due to shading by epiphytes even prior to effects of phytoplankton shading (Eminson and Phillips 1978; Phillips et al. 1978; Moss 1981; Sand-Jensen and Sondergaard 1981; also see Jones et al. 1983). It is quite possible that as nutrient loads to prairie wetlands increase, so may the importance of algal production. By shading out submersed macrophytes, increased algal production could accelerate the development of the lake stage in northern prairie wetlands, during which time overall macrophyte production is low. However, information on the relative production of algae and macrophytes in northern prairie wetlands is scant and it is not clear to what extent extrapolations from other systems might apply.

Most studies of seasonal patterns of algae in prairie wetlands report increases in biomass and production in spring, especially for the diatoms. This can in part be attributed to the onset of improved growth conditions as light and temperature increase following spring thaw. Summer maxima of usually chlorophytes and cyanobacteria are also common, especially in more productive systems (Hickman 1971; Hutchinson 1975; Mason and Bryant 1975; Hooper and Robinson 1976; Hooper-Reid and Robinson 1978a; Cattaneo and Kalff 1978; Bohr 1981; Lazarek 1982; Jenkerson and Hickman 1983; Jones 1984). Prairie wetlands are fertile systems and summer blooms might be expected, especially in those systems receiving high nutrient loads from agriculture or other sources. In some cases, increased nutrients may contribute to increases in biomass and production in the fall (Landers 1982). Various factors are known to affect the dynamics of algae in wetlands and there has been some effort to delineate the relative importance of these factors. Increases are in large part attributed to the onset of improved growth conditions, increased nutrients, light, and temperature. Declines in biomass have been attributed to nutrient limitation (Jorgensen 1957; Brown and Austin 1973; Hooper-Reid and Robinson 1978b), environmental "shock" (Round 1971), and grazing (Mason and Bryant 1975; Cattaneo and Kalff 1980; Cattaneo 1983).

There is some indication that northern prairie wetlands may sustain populations of phytoplankton typical of lakes and that these populations may exhibit patterns not unlike those of phytoplankton in temperate lakes, at least in eutrophic systems (Nicholls and MacCrimmon 1974; Kling 1975; Nicholls 1976; Kalff and Knoechel 1978; Wetzel 1983a). In more fertile systems, changes are accelerated and midsummer blooms of chlorophytes and cyanobacteria are common. Northern prairie wetlands are naturally fertile systems and many are increasingly fertile due to nutrient loads from agriculture (Neely and Baker, Chap. 4). Summer blooms of cyanobacteria are apparently characteristic of prairie pothole lakes. Northern prairie wetlands generally receive substantial nitrate and phosphate loads from agriculture (Neely and Baker, Chap. 4). Nitrate may be lost through denitrification in prairie wetlands, and with continued phosphate loading many of these systems may develop low N:P ratios (cf. Barica et al. 1980). The resulting nitrogen deficit favors blooms of N_2-fixing cyanobacteria (Barica et al. 1980). If N:P ratios are maintained at higher levels, N_2-fixing species are suppressed in favor of non-N_2-fixing cyanobacteria and chlorophytes.

Blooms of N_2-fixing cyanobacteria in northern prairie wetlands are of particular concern. These blooms can be so intense that their collapse may precipitate "summerkill" of fish populations in prairie pothole lakes (Barica 1975; Barica et al. 1980; Papst et al. 1980; Coulombe and Robinson 1981). The exact mechanisms involved in bloom collapse are not always clear. There is some indication that nutrient stress may precede and perhaps set the conditions for collapse (Healey and Hendzel 1976). However, combinations of photo-oxidation, O_2 toxicity, and cyanophage-induced cell lysis have all been identified as probable factors in bloom collapse, and it is likely that there is no single triggering mechanism (Coulombe and Robinson 1981). Regardless of the triggering mechanism, bloom collapse can result in O_2 depletion throughout the water column and massive fish kills. This result is dependent on thermal instability of the water column during or following bloom collapse, a likely condition in such shallow systems (Papst et al. 1980).

Patterns of epiphytic algal growth are made more complex by temporal and spatial variation in macrophytes which provide the substrata for colonization and growth (Sheldon and Boylen 1975; Gons 1982; Morin and Kimball 1983; Riber et al. 1984). This dependence is demonstrated by the development of epiphytic algae on successive leaves of aquatic macrophytes, with, of course, less algae on the youngest leaves (Hutchinson 1975; Sheldon and Boylen 1975; Morin and Kimball 1983; also see Riber et al. 1984). An additional complication in prairie glacial marshes is the cyclic nature of the vegetation, related to water-level fluctuations in these systems (van der Valk and Davis 1978; Hosseini 1986). In addition, recent studies have renewed the controversy over the relationship between periphytic algae and the substrata (Cattaneo 1978; Cattaneo and Kalff 1979; Eminson and Moss 1980; Cattaneo and Kalff 1981; Gough and Gough 1981). Goldsborough and Robinson (1985) found that the epiphytic algae associated with the underside of *Lemna* in a prairie wetland were ubiquitous throughout the marsh in spring and fall but were very host-specific during midsummer. Sufficiently detailed population studies leave little doubt that the dynamics and to some extent occurrence of algal taxa are related to the macrophyte host (Pip and Robinson 1982; Shamess et al. 1985). However, the bases of these relationships are unclear and it is possible that the relationships themselves may become blurred as systems become more productive (Moss 1981).

Metaphyton are perhaps the least well studied and most conspicuous algal assemblage in prairie wetlands. Although blooms of metaphyton can be rapid and extensive, their occurrence can also be highly variable both spatially and temporally, perhaps due to the inherent variation in littoral and marsh habitats (Pieczynska 1971; Hosseini 1986; Gurney and Robinson 1987). Floating masses of filamentous metaphyton derived from the periphytic community are especially common in eutrophic systems (Hillebrand 1983). In such cases, a mat of these algae may develop sufficiently to trap oxygen bubbles evolved during photosynthesis. As growth continues, bubbles can accumulate in sufficient quantities to literally buoy the algal mat to the surface. When production is low as on cloudy days, mats may sink and be much less conspicuous. Hosseini (1986) reported much higher metaphyton biomass in marshes flooded for one or two years than in unflooded marshes. He suggested that reduced shading by emergent macrophytes in flooded marshes was the primary reason for differences in metaphyton biomass. Subsequent studies in the same marshes demonstrated a significant negative correlation between metaphyton cover and the density of emergent vegetation, again suggesting the importance of shading (Gurney and Robinson 1987). Although there have been few attempts to quantify the production of metaphyton, their importance apparently increases during extreme high-water stages in northern prairie wetlands (Hosseini 1986).

However, it is not clear that this would be true for the lake stage of a cycling wetland, since metaphyton production is lowest in open-water areas (Gurney and Robinson 1987).

CONCLUSIONS

It is probably premature to draw specific conclusions regarding either the role of algae in northern prairie wetlands or the role of various factors affecting algal production. However, it is clear that algae are much more important in prairie wetlands than the amount of research devoted to them might imply. In addition, physical and chemical characters of wetlands are important determinants not only of production but also of the balance between different autotrophic components. Any substantial progress in our understanding of algae in prairie wetlands will require consideration of these interactions as well as the spatial and temporal heterogeneity that is an inherent and essential character of freshwater wetlands.

REFERENCES

Allanson, B. R. 1973. The fine structure of the periphyton of *Chara* sp. and *Potamogeton natans* from Wytham Pond, Oxford and its significance to the macrophyte-periphyton metabolic model of R. G. Wetzel and H. L. Allen. Freshwater Biol. 3:535–41.

Allen, H. L. 1971. Primary productivity, chemo-organotrophy, and nutritional interactions of epiphytic algae and bacteria on macrophytes in the littoral of a lake. Ecol. Monogr. 41:97–127.

Austin, A., S. Lang, and M. Pomeroy. 1981. Simple methods for sampling periphyton with observations on sampler design criteria. Hydrobiol. 85:33–47.

Barica, J. 1975. Collapses of algal blooms in prairie pothole lakes: Their mechanism and ecological impact. Internat. Ver. Theor. Angew. Limnol. Verh. 19:606–15.

Barica, J., H. Kling, and J. Gibson. 1980. Experimental manipulation of algal bloom composition by nitrogen addition. Can. J. Fish. Aquat. Sci. 37:1175–83.

Begres, F. M. 1971. The diatoms of Clear Lake and Ventura Marsh, Iowa. Ph.D. diss., Iowa State Univ., Ames.

Bohr, R. 1981. Do climax algal systems exist? Internat. Ver. Theor. Angew. Limnol. Verh. 21:1481–83.

Brandl, Z., J. Brandlova, and M. Postolkova. 1970. The influence of submerged vegetation on the photosynthesis of phytoplankton in ponds. Rozpr. Cesk. Akad. Ved. Rada Mat. Prir. Ved. 80:33–62.

Brock, T. D. 1970. Photosynthesis by algal epiphytes of *Utricularia* in Everglades National Park. Bull. Mar. Sci. 20:952–56.

Brown, D. J. 1972. Primary production and seasonal succession of the phytoplankton component of Crescent Pond, Delta Marsh, Manitoba. Master's thesis, Univ. Manitoba, Winnipeg.

Brown, S. D. 1973a. Site variation in littoral periphyton populations: Correlation and regression with environmental factors. Internat. Rev. Gesamten Hydrobiol. 58:437–61.

_____. 1973b. Species diversity of periphyton communities in the littoral of a temperate lake. Internat. Rev. Gesamten Hydrobiol. 58:787–800.

Brown, S. D., and A. P. Austin. 1973. Spatial and temporal variation in periphyton and physio-chemical conditions in the littoral of a lake. Arch. Hydrobiol. 71:183–232.

Carignan, R., and J. Kalff. 1982. Phosphorus release by submerged macrophytes: Significance to epiphyton and phytoplankton. Limnol. Oceanogr. 27:419–27.

Cattaneo, A. 1978. The microdistribution of epiphytes on the leaves of natural and artificial macrophytes. Br. Phycol. J. 13:183–88.

_____. 1983. Grazing on epiphytes. Limnol. Oceanogr. 28:124–32.

Cattaneo, A., and J. Kalff. 1978. Seasonal changes in the epiphyte community of natural and artificial macrophytes in Lake Memphremagog (Que. & Vt.). Hydrobiol. 60:135–44.

_____. 1979. Primary production of algae growing on natural and artificial aquatic plants: A study of interactions between epiphytes and their substrate. Limnol. Oceanogr. 24:1031–37.

_____. 1980. The relative contribution of aquatic macrophytes and their epiphytes to the production of macrophyte beds. Limnol. Oceanogr. 25:280–89.

_____. 1981. Reply to comment by Gough and Gough. Limnol. Oceanogr. 26:988–89.

Coulombe, A., and G. G. C. Robinson. 1981. Collapsing *Aphanizomenon flos-aquae* blooms: O_2 toxicity, and cyanophages. Can. J. Bot. 59:1277–84.

Cuker, E. 1983. Grazing and nutrient interactions in controlling the activity and composition of the epilithic algal community of an arctic lake. Limnol. Oceanogr. 28:133–41.

Eminson, D., and B. Moss. 1980. The composition and ecology of periphyton communities in freshwaters. I: The influence of host type and external environment and community composition. Br. Phycol. J. 15:429–46.

Eminson, D., and G. Phillips. 1978. A laboratory experiment to examine the effects of nutrient enrichment on macrophyte and epiphyte growth. Internat. Ver. Theor. Angew. Limnol. Verh. 20:82–87.

Fee, E. J. 1979. A relation between lake morphometry and primary productivity and its use in interpreting whole-lake eutrophication experiments. Limnol. Oceanogr. 24:401–16.

_____. 1980. Comment on "A relation between lake morphometry and primary productivity and its use in interpreting whole-lake eutrophication experiments." Limnol. Oceanogr. 25:1147–49.

Fitzgerald, G. P. 1969. Some factors in the competition or antagonism between bacteria, algae, and aquatic plants. J. Phycol. 5:351–59.

Goldsborourgh, L. G., and G. G. C. Robinson. 1985. Seasonal succession of diatom epiphyton on dense mats of Lemna minor. Can. J. Bot. 63:2332–39.

Gons, H. J. 1982. Structural and functional characteristics of epiphyton and epipelon in relation to their distribution in Lake Vechten. Hydrobiol. 95:79–114.

Gough, S. B., and L. P. Gough. 1981. Comment on "Primary production of algae growing on natural and artificial plans: A study of interactions between epiphytes and their substrate." Limnol. Oceanogr. 26:987–88.

Goulder, R. 1969. Interactions between the rates of production of a freshwater macrophyte and phytoplankton in a pond. Oikos 20:300–309.

Gurney, S. E., and G. G. C. Robinson. 1987. The influence of water level manipulation on metaphyton production in a temperate freshwater marsh. Internat. Ver. Theor. Angew. Limnol. Verh. 23:in press.

Healey, F. P., and L. L. Hendzel. 1976. Physiological changes during the course of blooms of *Aphanizomenon flos-aquae*. J. Fish. Res. Board Can. 33:36–41.

Hickman, M. 1971. The standing crop and primary productivity of the epiphyton attached to *Equisetum fluviatile* L. in Priddy Pool, North Somerset. Br. Phycol. J. 6:51–59.

———. 1978. Ecological studies on the epipelic algal community in five prairie-parkland lakes in central Alberta, Canada. Can. J. Bot. 56:991–1009.

Hickman, M., and C. G. Jenkerson. 1978. Phytoplankton primary productivity and population efficiency studies in a prairie parkland near Edmonton, Alberta, Canada. Internat. Rev. Gesamten Hydrobiol. 63:1–24.

Higashi, M., T. Miura, K. Tanimizu, and Y. Iwasa. 1981. Effect of the feeding activity of snails on the biomass and productivity of an algal community attached to a reed stem. Internat. Ver. Theor. Angew. Limnol. Verh. 21:590–95.

Hillebrand, H. 1983. Development and dynamics of floating clusters of filamentous algae. *In* Periphyton of freshwater ecosystems, ed. R. G. Wetzel. Dev. Hydrobiol. 17:31–39.

Hooper, N. M., and G. G. C. Robinson. 1976. Primary production of epiphytic algae in a marsh pond. Can. J. Bot. 54:2810–15.

Hooper-Reid, N. M., and G. G. C. Robinson. 1978a. Seasonal dynamics of epiphytic algal growth in a marsh pond: Productivity, standing crop, and community composition. Can. J. Bot. 56:2434–40.

———. 1978b. Seasonal dynamics of epiphytic algal growth in a marsh pond: Composition, metabolism, and nutrient availability, Can. J. Bot. 56:2441–48.

Hosseini, S. Y. 1986. The effects of water level fluctuations on algal communities of freshwater marshes. Ph.D. diss., Iowa State Univ., Ames.

Howard-Williams, C. 1981. Studies on the ability of a *Potamogeton pectinatus* community to remove dissolved nitrogen and phosphorus compounds from lake water. J. Appl. Ecol. 18:619–37.

Howard-Williams, C., and B. R. Allanson. 1981. An integrated study on littoral and pelagic primary production in a Southern African coastal lake. Arch. Hydrobiol. 92:507–34.

Hutchinson, G. E. 1975. A treatise on limnology. III: Limnological Botany. New York: John Wiley and Sons.

Jansson, M. 1980. Role of benthic algae in transport of nitrogen from sediment to lake water in a shallow clearwater lake. Arch. Hydrobiol. 89:101–9.

Jenkerson, C. G., and M. Hickman. 1983. The spatial and temporal distribution of an epiphytic algal community in a shallow prairie-parkland lake, Alberta, Canada. Holarctic Ecol. 6:41–58.

Jones, R. C. 1980. Productivity of algal epiphytes in a Georgia U.S.A. salt marsh: Effect of inundation frequency and implication for total marsh productivity. Estuaries 3:315–17.

————. 1984. Application of a primary production model to epiphytic algae in a shallow, eutrophic lake. Ecol. 65:1895–1903.

Jones, R. C., and M. S. Adams. 1982. Seasonal variations in photosynthetic response of algae epiphytic on *Myriophyllum spicatum* L. Aquat. Bot. 13:317–30.

Jones, R. C., K. Walti, and M. S. Adams. 1983. Phytoplankton as a factor in the decline of the submersed macrophyte *Myriophyllum spicatum* L. in Lake Wingra, Wisconsin, U.S.A. Hydrobiol. 107:213–19.

Jorgensen, E. G. 1957. Diatom periodicity and silicon assimilation. Dansk Bot. Ark. 18:1–54.

Kairesalo, T. 1980. Comparison of in situ photosynthetic activity of epiphytic, epipelic and planktonic algal communities in an oligotrophic lake, southern Finland. J. Phycol. 16:57–62.

Kalff, J. Phytoplankton and their dynamics in oligotrophic and eutrophic lakes. Annu. Rev. Ecol. Sys. 9:475–95.

Kalff, J., and R. Knoechel. 1978. Phytoplankton and their dynamics in oligo-trophic and eutrophic lakes. Annu. Rev. Ecol. Syst. 9:475–95.

Kling, H. 1975. Phytoplankton successions and species distribution in prairie ponds of the Erickson-Elphinstone district, Southwestern Manitoba. Res. and Dev. Dir. Freshwater Inst. No. 512.

Kowalczewski, A. 1975. Periphyton primary production in zone of submerged vegetation of Mikolajskie Lake. Ekol. Pol. 23:509–43.

Landers, D. H. 1982. Effects of naturally senescing aquatic macrophytes on nutrient chemisty and chlorophyll *a* of surrounding waters. Limnol. Oceanogr. 27:428–39.

Lazarek, S. 1982. Structure and productivity of epiphytic algal communities on *Lobelia dortmanna* L. in acidified and limed lakes. Water, Air, Soil Pollut. 18:333–42.

Mason, C. F., and H. J. Bryant. 1975. Periphyton production and grazing by chironomids in Alderfen Broad, Norfolk. Freshwater Biol. 5:271–77.

Millie, D. F., and R. L. Lowe. 1981. Diatoms new to Ohio and the Laurentian Great Lakes. Ohio J. Sci. 81:195–206.

Moore, J. W. 1980. Attached and planktonic algal communities in some inshore areas of Great Bear Lake. Can. J. Bot. 58:2294–2308.

Morin, J. O., and K. D. Kimball. 1983. Relationship of macrophyte-mediated changes in the water column to periphyton composition and abundance. Freshwater Biol. 13:403–14.

Moss, B. 1968. The chlorophyll-a content of some benthic algal communities. Arch. Hydrobiol. 65:51–62.

————. 1976. The effects of fertilization and fish on community structure and biomass of aquatic macrophytes and epiphytic algal populations: An eco-system experiment. J. Ecol. 64:313–42.

————. 1981. The composition and ecology of periphyton communities in freshwater. II: Inter-relationships between water chemistry, phytoplankton populations in a shallow lake and associated reservoirs ('Lund tubes'). Br. Phycol. J. 16:59–76.

Nicholls, K. H. 1976. Nutrient-phytoplankton relationships in the Holland Marsh, Ontario. Ecol. Monogr. 46:179–99.

Nicholls, K. H., and H. R. MacCrimmon. 1974. Nutrients in subsurface and runoff waters of the Holland Marsh, Ontario. J. Environ. Qual. 3:31–35.

Nichols, S. A. 1973. The effects of harvesting aquatic macrophytes on algae. Wis. Acad. Sci., Arts and Letters 61:165–72.

Papst, M. H., J. A. Mathias, and J. Barica. 1980. Relationship between thermal stability and summer oxygen depletion in a prairie pothole lake. Can. J. Fish. Aquat. Sci. 37:1433–38.

Phillips, G. L., D. Eminson, and B. Moss. 1978. A mechanism to account for macrophyte decline in progressively eutrophicated freshwaters. Aquat. Bot. 4:103–26.

Pieczynska, E. 1971. Mass appearance of algae in the littoral of several Mazurian lakes. Internat. Ver. Theoret. Angew. Limnol., Mitt. 19:59–69.

Pip, E., and G. G. C. Robinson. 1982. A study of the seasonal dynamics of three phycoperiphytic communities using nuclear track autoradiography. I: Inorganic carbon uptake. Arch. Hydrobiol. 94:341–71.

Prowse, G. A. 1959. Relationship between epiphytic algal species and their macrophytic hosts. Nature 186:1204–5.

Riber, H. H., J. P. Sorensen, and H. H. Schierup. 1984. Primary productivity and biomass of epiphytes on *Phragmites australis* in a eutrophic Danish lake. Holarctic Ecol. 7:202–10.

Robinson, G. G. C. 1983. Methodology: The key to understanding periphyton. *In* Periphyton of freshwater ecosystems, ed. R. G. Wetzel. Dev. Hydrobiol. 17:245–52.

Roos, P. J. 1981. Dynamics and architecture of reed periphyton. Internat. Ver. Theoret. Angew. Limnol. Verh. 21:948–53.

_____. 1983. Dynamics of periphytic communities. *In* Periphyton of freshwater ecosystems, ed. R. G. Wetzel. Dev. Hydrobiol. 17:5–10.

Round, F. E. 1971. The growth and succession of algal populations in freshwaters. Internat. Ver. Theoret. Angew. Limnol., Mitt. 19:70–99.

_____. 1972. Patterns of seasonal succession of freshwater epipelic algae. Br. Phycol. J. 7:213–20.

_____. 1981. The ecology of algae. Cambridge: Cambridge Univ. Press.

Sand-Jensen, K., and M. Sondergaard. 1981. Phytoplankton and epiphyte development and shading effect on submerged macrophytes in lakes of different nutrient status. Internat. Rev. Gesamten Hydrobiol. 6:529–52.

Shamess, J. J., G. G. C. Robinson, and L. G. Goldsborough. 1985. The structure and comparison of periphytic and planktonic algal communities in two eutrophic prairie lakes. Arch. Hydrobiol. 103:99–116.

Sheldon, R. B., and C. W. Boylen. 1975. Factors affecting the contribution by epiphytic algae to the primary productivity of an oligotrophic freshwater lake. Appl. Microbiol. 30:657–67.

Smirnov, N. N. 1958. Same data about food consumption of plant production of bogs and fens by animals. Internat. Ver. Theoret. Angew. Limnol. Verh. 13:363–68.

Sozska, G. J. 1975. Ecological relations between invertebrates and submerged macrophytes in the lake littoral. Ekol. Pol. 23:393–415.

Straskraba, M., and E. Piezynska. 1970. Field experiments on shading effect by emergents on littoral phytoplankton and periphyton production. Rozpr. Cesk. Akad. Ved. Rada Mat. Prir. Ved. 80:7–32.

Sumner, W. T., and C. D. McIntyre. 1982. Grazer-periphyton interactions in laboratory streams. Arch. Hydrobiol. 93:135–57.

van der Valk, A. G., and C. B. Davis. 1978. The role of the seed bank in the vegetation dynamics of prairie glacial marshes. Ecol. 59:322–35.

Wetzel, R. G. 1964a. A comparative study of the primary productivity of higher aquatic plants, periphyton, and phytoplankton in a large, shallow lake. Internat. Rev. Gesamten Hydrobiol. 49:1–61.

_____. 1964b. Primary productivity of aquatic macrophytes. Internat. Ver. Theoret. Angew. Limnol. Verh. 15:426–36.

_____. 1983a. Limnology. 2d ed. Philadelphia: W. B. Saunders.

_____. 1983b. Periphyton of freshwater ecosystems. Dev. Hydrobiol. 17:346ff.

BRUCE D. J. BATT, MICHAEL G. ANDERSO

7 THE USE OF PRAIRI

ABSTRACT

FOR many species of ducks, the prairie pothole region is considered to be their most important production area in North America. Each spring, throughout a large portion of the waterfowl production areas of Canada and the United States, the population of ducks, their reproductive success, and the condition of the habitat are estimated using comparable methodology. We analyzed this data set to determine the numbers, proportions, productivity, and sources of variation, for the 12 species of ducks that commonly breed in the prairie pothole region portion of the total surveyed area.

Between 1955 and 1985, an average of 21.6 million ducks used the region, representing about 51.1% of the total estimated surveyed population. Over 50% of the total numbers of 8 of the 12 species are found in the region. There is striking variation in bird use within and among years and among subdivisions of the region. Habitat quantity and quality, as measured by the number of ponds available in May, seem to be the dominant factors controlling duck numbers; correlating positively with the distribution, abundance, and reproductive success of ducks. There have been significant shifts in the relative abundance and total numbers of individual species within subdivisions and for the whole region. Massive changes in land-use are dominant factors producing these changes, but extrinsic factors during the nonbreeding season also may be operant. Conservation of waterfowl in North America is closely tied to the fate of the prairie pothole region.

KEY WORDS: prairie pothole region, ducks, temporal variation, regional variation, productivity, May ponds, waterfowl populations.

C. DIANE ANDERSON, and F. DALE CASWELL

POTHOLES BY NORTH AMERICAN DUCKS

INTRODUCTION

WETLANDS of the prairie pothole region of North America are intimately linked to the life cycles of a great variety of wildlife. There are species representing all five classes of vertebrates that are obligate users of prairie wetlands and the mosaic of land and water that they form (Clark 1978; Murkin and Batt 1987). Perhaps the most widely recognized wildlife species using this habitat are waterfowl (e.g., Sugden 1984), although other chapters in this volume identify the importance of prairie wetlands to fish (Peterka, Chap. 10) and mammals (Fritzell, Chap. 9).

Historically, prairie potholes have not received much attention from scientists, perhaps because they produce few obvious economic benefits in a region where land that is not in agricultural production is considered to be "wasteland" by most of society. The greatest efforts by individuals, industries, and governments have been focused on removing wetlands by filling or draining. The only opposition to this has come from the politically weaker voices of sports enthusiasts and naturalists who defend these areas for their importance to wildlife.

For most species of ducks, this region is considered to be the most important production habitat in North America (Canadian Wildlife Service 1986). The region frequently is touted as producing from 50 to 80% of the continent's main game species. These claims form the basis of numerous, but as yet largely ineffective, programs to preserve this resource.

BRUCE D. J. BATT, MICHAEL G. ANDERSON, and C. DIANE ANDERSON, Delta Waterfowl and Wetlands Research Station, Delta, Manitoba RIN 3A1. F. DALE CASWELL, Canadian Wildlife Service, 501 University Crescent, Winnipeg, Manitoba R3T 2N2.

The prairie pothole region extends over approximately 300,000 square miles in the western plains of Canada ($\cong 80\%$) and the United States ($\cong 20\%$). This huge area is not homogeneous as there are major differences among regions in geological history and soil types, topography, climate (e.g., precipitation, frost-free period), the history of human settlement, and intensity of land-use. Several of these elements have not been stable over long periods of time. Human factors have changed dramatically throughout the region during the past several decades. Furthermore, waterfowl using different portions of the region may winter in widely different localities across the continent (Bellrose 1980; Johnson 1986), and these areas too have been impacted by humans in disparate ways, which may affect the survival or condition of wintering ducks. Finally, natural climatic variation has resulted in distinct but nonuniform wet and dry periods.

This chapter will attempt to quantify the use and significance of this region for breeding waterfowl. We will describe trends in individual species populations and productivity over the last three decades, explore possible cause-and-effect relationships of these trends, and describe year-to-year variations in use patterns. We will offer some thoughts on future prospects for waterfowl in this region, particularly in relation to conflicts with agriculture.

BASIC ECOLOGICAL RELATIONSHIPS OF WATERFOWL AND PRAIRIE WETLANDS

Before examining data on the region's duck populations, it seems useful to describe briefly those species that use it and factors that make this area especially attractive to breeding ducks. Of the 34 species of ducks breeding in North America, 12 are common in the region. These are discussed under the general categories of dabbling ducks (*Anas* spp.) and diving ducks (*Aythya* spp. and *Oxyura* sp.). Seven of the 12 are dabbling ducks: mallard (*Anas platyrhynchos*), northern pintail (*A. acuta*), gadwall (*A. strepera*), blue-winged teal (*A. discors*), northern shoveler (*A. clypeata*), green-winged teal (*A. crecca carolinensis*), and American wigeon (*A. americana*). Five are diving ducks: canvasback (*Aythya valisineria*), redhead (*A. americana*), lesser scaup (*A. affinis*), ring-necked duck (*A. collaris*), and ruddy duck (*Oxyura jamaicensis*). The greater scaup (*Aythya marila*) is also present in the area and is not separated from the lesser scaup during population inventories. However, only a very low proportion of the scaup counted are known to be greater scaup. Other species that occur, but never beyond trace numbers in continental surveys, are: cinnamon teal (*Anas cyanoptera*), black duck (*A.*

rubripes), wood duck (*Aix sponsa*), white-winged scoter (*Melanitta fusca*), common goldeneye (*Bucephala clangula*), bufflehead (*B. albeola*), and mergansers (*Mergus merganser* and *M. serrator*). Data from these species are not included in this analysis.

For prairie ducks, several critical events occur in pothole habitat. Reproduction is the most important of these; indeed, all other events (e.g., feather molt) appear to adjust to the timing and success of reproduction.

Different species exploit the mosaic of prairie wetlands in different ways (e.g., Stewart and Kantrud 1973; Kantrud and Stewart 1977) and waterfowl communities vary considerably across the prairies (e.g., Stewart and Kantrud 1974; Nudds 1983) and over time (e.g., Smith 1971; Stoudt 1971; Trauger and Stoudt 1978; Leitch and Kaminski 1985; Johnson 1986). However, for all species carefully studied thus far, the birds appear to be attracted to the high levels of primary and secondary productivity characteristic of pothole basins (e.g., Murkin, Chap. 11). The high productivity of prairie potholes is likely a result of the fortuitous combination of fertile soils, diverse complexes of mostly shallow basins, moderately long growing seasons, and seasonal and year-to-year variability in water levels (Williams 1947; Smith 1971; Sugden 1984).

During the breeding period, including brood-rearing, all species appear to exploit the protein-, lipid-, and calcium-rich food provided by abundant aquatic invertebrates (Murkin and Batt 1987; Swanson, Chap. 8). Invertebrates appear to be critical for breeding females as sources of nutrients for egg production and body maintenance (e.g., Bartonek and Hickey 1969; Swanson et al. 1979; Swanson, Chap. 8) and for developing young waterfowl (Sugden 1973). Invertebrate communities themselves are dependent upon wetland dynamics in the prairie ecosystem (e.g., Voigts 1976; Murkin 1983).

Another commonly cited characteristic of potholes, which makes them attractive to breeding waterfowl, is their physical heterogeneity that allows breeding pairs to isolate themselves in defensible pieces of habitat where they can secure resources for breeding and are relatively undisturbed by other birds (e.g., Hochbaum 1944). Selection for reduced competition is probably relevant in a broader sense, too, for ducks and other migratory birds presumably journey to such breeding areas partly because there are fewer resident competitors for necessary resources than at low latitudes (e.g., Lack 1968).

Following breeding, most ducks quickly leave the potholes for larger lakes and marshes where they undergo a complete change in body plumage and prepare for fall migration. With some exceptions (e.g., molting blue-winged teal), males of most species leave the potholes as soon as there is no longer a chance to breed (Hochbaum 1944; Salomonsen 1968; Bergman 1973; Dubowy 1980; Stoudt 1982; Anderson 1985). Some nonbreeding females and those whose nests have been lost also join these postbreeding flocks (Bailey 1981). By midsummer, the only birds left in most potholes are incubating and brood-rearing females and young-of-the-year. Soon after fledging, even these birds abandon small potholes for larger water, usually long before freeze-up makes small wetlands unavailable.

SOURCES OF THE DATA

The data analyzed in this report were obtained during the May waterfowl breeding-ground surveys and the July waterfowl production surveys conducted annually by the U.S. Fish and Wildlife Service (USFWS) and the Canadian Wildlife Service (CWS) (CWS and USFWS 1977). These aerial surveys of waterfowl breeding habitat are arranged in 50 strata (Fig. 7.1), encompassing 50,000 linear miles of transects from South Dakota to Alaska, and have been surveyed annually since 1955. July production surveys have been flown on a variable subset of these transects over a shorter period of time. The 50 survey strata include the majority of the total area used by most of the species, but there is increased evidence that a significant proportion of the mallards may occur outside the surveyed area (Trost, Blohm, and Boyd pers. comm.). The other species for which this factor may be important are: northern pintail, green-winged teal, lesser scaup, and ring-necked duck.

Counts are flown with light aircraft at an altitude of 30–50 m, using two observers (Hanson and Hawkins 1975). Simultaneous ground surveys are run over a portion of the transect route to generate corrections for visibility of various species, pond conditions, etc. (Martinson and Kaczynski 1967). Henny et al. (1972) and Pospahala et al. (1974) provide more detailed discussions of survey techniques and the resulting data.

May breeding pair counts typically included all 50 strata (although long-term means were used for northern Ontario from 1974 to 1985). In the event that weather or other exigencies prevented flying a transect, long-term averages were substituted for missing values. We calculated from CWS files that this occurred with about 7% of the total data set, mostly in the early years of the survey. Data from outside the 50 strata surveyed area have been added by the USFWS to yield total estimated populations for northern pintails and mallards beginning at various times during the 31-year interval. These data were not used because they represent an unequal expansion of the information base and bias comparisons over the full period of this analysis. July production surveys as of 1985 included 31 of 50 strata but past coverage was variable. Brood

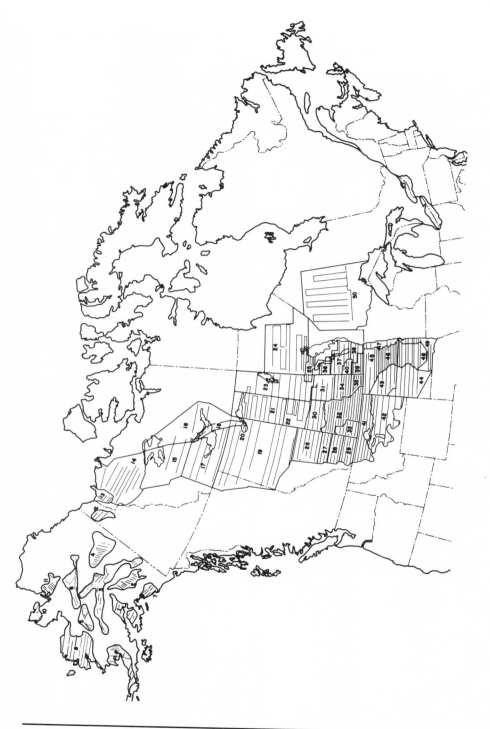

FIG. 7.1. Transects and strata of annual aerial surveys of waterfowl breeding grounds by the U.S. Fish and Wildlife Service and the Canadian Wildlife Service.

data are not available for all regions in all years. Consequently, opportunities for comparisons are more limited with brood data. In all cases where we made comparisons (See Tables 7.7–7.10), available brood data were matched with breeding pair and habitat data for the same individual strata and year, thus providing comparable, consistent comparisons despite imbalances in the data set. We assumed that, although regional coverage varied among years, each sample within each region provided unbiased samples of that region, which would thus allow comparisons among regions and over time.

For purposes of this report, we define the prairie pothole region to be 24 of the 50 strata of the total surveyed area, including southern Alberta (strata 26–29), southern Saskatchewan (30–35), southern Manitoba (36–40), eastern Montana (41–42), North Dakota (43, 45–47) and South Dakota (44, 48–49). This region includes some habitats (lakes, rivers) that do not fit the definition of potholes, but these are of relatively minor importance. Also, portions of Minnesota, Nebraska, and Iowa include important prairie wetland habitat and many breeding ducks, but data for these regions are scattered and lack long-term consistency that allows clear comparisons. Similarly, we did not include data from the earliest comprehensive surveys (1947–1954), which are not strictly comparable with the present data set. For habitat comparisons, we used May pond counts unadjusted for visibility biases, because annually adjusted data are not available before 1961. The timing of the annual surveys obtains the best data for mallard, northern pintail, and canvasback. The other species typically nest later in the season, and during the survey period they may not yet have arrived to be enumerated, or may be on their way to breeding grounds elsewhere. This fact will account for some of the variability obtained in annual population estimates.

Statistical tests follow Sokal and Rohlf (1981) and Wilkinson (1985). Percentage data were arcsine transformed before regressions or analyses of variance. Tukey's HSD test was used when comparisons of means were made after analysis of variance. Smoothing and time series analyses, based on three-year moving averages, were done to search for patterns in certain highly variable population data (Velleman and Hoaglin 1981).

RESULTS

Duck Populations

There has been considerable variation in mean total duck numbers (combined total for all surveyed species) in the region between 1955 and

1985 (21.6 ± 4.75 million, CV 22.1%), and in the mean proportion of all ducks estimated to be in the prairie pothole region portion of the 50 surveyed strata (51.1 ± 1.4%, CV 15.2%) (Table 7.1). The peak estimated population of 33.6 million birds occurred in 1956 and was followed by a rapid decline to 17.6 million in 1959. Populations since then have varied greatly, with the lowest population of 15.3 million recorded in 1985.

Species Composition

The number of ducks present varied considerably within and among species over the 31-year period for which comparable data are available (Table 7.1). The most abundant ducks were the mallard, blue-winged teal, and northern pintail, which together averaged 62% of the birds present. Annual fluctuations in numbers were considerable, with coefficients of variation falling between 20.3 and 71.4%. The most uncommon species, the ring-necked duck, was the most variable in number. On average, about 87% of the ducks were dabbling ducks and 13% were diving ducks.

While the relative numbers of each species present give the clearest picture of the community of ducks, a different picture is obtained when the importance of the region to each species is considered (Table 7.1). For 8 of the 12 species, over 50% of their mean total estimated numbers occurred in the region. The American wigeon approached this category at 49.3%.

Coefficients of variation for the proportion of the estimated populations of various species in the prairie pothole region ranged widely from

TABLE 7.1. Average duck populations in the prairie pothole region and the percentage of each species' total surveyed population found in the region (1955–1985)

Species	Breeding population (x10⁶) $\overline{X} \pm SD\ (CV)$	Percent of total surveyed population $\overline{X} \pm SD\ (CV)$
Mallard	5.4 ± 1.67 (31.1)	67.3 ± 7.6 (11.3)
Blue-winged teal	4.3 ± 0.95 (21.8)	88.1 ± 6.7 (7.6)
Northern pintail	3.7 ± 1.75 (47.8)	62.1 ± 16.4 (26.4)
Northern shoveler	1.6 ± 0.37 (23.2)	80.9 ± 10.6 (13.2)
American wigeon	1.6 ± 0.32 (20.3)	49.3 ± 8.1 (16.5)
Gadwall	1.4 ± 0.32 (22.9)	94.7 ± 3.4 (3.6)
Green-winged teal	0.7 ± 0.21 (28.6)	35.5 ± 9.4 (26.3)
Scaup	1.1 ± 0.38 (32.9)	16.9 ± 4.8 (28.5)
Redhead	0.6 ± 0.19 (31.4)	81.8 ± 11.5 (14.0)
Canvasback	0.4 ± 0.10 (28.3)	64.3 ± 12.6 (19.5)
Ring-necked duck	0.1 ± 0.05 (71.4)	13.9 ± 7.9 (56.8)
Ruddy duck	0.5 ± 0.21 (43.5)	86.7 ± 8.5 (9.8)
Total ducks[a]	21.56 ± 4.75 (22.1)	51.1 ± 7.8 (15.2)

[a]Combined total for all surveyed species.

3.6 to 56.8% (Table 7.1). This could be considered as an additional index of the dependence of a species on the region. Presumably, birds not tied to it, or to a strategy of precise homing, may successfully settle in other areas readily when habitat conditions are adequate. Obligate users could not do so. Thus, species least dependent on the region should show the greatest year-to-year variation (higher CV). Those species most closely tied to it should show the least variation among years (lower CV). This prediction is supported by a significant Spearman Rank Correlation ($r = 0.938$, $P < .001$) between ranks of the mean percentage of species present and ranks of coefficients of variation. Thus, the mean percentage of a species' population present in the region seems to be a strong indication of the dependence of that species on it, regardless of its comparative abundance. Using this criterion, the rank of dependence is (from most to least dependent): gadwall, blue-winged teal, ruddy duck, redhead, northern shoveler, mallard, canvasback, northern pintail, American wigeon, green-winged teal, scaup, and ring-necked duck.

Historical Trends in Duck Use

The proportions of each species present in the prairie pothole region over the 1955–1985 period were plotted (Fig. 7.2) and simple linear regressions were calculated (Table 7.2). These standardize the size of the total estimated population of each species and are thus a relative measure of bird distribution during the survey period. The distribution of total ducks, and of 9 of the 12 species, showed no significant temporal ($P > .05$) change. Only redheads showed a significant ($P < .01$) increase, while gadwalls ($P < .05$) and American wigeons ($P < .05$) significantly declined. Significant decreases were approached by total ducks, mallards ($P < .06$) and blue-winged teal ($P < .07$).

TABLE 7.2. Regressions of the proportions of each species' total surveyed population present in the prairie pothole region (1955–1985)

Species	Slope	r^2	P
Mallard	−0.292	0.121	.055
Blue-winged teal	−0.245	0.110	.069
Northern pintail	−0.291	0.026	.386
Northern shoveler	−0.151	0.017	.488
American wigeon	−0.393	0.193	.013
Gadwall	−0.168	0.198	.012
Green-winged teal	−0.197	0.037	.302
Scaup	−0.049	0.009	.617
Redhead	+0.601	0.227	.007
Canvasback	+0.046	0.001	.859
Ring-necked duck	+0.231	0.071	.148
Ruddy duck	+0.055	0.003	.753
Total ducks[a]	−0.286	0.112	.066

[a]Combined total for all surveyed species.

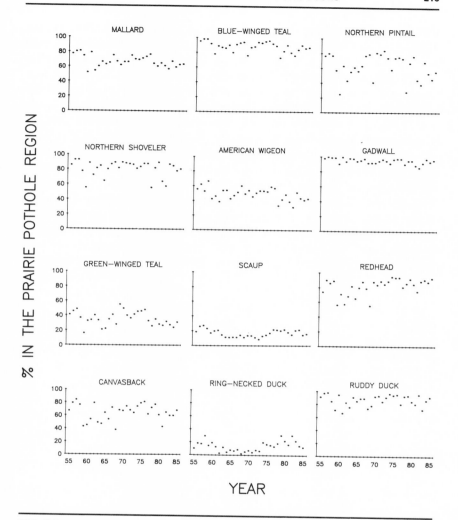

FIG. 7.2. Scatterplots of the percentage of a species' total population from the surveyed area estimated to be in the prairie pothole region each year for 1955–1985.

Because of the wide scatter in these data (Fig. 7.2), we searched further for patterns in proportion of each species settling in the region by using time-series analysis with three-year moving averages (the first and last data points of the series, 1955 and 1985, are only two-year averages) and included the data for the number of ponds present each May. Smoothed plots for the marginally declining species (mallards, blue-winged teal, and total ducks) look very different than plots of raw data. Although the raw data were suggestive of declines, the smoothed plots

are distinctly nonlinear and resemble smoothed data for May ponds
(Fig. 7.3). Smoothed plots for other species more closely resembled plots
of raw data (Fig. 7.2), though the scaup, ring-necked duck, northern
pintail, and green-winged teal series also appeared more nonlinear. The
steady declines in American wigeon and gadwall and the rise in redhead
proportions remained distinct in the smoothed data.

Relationship to Wetland Numbers

The most probable factor affecting the proportions of each species
using the region in a given year is habitat quality (Fretwell and Lucas
1969). However, variation in female philopatry and over-winter survival
of birds from different portions of the breeding range may also have
effects (Johnson 1986). The breeding ground surveys provide only a
single index of habitat quality, the number of May ponds, collected at
the same time as the data for breeding population estimates. Pond and
duck numbers have varied greatly over the 31-year period of the survey

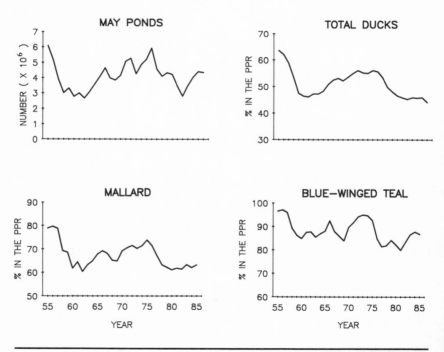

FIG. 7.3.   Moving-average plots of the estimated number of May ponds and the percentages of total ducks, Mallard, and Blue-winged Teal present in the prairie
pothole region for 1955–1985. Each point is the mean of years t, $t - 1$, and $t
+ 1$; for 1955 the point is the mean of t and $t + 1$; for 1985 the point is the
mean of t and $t - 1$.

(Fig. 7.4). There is a significant linear relationship between the total number of ducks and the number of May ponds ($y = 13.0 + 0.002x$, where y = total ducks and x = May ponds, $r^2 = 0.41$, $P < .001$). The proportions of total ducks and of all species individually, except the lesser scaup and ring-necked duck, also showed significant positive relationships to May ponds (Table 7.3). For significant relationships, coefficients of determination (r^2) ranged between 0.19 for the American wigeon and 0.57 for the northern pintail. The five strongest ($P < .001$)

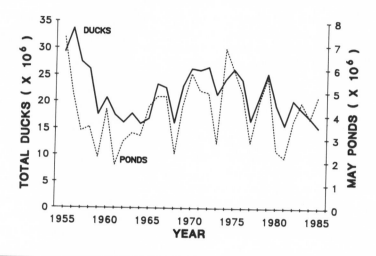

FIG. 7.4. Estimated number of unadjusted May ponds and total ducks present in the prairie pothole region for 1955–1985.

TABLE 7.3. **Regressions of the proportions of each species' total surveyed population present in the prairie pothole region in relation to the numbers of May ponds**

Species	Slope ($\times 1000$)	r^2	P
Mallard	0.030	0.296	.002
Blue-winged teal	0.030	0.371	.001
Northern pintail	0.089	0.571	.001
Northern shoveler	0.048	0.392	.001
American wigeon	0.026	0.191	.014
Gadwall	0.013	0.267	.003
Green-winged teal	0.032	0.229	.006
Scaup	−0.001	0.000	.965
Redhead	0.047	0.320	.001
Canvasback	0.048	0.285	.002
Ring-necked duck	0.005	0.007	.650
Ruddy duck	0.037	0.359	.000
Total ducks[a]	0.037	0.446	.001

[a]Combined total for all surveyed species.

relationships were for the northern pintail, northern shoveler, blue-winged teal, ruddy duck, and redhead.

Geographic and Temporal Variations

To search for patterns of change within the region, we calculated the relative proportion of each species in the community (number of each species x/number of all species combined) for the six administrative regions: Montana, North Dakota, South Dakota, southern Manitoba, southern Saskatchewan, and southern Alberta. Three ten-year time periods were selected (1955–1964, 1965–1974, 1975–1985) for statistical comparisons. The data then are measures of the relative abundance of each species at a given time and place. Two-way ANOVAs for each species showed that there were significant differences for both major factors and interaction effects for all but 6 of 36 possible comparisons (Table 7.4). All species varied significantly among the subdivisions of the region. All species, except the American wigeon, varied significantly among time periods and 7 of the 12 possible interaction comparisons yielded significant effects.

The data were regrouped by the three time periods for analysis of trends in relative proportion of each species summed over the entire region. All species, except the blue-winged teal and the American wigeon, showed significant changes (Table 7.5) over time periods. Mallards and northern pintails showed significant declines over the three periods, while the other six species were found in higher proportions in the later years.

Table 7.6 presents the relative abundance of 12 species in 6 subdivisions of the region summed over all years. For each species, regional averages differed greatly ($P < .001$).

TABLE 7.4.   **Significance of ANOVA comparisons for six regions of the prairie pothole region over three time periods of the relative abundance of each species in the regional population**

Species	Comparisons		
	region	period	region × period
Mallard	***	***	*
Blue-winged teal	***	***	***
Northern pintail	***	***	NS
Northern shoveler	***	***	**
American wigeon	***	NS	***
Gadwall	***	**	NS
Green-winged teal	***	***	**
Scaup	***	***	**
Redhead	***	***	NS
Canvasback	***	**	NS
Ring-necked duck	***	***	***
Ruddy duck	***	***	NS

Note: * $P < .05$, ** $P < .01$, *** $P < .001$.

... percentage composition of each species in the prairie pothole region for three time periods

Species	Period			P^a	Pattern of change
	1955–1964	1965–1974	1975–1985		
Mallard[b]	27.8 ± 3.9 (a)	24.2 ± 2.7 (b)	22.4 ± 3.1 (b)	.002	decrease
Blue-winged teal	21.4 ± 2.3 (a)	20.3 ± 2.4 (a)	19.2 ± 2.0 (a)	.095	no change
Northern pintail	16.5 ± 4.7 (ab)	18.7 ± 3.9 (a)	13.5 ± 3.9 (b)	.029	decrease
Northern shoveler	6.4 ± 1.2 (a)	7.9 ± 0.9 (b)	8.5 ± 1.8 (b)	.006	increase
American wigeon	7.5 ± 1.1 (a)	7.3 ± 0.9 (a)	7.2 ± 1.1 (a)	.857	no change
Gadwall	5.5 ± 2.6 (a)	7.4 ± 2.0 (ab)	7.6 ± 1.2 (b)	.041	increase
Green-winged teal	2.9 ± 0.6 (a)	3.7 ± 0.8 (b)	3.7 ± 0.5 (b)	.008	increase
Scaup	5.7 ± 1.4 (a)	3.6 ± 0.7 (b)	7.2 ± 1.3 (c)	.000	decrease/increase
Redhead	2.1 ± 0.4 (a)	2.5 ± 0.5 (a)	3.8 ± 0.7 (b)	.000	increase
Canvasback	1.6 ± 0.3 (a)	1.6 ± 0.3 (a)	1.9 ± 0.3 (b)	.025	increase
Ring-necked duck	0.2 ± 0.2 (a)	0.2 ± 0.1 (a)	0.6 ± 0.2 (b)	.000	increase
Ruddy duck	1.8 ± 0.6 (a)	2.1 ± 0.5 (ab)	3.1 ± 1.5 (b)	.018	increase

[a] Probability for overall F statistic for test of hypothesis that means do not differ among time periods.

[b] In each row, means followed by the same letter are not significantly different ($P > .05$).

TABLE 7.6. Relative abundance (mean ± SD percentage composition) of each species in six subdivisions of the prairie pothole region summed over all years (1955–1985)

Species	Region					
	Southern Alberta	Southern Saskatchewan	Southern Manitoba	Montana	North Dakota	South Dakota
Mallard[a]	25.7 ± 4.6 (a)[b]	27.9 ± 5.4 (ad)	21.3 ± 5.6 (b)	29.6 ± 5.0 (cd)	18.3 ± 4.6 (b)	19.8 ± 4.4 (b)
Blue-winged teal	13.6 ± 4.0 (ac)	17.1 ± 3.3 (a)	25.9 ± 8.1 (b)	11.3 ± 4.0 (c)	28.4 ± 6.6 (b)	38.1 ± 9.2
Northern pintail	19.2 ± 6.5 (a)	16.6 ± 5.3 (ab)	8.3 ± 3.8	18.7 ± 4.0 (ac)	15.3 ± 5.8 (bcd)	12.5 ± 4.5 (d)
Northern shoveler	7.3 ± 1.5 (a)	7.2 ± 1.8 (a)	5.4 ± 1.6	7.4 ± 2.9 (a)	9.0 ± 3.0 (a)	8.4 ± 3.1 (a)
American wigeon	7.5 ± 2.1 (ac)	8.6 ± 2.3 (a)	3.9 ± 2.0 (b)	12.1 ± 4.1	4.9 ± 3.8 (b)	5.1 ± 4.8 (bc)
Gadwall	6.4 ± 2.3 (a)	6.6 ± 2.7 (a)	3.8 ± 2.1	7.6 ± 2.8 (a)	10.0 ± 3.4	7.4 ± 2.7 (a)
Green-winged teal	4.3 ± 1.3 (a)	3.5 ± 1.0 (a)	4.7 ± 2.8 (a)	4.9 ± 2.3 (a)	1.6 ± 1.2 (b)	2.0 ± 1.6 (b)
Scaup	8.5 ± 2.9 (a)	5.4 ± 2.6 (b)	8.7 ± 3.9 (a)	4.3 ± 2.0 (b)	2.1 ± 1.8 (c)	1.6 ± 1.0 (b)
Redhead	2.6 ± 1.3 (a)	2.4 ± 1.1 (ab)	4.0 ± 1.5 (c)	1.4 ± 1.6 (bd)	4.6 ± 2.0 (c)	2.3 ± 1.1 (ad)
Canvasback	1.6 ± 0.5 (a)	2.2 ± 0.6	3.4 ± 1.4	0.5 ± 0.3 (b)	1.1 ± 0.5 (a)	0.4 ± 0.2 (b)
Ring-necked duck	0.1 ± 0.1 (a)	0.4 ± 0.3 (a)	1.2 ± 1.1	0.2 ± 0.4 (a)	0.4 ± 0.4 (a)	0.3 ± 0.5 (a)
Ruddy duck	1.6 ± 0.8 (a)	1.4 ± 0.9 (a)	6.7 ± 3.4	1.7 ± 1.8 (a)	4.3 ± 3.0	2.2 ± 2.6 (a)

[a] For each species, regional means are significantly different (ANOVA, $P < .001$) overall.

[b] For each species, regional means followed by the same letter are not significantly different (Tukey's HSD test, $P > .05$).

Occupancy Rates of Ponds

To test for possible changes in use of prairie pothole region habitat, we divided the total estimated number of ducks in the region by the total number of unadjusted May ponds estimated for the same region each year. A simple linear regression over time yielded the equation: $y = 128.164 - 0.062x$, where y = occupancy rate and x = years, $r^2 = 0.13$, $P < .05$. This relationship is relatively weak but indicates an overall decline in pond occupancy rate over the 31-year time period.

In an effort to deal with the extreme variation in these data, we ran linear and quadratic regression models on three-year running means (i.e., each point represented the mean of itself plus the population estimate of the year before and the year after). Both simple linear regression ($y = 11.90 - 0.0924x$, where y = occupancy rate and x = three-year running mean, $r^2 = 0.75$, $P < .001$) and quadratic models ($y = 37.276 - 0.829x + 0.005x^2$, $r^2 = 0.906$, $P < .001$) explained a much greater proportion of the variation present in the smoothed data than in the raw data.

Testing for functional relationships using "built-in" sampling correlations or correlated estimators may yield regression results that reflect sampling covariation as well as true correlation between the variables of interest. Thus, these large increases in r^2 should be interpreted cautiously. Nevertheless, we conclude that there has been a decline in pond occupancy rate since the beginning of the data set. The best-fit of the quadratic equation indicated a steeper decline until the mid-1960s and a decreasing rate of change since that time.

Patterns of Duck Productivity

We examined survey data for the entire region for relationships between productivity indices and wetland abundance, and trends over the time span of the data set. Two statistics were available: an index of class II and III broods (Gollop and Marshall 1954) (all ducks combined), and average brood size. Regressions of mean brood size and May ponds showed a significant positive relationship for three of six subdivisions of the region but not for all regions combined (Table 7.7). Brood index/ total ducks showed no relationship to water conditions.

To standardize the brood index among years, we matched data across transects for May and July surveys within the same year and calculated brood index/total ducks as a crude index of productivity for all ducks in the population. Regression analyses were run to test for trends over time for each region.

Brood index/total ducks has declined significantly both for the whole region and for northern Canada (though data there are less extensive) (Table 7.8). A steep decline in productivity in southern Alberta was the primary cause of the significant decline in the region as the other five subdivisions showed no significant changes. Northern Saskatchewan and northern Manitoba combined also showed a significant decline over this time period but northern Alberta, British Columbia, and the Northwest Territories did not.

Average brood size has declined in the prairie pothole region overall but not in northern Canada (Table 7.9). The steepest declines occurred in southern Alberta, South Dakota, southern Saskatchewan, and southern Manitoba.

TABLE 7.7. Results of regression analyses for changes in brood index/total ducks and mean brood size in relation to the number of May ponds

Parameter	Region	Years of data	Slope	r^2	P
Brood index/	S. Alberta	31	+0.95[a]	0.020	.456
total ducks	S. Saskatchewan	31	+0.08	0.012	.566
	S. Manitoba	31	−0.44	0.050	.234
	Montana	19	+1.43	0.006	.768
	North Dakota	28	−0.39	0.018	.498
	South Dakota	27	+0.89	0.033	.372
	Total	31	−0.07	0.040	.279
Mean brood size	S. Alberta	31	+0.95[b]	0.127	.053
	S. Saskatchewan	31	+0.30	0.171	.023
	S. Manitoba	31	+0.47	0.063	.184
	Montana	19	+2.41	0.235	.041
	North Dakota	28	+1.29	0.200	.019
	South Dakota	27	+0.17	0.001	.872
	Total	31	+0.11	0.084	.113

[a]For brood index/total ducks calculated slope is × 10^5.
[b]For mean brood size calculated slope is × 10^3.

TABLE 7.8. Results of regression analyses for changes in brood index/total ducks for the prairie pothole region and northern survey regions (1955–1985) (Brood data are not available for all regions in all years)

Region	Slope (× 100)	N[a]	r^2	P
Prairie pothole region				
S. Alberta	−0.155	31	0.79	.000
S. Saskatchewan	−0.019	31	0.07	.152
S. Manitoba	+0.011	31	0.03	.354
Montana	−0.075	19	0.14	.119
North Dakota	−0.005	28	0.01	.727
South Dakota	−0.011	27	0.02	.455
Total	−0.033	31	0.34	.001
Northern region				
N. Alberta, B.C., and N.W. Territories	−0.065	17	0.22	.061
N. Saskatchewan and N. Manitoba	−0.088	24	0.36	.001
Total	−0.075	24	0.39	.002

[a]Years of available brood data for each region.

These data were examined further by ANOVA to isolate better the nature of these declines. Data were divided by region and time period. Only two time periods were used because of limited brood data available for the north and other areas (e.g., strata 41, 42, etc.) early in the study period. Two-way ANOVA revealed that brood index/total ducks differed between time periods ($P < .001$) and in time $\times$ region interaction ($P = .032$) but not between regions ($P = .082$). Mean brood size did not differ by regions ($P = .178$) but did differ by time period ($P = .001$) and time $\times$ region interaction ($P < .001$). Individual pairwise comparisons are presented in Table 7.10.

TABLE 7.9. Results of regression analyses for changes in average brood size for the prairie pothole region and northern survey regions (1955–1985) (Brood data are not available for all regions in all years)

Region	Slope ($\times 10$)	N^a	r^2	P
Prairie pothole region				
S. Alberta	−0.504	31	0.55	.000
S. Saskatchewan	−0.325	31	0.22	.008
S. Manitoba	−0.286	31	0.23	.007
Montana	−0.086	19	0.02	.528
North Dakota	−0.162	28	0.05	.258
South Dakota	−0.431	27	0.29	.004
Total	−0.426	31	0.64	.000
Northern region				
N. Alberta, B.C., and N.W. Territories	−0.588	17	0.28	.030
N. Saskatchewan and N. Manitoba	−0.017	24	0.00	.907
Total	−0.050	24	0.01	.576

[a]Years of available brood data for each region.

TABLE 7.10. Mean ($\pm$ SD) brood index/total ducks and average brood size for the prairie pothole region and northern Canada for the first and second halves of the survey period

Parameter	Region	1955–1969	1970–1985
Brood index ($\times 100$)/total ducks	Prairie	2.10 ± 0.58 (a)[a](A)[b]	1.58 ± 0.27 (b)(A)
	North	2.71 ± 0.90 (a)(B)	1.51 ± 0.44 (b)(A)
Mean brood size	Prairie	5.72 ± 0.37 (a)(A)	5.03 ± 0.30 (b)(A)
	North	5.23 ± 0.26 (a)(B)	5.26 ± 0.39 (a)(A)

[a]For each parameter, values in each row followed by the same lowercase letter are not significantly different ($P > .05$).

[a]For each parameter, values in each column followed by the same uppercase letter are not significantly different ($P > .05$).

DISCUSSION

A striking feature of the prairie pothole region for ducks is the variability of habitat conditions, as indexed by the number of pothole basins flooded in May, and associated variations in duck use and productivity. The first year of the series, 1955, was a year of peak pond numbers and waterfowl populations, unmatched in any year since. The 31-year period has included dramatic changes in water and duck abundance. Our analyses support a great deal of earlier work by others that indicates that population variations result from several, presumably interacting, factors: the habitat preferences and basic characteristics of each species, natural variations of climate and geological history within the region, and man-induced changes in the landscape. To these must be added extrinsic factors that impact duck numbers in diverse ways during the portion of the year (more than half for most species) that birds are not present in the prairie pothole region.

Each species has a unique set of habitat requirements that cause birds to prefer particular regions over others during the breeding season, and the availability of these habitats presumably will affect settling patterns in spring. Resources that are important for ducks are assumed to fluctuate widely, more or less correlated with the only available long-term measure of habitat quality, May ponds. The portions of all species, except scaups and ring-necked ducks, settling in the region showed significant positive relationships to the number of May ponds. These two species appear to be the least closely tied to the region during the breeding season as only 16.9% of scaups and 13.9% of ring-necked ducks are found there in the spring. The main breeding range of these two species is further north in the forested region (Bellrose 1980).

Correlations between the percentage of a species' population settling and spring water conditions are highest in species that are only poorly, or variably, philopatric (northern pintails, blue-winged teal, and redheads, but not northern shovelers) (Table 7.3). There are almost no data on dispersal of ruddy ducks (for reviews, see Johnson 1986; Anderson et al. in press).

In a separate analysis, Johnson (1986) showed that 10 of the 12 species included in our analyses (excluding ring-necked ducks and ruddy ducks) exhibited some degree of displacement to other areas when the region was dry. This was usually in a northerly direction, but one species, the American wigeon, was displaced in a southeasterly direction. Overflights to northern areas during drought have been described previously by Hansen and McKnight (1964), Smith (1970), and Derksen and Eldridge (1980). Johnson (1986) suggested that three general strategies are used by breeding ducks to decide where to settle: a homing strategy wherein adults return to the area used the previous year and yearlings return to their natal area; an opportunistic strategy by which birds simply settle in the first suitable area encountered during spring migration; or a mixed strategy in which birds first home, but if the habitat is not suitable, they move on to other areas.

The data show significant differences in the relative abundance of all 12 species among six administrative subregions, and for 11 of 12 species, among the three time periods analyzed. The details of relative abundance by species for each time period and each region are presented in Tables 7.5 and 7.6. We did not search for detailed correlations between these data and possible cause-and-effect factors. However, it seems most likely that consistent regional differences are the product of species-specific habitat requirements. Changes in relative abundance over time might be the result of land-use changes that favor some species over others, or due to species-specific imbalances in factors extrinsic to the region, such as winter survival. For instance, all the diving ducks, which nest over water and generally are more successful than upland nesting ducks on intensively farmed land, have increased in relative abundance (Table 7.5). Shifts in relative abundance of individual species on small study areas across the prairies have been discussed by Trauger and Stoudt (1978), Leitch and Kaminski (1985), and others.

Along with annual variation in water abundance, the intensification of agriculture, which has resulted in drainage of potholes and destruction of upland nesting cover, probably has been the most dominant factor affecting the distribution, abundance, and reproductive success of the region's ducks. For the Dakotas and the three prairie provinces, estimates of pothole loss due to drainage range from 17 to 71% (Kiel et al. 1972; Schick 1972; Adams and Gentle 1978; Millar 1981; Rounds 1982; Rakowski and Chabot 1984; Tiner 1984; Turner et al. 1987). Conversion of native cover to small grain production and pasture has been extensive throughout the region (Cowardin et al. 1983; Sugden and Beyersbergen 1984; Boyd 1985). Other more subtle changes have occurred on the pothole margins through road construction (Kiel et al. 1972), burning (Fritzell 1975), and soil erosion (Canada 1984).

The result most obvious for waterfowl has been a massive loss and deterioration of habitat, both aquatic and upland. Associated effects result from the concentration of nesting ducks in very limited habitat, such as fence rows, roadsides, and narrow fringes around potholes, and from shifts in predator communities with intensive farming. The most alarming consequence has been the widespread decline of nesting success, and therefore recruitment, documented at numerous intensive study sites (Sellers 1973; Higgins 1977; Johnson and Sargeant 1977;

Cowardin et al. 1985; Greenwood et al. 1987).

Evidence of decreased reproductive success also was found in our analysis of brood production relative to population size and of average brood size. The brood index/total ducks decreased dramatically in southern Alberta and to a lesser degree throughout the region and in survey strata across northern Canada. Average brood size also decreased throughout the prairie pothole region but not in the northern regions. Similar results have been reported from an independent analysis of recent production data (Reynolds 1987).

The data show some significant positive relationships between May ponds and average brood sizes, suggesting that factors that cause birds to settle and breed are also related to the productivity of individual successful nesting attempts. That is, in wetter years, more birds settle and successful nests produce more young than in drier years. However, the brood index/total ducks parameter and May ponds showed no relationship, indicating that the effect of water availability is primarily on settling rates. Subsequently, the relative hatching success of the birds that do settle appears to be unchanged between wet and dry years. Alternatively, broods may be less visible to surveyors in wet years, thereby biasing comparisons of productivity and water levels (Blohm pers. comm.; Anderson pers. obs.). Field studies are needed to examine these biases.

The lower brood index/total ducks and the smaller brood size in recent times are consistent with the general pattern of reduced nesting success resulting from agricultural impacts. However, the lower index in the north cannot be explained by this relationship. The latter finding is somewhat surprising and will require a more intensive analysis to search for potential cause-and-effect relationships. Some extrinsic factor(s) during the wintering or spring migration periods may be affecting these parameters.

Agricultural impacts should be greatest on early nesting species (those that nest before there is appreciable new growth by crops or pasture grasses). Correspondingly, the earliest nesters, northern pintail and mallard, were the only two species that showed a significant decline in relative abundance over the three time periods of this analysis. Furthermore, upland nesters, in general, tended to settle in the region in declining proportions (Table 7.2). The species showing the steepest decline, the American wigeon, is often associated with grasslands (Bellrose 1980; Wishart 1983). Only species nesting over water showed any tendency to settle on the prairies in increasing proportions (Table 7.2). The lower average brood size in recent years may be related to a much larger portion of annual production coming from birds that had lost their first nests to predators or agriculture, and were forced to renest later in the season. Renest clutches are smaller in size and thus will produce fewer ducklings per successful hen (Sowls 1955; Johnsgard 1973; Batt and Prince 1979).

Among waterfowl biologists, there is considerable discussion about whether empty habitat exists in the prairie pothole region (i.e., areas with populations far below their presumed carrying capacity). Our analysis shows a reduced occupancy rate of potholes by ducks since 1955. The debate is whether this is simply a result of there being too few birds to fill the available habitat, or a result of the real carrying capacity being far below the apparent carrying capacity, as indexed only by May ponds. In view of escalating human impacts, there can be little doubt that this landscape should not be as productive as during the early years of the survey. However, there are also data to support the contention that at least some effects on populations have resulted from lower duck survival away from the prairie pothole region (Caswell et al. 1985).

These questions cannot be answered clearly with simple correlation studies such as this, but rather require direct experimentation with recruitment and survival. We consider this to be a critical issue that must be resolved if future waterfowl management is to be effective. We concur with Cowardin et al. (1985) that in order for waterfowl to thrive on the prairies, management must succeed in three areas: preservation and management of essential habitat, regulation of harvest, and maintenance of a recruitment rate that will compensate for annual mortality.

ACKNOWLEDGMENTS

We thank George Hochbaum for assistance during the early stages of data analysis; Bob Emery for the preparation of the figures; Hugh Boyd, Bob Blohm, Ron Reynolds, and Rich Crawford for helpful comments on the manuscript; and Arnold van der Valk for his patience. Data used in this report were kindly provided from unpublished CWS and USFWS files. This study was supported by the North American Wildlife Foundation through the Delta Waterfowl and Wetlands Research Station.

REFERENCES

Adams, G. D., and G. C. Gentle. 1978. Spatial changes in waterfowl habitat. Can. Wildl. Serv. Occas. Paper 38.

Anderson, M. G. 1985. Variations on monogamy in canvasbacks (*Aythya valisineria*). Ornithol. Mongr. 37:57–67.

Anderson, M. G., J. R. Rhymer, and F. C. Rohwer. In press. Philopatry, dispersal and the genetic structure of waterfowl populations. *In* Ecology and management of breeding waterfowl, ed. B. D. J. Batt et al. Minneapolis: Univ. Minn. Press.

Bailey, R. O. 1981. Post-breeding ecology of the redhead duck. Ph.D. diss., Macdonald College, Montreal, Quebec.

Bartonek, J. C., and J. J. Hickey. 1969. Food habits of canvasbacks, redheads, and lesser scaup in Manitoba. Condor 71:280–90.

Batt, B. D. J., and H. H. Prince. 1979. Laying dates, clutch size and egg weight of captive mallards. Condor 81:34–41.

Bellrose, F. C. 1980. Ducks, geese and swans of North America. 3d ed. Harrisburg, Pa.: Stackpole.

Bergman, R. D. 1973. Use of southern boreal lakes by postbreeding canvasbacks and redheads. J. Wildl. Manage. 37:160–70.

Boyd, H. 1985. The large-scale impact of agriculture on ducks in the prairie provinces, 1956–1981. Can. Wildl. Serv. Prog. Note 149.

Canada. Senate. 1984. Standing Committee on Agriculture, Fisheries, and Forestry. Soils at risk: Canada's future eroding.

Canadian Wildlife Service. 1986. North American waterfowl management plan: A strategy for cooperation. Minis. Supply Serv. Can. Cat. No. CW 66-80/ 1986E.

Canadian Wildlife Service and U.S. Fish and Wildlife Service. 1977. Standard operating procedures for aerial waterfowl breeding ground and habitat surveys in North America. Mimeo.

Caswell, F. D., G. S. Hochbaum, and R. K. Brace. 1985. The effect of restrictive regional hunting regulations on survival rates and local harvests of southern Manitoba mallards. N. Amer. Wildl. Nat. Resour. Conf. 50:549–56.

Clark, J. 1978. Freshwater wetlands: habitats for aquatic invertebrates, amphibians, reptiles, and fish. *In* Wetland functions and values: The state of our understanding, ed. P. E. Greeson et al., 330–43. Amer. Water Resour. Assoc. Tech. Publ. TPS79-2.

Cowardin, L. M., D. H. Johnson, A. M. Frank, and T. D. Klett. 1983. Simulating results of management actions on mallard production. N. Amer. Wildl. Nat. Resour. Conf. 48:257–71.

Cowardin, L. M., D. S. Gilmer, and C. W. Shaiffer. 1985. Mallard recruitment in the agricultural environment of North Dakota. Wildl. Mongr. 92:1–37.

Derksen, D. U., and W. D. Eldridge. 1980. Drought-displacement of pintails to the Arctic coastal plain, Alaska. J. Wildl. Manage. 44:224–29.

Dubowy, P. J. 1980. Optimal foraging and adaptive strategies of post-breeding male blue-winged teal and northern shovelers. Master's thesis, Univ. N. Dak., Grand Forks.

Fretwell, S. D., and H. H. Lucus. 1969. On territorial behavior and other factors influencing habitat distribution in birds. I: Theoretical development. Acta Biotheor. 19:16–36.

Fritzell, E. K. 1975. Effects of agricultural burning on nesting waterfowl. Can. Field-Naturalist 89:21–27.

Gollop, J. B., and W. H. Marshall. 1954. A guide for aging duck broods in the field. Miss. Flyway Counc. Tech. Comm. Unpubl. Rep.

Greenwood, R. J., A. B. Sargeant, D. H. Johnson, L. M. Cowardin, and T. L. Shaffer. 1987. Mallard nest success and recruitment in prairie Canada. N. Amer. Wildl. Nat. Resour. Conf. 52:298–302.

Hansen, H. A., and D. E. McKnight. 1964. Emigration of drought-displaced ducks to the Arctic. N. Amer. Wildl. Nat. Resour. Conf. 29:119–27.

Hanson, R. C., and A. S. Hawkins. 1975. Counting ducks and duck ponds in prairie Canada: How and why. Naturalist 25:8–11.

Henny, C. J., D. R. Anderson, and R. S. Pospahala. 1972. Aerial surveys of waterfowl production in North America, 1955–1971. U.S. Fish and Wildl. Serv. Spec. Sci. Rep. Wildl. 160.

Higgins, K. F. 1977. Duck nesting in intensively farmed areas of North Dakota. J. Wildl. Manage. 41:232–42.

Hochbaum, H. A. 1944. The canvasback on a prairie marsh. Harrisburg, Pa.: Stackpole.

Johnsgard, P. A. 1973. Proximate and ultimate determinants of clutch size in Anatidae. Wildfowl. 24:144–49.

Johnson, D. H. 1986. Determinants of the distributions of ducks. Ph.D. diss., N. Dak. State Univ., Fargo.

Johnson, D. H., and A. B. Sargeant. 1977. Impact of red fox predation on the sex ratio of prairie mallards. U.S. Fish and Wildl. Serv. Wildl. Res. Rep. 6.

Kantrud, H. A., and R. E. Stewart. 1977. Use of natural basin wetlands by breeding waterfowl in North Dakota. J. Wildl. Manage. 41:243–53.

Kiel, W. H., A. S. Hawkins, and N. G. Perret. 1972. Waterfowl habitat trends in the aspen parkland of Manitoba. Can. Wildl. Serv. Rep. Ser. 18.

Lack, D. 1968. Ecological adaptations for breeding in birds. London: Methuen.

Leitch, W. G., and R. M. Kaminski. 1985. Long-term wetland-waterfowl trends in Saskatchewan prairies. J. Wildl. Manage. 49:212–22.

Martinson, R. K., and C. F. Kaczynski. 1967. Factors influencing waterfowl counts on aerial surveys, 1961–1966. U.S. Fish and Wildl. Serv. Spec. Sci. Rep. Wildl. 105.

Millar, J. B. 1981. Habitat changes in Saskatchewan waterfowl strata 30 to 33 between fall 1978 and fall 1980. Can. Wildl. Serv. Unpubl. Proj. Rep.

Murkin, H. R. 1983. Responses of aquatic macroinvertebrates to prolonged flooding of marsh habitat. Ph.D. diss., Utah State Univ., Logan.

Murkin, H. R., and Batt, B. D. J. 1987. The interactions of vertebrates and invertebrates in peatlands. Mem. Entomol. Soc. Can. 140:15–30.

Nudds, T. D. 1983. Niche dynamics and organization of waterfowl guilds in variable environments. Ecol. 64:319–30.

Pospahala, R. S., D. R. Anderson, and C. J. Henny. 1974. Population ecology of the mallard. II: Breeding, habitat conditions, size of the breeding populations, and production indices. U.S. Fish and Wildl. Serv. Resour. Publ. 115.

Rakowski, P. W., and B. P. Chabot. 1984. Changes in land-use in the Minnedosa district of southwestern Manitoba; an update on the Kiel-Hawkins transects. Can. Wildl. Serv. Unpubl. Rep.

Reynolds, R. E. 1987. Breeding duck population, production and habitat surveys 1979–85. N. Amer. Wildl. Nat. Resour. Conf. 52:186–205.

Rounds, R. C. 1982. Land use changes in the Minnedosa pothole region of southwestern Manitoba. Blue Jay 40:6–12.

Salomonsen, F. 1968. The moult migration. Wildfowl 19:5–24.

Schick, C. D. 1972. A documentation and analysis of wetland drainage in the Alberta parkland. West. North. Reg., Can. Wildl. Serv. Unpubl. Rep.

Sellers, R. A. 1973. Mallard releases in understocked prairie pothole habitat. J. Wildl. Manage. 37:10–32.

Smith, A. G. 1971. Ecological factors affecting waterfowl production in the Alberta parklands. U.S. Fish and Wildl. Serv. Resour. Publ. 98.

Smith, R. I. 1970. Response of pintail breeding populations to drought. J. Wildl. Manage. 34:943–46.

Sokal, R. R., and R. J. Rohlf. 1981. Biometry. 2d ed. San Francisco: W. H. Freeman and Co.

Sowls, L. K. 1955. Prairie ducks: A study of their behavior, ecology and management. Harrisburg, Pa.: Stackpole.

Stewart, R. E., and H. A. Kantrud. 1973. Ecological distribution of breeding waterfowl populations in North Dakota. J. Wildl. Manage. 37:39–50.

———. 1974. Breeding waterfowl populations in the prairie pothole region of North Dakota. Condor 76:70–79.

Stoudt, J. H. 1971. Ecological factors affecting waterfowl production in the Saskatchewan parklands. U.S. Fish and Wildl. Serv. Resour. Publ. 99.

———. 1982. Habitat use and productivity of canvasbacks in southwestern Manitoba, 1961–1972. U.S. Fish and Wildl. Serv. Spec. Sci. Rep. Wildl. 248.

Sugden, L. G. 1973. Feeding ecology of pintail, gadwall, American wigeon and lesser scaup ducklings. Can. Wildl. Serv. Rep. Ser. 24.

———. 1984. The waterfowl resource of the Canadian plains. Prairie Forum 9:299–314.

Sugden, L. G., and G. W. Beyersbergen. 1984. Farming intensity on waterfowl breeding grounds in Saskatchewan parklands. Wildl. Soc. Bull. 12:22–26.

Swanson, G. A., G. L. Krapu, and J. R. Serie. 1979. Foods of female dabbling ducks on the breeding grounds. In Waterfowl and wetlands—an integrated review, ed. T. A. Bookhout, 47–57. La Crosse, Wis.: La Crosse Printing.

Tiner, R. W., Jr. 1984. Wetlands of the United States: Current status and recent trends. U.S. Fish and Wildl. Serv. Nat. Wetlands Inventory.

Trauger, D. L., and J. H. Stoudt. 1978. Trends in waterfowl populations and habitats on study areas in Canadian parklands. N. Amer. Wildl. Nat. Resour. Conf. 43:187–205.

Turner, B. C., G. S. Hochbaum, F. D. Caswell, and D. J. Nieman. 1987. Agricultural impacts on wetland habitats on the Canadian prairies, 1981–85. N. Amer. Wildl. Nat. Resour. Conf. 52:206–15.

Velleman, P. F., and D. C. Hoaglin. 1981. Applications, basics, and computing of exploratory data analysis. Belmont, Calif.: Duxbury Press.

Voigts, D. K. 1976. Aquatic invertebrate abundance in relation to changing marsh vegetation. Amer. Midl. Nat. 95:313–22.

Wilkinson, L. 1985. Systat: The system for statistics. Evanston, Ill.: Systat Inc.

Williams, C. S. 1947. Waterfowl breeding conditions—summer 1947. U.S. Fish and Wildl. Serv. Spec. Sci. Rep. Wildl. 45.

Wishart, R. A. 1983. The behavioral ecology of the American wigeon (*Anas americana*) over its annual cycle. Ph.D. diss., Univ. Manitoba, Winnipeg.

GEORGE A. SWANSON and HAROLD F. DUEBBEF

⑧ WETLAND HABITATS OF WATERFOW

ABSTRACT

INVESTIGATIONS of wetland use by waterfowl have demonstrated the importance of the wetland complex in providing the habitat requirements of breeding
birds. Seasonally flooded wetlands provide pair habitat and feeding sites for
breeding dabbling ducks. They also provide nest sites for diving ducks and
feeding sites for broods during years of high water. Investigations of foods
consumed by breeding birds, particularly laying females and broods during early
development, demonstrate high consumption of aquatic invertebrates. The diet
selected by Anatinae is influenced by the current physiological demands of the
birds; their adaptations for feeding; the nutritional value, abundance, and distribution of food items; and behavior of invertebrates.

Components of the wetland complex can be evaluated by the role that each
basin plays in the ecology of waterfowl during migration, reproduction, and
molting. Large semipermanent wetlands that contain vast stands of deep marsh
interspersed with open water provide ideal habitat for waterfowl during breeding
and molting. Lakes with higher concentrations of salts provide migration and
staging habitat for a variety of waterfowl species.

KEY WORDS: ducks, chemistry, hydrology, migration, molting,
nesting, ponds, prairie, staging, waterfowl, wetlands.

INTRODUCTION

A N assessment of relationships between waterfowl and aquatic habitats that support them requires an understanding of the re- quirements of the birds and wetland conditions that satisfy these requirements. Knowledge of feeding ecology provides a basis for defin- ing the role of specific food items in satisfying the nutritional require- ments of each species. Information derived from studies of habitat use, nest site selection, nesting chronology, and renesting characteristics can be used to define phenological events and cyclic characteristics of wetlands that correspond to use of aquatic habitats during critical stages in the reproductive cycle.

One of the least understood aspects of the relationship between wetland ecology and waterfowl use is the role that hydrology plays in regulating environmental factors that satisfy the requirements of breed- ing birds. Hydrology, a major force behind wetland ecology, dictates hydroperiods and chemical characteristics that control aquatic biotic communities. Availability of key food items, overwater nesting cover, sites for pair isolation, escape cover, and suitable water quality are con- trolled by hydrologic factors.

The role of prairie wetlands in the maintenance of key species of North American waterfowl has been emphasized by waterfowl biologists (Leitch 1964; Smith et al. 1964). Wetlands in the northern prairie of North America provide a variety of aquatic habitats that satisfy the requirements of breeding and migrating waterfowl and are essential for maintaining traditional population levels. Duck use of prairie wetlands

GEORGE A. SWANSON and HAROLD F. DUEBBERT, U.S. Fish and Wildlife Service, Northern Prairie Wildlife Research Center, Jamestown, North Dakota 58401.

depends on those areas' ability to provide the spacing requirements of breeding pairs; nutritional requirements during reproduction, molting, and migration; suitable nesting cover; escape cover; and a source of adequate drinking water. The wetland complex as well as land use associated with wetland basins and the surrounding uplands has been recognized as an important factor influencing recruitment in the prairie pothole region. To adequately describe the role of prairie wetlands in satisfying the requirements of waterfowl, it is necessary to identify the aquatic habitats that satisfy waterfowl requirements during spring migration, laying, brood rearing, molting, staging, and fall migration.

The ecological relationships between waterfowl and their aquatic habitats in the prairie pothole region have been investigated through studies of pair use of different wetland classes, feeding ecology, and nutritional requirements. Although descriptions of duck use provide a means of associating birds with different types of aquatic habitat, this approach does not identify the specific requirements satisfied by the habitats used. More recent investigations have focused on feeding ecology, physiological requirements, and condition indices (Swanson et al. 1974; Krapu 1974a, 1974b; Sugden 1973; Krapu 1979, 1981; Johnson et al. 1985; Hohman 1985; Swanson et al. 1986) to understand the cause-and-effect relationships between breeding birds and their aquatic habitats. This information is needed to establish guidelines for preservation and management of wetland habitats and mitigation of wetland losses. Our objective is to summarize the wetland habitat requirements of waterfowl in the Northern Prairies. Most of the available information, however, applies to the prairie pothole region.

DISCUSSION

Characteristics of Prairie Wetlands

The northern prairie wetlands area of North America contains a high density of shallow wetland basins that are influenced by annual moisture regimes that manipulate water levels and dissolved salts. Plant and animal communities must continually adjust to fluctuations in water depth and salt content. This dynamic water regime, and periodic changes in the biota that it produces, is a dominant factor influencing wetland use by waterfowl (Weller 1978, 1981).

The characteristics of prairie wetlands have been described in several classification systems (Kantrud 1986a). A regional classification system developed by Stewart and Kantrud (1971) used vegetative community types, water chemistry, and cover interspersion to differentiate classes, subclasses, and cover types of wetland basins in the glaciated prairie. Classes and subclasses were based on hydrological and chemical features, respectively. Cover types, which respond to climatic trends and land-use, are dynamic and have an important influence on wetland use by waterfowl (Weller 1981). Prairie wetlands occupy shallow basins with dynamic water regimes that tend to be nonintegrated and, as a result, are high in dissolved salts (Swanson et al. 1988).

Wetland communities are controlled hydrologically by (1) annual fluctuations in water levels that establish and maintain different wetland zones, (2) long-term trends in climatic conditions that cycle semipermanent lakes between extremes of flooding and drawdown, and (3) surface and groundwater flow systems that interact with climatic conditions, basin topographic setting, and geologic conditions to influence salt concentrations (LaBaugh et al. 1987, Swanson 1986b). As salt concentrations increase, salt-tolerant species dominate and wetland zones and their species composition change.

Water Chemistry

Wide variability in the chemistry of lakes and wetlands has been reported for the north-central United States (Moyle 1956; Stewart and Kantrud 1972; Gorham et al. 1983; Swanson et al. 1984; Sloan 1972) and Canada (Barica 1975; Rozkowski 1969). Recent results from the Cottonwood Lake study area, Stutsman County, North Dakota (LaBaugh et al. 1987) indicate that the chemistry of each wetland is dependent on the position that it occupies with respect to groundwater flow systems. Lakes that receive discharge from both regional and local groundwater flow systems, and that do not lose water to seepage, are highly saline (Swanson et al. 1988).

The chemical characteristics of prairie lakes and wetlands play a major role in determining the species composition, structure, and distribution of the plant and animal communities that occupy a wetland basin. Stewart and Kantrud (1971) described plant communities associated with various dissolved salt concentrations in waters of prairie lakes, and used specific conductance as a means of developing subclasses for a prairie wetland classification system.

The influence of chemical characteristics on use of prairie lakes by waterfowl has been noted by Swanson et al. (1984), Swanson (1986a), and Swanson et al. (1988). Chemical characteristics of prairie lakes influence duck use by controlling the abundance and distribution of key food items (Swanson 1986a) and potential competitors (Swanson and Nelson 1970), over-water nesting cover, the quality of drinking water, and escape cover for flightless birds (Swanson et al. 1984).

Prairie lakes tend to be shallow, highly eutrophic, and high in dissolved salts, which are factors that limit potential competition by fish populations (Nickum 1970; Schoenecker 1970). Fathead minnows (*Pimephales promelas*) and brook sticklebacks (*Culaea inconstans*) are more resistant to the chemical conditions associated with winterkill and high salinity than are game fish species (Burnham and Peterka 1975; Held 1971). Game fish are restricted to fresher, deeper lakes that are not abundant in the prairie pothole region. Burnham and Peterka (1975) studied the effects of sodium sulfate and sodium chloride on hatching success and survival of fathead minnow eggs and sac fry and found that different salts can have different effects.

Except for the European carp (*Cyprinus carpio*), the influence of fish species on use of prairie wetlands by nonpiscivorous ducks has not been well documented. On the basis of food selection one would expect to find different reactions, depending on the duck and fish species involved, their age and reproductive condition, diet, and the abundance and distribution of key food items (Swanson and Nelson 1970). Hurlbert et al. (1986) summarized some of the literature on the potential for fish-waterbird competition.

The hydrologic characteristics of prairie wetlands, principally those that determine salt concentrations and the availability of freshwater, determine whether saline lakes are suitable for rearing ducklings (Swanson et al. 1984). Cooch (1964) suggested that high salt levels in wetlands can contribute to a botulism outbreak because the toxin influences the function of supraorbital salt glands in birds.

Female dabbling ducks of some species nest on islands located on saline lakes (Duebbert et al. 1983; Lokemoen et al. 1984) that provide attractive nest sites secure from mammalian predators. Recently hatched ducklings, however, cannot tolerate salt levels that exceed 20,000 microsiemens per cm (μS/cm). Swanson et al. (1984) reported that some mortality occurred in ducklings exposed to 16,000 μS/cm and that growth was retarded at 17,000 μS/cm. Duckling use of saline lakes that exceeded 20,000 μS/cm was restricted to lakes that contained freshwater springs along the shoreline. Prairie saline lakes contain high concentrations of sulfates and magnesium (Table 8.1) that do not appear to be processed by the supraorbital salt glands as efficiently as sodium chloride (Schmidt-Nielson 1960). Hens that hatch nests located on islands in lakes with high salt levels move their broods to freshwater springs or other wetlands that contain suitable water quality (Duebbert et al. 1983). Duckling use of saline lakes was dominated by gadwall (Table 8.1).

Understanding the hydrologic conditions that control the chemical characteristics of prairie lakes, as well as the effect of water chemistry on plant and invertebrate communities and bird physiology, provides knowledge that can be used to preserve and manage wetlands for waterfowl production and migrational habitat.

TABLE 8.1. Hydrographic features, chemical characteristics, duckling species composition (%), and duckling use of saline lakes in the glacial outwash of Stutsman and Kidder counties, North Dakota

| | Lake designation | | | |
| | Permanent lakes | | Semipermanent lakes | |
	A	B	C	D
Hydrographic features				
Length, km	4.5	3.0	1.4	1.4
Shore length, km	20.7	10.5	4.5	3.8
Surface area, ha	828	440	73	52
Maximum depth, m	1.5	30.0	1.0	1.0
Chemical characteristics[a]				
pH	9.2	9.5	9.5	9.5
Specific conductivity[b]	40,000	23,400	29,000	15,900
Chloride	1,815	1,360	3,115	1,295
Sulfate	27,500	8,750	12,000	5,000
Total alkalinity	1,480	1,870	670	570
Sodium	9,240	6,300	7,500	3,200
Potassium	712	512	652	250
Calcium	35	12	49	30
Magnesium	4,288	688	1,360	816
Species composition (%)				
Gadwall	67	52	53	63
Blue-winged teal	0	0	13	24
Redhead	19	48	8	3
Mallard	12	0	8	6
Northern pintail	2	0	7	2
Northern shoveler	0	0	3	2
American wigeon	0	0	8	0
Duckling use				
N/ha	0.1	0.1	0.6	3.1
N/km of shoreline	4.1	2.5	9.8	41.7

Source: Adapted from Swanson et al. 1984.
[a]Data expressed in mg/l.
[b]μS/cm at 25°C.

Vegetation Dynamics

Emergent vegetation that occurs in wetlands in the prairie pothole region was originally manipulated by natural forces such as climate, grazing, and fire (Kantrud 1986c). Current land-use practices, however, have greatly modified these original ecological factors through suppression of fire, controlled grazing, selective drainage, and tillage. Wetlands that were originally nonintegrated have been converted to integrated systems by selectively draining shallow wetlands into larger basins. This process tends to lower dissolved salts, deposit silt in the remaining basins, and stabilize water levels. These changes favor the growth and development of cattails (*Typha* spp.) that are well adapted to form extensive monotypes in shallow, stable water that is low in dissolved salts (Kantrud 1986c).

A wetland complex made up of seasonally and semipermanently flooded basins (Winter and Carr 1980; Swanson 1987a), was observed over a 19-year period (1967–1986) on the Cottonwood Lake study area in Stutsman County, North Dakota. Information from this study combined with previous descriptions of wetlands in this area (Stewart and Kantrud 1971; Eisenlohr 1972), can be used to describe changes that have occurred over a 25-year period (1961–1986). Changes in emergent vegetation were documented using ground and low level aerial photography. A hydrology study was initiated during the summer of 1978 (Winter and Carr 1980) to define the influence of hydrology and chemistry on plant and invertebrate communities (LaBaugh et al. 1987).

Semipermanent wetlands have cycled during 1961–1986 on the study area between extremes in water level that drowned emergent vegetation and established open-water lakes to drawdowns that exposed mudflats and reestablished emergent vegetation (Swanson 1987b). Rapid changes occurred when an increase in water level persisted long enough to drown out emergent vegetation or when drawdown exposed mudflats during the growing season. If annual fluctuations in water level did not exceed the depth tolerance of emergent vegetation or did not expose mudflats by drawdown during the growing season vegetation zones remained stabilized.

Semipermanent basins with similar hydrologic functions responded to climatic trends to produce salt concentrations and zones of emergent vegetation that were similar in species composition. Basins with surface water outflow and high turnover rates of water volume tended to have stable water levels and low dissolved salts. Nonintegrated basins without surface outflow tended to be dynamic in both water-level changes and salt concentrations as they responded to climatic trends. Seeds of salt-tolerant species such as alkali bulrush (*Scirpus maritimus*) and whitetop rivergrass (*Scolochloa festucacea*) (Stewart and Kantrud 1971) germinated during drawdown in closed semipermanently flooded basins. In 1977, specific conductance of water in wetland P1 (Swanson 1987b) was 8,000 (μS/cm) just prior to drawdown. After this wetland reflooded in 1978, a shallow-marsh species (whitetop rivergrass) that germinated during drawdown in 1977 dominated the center of the basin until it drowned in 1980 and an open-water zone was reestablished. Cattail, on the other hand, germinated in 1974 on the exposed mudflat of wetland P4 (Swanson 1987b), a flow-through system lower in salt content, and this wetland is currently dominated by cattail (Fig. 8.1). Invertebrate populations are also influenced by wetland hydrologic cycles (Swanson 1984).

A qualitative model of plant succession in freshwater wetlands proposed by van der Valk (1981) provides a framework for understanding and predicting the vegetation dynamics of wetlands. Van der Valk and Davis (1978) described the role of seed banks in the vegetation dynamics

FIG. 8.1. Previously open-water wetland dominated by cattail for 13 years following drawdown in 1974.

of glacial prairie marshes in northern Iowa. Species present in prairie marsh seed banks contained seeds that germinate on exposed mudflats or in very shallow water, those that survive on exposed mudflats and germinate when there is standing water, and those that can only germinate on exposed mudflats without standing water. Weller (1981) described changes in wetland vegetation related to trends in water depth and the activity of muskrats (*Ondatra zibethicus*). Plant species composition, zonation, and cover types as influenced by hydroperiod and salinity were described by Stewart and Kantrud (1971) in their classification of natural ponds and lakes in the glaciated prairie pothole region. They described response of plant communities to drawdown and flooding. Plant species composition, structure, and distribution influence bird use as marshes change from dense vegetation established during drawdown to open water when vegetation is removed by rising water and herbivore activity (Weller 1981).

Waterfowl Response to Cover
Kantrud (1986c) reviewed the literature on effects of vegetational changes on use of wetlands by breeding waterfowl in the prairie pothole region. Wetlands covered by dense stands of tall emergent vegetation exhibit decreased use by waterfowl as compared to wetlands with open areas of shallow water, those sparsely vegetated with short emergents, or those with exposed shorelines and mudflats. Both dabbling ducks

(Anatini) and diving ducks (Aythyini) prefer wetlands with openings in the marsh canopy or flooded emergent vegetation of a shorter type (Kantrud 1986c).

The response of waterfowl to changes in the structure and density of wetland vegetation has been attributed to the quality and accessibility of overwater nesting cover, pair isolation, security of flightless birds, and availability of aquatic foods. Mallards (*Anas platyrhynchos*) and gadwalls (*A. strepera*) were observed to concentrate during dry years on semipermanent wetlands that contained an interspersion of deep marsh and open water. Breeding pairs were observed to make repeated attempts to land on wetlands that appeared to be saturated with pairs because they were immediately repelled by a paired male when they attempted to land. A pair of gadwall attempted to land four times on a semipermanent wetland but was repelled each time until they left the area. During each chase they flew over adjacent open-water wetlands but did not attempt to land. Paired gadwall collected on this wetland were consuming large midge larvae that were abundant and highly available in the shallow water between clumps of emergent vegetation.

Midges (Chironomidae) and Cladocera appear to respond to rising water levels that drown out emergent or upland vegetation and, as a result, establishes a detritus food chain (McKnight and Low 1969). Open pools that are established by an increase in water depth may provide abundant foods for several years. The role of organic detritus and algae in supporting high populations of Cladocera and midges in prairie wetlands has not been well defined. Cladocera and midges, however, respond to an increase in the organic content that supports aquatic food chains (Swanson 1977). Kaminski and Prince (1981) and Murkin et al. (1982) examined responses of dabbling ducks and aquatic invertebrates to manipulated vegetation. Kaminski and Prince (1981) suggest that breeding dabbling ducks use cover-water interspersion as a proximate cue to wetland habitats that produce abundant aquatic invertebrate populations. Murkin et al. (1982) suggest that visual isolation associated with cover-water interspersion also determines waterfowl densities. Nelson and Kadlec (1984) provide a functional basis for structural cues potentially used by female waterfowl to assess invertebrate food resource suitability.

Waterfowl broods also prefer semi-open or open emergent vegetative cover (Kantrud 1986c). Duck broods observed by Duebbert and Frank (1984) during 1958–1963 and 1967–1978 in North Dakota used primarily semipermanent (58%) and seasonal (24%) wetlands. Although cover has been described as important to broods, large numbers of broods are often found on open seasonally flooded wetlands (Fig. 8.2)

FIG. 8.2. Large concentration of broods on the Big Meadow Waterfowl Production Area, an open, seasonally flooded wetland near Wildrose, North Dakota.

and waste-stabilization ponds where overwater cover is absent but midges and Cladocera are abundant (Swanson 1977).

Bird Use of Wetlands

Studies of breeding pair use in the prairie pothole region have demonstrated the importance of a variety of wetlands in supplying pair requirements (Stewart and Kantrud 1973; Sugden 1978; Stoudt 1971, 1982; Ruwaldt et al. 1979).

Large semipermanent wetlands that contain vast areas of deep marsh vegetation interspersed with open water as well as shallow marsh, wet meadow, and low prairie vegetation (Fig. 8.3) provide ideal habitat for waterfowl and other wetland wildlife (Weller 1981; Krapu and Duebbert 1974). When emergent nesting cover is located in the center of large marshes, predation appears to be less severe on overwater nests, and bird colonies persist that do not occur on small marshes. Kraft Slough, a

FIG. 8.3. Kraft Slough, a large semipermanent marsh located in western Sargent County, North Dakota, showing areas of deep-marsh vegetation interspersed with open water.

large semipermanent marsh in western Sargent County in North Dakota, contained an estimated 3,323 pairs of all species of breeding birds in 1974 (Krapu and Duebbert 1974). Large semipermanent and permanent marshes that contain extensive stands of deep marsh vegetation such as common reed (*Phragmites communis*), bulrush (*Scirpus* spp.), and cattail provide essential habitat for concentrations of flightless adult ducks during the molting period.

Large saline lakes that contain extensive beds of sago pondweed (*Potamogeton pectinatus*) provide fall staging and conditioning habitat for tundra swans (*Cygnus columbianus*), canvasbacks (*Aythya valisineria*), and several other species of waterfowl (Kantrud 1986b).

Waterfowl use of different wetlands classified by hydroperiod and salinity have been described by Drewien and Springer (1969), Stewart and Kantrud (1973), Kantrud and Stewart (1977), Flake (1978), and Ruwaldt et al. (1979). The method of expressing pair use data will influence interpretation of study results. Wetland use expressed as pairs/ km² by wetland type tends to emphasize use of small ephemeral, temporary, and seasonal basins; whereas pair use expressed as pairs per wetland basin tends to indicate greater use of larger basins with more permanent water (Kantrud and Stewart 1977). Pair use expressed as pairs/km² for basins containing ponded water tends to elevate use of ephemeral and temporary wetlands; whereas pair use expressed as pairs/ km², without regard to presence or absence of ponded water, tends to elevate use of wetlands that contain water for longer periods (Kantrud and Stewart 1977).

Seasonally flooded wetlands that flood in early spring and dry by midsummer receive high use by breeding dabbling ducks. If first nesting attempts are highly successful, shallow wetlands that receive high pair use in early spring increase in importance. As nest losses increase and renesting birds are forced to lay clutches in June or early July, wetlands that hold water longer increase in importance to breeding females.

The length of time that wetlands contain water in any given year influences their role in providing the requirements of breeding pairs. Evans and Black (1956), Jenni (1956), Drewien and Springer (1969), Stewart and Kantrud (1973), Krapu (1974a), and Swanson et al. (1974) stressed the importance of seasonally flooded wetlands to breeding dabbling ducks.

Ducks that nested on Miller Lake island in dense concentrations were closely associated with a complex of 97 natural basin wetlands that existed within 3 km of the island (Duebbert et al. 1983). Of the 97 wetlands, 13% were ephemeral, 35% were temporary, 41% were seasonal, and 7% were semipermanent according to the classification of Stewart and Kantrud (1971). Breeding pairs and hens with broods made heavy use of temporary and seasonal wetlands and it is doubtful whether the dense nesting concentration could have been maintained without them.

Temporary and seasonal wetlands were a major component of the aquatic habitat that supported a highly productive duck nesting population at Hosmer, South Dakota, during 1969–1974 (Duebbert and Loke-moen 1980). In 6 years, a minimum of 7,250 ducklings hatched on a 51 ha field of prime nesting cover in an area where predators were rigidly controlled. In a circular area of 8.13 km² surrounding the nesting field there were 74 natural basin wetlands of which 19% were ephemeral, 28% were temporary and 53% were seasonal.

Breeding pairs of dabbling ducks used seasonal wetlands in North Dakota as follows: mallards 44%, gadwalls 41%, northern pintails (*Anas acuta*) 40%, green-winged teal (*A. crecca*) 54%, blue-winged teal (*A. discors*) 52%, northern shovelers (*A. clypeata*) 40%, and American wigeons (*A. americana*) 42% (Stewart and Kantrud 1973). Diving duck pair use was greater on semipermanent wetlands: 63% in redheads (*Aythya americana*), 69% in ring-necked ducks (*A. collaris*), 71% in canvasbacks, 53% in lesser scaup (*A. affinis*), and 67% in ruddy ducks (*Oxyura jamaicensis*), respectively.

Ruwaldt et al. (1979) used the wetland classification system of Stewart and Kantrud (1971) to describe pair use of prairie wetlands in South Dakota. When surface water was abundant in 1973, some of the highest pair densities (pairs per hectare) observed on natural wetlands occurred on ephemeral, temporary, and seasonal basins (Ruwaldt et al. 1979).

Response to Drought

Use observed by Ruwaldt et al. (1979) was influenced by water conditions that were in turn altered by a drought that started in 1973 and persisted into 1974. Declines in pair density observed by Ruwaldt et al. (1979) in 1974 on the more permanent wetlands were attributed to a change in the wetland complex resulting from loss of shallow wetlands. Overall pair use decreased 59% in 1974 in response to drought conditions. Species most sensitive to drought were northern pintail, blue-winged teal, and northern shoveler. Mallard, gadwall, and American wigeon were less sensitive.

When shallow wetlands within the wetland complex are not available to breeding birds in drought years, breeding strategies and production are altered (Hansen and McKnight 1964; Smith 1969; Smith 1970; Henny 1973; Derksen and Eldridge 1980; Krapu et al. 1983; Swanson et al. 1985). Some birds migrate to different geographic areas in response to drought (Hansen and McKnight 1964; Smith 1970; Calverley and Boag 1977) while others remain on permanent lakes in traditional breeding areas in a nonbreeding status (Smith et al. 1964; Smith 1969; Kaminski and Prince 1981).

Depending on the severity of drought in any given year, a portion of the birds may attempt to nest. Females that initiate nests in dry years do not persistently renest as they do in wet years (Stoudt 1969; Pospahala et al. 1974; Calverley and Boag 1977) but join flocks of molting drakes early in the breeding season (Swanson et al. 1985). Displacement of ducks by drought have been documented through increases in bird numbers north of the prairies and decreases on the northern prairie breeding grounds (Stewart and Kantrud 1973; Ruwaldt et al. 1979; Krapu et al. 1983). When seasonally flooded wetlands are dry, the biomass of invertebrates available to support breeding birds is greatly reduced (Smith et al. 1964; Swanson et al. 1985, 1986). Jessen et al. (1964) suggested that high use by breeding pairs is related to standing crops of food and is modified by the territorial requirements of each species.

Wetland Use by Breeding Females

Dwyer et al. (1979) described the use of prairie wetlands by radio-marked, breeding mallards. Feeding time by hens increased from 18 to 55% from prelaying to laying and mallard hens spent 45% of their time foraging in seasonal wetlands. Krapu (1974a), Serie and Swanson (1976), and Swanson et al. (1985) described a significant increase in invertebrates in the diet of laying versus prelaying northern pintails and gadwalls and nonlaying mallards. Laying blue-winged teal (Swanson and Meyer 1977) and northern shovelers (Swanson et al. 1979) also consumed a diet dominated by invertebrates (Fig. 8.4).

Drewien and Springer (1969) noted that pairs demonstrated intraspecific strife when nesting began. When egg laying was initiated, pair use shifted to small, shallow wetlands. High use of seasonally flooded wetlands coincides with initiation of laying when increased feeding is required to satisfy protein demands for egg production (Krapu and Swanson 1975). Laying female dabbling ducks satisfy protein demands by consuming invertebrates that are abundant and highly available in seasonally flooded wetlands (Swanson et al. 1974).

Swanson et al. (1979) summarized the foods consumed by laying female dabbling ducks in south-central North Dakota. Feeding ecology studies have defined the diet of laying northern pintails (Krapu 1974a), blue-winged teal (Swanson and Meyer 1977), gadwalls (Serie and Swanson 1976; Swanson et al. 1979), northern shovelers (Swanson et al. 1979), and mallards (Swanson et al. 1985). Hohman (1985) recently

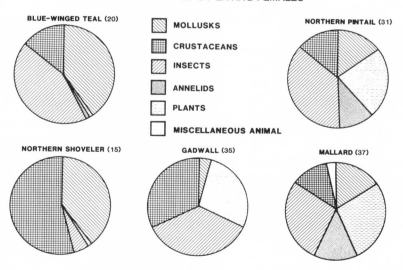

FOODS CONSUMED BY LAYING FEMALES

FIG. 8.4. Proportions of plant and animal foods consumed by laying female blue-winged teal (*Swanson and Meyer 1977*), northern pintails (*Krapu 1974a*), northern shovelers (*Swanson et al. 1979*), gadwalls (*Swanson et al. 1979*), and mallards (*Swanson et al. 1985*). Number of birds examined shown in parentheses.

described the diet of prelaying and laying ring-necked ducks in the prairie-boreal forest transition zone of northwestern Minnesota. Studies of the diet of laying female canvasbacks in the Minnedosa area (J. R. Serie, pers. commun.) and redheads and ruddy ducks in the vicinity of Jamestown, North Dakota (M. C. Woodin, pers. commun.), have been completed but the data are not currently available. Several studies have examined the nutrient content of foods consumed by laying females (Krapu and Swanson 1975) and the reproductive performance of laying females exposed to changes in diet and food availability (Krapu 1979; Swanson et al. 1986).

Species differences in the foods consumed by laying females cannot be readily ascertained due to differences in nesting chronology (Swanson et al. 1979) and annual changes in renesting effort that expose each species to different food resources. Invertebrate populations and their availability to breeding birds change rapidly with time (Swanson et al. 1974) and wetland basins with different hydrologic characteristics selectively dry as the season progresses.

Similar proportions of invertebrates were consumed by laying mallards, pintails, and gadwalls (Fig. 8.4). Gadwalls substituted plant material for the seed component consumed by the other two species (Swanson 1985). Laying female northern shovelers and blue-winged teal consumed 99% animal material. Snails were a major food item in the diet of blue-winged teal and northern shovelers. Gadwalls, however, selected few aquatic snails.

Insects were a major food item in the diet of laying blue-winged teal, gadwalls, mallards, and northern pintails, but were generally not consumed by northern shovelers. Crustaceans were a dominant food item in the diet of laying northern shovelers and were an important food item in the diet of gadwalls.

Earthworms (Oligochaeta) were important in the diet of the two early nesting species, mallard and northern pintail. Terrestrial earthworm availability depended on the amount of rainfall during early spring. Seasonal changes in the diet of laying female mallards reflected changes in food availability (Swanson et al. 1985).

Nest loss is often high in ground-nesting ducks in the prairie pothole region (Cowardin et al. 1985). Renesting is influenced by water conditions and, subsequently, food availability (Swanson et al. 1986) as well as the nutrient reserves and photoperiod. Mallards are physiologically capable of producing 50 eggs during the breeding season when they have access to an unlimited food supply (Swanson et al. 1986).

The role of food availability as a factor influencing the reproductive characteristics of prairie dabbling ducks was investigated on experimental ponds (Swanson et al. 1986). An important breeding strategy of prairie nesting ducks is to renest following nest loss (Sowls 1955; Strohmeyer 1967; Cowardin et al. 1985; Swanson et al. 1986). The importance of renesting to annual production has been discussed by Gates (1962), Pospahala et al. (1974), Donham et al. (1976), and Swanson et al. (1986). Early-nesting species such as the mallard initiate laying in mid-April and renesting may continue until late June or early July. Climatic conditions and, subsequently, water levels in wetlands influence the renesting effort in any given year (Cowardin et al. 1985). Three-year-old mallards are physiologically capable of producing four and five clutches during the breeding season. When food availability was reduced, clutch size dropped, renesting intervals increased, and the number of renesting attempts was reduced (Swanson et al. 1986). The relationship between stage of incubation when mallard clutches were removed and renesting intervals is expressed as a linear and quadratic equation in Figure 8.5 (Swanson et al. 1986). Birds incubating clutches to the pipping stage were able to renest in 11 days when exposed to an unlimited food supply.

Feeding Ecology

Nutrient requirements for reproduction, growth, and migration are prerequisite information for understanding the role of wetland habitat in waterfowl population dynamics. Swanson and Meyer (1973) reviewed

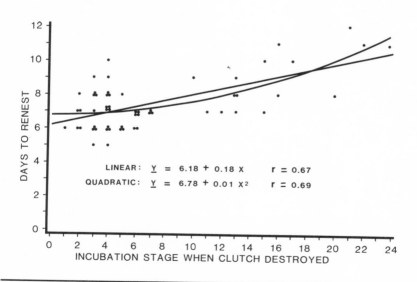

LINEAR: $Y = 6.18 + 0.18 X$ $r = 0.67$

QUADRATIC: $Y = 6.78 + 0.01 X^2$ $r = 0.69$

FIG. 8.5. Incubation stage when mallard clutches were destroyed plotted against number of days required to renest showing linear and quadratic rates of increase in renesting interval (*Swanson et al. 1986*).

the literature on foods consumed by breeding diving and dabbling ducks and their broods. Newer studies, however, have been completed since their report was written. Most of the published studies of feeding ecology in the prairie pothole region have been undertaken in the vicinity of Minnedosa, Manitoba, and Jamestown, North Dakota (Fig. 8.6). The work of Sugden (1973) in Alberta, Dirschl (1969) in Saskatchewan, and Hohman (1985) in northwestern Minnesota are exceptions.

Perret (1962) described foods of breeding and immature mallards on a study area south of Minnedosa, Manitoba, and pointed out some of the deficiencies in previous food habit studies. Rogers and Korschgen (1966), Bartonek and Hickey (1969a, 1969b), and Siegfried (1973) examined foods consumed by diving ducks near Minnedosa, Manitoba. Dirschl (1969) described the diet of lesser scaup and blue-winged teal on a marsh complex located in the Saskatchewan River Delta. Sugden (1973) described the diet of northern pintail, gadwall, American wigeon, and lesser scaup ducklings on wetlands near Strathmore, Alberta. The diet of males and females was analyzed separately in some of the studies but the reproductive condition of the female was not defined.

Foods Consumed by Breeding Pairs

Adult female diving ducks in the prairie pothole region primarily consume invertebrates during spring and summer (Table 8.2). Lesser scaup consistently selected scuds (Amphipoda) as a major component of their diet, leeches (Hirudinea) being a second choice. Other diving duck species do not select scuds even though this crustacean is abundant in semipermanent wetlands where diving ducks feed most often. Ruddy duck (Oxyurini) males and females concentrated on midge larvae and redheads and ring-necked ducks consumed caddis flies (Trichoptera) as a principal food. A small sample of redheads in North Dakota fed on midge larvae (Table 8.2). Canvasback and ruddy duck females (Siegfried 1973) selected snails (Gastropoda) which provide a rich source of calcium (Krapu and Swanson 1975). Male canvasbacks, on the other hand, consumed tubers of sago pondweed.

Adult dabbling ducks consumed relatively high proportions of invertebrates during the breeding season (Table 8.3). Northern pintail females selected a diet that contained a greater volume of invertebrates than paired males. Mallard females examined in Manitoba consumed a significantly greater volume of invertebrates than males (Perret 1962). Nonlaying female mallards examined in North Dakota selected a diet similar to males but laying females consumed a significantly greater volume of invertebrates (Swanson et al. 1985). Northern shovelers and gadwalls selected a diet relatively high in crustaceans.

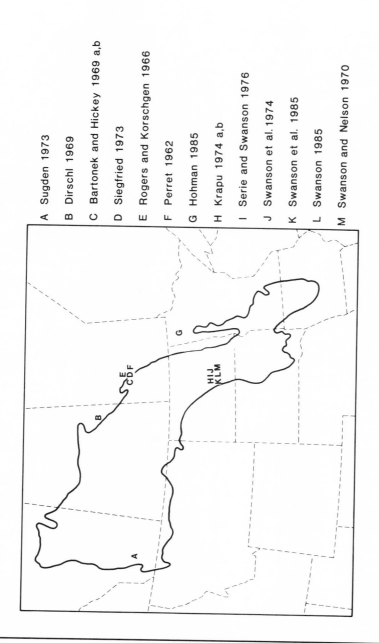

A Sugden 1973
B Dirschl 1969
C Bartonek and Hickey 1969 a,b
D Siegfried 1973
E Rogers and Korschgen 1966
F Perret 1962
G Hohman 1985
H Krapu 1974 a,b
I Serie and Swanson 1976
J Swanson et al. 1974
K Swanson et al. 1985
L Swanson 1985
M Swanson and Nelson 1970

FIG. 8.6. Prairie pothole region of North America showing the approximate locations of feeding ecology studies of breeding birds.

TABLE 8.2. Foods consumed by adult diving ducks during the breeding season

Species	Location	Sex	Number of birds	Invertebrates consumed (%)	A principal food (%)
Redhead[a]	North Dakota	F	3	95	Chironomidae (55)
Redhead[b]	Manitoba	F	6	81	Trichoptera (80)
		M	6	86	Trichoptera (62)
Canvasback[b]	Manitoba	F	16	92	Gastropoda (66)
		M	13	2	Potamogeton spp. (95)
Lesser scaup[b]	Manitoba	F	7	98	Amphipoda (46)
		M	7	99	Hirudinea (61)
Lesser scaup[c]	Saskatchewan	C[d] (May)	12	91	Amphipoda (66)
		C (June)	20	95	Amphipoda (67)
		C (July)	22	95	Hirudinea (49)
Lesser scaup[e]	Manitoba	C	39	91	Amphipoda (52)
Ring-necked duck[f]	Minnesota	F (Prelaying-laying)	11	63	Trichoptera (21)
		M (Post arrival)	10	63	Trichoptera (37)
Ruddy duck[g]	Manitoba	F	19	95	Chironomidae (63)
		M	23	90	Chironomidae (82)

Source: Adapted from Swanson and Meyer 1973.
[a]Swanson and Meyer 1973. Data expressed as percent by volume.
[b]Bartonek and Hickey 1969a. Data expressed as percent by volume.
[c]Dirschl 1969. Data expressed as percent by weight.
[d]Sexes combined.
[e]Rogers and Korschgen 1966. Data expressed as percent by volume.
[f]Hohman 1985. Data expressed as percent by weight.
[g]Siegfried 1973. Data expressed as percent by volume.

TABLE 8.3. Foods consumed by adult dabbling ducks during the breeding season

Species	Location	Sex	Number of birds	Invertebrates consumed (%)	A principal food (%)
Blue-winged teal[a]	North Dakota	F	61	91	Insecta (36)
					Gastropoda (36)
Blue-winged teal[b]	Saskatchewan	M	46	85	Insecta (33)
		C[c] (May)	17	66	Gastropoda (43)
		C (June)	23	68	Gastropoda (48)
		C (July)	6	81	Hirudinea (62)
Gadwall[d]	North Dakota (Saline lakes)	F	77	48	Crustacea (29)
Gadwall[e]	North Dakota (Wetlands)	M	30	40	Crustacea (32)
		F	72	62	Insecta (31)
Mallard[f]	Manitoba	M	36	45	Crustacea (26)
		F	46	64	Insecta (60)
Mallard[g]	North Dakota	M	50	46	Insecta (44)
		F (Nonlaying)	41	37	Seeds (59)
Northern shoveler[e]	North Dakota	M	39	38	Seeds (56)
		F	44	99	Crustacea (57)
Northern pintail[g]	North Dakota[h]	M	28	97	Crustacea (52)
		F	39	79	Diptera (28)
		M	14	30	Seeds (70)

Source: Adapted from Swanson and Meyer 1973.
[a] Swanson et al. 1974. Data expressed as percent by volume.
[b] Dirschl 1969. Data expressed as percent by weight.
[c] Sexes combined.
[d] Serie and Swanson 1976. Data expressed as percent by volume.
[e] Swanson, 1986b. Data expressed as percent by volume.
[f] Swanson et al. 1985. Data expressed as percent by volume.
[g] Krapu 1974b. Data expressed as percent by volume.
[h] Birds fed on nontilled wetlands.

247

Blue-winged teal during the breeding season selected a diet dominated by snails and insects (Table 8.3). Diet changes occurred following arrival on the breeding grounds in mid-May when laying was initiated; the birds at this time shifted from a diet high in seeds to one dominated by invertebrates (Swanson et al. 1974). Foods consumed varied with the wetland zone that birds selected to feed in (Table 8.4). Snails, insects, and seeds dominated the diet of birds that fed in wet-meadow and shallow-marsh zones and scuds, insects, and snails dominated the diet of birds that fed in deep-marsh zones. This shift was influenced by a change in hydroperiod. Seasonally flooded basins do not routinely support deep-marsh zones and scuds (Stewart and Kantrud 1971; Swanson 1984). Snails and insects were the major foods selected in open-water zones with submerged vascular plants that were in contact with the water surface. Copepoda, Anostraca, and Cladocera were consumed in the open-water zone (above littoral) and midges and mayflies (Ephemeroptera) dominated the diet of birds that fed on the water surface above deep open water.

Foods Consumed by Juveniles
Juvenile lesser scaup and redheads, class II (Gollop and Marshall 1954), ring-necked ducks, and one- to five-week-old ruddy ducks selected the same kinds of invertebrate foods that were consumed by breeding females (Tables 8.2, 8.5). Scuds, caddis flies, midges, and snails were dominant foods consumed by diving ducks during the breeding season in prairie wetlands and the prairie-boreal transition zone.

The diet of juvenile Anatini varied among species (Table 8.6). Gadwall and American wigeon ducklings in Alberta consumed stems and leaves of baby pondweed (*Potamogeton pusillus*) (Table 8.6). Northern pintail ducklings selected a diet of 67% animal foods dominated by snails. Mallard ducklings in Manitoba consumed a diet of animal foods dominated by insects. The diet of northern shoveler ducklings was composed of approximately 100% animal material dominated by Crustacea. Juvenile blue-winged teal selected a diet of invertebrates dominated by molluscs and insects.

Ducklings of all species during the early stages of development consumed a diet dominated by invertebrates (Table 8.7). The diet of northern pintail, gadwall, American wigeon, and lesser scaup ducklings from one- to five-days old exceeded 90% animal material. All species consumed a diet dominated by invertebrates for up to 15 days of age. After 15 days of age, gadwall and American wigeon ducklings shifted to a diet dominated by plants whereas northern pintail and lesser scaup continued to consume a diet high in invertebrates.

TABLE 8.4. Proportion (mean percent by volume) of plant and animal foods contained in the esophagi of breeding blue-winged teal collected while feeding within different zones of North Dakota wetlands[a]

Food items	Wet-meadow zone (17 birds)	Shallow-marsh zone (25 birds)	Deep-marsh zone (11 birds)	Open-water zone (17 birds)	Permanent open-water zone (above littoral) (12 birds)	Permanent open-water zone[b] (above profundal) (4 birds)
Animal						
Mollusca	68.2	88.2	99.9	95.5	93.9	100.0
Gastropoda	34.9	49.1	23.7	37.0		0.7
Lymnaeidae	34.9	49.1	23.7	35.3		0.7
Planorbidae	21.8	37.4	3.3	16.2		
Physidae	10.5	3.0	15.1	10.0		0.6
Pelecypoda	2.6	8.7	5.3	9.1		0.1
Crustacea				1.7		
Amphipoda	0.2	5.8	39.4	14.6	83.2	
Ostracoda		T[c]	36.3	3.9	5.5	
Copepoda			3.1	4.2		
Cladocera		T			24.7	
Conchostraca	0.2	5.7		4.2	29.3	
Anostraca	T	T	T	2.3		
Insecta	33.0	27.4	34.7	43.9	23.7	99.0
Ephemeroptera	T		T		10.7	24.1
Odonata		0.4	5.3	2.6		
Hemiptera		0.9	0.1	4.5		
Trichoptera	1.6	4.8	0.3	8.0		0.1
Coleoptera	14.2	7.4	1.0	8.4		1.1
Diptera	17.2	13.9	28.0	20.4	7.7	73.7
Culicinae			9.4	0.8	3.0	
Chironomidae		5.8	10.4	9.0		73.5
Annelida	3.2	3.2	2.1		2.4	
Misc. animal	0.1	0.1	T			
Plant	31.8	11.8	0.1	4.5	6.1	0.3
Seeds	31.8	11.6	T	4.1	6.0	T
Vegetative parts		0.2	T	0.2	0.1	T
Algae				0.2		

Source: Adapted from Swanson and Meyer 1973.
[a] Zones as defined by Stewart and Kantrud (1971) for aquatic vegetation.
[b] Birds sampled at night.
[c] T = < 0.1%.

TABLE 8.5. Foods consumed by juvenile diving ducks on the breeding grounds

Species	Location	Age class	Number of birds	Invertebrates consumed (%)	A principal food (%)
Lesser scaup[a]	Alberta	Class I–III	135	96	Amphipoda (52)
Lesser scaup[b]	Manitoba	Juvenile	25	99	Amphipoda (49)
Redhead[b]	Manitoba	Juvenile	37	43	Trichoptera (18)
Canvasback[b]	Manitoba	Juvenile	86	87	Trichoptera (59)
Ring-necked duck[c]	Minnesota	Class I	11	98	Chironomidae (48)
		Class II	29	80	Trichoptera (62)
Ruddy duck[d]	Manitoba	1–5 weeks	18	88	Chironomidae (73)

Source: Adapted from Swanson and Meyer 1973.
[a]Sugden 1973. Data expressed as percent by weight.
[b]Bartonek and Hickey 1969a. Data expressed as percent by volume.
[c]Hohman 1985. Data expressed as percent by weight.
[d]Siegfried 1973. Data expressed as percent by volume.

TABLE 8.6. Foods consumed by juvenile dabbling ducks on the breeding grounds

Species	Location	Age class	Number of birds	Invertebrates consumed (%)	A principal food (%)
Gadwall[a]	Alberta	I–III	167	10	Potamogeton pusillus (34)
American wigeon[a]	Alberta	I–III	129	11	Potamogeton pusillus (47)
Northern pintail[a]	Alberta	I–III	144	67	Gastropoda (36)
Mallard[b]	Manitoba	I–III[c]	62	91	Insecta (72)
Northern shoveler[d]	North Dakota	III	10	100	Crustacea (49)
Blue-winged teal[e]	North Dakota	Juvenile (flying)	61	90	Mollusca (41) Insecta (40)
Blue-winged teal[f]	North Dakota	I	24	100	Mollusca (48)
		II	20	92	Insecta (62)
		III	24	95	Insecta (48)

Source: Adapted from Swanson and Meyer 1973.
[a]Sugden 1973. Data expressed as percent by weight.
[b]Perret 1962. Data expressed as percent by volume.
[c]Includes eight flying birds.
[d]Swanson et al. 1972. Data expressed as percent by volume.
[e]Swanson 1985. Data expressed as percent by volume.
[f]Swanson 1986b. Data expressed as percent by volume.

TABLE 8.7. Changes in the percent of animal foods consumed by ducklings as related to age

Age (days)	Animal foods (%)			
	Northern pintail	Gadwall	American wigeon	Lesser scaup
0–5	98 (10)[a]	94 (22)	99 (8)	99 (19)
6–10	96 (25)	58 (32)	97 (29)	99 (22)
11–15	91 (18)	71 (35)	89 (13)	99 (15)
16–20	82 (14)	21 (31)	5 (12)	100 (16)
21–30	39 (38)	2 (15)	2 (20)	92 (24)
31–40	91 (14)	5 (14)	1 (25)	98 (23)
41+	50 (25)	1 (18)	5 (22)	95 (16)

Source: Adapted from Sugden 1973.
[a]Sample size in parentheses.

Foods Consumed by Postbreeding Ducks

Salomonsen (1968) described the behavior of molting diving and dabbling ducks. Some species migrate and concentrate on molting areas while others molt on wetlands used during the breeding season. DuBowy (1985) studied the feeding ecology and behavior of postbreeding male blue-winged teal and northern shovelers on the Delta Marsh in south-central Manitoba during 1977–1979. Northern shoveler males selected a diet dominated by Cladocera (85.5%) and midge pupae (12.9%). Blue-winged teal, on the other hand, selected principally snails (44.3%), Culicidae (29.2%), seeds and vegetation (15.5%), and midges (5.6%). Northern shovelers did not feed consistently during the summer flightless period, while blue-winged teal fed throughout the summer.

Bergman (1973) described feeding strategies on lakes used by postbreeding canvasbacks and redheads. Canvasbacks consumed 85% plant material dominated by tubers (17%) and root stalks (11%) of pondweed. Midge larvae accounted for 12% of the foods consumed. Redheads fed in different areas and consumed 96% plant food dominated by muskgrass (*Chara* spp.) (22%), sago pondweed root stalks (29%), and western wigeongrass (*Ruppia occidentalis*) leaves and stems (10%).

Bergman (1973) described a July concentration of 2,000 canvasbacks, redheads, and lesser scaup that responded to an emergence of mayflies on Dauphin Lake in southwestern Manitoba. The birds that he examined consumed 100% mayflies. When the emergence terminated, the birds moved on. Redheads examined by Bartonek and Hickey (1969a) in September and early October consumed a diet dominated by muskgrass, which accounted for 99% of the diet.

Bartonek and Hickey (1969a) summarized the fall and winter foods of canvasbacks. The September and early October diet consisted of 78% plant food dominated by pondweed tubers (71%) and 22% animal food dominated by mayflies (18%). Anderson and Low (1976) documented use of sago pondweed by waterfowl on the Delta Marsh of Lake Manitoba. Mallards and canvasbacks were the most commonly observed waterfowl on their study plots.

During fall migration, mallards and northern pintails feed extensively on grain in the uplands but they also feed in wetlands (Krapu and Swanson 1977; Swanson et al. 1985; Sugden and Driver 1980). Lakes with extensive beds of common wigeongrass (*Ruppia maritima*) are highly attractive to American wigeons, redheads, and northern pintails during fall staging and migration (Krapu and Swanson 1977). Lakes dominated by sago pondweed are attractive to canvasbacks, tundra swans, and mallards that consume pondweed tubers (Anderson and Low 1976; Kantrud 1986b). Gadwalls concentrate on wetlands with watermilfoil (*Myriophyllum* spp.), where they consume plant parts; blue-winged teal and green-winged teal consume scuds and midge larvae. Lesser scaup concentrate on lakes with scuds, where they select a diet dominated by this crustacean.

When fall rains fill seasonally flooded wetlands or semipermanent wetlands that were previously dry, dabbling ducks concentrate to feed on seeds of annual plants such as barnyardgrass (*Echinochloa* spp.) and goosefoot (*Chenopodium* spp.).

Factors Influencing Food Selection

Wetland foods consumed by waterfowl in the prairie pothole region are influenced by environmental factors that control availability. This is particularly true for dabbling ducks that are restricted as depth increases in their use of the water column and much of the benthos. Availability of invertebrate foods can be influenced by their life history and diel activity patterns, climatic conditions, water chemistry, and seasonal and annual trends in the distribution of water within the wetland complex (Swanson et al. 1974; Swanson 1977; Swanson et al. 1984; Nelson and Kadlec 1984).

Both bird-related and food-related factors have an influence on the food items that are consumed. Physiological demands that influence food consumption include the nutritional requirements for egg production, growth, molting, maintenance, and migration. Females during egg production and ducklings during early stages of growth have a high protein demand, which they satisfy by consuming invertebrates (Sugden 1973; Krapu and Swanson 1975). On the other hand, mallards during fall migration have a high energy demand, which they satisfy by consuming a diet dominated by grain and other seeds (Swanson et al. 1985).

The morphological adaptations of each species and their different foraging strategies also influence food selection (Swanson and Meyer 1973). For example, the spacing of the lamellae allow some species to feed on small microcrustaceans that are unavailable to other birds (Swanson et al. 1979). Diving ducks are able to feed on benthic midge larvae that are unavailable to surface feeding ducks.

A key food-related factor influencing food selection is the nutritional value of the food, which interacts with the current physiological demands of the bird. A second food-related factor is availability, which interacts with the bird's morphological adaptations and foraging strategies. Food availability is influenced by habitat conditions, the abundance and distribution of the food items, and the behavior of invertebrates. An invertebrate that swims to the surface to emerge becomes highly available to surface feeding birds, whereas an invertebrate that remains in the benthic area is unavailable to them.

Nest Site Selection

Redhead and canvasback hens generally select nest sites in semipermanent wetlands (Table 8.8). Preferred nesting covers are cattail or bulrush, especially hardstem bulrush (*Scirpus acutus*) or cattail. Nests are usually placed in small patches of vegetation or in stands of vegetation with a broken pattern. Large monotypic stands of dense vegetation without breaks seem to be avoided. Nests are sometimes placed in seasonal wetlands containing vegetation such as whitetop rivergrass or slough sedge (*Carex atherodes*). The presence of dead residual vegetation from the preceding year is an important component of nesting habitat and is essential for building a secure nest. Water depths at nest sites generally vary from 30 to 100 cm and nests of these species are rarely found in the uplands. Ruddy ducks nest over water in either seasonal or semipermanent, wetlands. Nest sites are similar to those of canvasbacks and redheads, but ruddy ducks may use wetlands with aquatic grasses and sedges to a greater extent. Ring-necked ducks prefer to nest in wet-meadow or shallow marsh zones adjacent to seasonal, semipermanent or

TABLE 8.8. Nest site selection by prairie nesting waterfowl

Species	Dense upland cover	Thin upland cover	Wet meadow/ sedge mat	Dry wetland	Over-water wetland
Green-winged teal[a]	1[b]	2[c]	...	...	...
Blue-winged teal[d]	2	1	2	3[e]	...
Northern shoveler[f]	2	1	...	3	...
Gadwall[g]	1	3	...	2	...
American wigeon[a]	1	2	...	3	...
Mallard[h]	1	2	...	2	3
Northern pintail[i]	2	1	...	...	...
Canvasback[j]	...	...	...	...	1
Redhead[k]	3	...	2	...	1
Ring-necked duck[l]	...	...	1	...	...
Lesser scaup[m]	1	3	2	...	...
Ruddy duck[j]	...	3	2	...	1

[a]Klett, personal communication.
[b]Preferred site.
[c]Frequently used site.
[d]Burgess et al. 1965; Glover 1956; Heiser 1971; Kaiser et al. 1979; Oetting and Cassel 1971; Sowls 1955.
[e]Occasional site.
[f]Sowls 1955.
[g]Duebbert and Lokemoen 1976.
[h]Cowardin et al. 1985; Duebbert and Lokemoen 1976; Dzubin and Gollop 1972; Smith 1971; Stoudt 1971.
[i]Higgins 1977; Lynch 1947; Sowls 1955.
[j]Stoudt 1982; Sugden 1978.
[k]Stoudt 1982.
[l]Townsend 1966.
[m]Townsend 1966; Hammell 1973; Rogers 1959, 1962.

permanent wetlands. Nests are usually on subirrigated sites with a moist substrate without standing water. Residual cover is an important component of nest site selection. Lesser scaup have a tendency to nest on small islands in large lakes or in the moist soil ecotone between the wetland and upland. Lesser scaup also frequently nest on upland sites in a wide variety of habitat types. Nests may be in tall, dense grasses or forbs, shrub cover, or occasionally in growing crops.

To assess the total reproductive habitat requirements of nesting dabbling ducks, consideration of both the quality of the wetland complex and the associated upland habitats is important. Adamus (1983) recognized the importance of an evaluation of upland habitats for wetland functional assessment. Most species of dabbling ducks nest in the uplands (Table 8.8). A wide variety of habitats are used; each waterfowl species has adapted to nesting in certain vegetative types. Nests are placed at varying distances from wetlands, generally proportional to the size of the duck. For example, nests of blue-winged teal and northern shovelers are generally within 1 km of water, whereas nests of mallards, gadwalls, and northern pintails may be placed up to 3 km from water.

Mallards and gadwalls prefer to nest in cover that is tall and dense, which may be grassy, herbaceous, or brushy. In native prairie, patches of brush composed of western snowberry (*Symphoricarpos occidentalis*) and/or Wood's rose (*Rosa woodsii*) are highly preferred (Duebbert et al. 1986). Tall, dense grasses such as smooth bromegrass (*Bromus inermis*) or intermediate wheatgrass (*Agropyron intermedium*) are used along with herbaceous vegetation such as alfalfa (*Medicago sativa*), sweet clover (*Melilotus* spp.) (Duebbert and Lokemoen 1976), or tall nettle (*Urtica gracilis*). Many other types of vegetation are used to a lesser extent. Nests of mallards and gadwalls are occasionally concentrated on islands in large lakes (Duebbert et al. 1983; Lokemoen et al. 1984). Mallard nests are sometimes found over water in stands of cattail or hardstem bulrush (Krapu et al. 1979). American wigeons also prefer the kinds of vegetation used by mallards and gadwalls.

Blue-winged teal, green-winged teal, northern shovelers, and pintails prefer to nest in grassy vegetation of short to medium height. Northern pintails accept closely grazed prairie grasslands and grain stubble fields for nest sites. In native mixed-grass prairie, green needlegrass (*Stipa viridula*) and western wheatgrass (*Agropyron smithii*) are frequently selected as nest sites by these species. In ecologically disturbed situations, Kentucky bluegrass (*Poa pratensis*) and smooth bromegrass are frequently used by hens of these four species. While these species prefer nest sites in short to medium height cover, they also accept tall, dense cover. As with diving ducks, the presence of residual cover (dead vegetation from the previous year) is an important component of attractive nest sites. Blue-winged teal, green-winged teal, northern shovelers, and northern pintails sometimes nest on islands, but they do not form dense concentrations of nests.

Dabbling ducks often place their nests in the relatively tall, dense cover found in dry wetlands containing vegetation such as cattail, bulrush, or whitetop grass.

Fields of no-till winter wheat (*Triticum aestivum*) provide nesting habitat for blue-winged teal, northern pintails, and mallards and to a lesser extent, northern shovelers and gadwalls (Duebbert and Kantrud 1987). Land-use influences on the availability of upland nesting cover for nesting waterfowl are shown in Table 8.9.

Waterfowl Predators

Predators routinely consume ducks when certain phases of the life cycle of the predator and prey interact. Incubating hens (Sargeant et al. 1984), molting adults (Oring 1964), ducklings (Talent et al. 1983), and eggs (Duebbert and Lokemoen 1976; Greenwood et al. 1987) are routinely consumed. Predators having the greatest impact on ducks in the prairie pothole region of the United States include the red fox (*Vulpes vulpes*), striped skunk (*Mephitis mephitis*), raccoon (*Procyon lotor*), mink (*Mustela vison*), and Franklin's ground squirrel (*Spermophilus franklinii*) (Cowardin et al. 1983). Predators having a lesser impact include the badger (*Taxidea taxus*), coyote (*Canis latrans*), long-tailed weasel (*Mustela frenata*), American crow (*Corvus brachyrhynchos*), and some gulls and raptors (Cowardin et al. 1983). Most of these predators prey on duck nests or adults occupying nests in upland habi-

TABLE 8.9.   Land-use impacts on selection of upland nesting cover by waterfowl

Species	Planted cover[a]	Pasture[b] (moderately grazed)	Haylands[c]	Stubble[d]	Fall seeded no-till[e]	Idle[f]
Green-winged teal	3	2	4	. . .[g]	5	1
Blue-winged teal	3	1	4	. . .	5	2
Northern shoveler	3	1	4	. . .	5	2
Gadwall	1	3	4	. . .	5	2
American wigeon	3	2	4	. . .	. . .	1
Mallard	1	3	4	6	5	2
Northern pintail	5	1	6	2	3	4
Lesser scaup	2	3	. . .	. . .	. . .	1

Note: Numbers are preference ranks (1–6).
[a]Duebbert and Lokemoen 1976; MacFarlane 1977.
[b]Burgess et al. 1965; Dzubin and Gollop 1972.
[c]Duebbert and Kantrud 1974.
[d]Duebbert and Kantrud 1974; Higgins 1977.
[e]Duebbert and Kantrud, unpublished; Cowan 1982.
[f]Duebbert and Lokemoen 1976.
[g]Rare use.

tats. Two exceptions are the mink and raccoon, which forage extensively in wetland basins (Eberhardt and Sargeant 1977; Fritzell 1978; Greenwood 1981; and Arnold 1986).

Eberhardt and Sargeant (1977) described foods consumed by mink families during April through August of 1972 and 1973 in semipermanent marshes on the Missouri Coteau of western Stutsman County, North Dakota. Ducks accounted for 11% of the foods consumed. Ruddy ducks were taken more frequently than expected based on waterfowl breeding pair counts. Thirty-three percent of dabbling ducks found at mink dens were females as compared to 78% females of diving ducks. Eggshells were found in small quantities in mink scats during the nesting season.

Arnold (1986) described the diet, habitat use, activity patterns, movements, and home ranges of male mink during the waterfowl breeding season in the aspen parkland of southwest Manitoba during 1984–1985. Ducks or their eggs made up 27% and 12%, respectively, of prey items identified and 15.6% of scat residues analyzed. Ducks were not an important item in the diet of male mink until summer. During wet years when seasonally flooded wetlands contain water long enough for broods to fledge, dabbling ducks are less likely to encounter predation by mink (Talent et al. 1983), which prefer semipermanent or permanent wetlands (Arnold 1986). Mink generally utilized wetlands that had higher proportions of diving ducks (canvasbacks, redheads, and ruddy ducks). Wetlands used by mink were avoided by dabbling ducks and duck broods. Sowls (1955) believed that coots (*Fulica americana*), muskrats, and small rodents act as buffer species reducing loss of ducks to mink predation.

Fritzell (1978) described movements, home range, and habitat use of raccoons during the waterfowl breeding season in Griggs and Barnes counties, North Dakota, during 1973–1975. Habitats preferentially used by raccoons were building sites, wooded areas, and wetlands that made up 10% of the study area. All wetland classes found on this study area were used by raccoons. Nocturnal use of wetlands increased from 30% in April to 56% in July; diurnal use of wetlands increased from 37% to 70% during the same period. Dense nesting cover in the upland was seldom used by raccoons.

Greenwood (1981) described foods consumed by raccoons during the waterfowl nesting season in Griggs and Barnes counties, North Dakota, during 1974–1976. Birds or eggs occurred in 34 and 29% of the scats, respectively. Of the remains of 64 large birds found in scats, 41% were waterfowl, which included blue-winged teal, mallard, pintail, lesser scaup, ring-necked duck, and ruddy duck.

Sowls (1955) examined 53 marsh hawk (*Circus cyaneus*) pellets collected near marsh hawk nests at Delta, Manitoba, in 1939. Marsh hawk pellets contained remains of ducklings, adult and juvenile coots, passerine birds, mammals, and insects. Sowls (1955) concluded that passerine birds and rodents were the most important food items identified in marsh hawk pellets.

Islands in large saline (Duebbert et al. 1983) and fresh lakes (Duebbert 1982) have demonstrated the advantage of removing predator impacts on ground nesting ducks (Cowardin et al. 1983). Duck nest success on islands in Audubon National Wildlife Refuge in central North Dakota and Miller Lake in northwestern North Dakota was 86 and 85%, respectively (Cowardin et al. 1983). During a five-year period, 2,561 duck nests of nine species were found on a 4.5 ha island in Miller Lake (Duebbert et al. 1983).

Land-use changes have favored the establishment and maintenance of predators that are adapted to prey on ducks and their eggs and young (Cowardin et al. 1983) in the prairie pothole region. Most of the predation that occurs in wetlands is limited to overwater nesting species, broods of diving and dabbling ducks, and molting birds. The abundance and distribution of emergent cover plays an important role in providing nesting cover for overwater nesting species (Weller 1981) but the influence of emergent cover on predation is not well understood.

Land-Use Impacts

Stewart and Kantrud (1973) examined the ecological distribution of breeding waterfowl populations in North Dakota during 1967–1969. Natural seasonal ponds with untilled soils and semipermanent lakes were the primary wetlands used by breeding waterfowl. The impact of tillage on wetlands was evidenced by the fact that during their study wetlands with tilled soils (mostly temporary and seasonal wetlands) comprised 29% of the area and 52% of the wetlands. Potential adverse effects of tillage on aquatic invertebrates include reduction of soil organic content, increased turbidity, destruction of invertebrate eggs, and loss of surface organic litter that supports detritus food chains. Swanson et al. (1974) suggested that spring flooding of summer and fall tilled basins produced wetlands that were less attractive to breeding birds than flooded stubble. The impact of tillage on wetland use by migrating birds that require high energy foods can be expected to differ depending on the condition of the wetland substrate when it is flooded. Flooded stubble can be expected to provide more abundant high energy foods as compared to recently tilled, barren soils.

Grue et al. (1986) reviewed the effects of agriculture on waterfowl and other wildlife inhabiting prairie wetlands with emphasis on agricultural chemicals. They pointed out the 94% of the managed Waterfowl

Production Areas within the Arrowwood Wetland Management District in central North Dakota had adjacent cropland on at least one boundary and 37% were completely surrounded by cropland. Much of the runoff from cropland flows into or through wetlands located within Waterfowl Production Areas.

Increased mechanization and reliance on small grain monocultures has increased tillage of wetland basins and the use of pesticides (Grue et al. 1986). Tilled wetlands are highly susceptible to chemical influence because they are usually relatively small and interspersed within agricultural fields, which increases the probability for chemical contamination from direct spraying and aerial drift (Grue et al. 1986). Use of herbicides increased 356% and insecticide use 170% between 1966 and 1982 in the northern plains of the United States (Grue et al. 1986).

Agricultural chemicals may impact waterfowl directly through lethal and sublethal effects, or indirectly by eliminating plant and invertebrate foods (Grue et al. 1986). Of the 27 insecticides applied to crops in North Dakota in 1984, 63% were organophosphates, 15% carbamates, 15% organochlorines, and 7% synthetic pyrethroids (Grue et al. 1986). Six of the most widely used insecticides in North Dakota in 1984 are either highly toxic to aquatic invertebrates or to birds (Grue et al. 1986). Grue et al. (1986) pointed out that a long-term research program is needed to evaluate the impacts of agricultural chemicals on wetlands and wildlife under field conditions.

Cowardin et al. (1981) examined the wetland characteristics of a 10,041 km² study area in central North Dakota during the summers of 1977–1979. Tillage was the most prevalent activity and affected 40% of the wetlands sampled.

CONCLUSIONS

Wetlands in the northern prairie area have developed in response to unique hydrologic regimes that are the product of interactions between climatic conditions and shallow depressions. The variety of landforms that have developed provide the basis for different wetland complexes with components that vary in hydroperiod and chemical characteristics. Plant and invertebrate communities respond to dynamic water regimes and associated salt concentrations to produce an abundant food resource that sustains a large waterfowl population during the breeding season.

Waterfowl migrating north in early spring encounter millions of shallow prairie wetlands filled with snow melt water. These shallow wetlands provide food to sustain migrating waterfowl and maintain fat reserves required for successful reproduction. Waterfowl breeding north of the prairie pothole region also benefit from food resources provided by prairie wetlands.

As the breeding season progresses, resident pairs disperse and use a variety of wetlands to satisfy their reproductive requirements. Wetland use during the breeding season may change with each nesting attempt. Dabbling ducks feed in wet-meadow and shallow-marsh zones of seasonal and semipermanent wetlands. Diving ducks feed in open-water zones of semipermanent wetlands where they have access to benthic invertebrates and tubers that are unavailable to surface-feeding ducks. Shallow temporary and seasonal wetlands warm early in the spring and provide an abundant invertebrate population that is used by laying female dabbling ducks. As temporary and seasonal wetlands dry, renesting dabbling ducks feed on open-water zones of semipermanent wetlands where insects are emerging and submerged vascular plants provide a substrate for invertebrates.

Early hatched broods feed on seasonal wetlands when they are available (Talent et al. 1982), whereas broods that hatch later tend to use semipermanent wetlands. Class I dabbling ducks feed on emerging insects (Sugden 1973); dates of emergence vary within and among wetlands. Hens move their broods and will concentrate on wetlands that have a highly abundant food supply (Swanson 1977). Broods of a variety of ages are present during the summer months and they require an abundance of high protein food from May through August. An abundance of seasonal and semipermanent wetlands insures that an invertebrate population is available for recently hatched broods during the summer.

Large semipermanent wetlands provide unique habitats for a variety of breeding birds. Saline lakes provide critical staging and conditioning habitat for tundra swans, canvasbacks, and several other species of waterfowl.

Research Needs

Weller et al. (1984) stressed the need for long-term studies of wetland complexes in the prairie pothole region. Studies should focus on the role of hydrology in determining the chemical characteristics of wetlands (LaBaugh et al. 1987) and the combined influences of hydrology and chemistry on plant and animal communities used by breeding and migrating waterfowl (Swanson 1986b). Climatic conditions are such that basins cycle between dry and wet conditions over extended periods (Weller 1978). Wetlands cycle at different rates depending on their individual response to changes in groundwater, surface runoff, and evaporation/precipitation ratios. The response of breeding and migrating birds to changes in plant and invertebrate communities caused by different hydroperiods and salinity should be part of a long-term study.

The value of prairie wetlands for conditioning or maintenance of migrating waterfowl that nest north of the prairie pothole region or in the northern part of the region has been generally overlooked. The role of prairie wetlands in providing the nutritional requirements of birds during spring migration requires additional study.

The role that prairie wetlands play in the conditioning of fall migrating birds also requires additional study. Traditional fall migration lakes east of the prairie pothole region in the Lake States have been degraded by stable water, rough fish populations, turbidity, and agricultural runoff, which have reduced or eliminated key foods such as sago pondweed and wildcelery (*Vallisneria americana*) that are used by diving ducks, especially canvasbacks. Hydrologically unique prairie lakes that maintain ideal chemical conditions for the production of sago pondweed still exist in the prairie pothole region, but their hydrological conditions are not well defined. Changes in hydrology that cause a rise or fall in water level and salt content above or below ideal conditions for sago pondweed will reduce their value to migrating waterfowl. Studies are needed to define the hydrology and chemistry of key waterfowl lakes that support most of the canvasbacks and tundra swans that migrate through this region during spring and fall. Studies of the chemical characteristics of prairie lakes suggest that road construction through saline lakes alters their hydrology, chemistry, and biota (Swanson et al. 1984).

Irrigation from well water, which has increased in the prairie pothole region, has potential to divert water from groundwater systems supporting prairie lakes that are groundwater discharge areas. Changes in the hydrology will alter water chemistry, and subsequently, the biota used by waterfowl.

Grue et al. (1986) stressed the need for laboratory and field studies in the United States and Canada to assess the potential impacts of agricultural chemicals on wetlands and the waterfowl that depend on them for survival. Tillage and selective drainage have potential to alter the characteristics of prairie wetland complexes through water consolidation, wetland basin integration, and siltation. Integrated wetland systems that are the result of these practices differ hydrologically, chemically, and biologically from the nonintegrated wetlands that are typical of much of the northern prairie. The impact of siltation and selective drainage on prairie wetland complexes requires additional study.

ACKNOWLEDGMENTS

The authors would like to thank J. T. Lokemoen for critical comments on this manuscript.

REFERENCES

Adamus, P. R. 1983. A method for wetland functional assessment. U.S. DOT Rep. FHWA-1P-82-23, Vol. I. and FHWA-1P-82-24, Vol. II. Washington, D.C.: GPO.

Anderson, M. G., and J. B. Low. 1976. Use of sago pondweed by waterfowl on the Delta Marsh, Manitoba. J. Wildl. Manage. 40:233–42.

Arnold, T. W. 1986. The ecology of prairie mink during the waterfowl breeding season. Master's thesis, Univ. Missouri, Columbia.

Barica, J. 1975. Geochemistry and nutrient regime of saline eutrophic lakes in the Erickson-Elphinstone district of southwestern Manitoba. Environ. Can. Fish. Mar. Serv. Res. Dev. Dir. Tech. Rep. 511. Winnipeg.

Bartonek, J. C., and J. J. Hickey. 1969a. Food habits of canvasbacks, redheads, and lesser scaup in Manitoba. Condor 71:280–90.

———. 1969b. Selective feeding by juvenile diving ducks in summer. Auk 86:443–57.

Bergman, R. D. 1973. Use of southern boreal lakes by postbreeding canvasbacks and redheads. J. Wildl. Manage. 37:160–70.

Burgess, H. H., H. H. Prince, and D. L. Trauger. 1965. Blue-winged teal nesting success as related to land use. J. Wildl. Manage. 29:89–95.

Burnham, B. L., and J. J. Peterka. 1975. Effects of saline water from North Dakota lakes on survival of fathead minnow (*Pimephales promelas*) embryos and sac fry. J. Fish. Res. Board Can. 32:809–12.

Calverley, B. K., and D. A. Boag. 1977. Reproductive potential in parkland and arctic nesting populations of mallards and pintails (Anatidae). Can. J. Zool. 55:1242–51.

Cooch, F. G. 1964. A preliminary study of the survival value of a functional salt gland in prairie Anatidae. Auk 81:380–93.

Cowan, W. F. 1982. Waterfowl production on zero tillage farms. Wildl. Soc. Bull. 10:305–8.

Cowardin, L. M., D. S. Gilmer, and L. M. Mechlin. 1981. Characteristics of central North Dakota wetlands determined from sample aerial photographs and ground study. Wildl. Soc. Bull. 9:280–88.

Cowardin, L. M., A. B. Sargeant, and H. F. Duebbert. 1983. Problems and potentials for prairie ducks. J. Nat. Hist. Soc. Minn. Special issue no. 4.

Cowardin, L. M., D. S. Gilmer, and C. W. Shaiffer. 1985. Mallard recruitment in the agricultural environment of North Dakota. Wildl. Monogr. 92.

Derksen, D. V., and W. D. Eldridge. 1980. Drought-displacement of pintails to the arctic coastal plain, Alaska. J. Wildl. Manage. 44:224–29.

Dirschl, H. L. 1969. Foods of lesser scaup and blue-winged teal in the Saskatchewan River Delta. J. Wildl. Manage. 33:77–87.

Donham, R. S., C. W. Dane, and D. S. Farner. 1976. Plasma luteinizing hormone and the development of ovarian follicles after loss of clutch in female mallards (*Anas platyrhynchos*). Gen. Comp. Endocrinol. 29:152–55.

Drewien, R. C., and P. F. Springer. 1969. Ecological relationships of breeding blue-winged teal to prairie potholes. Can. Wildl. Serv. Rep. Ser. 6.

DuBowy, P. J. 1985. Feeding ecology and behavior of postbreeding male blue-winged teal and northern shovelers. Can. J. Zool. 63:1292–97.

Duebbert, H. F. 1982. Nesting of waterfowl on islands in Lake Audubon, North Dakota. Wildl. Soc. Bull. 10:232–37.

Duebbert, H. F., and A. M. Frank. 1984. Value of prairie wetlands to duck broods. Wildl. Soc. Bull. 12:27–34.

Duebbert, H. F., and H. A. Kantrud. 1974. Upland duck nesting related to land use and predator reduction. J. Wildl. Manage. 38:257–65.

———. 1987. Use of no-till winter wheat by nesting ducks in North Dakota. J. Soil Water Conserv. 42:50–53.

Duebbert, H. F., and J. T. Lokemoen. 1976. Duck nesting in fields of undisturbed grass-legume cover. J. Wildl. Manage. 40:39–49.

———. 1980. High duck nesting success in a predator-reduced environment. J. Wildl. Manage. 44:428–37.

Duebbert, H. F., J. T. Lokemoen, and D. E. Sharp. 1983. Concentrated nesting of mallards and gadwalls on Miller Lake Island, North Dakota. J. Wildl. Manage. 47:729–40.

———. 1986. Nest sites of ducks in grazed mixed-grass prairie in North Dakota. Prairie Nat. 18:99–108.

Dwyer, T. J., G. L. Krapu, and D. M. Janke. 1979. Use of prairie pothole habitat by breeding mallards. J. Wildl. Manage. 43:526–31.

Dzubin, A., and J. B. Gollop. 1972. Aspects of mallard breeding ecology in Canadian parkland and grassland. U.S. Fish and Wildl. Serv. Wildl. Res. Rep. 2.

Eberhardt, L. E., and A. B. Sargeant. 1977. Mink predation on prairie marshes during the waterfowl breeding season. In Proc. 1975 Predator Symp. ed. R. L. Phillips and C. Jonkel, 33–43. Missoula, Mont.: Mont. For. Conserv. Exper. Stn., Univ. Mont.

Eisenlohr, W. S., Jr. 1972. Hydrologic investigations of prairie potholes in North Dakota, 1959–1968. U.S. Geol. Surv. Prof. Paper 585-A.

Evans, C. D., and K. E. Black. 1956. Duck production studies on the prairie potholes of South Dakota. U.S. Fish and Wildl. Serv. Spec. Sci. Rep. Wildl. 32.

Flake, L. D. 1978. Wetland diversity and waterfowl. In Wetland functions and values: The state of our understanding, ed. P. E. Greeson et al., Minneapolis, Minn.: Amer. Water Resour. Assoc.

Fritzell, E. K. 1978. Habitat use by prairie raccoons during the waterfowl breeding season. J. Wildl. Manage. 42:118–27.

Gates, J. M. 1962. Breeding biology of the gadwall in northern Utah. Wilson Bull. 74:43–67.

Glover, F. A. 1956. Nesting and production of the blue-winged teal (Anas discors Linnaeus) in northwest Iowa. J. Wildl. Manage. 20:28–46.

Gollop, J. B., and W. H. Marshall. 1954. A guide for aging duck broods in the field. Miss. Flyway Counc. Tech. Sect. Mimeo.

Gorham, E., W. E. Dean, and J. E. Sanger. 1983. The chemical composition of lakes in the north-central United States. Limnol. Oceanogr. 28:287–301.

Greenwood, R. J. 1981. Foods of prairie raccoons during the waterfowl nesting season. J. Wildl. Manage. 45:754–60.

Greenwood, R. J., A. B. Sargeant, D. H. Johnson, L. M. Cowardin, and T. L. Shaffer. 1987. Mallard nest success and recruitment in prairie Canada. Trans. N. Amer. Wildl. Nat. Res. Conf. 52:298–309.

Grue, C. E., L. R. DeWeese, P. Mineau, G. A. Swanson, J. R. Foster, P. M. Arnold, J. N. Huckins, P. L. Sheehan, W. K. Marshall, and A. P. Ludden, 1986. Potential impacts of agricultural chemicals on waterfowl and other wildlife inhabiting prairie wetlands: An evaluation of research needs and approaches. Trans. N. Am. Wildl. Nat. Resour. Conf. 51:357–83.

Hammell, G. S. 1973. The ecology of the lesser scaup (*Aythya affinis* Eyton) in southwestern Manitoba. Master's thesis, Univ. Guelph, Guelph, Ontario.

Hansen, H. A., and D. E. McKnight. 1964. Emigration of drought-displaced ducks to the Arctic. Trans. N. Amer. Wildl. Nat. Resour. Conf. 29:119–127.

Heiser, N. G. 1971. Nest site selection by blue-winged teal (*Anas discors*) in northwest Iowa. Master's thesis, Iowa State Univ., Ames.

Held, J. W. 1971. Some ecological aspects of the fathead minnow, *Pimephales promelas* R., in North Dakota saline lakes. Ph.D. diss., N. Dak. State Univ., Fargo.

Henny, C. J. 1973. Drought displaced movement of North American pintails into Siberia. J. Wildl. Manage. 37:23–29.

Higgins, K. F. 1977. Duck nesting in intensively farmed areas of North Dakota. J. Wildl. Manage. 41:232–42.

Hohman, W. L. 1985. Feeding ecology of ring-necked ducks in northwestern Minnesota. J. Wildl. Manage. 49:546–57.

Hurlbert, S. H., W. Loayza, and T. Moreno. 1986. Fish-flamingo-plankton interactions in the Peruvian Andes. Limnol. Oceanogr. 31:457–68.

Jenni, D. A. 1956. Pothole water levels in relation to waterfowl breeding populations and production. Master's thesis, Utah State Univ., Logan.

Jessen, R. L., J. P. Lindmeier, and R. E. Farmes. 1964. A study of duck nesting and production as related to land use in Mahnomen County, Minnesota. *In* Ducks and land use in Minnesota, ed. J. B. Moyle, 28–85. Minn. Dept. Conserv. Bull. 8.

Johnson, D. H., G. L. Krapu, K. J. Reinecke, and D. G. Jorde. 1985. An evaluation of condition indices for birds. J. Wildl. Manage. 49:569–75.

Kaiser, P. H., S. S. Berlinger, and L. H. Fredrickson. 1979. Response of blue-winged teal to range management on waterfowl production areas in southeastern South Dakota. J. Range. Manage. 32:295–98.

Kaminski, R. M., and H. H. Prince. 1981. Dabbling duck activity and foraging responses to aquatic macroinvertebrates. Auk 98:115–26.

Kantrud, H. A. 1986a. Classification systems for prairie wetlands. N. Dak. Acad. Sci. 40:43.

———. 1986b. Western Stump Lake, a major canvasback staging area in eastern North Dakota. Prairie Nat. 18:247–53.

———. 1986c. Effects of vegetation manipulation on breeding waterfowl in prairie wetlands—a literature review. U.S. Fish and Wildl. Serv. Tech. Rep. 3.

Kantrud, H. A., and R. E. Stewart. 1977. Use of natural basin wetlands by breeding waterfowl in North Dakota. J. Wildl. Manage. 41:243–53.

Krapu, G. L. 1974a. Feeding ecology of pintail hens during reproduction. Auk 91:278–90.

———. 1974b. Foods of breeding pintails in North Dakota. J. Wildl. Manage. 38:408–17.

———. 1979. Nutrition of female dabbling ducks during reproduction. *In* Waterfowl and wetlands—an integrated review, ed. T. A. Bookhout, 59–70. Madison, Wis.: N. Cent. Sect. Wildl. Soc.

———. 1981. The role of nutrient reserves in mallard reproduction. Auk 98:29–38.

Krapu, G. L., and H. F. Duebbert. 1974. A biological survey of Kraft Slough. Prairie Nat. 6:33–55.

Krapu, G. L., and G. A. Swanson. 1975. Some nutritional aspects of reproduction in prairie nesting pintails. J. Wildl. Manage. 39:156–62.

———. 1977. Foods of juvenile, brood hen, and post-breeding pintails in North Dakota. Condor 79:504–07.

Krapu, G. L., L. G. Talent, and T. J. Dwyer. 1979. Marsh nesting by mallards. Wildl. Soc. Bull. 7:104–10.

Krapu, G. L., A. T. Klett, and D. G. Jorde. 1983. The effect of variable spring water conditions on mallard reproduction. Auk 100:689–98.

LaBaugh, J. W., T. C. Winter, V. A. Adomaitis, and G. A. Swanson. 1987. Hydrology and chemistry of selected prairie wetlands in the Cottonwood Lake area, Stutsman County, North Dakota, 1979–1982. U.S. Geol. Surv. Prof. Paper 1431:26.

Leitch, W. G. 1964. Water. In Waterfowl tomorrow, ed. J. P. Linduska, 273–81. Washington, D.C.: U.S. Fish and Wildl. Serv.

Lokemoen, J. T., H. F. Duebbert, and D. E. Sharp. 1984. Nest spacing, habitat selection, and behavior of waterfowl on Miller Lake Island, North Dakota. J. Wildl. Manage. 48:309–21.

Lynch, J. J. 1947. Waterfowl breeding conditions in Saskatchewan, 1947. In U.S. Fish and Wildl. Serv. Spec. Sci. Rep. 45.

MacFarlane, R. J. 1977. Waterfowl production in planted nesting cover. Master's thesis, York Univ., Downsview, Ontario.

McKnight, D. E., and J. B. Low. 1969. Factors affecting waterfowl production on a spring-fed salt marsh in Utah. Trans. N. Amer. Wildl. Nat. Resour. Conf. 34:307–14.

Moyle, J. B. 1956. Relationships between the chemistry of Minnesota surface waters and wildlife management. J. Wildl. Manage. 20:303–20.

Murkin, H. R., R. M. Kaminski, and R. D. Titman. 1982. Responses by dabbling ducks and aquatic invertebrates to an experimentally manipulated cattail marsh. Can. J. Zool. 60:2324–32.

Nelson, J. W., and J. A. Kadlec. 1984. A conceptual approach to relating habitat structure and macroinvertebrate production in freshwater wetlands. Trans. N. Amer. Wildl. Nat. Resour. Conf. 49:262–70.

Nickum, J. G. 1970. Limnology of winterkill lakes in South Dakota. N. Cent. Div. Amer. Fish. Soc. Spec. Publ. 1.

Oetting, R. B., and J. F. Cassel. 1971. Waterfowl nesting on interstate highway right-of-way in North Dakota. J. Wildl. Manage. 35:774–81.

Oring, L. W. 1964. Predation upon flightless ducks. Wilson Bull. 76:190.

Perret, N. G. 1962. The spring and summer foods of the common mallard (Anas platyrhynchos platyrhynchos L.) in south central Manitoba. Master's thesis, Univ. of British Columbia, Vancouver.

Pospahala, R. S., D. R. Anderson, and C. J. Henny. 1974. Population ecology of the mallard. II: Breeding habitat conditions, size of the breeding populations, and production indices. U.S. Fish and Wildl. Serv. Resour. Publ. 115.

Rogers, J. P. 1959. Low water and lesser scaup reproduction near Erickson, Manitoba. Trans. N. Amer. Wildl. Conf. 24:216–24.

———. 1962. The ecological effects of drought on reproduction of the lesser scaup, Aythya affinis (Eyton). Ph.D. thesis, Univ. Mo., Columbia.

Rogers, J. P., and L. J. Korschgen. 1966. Foods of lesser scaups on breeding, migration, and wintering areas. J. Wildl. Manage. 30:258–64.

Rözkowski, A. 1969. Chemistry of ground and surface waters in the Moose Mountain Area, southern Saskatchewan. Geol. Surv. Can. Paper 67-9. Ottawa.

Ruwaldt, J. J., Jr., L. D. Flake, and J. M. Gates. 1979. Waterfowl pair use of natural and man-made wetlands in South Dakota. J. Wildl. Manage. 43:375–83.

Salomonsen, F. 1968. The moult migration. Wildfowl 19:5–24.

Sargeant, A. B., S. H. Allen, and R. T. Eberhardt. 1984. Red fox predation on breeding ducks in midcontinent North America. Wildl. Monogr. 89.

Schmidt-Nielson, K. 1960. The salt-secreting gland of marine birds. Circulation 21:955–67.

Schoenecker, W. 1970. Management of winterkill lakes in the Sandhill Region of Nebraska. N. Cen. Div. Amer. Fish. Soc. Spec. Publ. 1.

Serie, J. R., and G. A. Swanson. 1976. Feeding ecology of breeding gadwalls on saline wetlands. J. Wildl. Manage. 40:69–81.

Siegfried, W. R. 1973. Summer food and feeding of the ruddy duck in Manitoba. Can. J. Zool. 51:1293–97.

Sloan, C. E. 1972. Ground-water hydrology of prairie potholes in North Dakota. U.S. Geol. Surv. Prof. Paper 585-C.

Smith, A. G. 1969. Waterfowl-habitat relationships on the Lousana, Alberta, waterfowl study area. Can. Wildl. Serv. Rep. Ser. 6.

_____. 1971. Ecological factors affecting waterfowl production in the Alberta parklands. U.S. Fish and Wildl. Ser. Resour. Publ. 98.

Smith, A. G., J. H. Stoudt, and J. B. Gollop. 1964. Prairie potholes and marshes. In Waterfowl tomorrow, ed. J. P. Linduska, 39–50. Washington, D.C.: U.S. Fish and Wildl. Ser.

Smith, R. I. 1970. Response of pintail breeding populations to drought. J. Wildl. Manage. 34:943–46.

Sowls, L. K. 1955. Prairie ducks. Washington, D.C.: Wildl. Manage. Inst.

Stewart, R. E., and H. A. Kantrud. 1971. Classification of natural ponds and lakes in the glaciated prairie region. U.S. Fish and Wildl. Serv. Resour. Publ. 92.

_____. 1972. Vegetation of prairie potholes, North Dakota, in relation to quality of water and other environmental factors. U.S. Geol. Surv. Prof. Paper 585-D.

_____. 1973. Ecological distribution of breeding waterfowl populations in North Dakota. J. Wildl. Manage. 37:39–50.

Stoudt, J. H. 1969. Relationships between waterfowl and water areas on the Redvers Waterfowl Study Area. Can. Wildl. Ser. Rep. Ser. No. 6.

_____. 1971. Ecological factors affecting waterfowl production in the Saskatchewan parklands. U.S. Fish and Wildl. Serv. Resour. Publ. 99.

_____. 1982. Habitat use and productivity of canvasbacks in southwestern Manitoba, 1961–1972. U.S. Fish and Wildl. Serv. Spec. Sci. Rep. Wildl. No. 248.

Strohmeyer, D. L. 1967. The biology of renesting by the blue-winged teal (*Anas discors*) in northwest Iowa. Ph.D. thesis, Univ. Minn., Minneapolis.

Sugden, L. G. 1973. Feeding ecology of pintail, gadwall, American widgeon, and lesser scaup ducklings. Can. Wildl. Serv. Rep. Ser. 24.

_____. 1978. Canvasback habitat use and production in Saskatchewan parklands. Can. Wildl. Serv. Occas. Paper 34.

Sugden, L. G., and E. A. Driver. 1980. Natural foods of mallards in Saskatchewan parklands during late summer and fall. J. Wildl. Manage. 44:705–09.

Swanson, G. A. 1977. Diel food selection by Anatinae on a waste-stabilization system. J. Wildl. Manage. 41:226–31.

_____. 1984. Dissemination of amphipods by waterfowl. J. Wildl. Manage. 48:988–91.

_____. 1985. Invertebrates consumed by dabbling ducks (Anatinae) on the breeding grounds. J. Minn. Acad. Sci. 50:37–40.

_____. 1986a. Characteristics of prairie saline lakes and their influence on waterfowl use. N. Dak. Acad. Sci. 40:34.

_____. 1986b. Aquatic habitats of breeding waterfowl. In The Ecology and Management of Wetlands. Vol. 1. Ecology of Wetlands, ed. D. D. Hook, et al., 195–202. Portland: Timber Press.

_____. 1987a. An introduction to the Cottonwood Lake Area. N. Dak. Acad. Sci. 41:25.

_____. 1987b. Vegetation changes in wetlands of the Cottonwood Lake Area. N. Dak. Acad. Sci. 41:29.

Swanson, G. A., and M. I. Meyer. 1973. The role of invertebrates in the feeding ecology of Anatinae during the breeding season. Waterfowl Habitat Manage. Symp., Moncton, New Brunswick, Can., July 30–August 1.

_____. 1977. Impact of fluctuating water levels on feeding ecology of breeding blue-winged teal. J. Wildl. Manage. 41:426–33.

Swanson, G. A., and H. K. Nelson. 1970. Potential influence of fish-rearing programs on waterfowl breeding habitat. N. Cent. Div. Amer. Fish. Soc. Spec. Publ. 1.

Swanson, G. A., G. L. Krapu, and H. K. Nelson. 1972. Mercury levels in tissues of ducks collected in south-central North Dakota. Proc. N. Dak. Acad. Sci. 25:84–93.

Swanson, G. A., M. I. Meyer, and J. R. Serie. 1974. Feeding ecology of breeding blue-winged teal. J. Wildl. Manage. 38:396–407.

Swanson, G. A., G. L. Krapu, and J. R. Serie. 1979. Foods of laying female dabbling ducks on the breeding grounds. In Waterfowl and wetlands – an integrated review, ed. T. A. Bookhout, 47–57. Madison, Wis.: The Wildl. Soc.

Swanson, G. A., V. A. Adomaitis, F. B. Lee, J. R. Serie, and J. A. Shoesmith. 1984. Limnological conditions influencing duckling use of saline lakes in south-central North Dakota. J. Wildl. Manage. 48:340–49.

Swanson, G. A., M. I. Meyer, and V. A. Adomaitis. 1985. Foods consumed by breeding mallards on wetlands of south-central North Dakota. J. Wildl. Manage. 49:197–203.

Swanson, G. A., T. L. Shaffer, J. F. Wolf, and F. B. Lee. 1986. Renesting characteristics of captive mallards on experimental ponds. J. Wildl. Manage. 50:32–38.

Swanson, G. A., T. C. Winter, V. A. Adomaitis, and J. W. LaBaugh. 1988. Chemical characteristics of prairie lakes in south-central North Dakota – their potential for influencing use by fish and wildlife. U.S. Fish and Wildl. Tech. Rep. (in review).

Talent, L. G., G. L. Krapu, and R. L. Jarvis. 1982. Habitat use by mallard broods in south-central North Dakota. J. Wildl. Manage. 46:629–35.

Talent, L. G., R. L. Jarvis, and G. L. Krapu. 1983. Survival of mallard broods in south-central North Dakota. Cooper Ornithol. Soc. 85:74–78.

Townsend, G. H. 1966. A study of waterfowl nesting on the Saskatchewan River Delta. Can. Field Nat. 80:74–88.

van der Valk, A. G. 1981. Succession in wetlands: A Gleasonian approach. Ecol. 62:688–96.

van der Valk, A. G., and C. B. Davis. 1978. The role of seed banks in the vegetation dynamics of prairie glacial marshes. Ecol. 59:322–35.

Weller, M. W. 1978. Wetland habitats. *In* Wetland functions and values: the state of our understanding, ed. P.E. Greeson, et al., 210–34. Minneapolis, Minn.: Amer. Water Resour. Assoc.

_____. 1981. Freshwater marshes—ecology and wildlife management. Minneapolis, Minn.: Univ. Minn. Press.

Weller, M., E. J. Clairain, Jr., L. Fredrickson, J. Kadlec, H. Short, G. Swanson, and P. R. Stuber. 1984. Habitat panel. Proc. Nat. Wetland Values Assess. Workshop. U.S. Fish and Wildl. Serv., FWS/OBS-84/12.

Winter, T. C., and M. R. Carr. 1980. Hydrologic setting of wetlands in the Cottonwood Lake Area, Stutsman County, North Dakota. U.S. Geol. Surv. Water Resour. Invest. 80–99.

ERIK K. FRITZELL

9 MAMMALS IN PRAIRIE WETLANDS

ABSTRACT

BASED on a review of literature, the ecology of mammals associated with northern prairie wetlands is discussed. Species considered include terrestrial or semiaquatic mammals, whose current geographic range encompasses most of the prairie pothole region and which commonly use wetlands for cover or obtain a major portion of their diets from wetland-dependent organisms. Most occupy broad niches and are also commonly found in other environments. As the primary grazer in semipermanent marshes, muskrats (*Ondatra zibethicus*) affect vegetation structure, energy and nutrient dynamics, and invertebrate and bird communities. But the wet-dry cycle and associated ecological changes in northern prairie marshes may determine the fate of muskrat populations. Small mammals, especially meadow voles (*Microtus pennsylvanicus*), provide an important prey base for many carnivores; their cycle of abundance and scarcity is a proximate factor affecting life history patterns of other species. Mammalian carnivores throughout the prairie pothole region use wetlands as important habitats for obtaining food and shelter. As a result they have significant impact on the production of other important wetland wildlife resources, such as waterfowl. White-tailed deer (*Odocoileus virginianus*) may depend on wetlands for thermal cover to survive periods of extreme energetic stress common during the long winters. In some locations, wetlands are important fawning sites. Northern prairie wetlands play an important role in the life cycles of many prairie mammals and mammals may markedly affect other components of wetland ecosystems and the values humans extract from them.

KEY WORDS: carnivora, grazing, habitat, mammals, muskrats, rodents, wetlands, white-tailed deer.

INTRODUCTION

URSORY EXAMINATION of wetland faunas in the glaciated prairie region reveals invertebrate communities dominated by aquatic insects and vertebrate communities dominated by aquatic birds. Mammals, other than muskrats, typically have not been considered major elements of wetland ecosystems or major beneficiaries of wetland habitats. Detailed analysis of habitat use patterns and diets of many "terrestrial" mammals, however, strongly suggests that wetland habitats in the prairie pothole region are vital to the welfare of several mammalian species. Furthermore, the interactions of some mammals with other wetland species tie them intimately with the productivity of northern prairie wetlands. The objectives of this chapter are (1) to review the importance of wetlands to mammals in the prairie pothole region, (2) to describe relationships between mammals and other wetland-adapted organisms, and (3) to discuss the ecological and economic values of mammals associated with northern prairie wetland habitats.

I have limited the scope of this chapter to terrestrial or semiaquatic mammals whose current geographic range encompasses most of the prairie pothole region and that commonly use wetlands for cover or obtain a major portion of their diets from wetland-dependent organisms (Table 9.1). Most of these species occupy broad niches and are commonly found also in grasslands, forests, or other environments. Within the prairie pothole region, however, these mammals readily exploit the resources provided by wetlands; in some cases, viable populations within the region may be dependent upon the quantity, quality, and availability

ERIK K. FRITZELL, School of Forestry, Fisheries and Wildlife, 112 Stephens Hall, University of Missouri, Columbia, Missouri 65211.

TABLE 9.1.   Important mammals in northern prairie wetland ecosystems

Common name	Scientific name
Masked shrew	*Sorex cinereus*
Northern short-tailed shrew	*Blarina brevicauda*
Thirteen-lined ground squirrel	*Spermophilus tridecemlineatus*
Franklin's ground squirrel	*Spermophilus franklinii*
Beaver	*Castor canadensis*
Western harvest mouse	*Reithrodontomys megalotis*
Deer mouse	*Peromyscus maniculatus*
Meadow vole	*Microtus pennsylvanicus*
Muskrat	*Ondatra zibethicus*
Meadow jumping mouse	*Zapus hudsonius*
Red fox	*Vulpes vulpes*
Raccoon	*Procyon lotor*
Long-tailed weasel	*Mustela frenata*
Least weasel	*Mustela nivalis*
Mink	*Mustela vison*
Striped skunk	*Mephitis mephitis*
White-tailed deer	*Odocoileus virginianus*

Note: Species whose geographic ranges include only a small portion of the prairie pothole region are excluded.

of wetland habitat. Some species markedly affect the production of other wetland resources, such as waterfowl. Where appropriate, I have discussed these relationships.

I have arbitrarily excluded mammals whose geographic ranges include only a small portion of the prairie pothole region or whose distribution within the region is localized. For example, moose (*Alces alces*), snowshoe hares (*Lepus americanus*), and arctic shrews (*Sorex arcticus*) inhabit wetlands along the northern periphery of the region. These species are important components of wetland communities in the boreal forest and transition zones but are of minor significance when viewed from a regional perspective. I have also excluded the bat fauna. Being obligate insectivores, vespertilionid bats of the region are probably influenced by the abundance of insects emerging from wetlands. Yet bats are not common in the prairie pothole region and their distribution likely is influenced more by the availability of suitable roosting sites, such as trees and buildings, than by wetland resources. At Delta, Manitoba, bats of four species regularly fed along a narrow forested ridge rather than over the adjacent Lake Manitoba or extensive Delta Marsh (Barclay 1984).

On the basis of their ecological roles in prairie wetland ecosystems and their importance as resources within the region, four distinct groups of mammals will be considered: semiaquatic herbivores, small mammals, carnivores, and white-tailed deer.

SEMIAQUATIC MAMMALS

The prairie pothole region encompasses the distributions of two semiaquatic herbivorous mammals, the beaver and the muskrat. Beavers are primarily associated with lotic environments (Bailey 1926; Jones et al. 1983) but they may inhabit semipermanent and permanent wetlands close to rivers and streams throughout the region. Beavers occasionally occupy semipermanent wetlands in the southern portion of the prairie pothole region, but populations do not become established in these habitats. In the northern parkland portion of the region where woody vegetation is common, beavers regularly inhabit wetlands except during periods of extreme drought. It is not considered a major species associated with wetlands throughout the region; therefore, discussion here will center on the muskrat.

Perhaps more than any other animal, muskrats influence the structure and function of semipermanent wetlands in the northern prairie. Most, if not all, values linked to ecological processes emanating from prairie marshes are affected measurably by the presence, abundance, and activity of this dominant marsh herbivore. Yet the details of muskrat ecology in prairie wetlands are poorly quantified. Most published information on the species in the glaciated prairie is included in Errington (1963), which forms the basis for the following discussion except where noted. Since the completion of his lifelong studies, most research on muskrats has been conducted elsewhere (Willner et al. 1980; Perry 1982).

Muskrats may inhabit all types of wetlands temporarily, but they may only survive well in wetlands deep enough to sustain under ice activity throughout the winter. Therefore, semipermanent and permanent wetlands (Types IV and V of Stewart and Kantrud [1971]) are centers of muskrat abundance in the northern prairie region.

Activity of muskrats is centered around a conical lodge constructed of vegetation or a burrow system dug into a bank. Lodge building and burrowing activity occur in early summer and before freeze-up in late fall when it is conspicuously accelerated. Lodges may be of two kinds — nest houses and feeding houses (Fig. 9.1). The larger nest houses, which may be over 2 m high and 3 m in diameter, contain single or multiple chambers well above the water level. One or more entrances or "plunge holes" provide access from underwater. Smaller feeding houses do not always have a chamber. Several feeding houses may be located within 25–50 m of an occupied nest house. Bank burrows may be a short tunnel with room for only one individual or an elaborate maze of interconnected passageways and chambers extending up to 100 m from the water's edge.

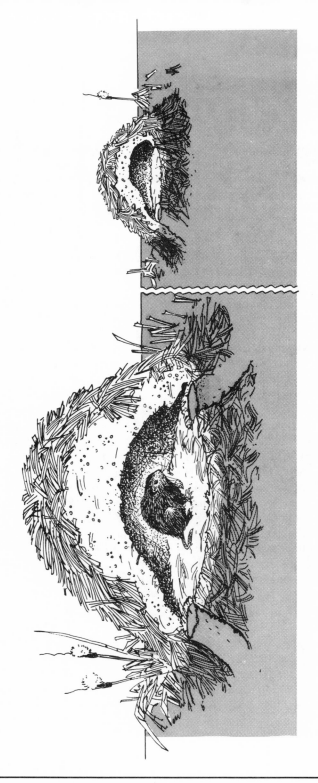

FIG. 9.1. Cross section of a muskrat nest lodge and feeding house in winter. Dimensions after MacArthur and Aleksiuk (1979).

In late fall and winter, muskrats construct "push ups" by carrying masses of submergent vegetation through cracks in the ice. An open plunge hole may be found adjacent to a resting shelf on the ice. Push ups and feed houses radiate from the nest house or burrow in a "stepping stone" fashion and are visited regularly during winter foraging activities (MacArthur 1978). MacArthur and Aleksuik (1979) described the characteristics and microenvironments of muskrat lodges at Delta, Manitoba. In winter, well-insulated, closely spaced nest houses and feed houses provided an equable microclimate moderated by the presence of open water in plunge holes. In summer, high lodge temperatures appeared to favor the use of burrows and open nests by adults. Burrows provided the coolest, most stable microclimates in summer.

The presence of muskrat lodges and bank burrows may influence prairie marsh ecology, although the impacts are minor compared to the effects of cutting and grazing. Kangas and Hannan (1985) found 26 taxa of plants on active and inactive muskrat lodges in a Michigan marsh. They concluded that muskrat lodges provided substrates for dense growths of otherwise minor marsh species and thus enhanced the diversity of the wetland. Active lodges and remnants of decomposing lodges also provide nesting substrates for some bird species such as black terns (*Chlidonias niger*), Forester's terns (*Sterna foresteri*) (Weller and Spatcher 1965), and Canada geese (Cooper 1978). Lodges and burrows provide den sites for other mammals, such as meadow voles (Errington 1963), raccoons (Dorney 1954) and minks (Errington 1963; Eberhardt and Sargeant 1977).

One family of muskrats usually occupies a single nest house or burrow and defends a territory around it. Movements are usually restricted to within 150 m of the nest house or burrow and most foraging is within 10 m of a lodge, burrow, or push up (MacArthur 1978). Both sexes defend the breeding territory, although females are more aggressive than males and sometimes kill an intruder. Aggression and fighting are most prevalent prior to and during the breeding season but also are common during the fall when subadults prepare to establish territories. Muskrats unable to hold territories are more vulnerable to predation and cannibalism.

Muskrats eat a wide variety of aquatic plants, but in the northern prairies, cattail (*Typha* spp.) and bulrushes (*Scirpus* spp.) seem to be the staple food. They prefer the roots and basal portions of the plant shoots and discard the tougher leaves and stems or use them in lodge construction. *Equisetum fluviatile* is a preferred food in Sweden (Danell 1978) and Errington (1963) suggested that it may be preferred over cattails in northern prairie marshes. Other plant genera incorporated into the diet include: *Sparganium, Sagittaria, Potamogeton, Salix, Carex,* and *Poly-*

gonum. Animal matter, such as fish and mussels may be eaten occasionally.

Muskrat populations are highly variable. For example, for the period 1939–1957, population estimates on 650 ha Wall Lake in Iowa ranged from 0, when the marsh was completely dry, to 9,000 when emergents covered the area (Errington 1963) (Fig. 9.2). Population densities greater than 50/ha are not unusual. The maximum winter population reported is 86/ha in an Iowa cattail marsh (Errington 1948). Where habitat conditions are good, population growth can be almost exponential. Females bear an average of 2.5 litters annually with a mean of 7.5 young/litter. Population declines may be equally precipitous. Mortality rates are largely dependent on the amount of quality wetland habitat available. When populations reach extremely high levels or suitable habitat is reduced through natural drought or artificial drawdown, interspecific interactions force some muskrats into marginal habitat where they become vulnerable to predation by mink, foxes, raptors, and other predators. Crowding may also result in cannibalism (especially of young), epizootics, and severe overgrazing. Muskrat "eat outs" (Figure 9.3) that decimate aquatic vegetation result in mass emigration and high

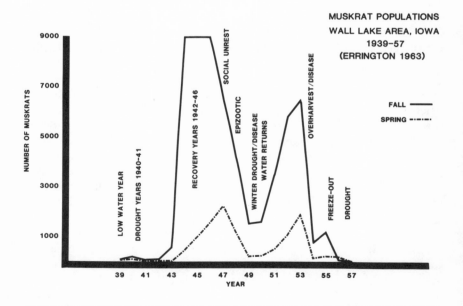

FIG. 9.2.   Muskrat populations and major environmental and demographic events on the Wall Lake Area, Iowa, 1939–57 (*Adapted from Errington 1963*).

FIG. 9.3. The southern end of Goose Lake, Iowa, in the summer of 1959 (upper) and again in the summer of 1962 (lower) after a severe muskrat eat out. Taken from Weller and Spatcher (1965).

mortality. Severe cold may affect overwinter survival in northern latitudes. "Freeze outs" occur when ice becomes thick enough to prevent foraging. Seabloom and Beer (1963) documented the almost complete decimation of a local muskrat population in North Dakota as a result of winter drought and the associated heavy ice formation.

Semipermanent prairie marshes exhibit a cycle of vegetative change lasting anywhere from 5 to 30 years, depending on precipitation and resultant water level changes (Kantrud et al. Chap. 5) Based on observed changes in muskrat populations and vegetation throughout the cycle, muskrat activity has been considered an important influence on primary production (van der Valk and Davis 1978a), decomposition rates (Davis and van der Valk 1978), vegetative structure (Weller and Spatcher 1965; Weller and Fredrickson 1973; van der Valk and Davis 1978b), invertebrate communities (Voights 1976; Kaminski and Prince 1981), and bird populations and communities (Weller and Spatcher 1965; Weller and Fredrickson 1973; Murkin et al. 1982).

During the dry marsh stage when wetland basins become partially or completely dry, most muskrats emigrate or die in situ. Remnant populations may survive wherever water, food, and cover remain. This may be in the deeper central portions of large marshes or in isolated areas holding permanent water. Seeds of mudflat annuals and emergent perennials germinate while the marsh bottom is exposed. When precipitation returns to normal, water levels rise and mudflat plant species disappear. During this regenerating phase, emergents (especially cattails) increase in density through vegetative growth and soon dominate the plant community in relatively homogenous stands. Muskrats that survived the dry periods in remnants of suitable habitat immigrate to colonize this optimal but vacant habitat. Muskrat populations increase rapidly as they exploit the expanding populations of emergents (Weller and Spatcher 1965; Weller and Fredrickson 1973; Bishop et al. 1979).

Disease, insect damage, high water, senescence, and muskrat grazing and cutting have all been suggested as contributing causes to the halt of the regenerating phase and onset of the degenerating phase, although the relative importance of each has not been well quantified. Dense emergent cover decreases in a mosaic pattern, largely because muskrats concentrate their cutting and grazing near lodges, which are well dispersed as a result of the species' territoriality. Openings in the emergents increase in size and number as muskrat populations respond functionally and numerically to the abundant forage. Excellent interspersion of cover and water is provided when cover to water ratios have declined to approximately 50%–the hemi-marsh condition of Weller and Spatcher (1965). Ducks and many other marsh-dwelling birds attain their highest breeding densities under these conditions (Weller and Spatcher 1965; Weller and Fredrickson 1973; Kaminski and Prince 1981; Murkin et al. 1982). Preference of birds for the hemi-marsh condition has been related to increased accessibility of nesting cover (Weller and Spatcher 1965), increased diversity of vegetation types (Weller and Fredrickson 1973), and increased macroinvertebrate production (Voights 1976). Nelson and Kadlec (1984) discussed waterfowl habitat selection in relation to macroinvertebrate production and patterns of emergent vegetation.

Continued high water levels and the still expanding muskrat population lead to the eventual destruction of the emergent community and associated reductions in the populations of macroinvertebrates and breeding birds. Because muskrat populations have increased since the regenerating phase, they have been considered the principal factor in the total destruction of emergent cover. Abrupt and dramatic muskrat "eat outs" (Fig. 9.3) result in subsequent emigration or high in situ mortality (Errington et al. 1963). The lake marsh phase begins when remaining emergents disappear from all but the periphery of the marsh and submersed and free-floating plants dominate. The marsh will then remain in the lake stage until water levels decline and expose the moist substrate allowing the germination of annuals and emergent perennials.

Grazing and cutting of stems by muskrats has a major impact on the rate and pattern of emergent destruction although empirical data on the effects of muskrat grazing are scarce. Daily consumption of *Typha latifolia* by muskrats has been estimated to be 1.4 kg fresh mass per kg muskrat fresh mass (Krasovskij in Pelikan et al. 1970) and mass of cattail destroyed but not consumed to be 2–3 times that consumed (Lavrov in Pelikan et al. 1970). In a Czechoslovakia wetland, with cover of 48.8% *Typha latifolia,* 48.7% *Phragmites australis,* and 2.5% open water, Pelikan et al. (1970) estimated the fall muskrat population to be 28–55 muskrats/ha, a situation approximating a prairie marsh in the late regenerating or early degenerating phase. Here, they estimated that muskrats destroyed an average of 3,565 shoots within a 14 m radius of each lodge or 20.2% of the net production in the same area. Overall, this represented a 5–10% destruction of cattail net production within the marsh. At another location, muskrats consumed 0.9% of the aboveground production and 1.3% of the underground production, but destroyed an estimated 6.6–8.8% of the primary production (Pelikan 1978). During the fall when house building begins, muskrats in *Sagittaria* spp. marshes along the Mississippi River removed about 75% of the aboveground standing crop in areas 4–5 m in diameter around lodges; however, this represented <1% of the total standing crop in the marsh. (W. R. Clark, pers. commun.). Smith and Kadlec (1985) found that waterfowl and muskrats (of unknown densities) reduced the production and standing crop of emergent macrophytes in a Utah marsh, especially in areas that had been burned. Grazing intensity on the aboveground biomass in burned areas was 48% for *Typha* spp., 25% for *Scirpus lacustris,* and 9% for *S. maritimus.* Clearly the effect of muskrat grazing and associated destruction of emergents cannot be ignored as major influence of marsh structure and dynamics.

SMALL MAMMALS

Considering the wealth of research on small mammals (mice, voles, and insectivores) worldwide, this component of northern prairie wetland ecosystems is poorly studied. Although descriptive narratives are available in regional or local summaries of mammals (e.g., Jones et al. 1984; Wilhelm et al. 1981), quantitative information largely is limited to unpublished theses and reports. Details of the functional roles of small mammals in northern prairie wetlands must be inferred from studies conducted in other environments.

Frequency distributions of small mammals trapped in wetlands throughout the prairie pothole region reflect the structure of the community (Table 9.2), although caution must be used in interpreting these data. Furthermore, differences in methodology and study design do not permit detailed comparisons among locations.

Six species typically make up the small mammal community in most northern prairie wetlands: masked shrew, northern short-tailed shrew, thirteen-lined ground squirrel, deer mouse, meadow vole, and meadow jumping mouse. These small mammals are habitat generalists, and have no unique adaptations to wetland habitats. They have relatively large geographic ranges. The life history traits of these mammals are diverse, however, suggesting a high potential for niche separation among them within wetland ecosystems (Table 9.3).

Meadow voles are usually the most abundant of the wetland small mammals, often accounting for >40% of the individuals. Their populations fluctuate dramatically and often exhibit characteristic cycles of three- to five-year periodicity. Meadow vole populations may exceed 600 voles/ha during a cyclic high (Tait and Krebs 1985). The other five major small mammal species are found in wetlands throughout the region but usually in lower densities than *Microtus*. Various "minor" species (e.g., see Table 9.2) occasionally are captured in wetlands but most are typically associated with more xeric habitats. The distribution of small mammals within prairie wetlands is probably influenced by soil moisture and the associated continuum of vegetation types (Fig. 9.4). Pendleton (1984) studied habitat selection by small mammals in numerous wetlands in eastern South Dakota. Meadow voles were most commonly associated with sites having higher soil moisture. Deer mice predominated at drier trap sites at the edges of wetland basins. Both masked and short-tailed shrews were found in transitional habitats intermediate in moisture. Meadow jumping mice seemed to use mesic and hydric habitats similar to that of meadow voles, and thirteen-lined ground squirrels used upland habitats similar to those occupied by deer mice, although data were limited for these two species. Pendleton's quantitative analysis of habitat

TABLE 3.2. Proportions of small mammal species trapped in prairie wetlands reported in published and unpublished sources

A

	Sorex cinereus	Blarina brevicauda	Spermophilus tridecemlineatus	Thomomys talpoides	Reithrodontomys megalotis	Peromyscus maniculatus
South Dakota						
Marshall, Day, Clark, and Lake counties[a]	0.12	0.00	0.03	0.00	0.01	0.22
Brookings County[a]	0.24	0.01	0.06	…	…	0.19
Moody County[a]	0.15	0.35	0.04	…	…	0.08
Clay and Union counties[b]	0.10	0.19	…	…	0.18	0.20
Iowa						
Clay County[c]	0.53	0.02	0.07	…	…	0.02
North Dakota						
Stutsman County[d]	0.05	0.05	…	…	…	0.09
Benson and Eddy counties[e]	…	…	0.01	…	…	0.17
Benson and Eddy counties[f]	0.06	…	0.02	…	…	0.07
Manitoba						
Odanah Municipality[g]	0.24	…	0.01	…	…	0.18

[a]Pendleton 1984.　[e]USDI 1979.
[b]Lindell 1971.　[f]USDI 1980.
[c]Weller 1979.　[g]Fritzell 1972.
[d]Eberhardt 1974.

B

	Onychomys leucogaster	Clethrionomys gapperi	Microtus ochrogaster	Microtus pennsylvanicus	Mus musculus	Zapus hudsonius	Mustela nivalis
South Dakota							
Marshall, Day, Clark, and Lake counties[a]	0.00	0.01	…	0.48	0.00	0.13	…
Brookings County[a]	…	…	…	0.48	…	0.03	…
Moody County[a]	…	…	…	0.33	0.01	0.05	0.01
Clay and Union counties[b]	…	…	…	0.18	0.15	…	…
Iowa							
Clay County[c]	…	…	…	0.34	0.07	0.02	…
North Dakota							
Stutsman County[d]	…	…	…	0.75	…	0.06	…
Benson and Eddy counties[e]	0.01	…	0.06	0.64	…	0.17	…
Benson and Eddy counties[f]	0.07	…	…	0.71	…	…	…
Manitoba							
Odanah Municipality[g]	…	0.11	…	0.41	…	0.05	…

[a]Pendleton 1984.　[e]USDI 1979.
[b]Lindell 1971.　[f]USDI 1980.
[c]Weller 1979.　[g]Fritzell 1972.
[d]Eberhardt 1974.

TABLE 9.3. Life history categories of small mammals commonly found in prairie wetlands

Species	Size[a]	Reproductive index[b]	Life form[c]	Seasonality activity[d]	Diet[e]
Sorex cinereus	1	2	2	1	2
Blarina brevicauda	2	2	2	1	2
Spermophilus tridecemlineatus	5	1	3	2	3
Peromyscus maniculatus	2	2	3	1	3
Microtus pennsylvanius	3	3	2	1	1
Zapus hudsonius	2	2	3	2	1

Source: Adapted from Grant and Birney 1979; Risser et al. 1981.

[a]1 = ≤ 15 g; 2 = 16–30 g; 3 = 31–45 g; 4 = 46–60 g; 5 = > 60 g.

[b]Reproductive = $\dfrac{\text{(mean litter size) (maximum no. of litters in 180 days)}}{\text{minimum age of initial breeding}}$; Index (RI):

1 = RI < 0.1; 2 = 0.1<RI<0.5; E = RI > 0.5.

[c]1 = fossorial; 2 = subsurface or litter; 3 = surface.

[d]1 = year-round; 2 = seasonal.

[e]1 = herbivore; 2 = carnivore; 3 = omnivore.

SMALL MAMMALS

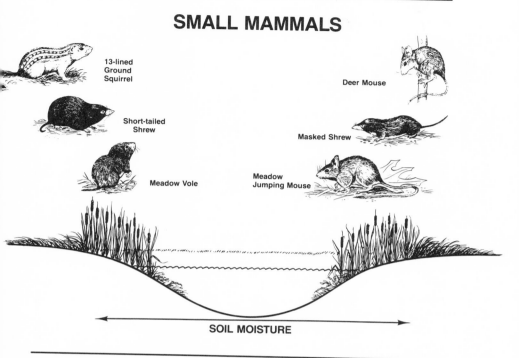

13-lined
Ground
Squirrel

Deer Mouse

Short-tailed
Shrew

Masked Shrew

Meadow Vole

Meadow
Jumping Mouse

SOIL MOISTURE

FIG. 9.4. Distribution of small mammals related to habitat in northern prairie wetlands
(*Adapted from Pendleton 1984*).

selection is supported by research conducted on the same species on
other environments (Getz 1961a, 1961b, 1961c, 1970; Spencer and Pettus
1966; Birney et al. 1976; Douglass 1976; Wrigley et al. 1979).

The role of small mammals in the energy and nutrient dynamics of
wetland ecosystems is poorly understood. Their relative contribution to
ecosystem energetics and nutrient processing has not been measured in
North American wetlands, but it is probably not of great importance. In
a Czechoslovakian wetland composed of about 50% *Typha* and 50%
Phragmites, consumption by the rodent community (excluding
muskrats) was estimated to be 0.55% of the aboveground and about
0.18% of the underground plant production (Pelikan 1978). That Czechoslovakian rodent community was more diverse (eight species) and
probably had more individuals and biomass (mean annual density =
57.3 individuals/ha^{-1}; mean annual dry mass = 0.19 gr/m^{-2}) than typical rodent communities in the prairie pothole region. The species composition of the small mammal community within the northern true prairie

ecosystem (as described from Isanti County, Minnesota) (Grant and Birney 1979; Risser et al. 1981) is similar to that found in wetlands of the prairie pothole region. This is not surprising because wetlands within the northern mixed-grass prairie (i.e., prairie pothole region) occupy mesic or hydric sites in a drier climate, whereas tallgrass prairies in eastern Minnesota occupy a xeric site within a moister climate. The energetics of that and similar small mammal communities (French et al. 1976; Risser et al. 1981) may provide important clues to understanding energetics in northern prairie wetlands, even though the environments are not identical.

Despite the probable lack of importance to wetland energy and nutrient budgets, the production of rodents is important to the presence and abundance of other conspicuous and economically important secondary and tertiary consumers using northern prairie wetlands. Meadow voles, in particular, figure prominently in the diets of red foxes (Scott 1943, 1947), mink (Waller 1962; Cowan and Reilly 1973; Eberhardt and Sargeant 1977), short-eared owls (*Asio flammeus*) (Walley 1972; Clark 1975), northern harriers (*Circus cyaneus*) (Errington and Breckenridge 1936) and other wetland species. Vole populations undergo dramatic fluctuations, often with a three- to five-year periodicity (Krebs and Myers 1974). Some consumers, in turn, are adapted to exploit periodic abundances and to survive during scarcities of the species. For example, in 1968 when meadow voles were scarce, Clark (1975) found only one breeding pair of short-eared owls throughout southern Manitoba. In 1969, after an estimated ten-fold increase in voles, owls bred in large numbers. After 25 years of study, Hamerstrom et al. (1985) concluded that the abundance of voles governed not only the abundance of northern harriers in a Wisconsin marsh, but also their mating system.

Birney et al. (1976) advanced the hypothesis "that some threshold of cover is necessary for a population of *Microtus* to increase in numbers sufficiently to undergo a multi-year cycle. . . . and [the threshold] is site specific. . . . Above the threshold, quantity of cover probably influences the amplitude and perhaps the duration between peaks of a cycle." They suggested that only under conditions provided by a level of cover above the threshold will reproduction and survival be sufficient to permit the attainment of high populations characteristic of cycles. After presenting data supporting the hypothesis from tallgrass prairies, Lemen and Clausen (1984) concluded the 700 g/m^2 of grass cover was required to support "high" densities of voles. In advancing their hypothesis Birney et al. (1976) suggested that an upland site in Minnesota with low cover levels was not able to support a cycling population of *Microtus* and a wetland site with high levels of cover probably would support cycles. A local "patch" of dense cover, such as found in wetlands, could serve as a reservoir out of which dispersing individuals will colonize low cover habitats. Such a view of vole populations is consistent with the model presented by Smith et al. (1978) who offered testable hypotheses about the demographic and genetic characteristics of these "primary" and "secondary" populations. A mosaic of high cover wetlands interspersed among lower cover uplands is characteristic of the prairie pothole region. If the hypothesis of Birney et al. (1976) holds, then wetlands, by providing high cover loci, may markedly affect the very nature of *Microtus* population dynamics and, in turn, affect the dynamics of secondary and tertiary consumers.

Franklin's ground squirrels also inhabit wetlands throughout the prairie pothole region. But because of their relatively large size (300–600 g) they are not commonly trapped during inventories of small mammal communities. They are one of the least studied of the Nearctic ground squirrels. The paucity of information largely results from their preference for tall, dense vegetation where they are seldom seen.

Population estimates vary throughout the region. Two studies at Delta, Manitoba, reported densities of 9.9–12.4 squirrels/ha (Sowls 1948) and 4.2–5.7 squirrels/ha (Lynch 1972). Such high densities are probably quite exceptional. In Alberta, Murie (1973) reported a density of 1.3–2.5 adults/ha, and in Minnesota, Haggerty (1968) estimated 0.2–1.5 adults/ha. A minimum density of 3 adults/ha was documented in the pothole region of North Dakota (Choromanski-Norris 1983).

Choromanski-Norris (1983) studied the movements and habitat selection of Franklin's ground squirrels in managed waterfowl habitat using radio-telemetry. Annual home-range sizes averaged 24.6 ha for males and 8.7 ha for females. Ground squirrels used wetland edges only and most of their activity was concentrated in upland habitats.

Although vegetative material comprises two-thirds or more of the diet of Franklin's ground squirrels, insects, small mammals and bird eggs are also consumed (Bailey 1926; Lyon 1932; Sowls 1948; Haggerty 1968). Severe predation on the eggs of upland nesting ducks by Franklin's ground squirrels was documented at Delta Marsh, Manitoba (Sowls 1948), where ground squirrels were responsible for the destruction of 19% of the duck nests accessible to them. Studies regarding the feasibility of predator control, using strychnine-treated eggs, have also identified the Franklin's ground squirrel as a potential waterfowl nest predator (Balser et al. 1968; Lynch 1972). In North Dakota, recent evidence suggests that predation by Franklin's ground squirrels on upland duck nests in managed prairie habitat can be significant (R. Greenwood, pers. commun.).

CARNIVORES

Red Fox

Red foxes typically are not considered inhabitants of wetland environments. Yet because the impact of fox predation on waterfowl populations can be substantial, brief discussion of this mammal is warranted.

Sargeant's (1982) excellent chronicle of midwestern red fox populations describes changes in abundance over almost two centuries. Fox populations apparently were sparse prior to settlement of the prairie pothole region. As the region was settled in the late 1800s, populations further declined, probably from overexploitation. Foxes were extirpated from some areas. But, after the late 1930s, their numbers increased and their range expanded dramatically because of changes in habitat, reduced interspecific competition with other canids, and reduction in harvest pressure. More recently populations have fluctuated but remain relatively high. Spring fox densities for the prairie pothole region of North Dakota from 1963 to 1980 ranged from one family/15.7 km² to one family/127.9 km² (Sargeant et al. 1984). Foxes tend to be less numerous in western areas of the region than in the east probably because of competition with coyotes (*Canis latrans*) which are more abundant there (Sargeant 1982; Voight and Earle 1983).

A red fox family, the basic social unit of the species, typically consists of a mated pair and their offspring from whelping through dispersal. Each family occupies a territory of 2.6–8.0 km² (Scott 1943; Sargeant 1972; Sargeant et al. 1975; Johnson and Sargeant 1977). Within this territory four to six young typically are reared (Allen 1984). Parents provide the young with food throughout the 13-week denning season (1 April–30 June), a period that coincides with the nesting season of prairie waterfowl. During the denning period foxes feed on ducks, passerine birds, lagomorphs, rodents, carrion, and a wide variety of other organisms mainly obtained in upland habitats.

Sargeant et al. (1984) estimated that ducks averaged 15.8 and 17.0% of the total prey biomass consumed by foxes during the annual denning season in the Drift Plain and Missouri Coteau portion of central North Dakota, respectively. Consumption of duck varied annually from 7.7 to 31.5% of the diet. Female dabbling ducks particularly provided a major portion of the diet. Fox predation accounted for a reduction in 13.5% of the female and 4.5% of the male duck populations, resulting in an average annual take of 900,000 adult ducks in midcontinent North America (primarily the prairie pothole region).

Red foxes prey selectively on female dabbling ducks (and duck eggs) undoubtedly because they are vulnerable while nesting in upland habitats. The degree of hen-selective predation by foxes varies among duck species and geographic location (Sargeant et al. 1984). Sixty-four percent of the gadwalls (*Anas strepera*) taken by foxes were females, whereas 90% of the shovelers (*A. clypeata*) were females. Sixty-five percent of the mallards (*A. platyrynchos*) and northern pintails (*A. acuta*) taken in the western Dakotas were hens compared to 76% hens taken in the eastern Dakotas. Differences in sex-selectivity among species may relate to the behavior and nesting chronology of the ducks, but wetland characteristics may affect geographic differences. Man-made stockponds with steep shorelines and little emergent vegetation predominate in western areas, whereas natural marshes with gradual shorelines and much emergent vegetation predominate in the east. The sexes may be more equally vulnerable to predation in western areas because they are relatively more accessible to foxes while in those wetland habitats (Sargeant et al. 1984).

Raccoon

Raccoons inhabited eastern river valleys of the prairie pothole region prior to settlement by Europeans (Coues 1897). In the early twentieth century, they were found in low densities along wooded watercourses (Bailey 1926). Today they are common throughout the region in all habitat types. The expansion of the raccoon range has been well documented (Sowls 1949; Sutton 1964; Lynch 1971; Kiel et al. 1972; Houston and Houston 1973). In general, populations expanded northwesterly across the region. They were established by the late 1940s in North Dakota, by the mid-1950s in Manitoba and by the mid-1960s in Saskatchewan. The immediate causes for the establishment of raccoons in the region are unknown. Several cultural changes to the landscape during this period, however, may have been major influences including: the abandonment of farm buildings that served as important den sites; an increased availability of stored grain and associated insects that served as important foods in late fall, winter, and early spring; and the reduction in coyote populations through predator control programs. Wherever they have been found, raccoons have exploited wetlands intensively.

Knowledge of raccoon biology in prairie pothole landscapes comes from two studies. Cowan (1973) described the life history of raccoons near Minnedosa in southwestern Manitoba in the late 1960s, and they were studied intensively near Walum in east-central North Dakota from 1973 to 1976 (Fritzell and Matthews, 1975; Fritzell 1977, 1978a, 1978b, 1978c; Greenwood 1979, 1981, 1982; Fritzell and Greenwood 1984). Both study areas are dominated by agricultural land devoted primarily to small grain production. The Minnedosa area included more wooded areas and wetlands than found at Walum, but marshes at Minnedosa are much smaller and are well interspersed with upland vegetation types. Raccoon populations during spring were estimated to be 1.5–3.2/km^2 at Minnedosa (Cowan 1973) and 0.5–1.0/km^2 at Walum (Fritzell 1978a). These densities are considerably sparser than those recorded from other habitats in North America (Kaufmann 1982).

During the spring and summer individual raccoons exploit the prairie pothole environment differently depending on their social status (Fritzell 1978a, 1978b; Greenwood 1982). Adult males occupied exclusive territories averaging 2,560 ha and traveled regularly throughout this large area. Yearling males had smaller home ranges ($\bar{x} = 1,139$ ha) when resident, but many of them dispersed between May and July often reestablishing home ranges elsewhere. Adult females typically rear young during this period. Their home ranges averaged 806 ha, and were much compressed around the litter site when young were less than four weeks of age. Yearling females, which rarely reproduce, had home ranges averaging 656 ha, and showed little evidence of dispersal. Lactating females and yearlings obtained their nutritional requisites with considerably less travel and energy expenditure than did adult males (Greenwood 1982).

Wetlands were the most commonly used habitat type at night when raccoons were active at both Minnedosa (Cowan 1973) and Walum (Fritzell 1978a). All classes of northern prairie wetlands (Stewart and Kantrud 1971) were used extensively by raccoons at Walum; but types III and IV marshes were centers of raccoon activity, probably due to their greater availability (Fritzell 1978a). Ninety-four percent of nocturnal raccoon activity in wetlands was related to foraging (Greenwood 1982). Early in the spring raccoons often foraged near building sites, but as natural foods became more available the use of wetlands increased. Frequency of use of wetlands increased from 30% in April to 56% in July (Fritzell 1978a). Few data describing habitat use patterns after midsummer are available, but wetland use probably remains significant as it does in other regions (Schneider et al. 1971).

An efficient omnivore, the raccoon readily adapts to temporal changes in food availability. Their diets are consistent with the foraging pattern described above and are often dominated by wetland organisms. Plant and animal matter were identified in about equal numbers of the 586 raccoon scats collected April to July in North Dakota (Greenwood 1981). Wheat, barley, and sunflowers were important plant foods especially in the early spring. Aquatic insects, birds and bird eggs, snails, and crustaceans comprised important animal foods. Significantly, almost all animal foods were derived from wetlands and their use increased during the summer months. Food habits of raccoons near Minnedosa were very similar except that various wild fruits commonly were eaten during summer and fall (Cowan 1973). Greenwood's (1982) detailed analysis of foraging behavior of individual raccoons substantiated the intensive use of grain from farmyards and aquatic organisms from wetlands.

Raccoons in the glaciated prairies spend the daylight hours at various resting sites throughout their home ranges. Except females attending litters, they seldom were found in the same location on consecutive days from April to July. Approximately one-third of the resting sites were used more than once by the same raccoon (Fritzell 1978a). Forty-three percent of the resting sites used by raccoons on the Walum study area were located in wetlands and 44% were in building sites. Similar to foraging patterns, use of wetlands as resting sites increased throughout the spring and summer as use of building sites decreased. Seventy percent of the resting locations in July were in wetlands. Similar shifts to wetland locations during the summer were observed by Cowan (1973) and Schneider et al. (1971).

Well-insulated den sites where raccoons spend the winter months may be especially important to raccoon survival at northern latitudes. Buildings, burrows, and "scrub piles" were used as winter dens on the Minnedosa area (Cowan 1973), as were abandoned buildings on the Walum area (personal observation). Apparently raccoons will den in frozen wetlands in the southern portions of the prairie pothole region. I have received reliable reports of groups of raccoons being encountered in thick "cattail teepees" in South Dakota during the winter, and occasionally they have been found denning in muskrat lodges in marshes outside the prairie region (Dorney 1954; Urban 1970).

Both Cowan (1973) and Greenwood (1981, 1982) documented extensive depredation by raccoons on waterfowl eggs. Waterfowl nesting success in the prairie pothole region has declined markedly over the past 40 years (Miller 1971). Raccoons have been considered a major influence in that decline (Duebbert and Kantrud 1974; Duebbert and Lokemoen 1976; Trauger and Stoudt 1974; Kiel et al. 1972; Sargeant and Arnold 1984). The proclivity of raccoons to forage and den in and near wetlands provides them many opportunities for destroying nests, especially those of diving ducks and other birds that nest over water. Although the total impact of nest depredation by raccoons on waterfowl populations is not known, its importance will likely increase because of desires to produce more ducks from a smaller habitat base.

Mink

The mink is a common carnivore throughout the prairie pothole region and is more closely associated with wetlands than is any other mammalian carnivore. Although they may be found in other habitats, mink are seldom found far from water. The abundance and diversity of wetlands in the prairie region provide excellent mink habitat. No reliable population estimates from the northern prairie region are available, but densities likely vary considerably. For example, Errington (1943) thought five different families (females with young) inhabited half of the 182 ha Little Wall Lake, Iowa, in 1935, but no families were found on the entire marsh in 1939. Whether his estimates were accurate is unknown, but they suggest marked fluctuations. Although it is not well documented, many biologists suggest that drought conditions result in reduced reproduction by mink (Eberhardt 1974; Arnold 1986; A. B. Sargeant, pers. commun.).

Mink are solitary and primarily nocturnal (Gerell 1969). Adult males occupy large territories exclusive of other males. Their territories may be several times the size of female home ranges (Marshall 1936; Ritchey and Edwards 1956; Gerell 1970). Female ranges overlap those of males and other females (Gerell 1970). Juvenile males disperse from their natal areas beginning in late summer and may move up to 45 km (Gerell 1970).

Dens serve as refugia for mink during the day and are usually located along shorelines in abandoned muskrat burrows (Schladweiler and Storm 1969; Sargeant et al. 1973; Eberhardt 1973; Eberhardt and Sargeant 1977). During the spring and summer, males roam widely while females center their activity around rearing dens where they alone rear an average of 3.5 young from May through July. The denning habits of two families of mink studied intensively by Eberhardt and Sargeant (1977) are probably typical. One family used a minimum of five rearing dens; the other used at least nine. Each female centered its activity on a single semipermanent marsh of 19 or 16 ha. Most, if not all, food was obtained within this area. Concentrated foraging by females during the rearing period often had severe impacts on prey populations in the vicinity of den sites (Sargeant et al. 1973; Eberhardt and Sargeant 1977). Arnold (1986) studied the foraging ecology of male mink in southwestern Manitoba. Nightly foraging commenced from any one of numerous dens scattered throughout each home range. Individuals regularly shifted dens and associated foci of activity to different semipermanent and permanent wetlands within their home ranges, all of which were larger than 270 ha. In contrast to females, the effects of male mink on prey populations was dispersed over a greater area.

Throughout their geographic range, mink are efficient predators capable of taking a variety of prey when available, mainly aquatic and semiaquatic vertebrates and invertebrates (see review in Linscombe et al. 1982). The food habits of mink inhabiting northern prairie wetlands have been well documented (Waller 1962; Cowan and Reilly 1973; Eberhardt 1973; Eberhardt and Sargeant 1977; Arnold 1986). The most notable difference between mink food habits in prairie wetlands and other habitats is the lack of fish and abundance of marsh birds in the prairie mink diet.

Birds and mammals comprise the major portion of the diet throughout the northern prairie region. Waller (1962 and summarized in Linscombe et al. 1982) compared the seasonal diets of mink in Iowa by measuring frequencies of occurrence in droppings. In winter, birds and mammals made up about equal proportions of the diet (48% and 49.6%, respectively) and no other category appeared in more than 10% of the droppings. Birds dominated the diet in spring (71.6%), mammals were less important (34.0%), and other categories remained low. In summer, mammals were of greatest importance (50.2%); birds second (32.2%); but fish, frogs, crayfish, and insects all were taken more extensively (12.5–22.8%). Mammals (47.7%), birds (40.5%), and frogs (30.0%) were the major food items during the autumn months. Several studies of the summer foods of mink in North Dakota (Cowan and Reilly 1973; Eberhardt 1973; Sargeant et al. 1973; Eberhardt and Sargeant 1977; Arnold 1986) emphasize the importance of marsh birds as mink prey. The predominance of birds in the diet likely is due to the high densities of vulnerable avian species on northern prairie marshes and to the scarcity of other potential prey, especially fish and crayfish (Eberhardt and Sargeant 1977, Peterka Chap. 10).

Mink predation may have an important impact on marsh bird production. Eberhardt and Sargeant (1977) estimated that a single mink family killed 8% of the adult and 52% of the juvenile coots (*Fulica americana*), as well as 20% of the adult and 6% of the juvenile pied-billed grebes (*Podilymbus podiceps*) on one semipermanent marsh. The impact of mink on duck populations may be substantial also, especially predation on ducklings (Arnold 1986). Eberhardt and Sargeant (1977) found an average of 12.6 ducks (6.3 adults, 5.3 juveniles) were taken per mink family. Mink predation on female diving ducks may contribute to the disparate sex ratios favoring males commonly observed among waterfowl (Eberhardt and Sargeant 1977).

Weasels

Two species of weasels inhabit the prairie pothole region, the long-tailed weasel and the least weasel. Few ecological data are available for either species within the region. Weasels prey primarily on voles; therefore their populations respond numerically and functionally to the cyclic changes in vole populations (Polderboer et al. 1941; Fitzgerald 1977). Because wetlands provide excellent vole habitat in the prairie region, they may be a key component of weasel habitat. The diet of the long-tailed weasel may include larger prey, such as ground squirrels and young lagomorphs, as well. Predation by long-tailed weasels on nesting ducks and their eggs has been documented (Keith 1961; Teer 1964), but the impact of weasel predation on waterfowl populations is probably minimal.

Striped Skunks

Striped skunks are ubiquitous predators throughout the prairie pothole region and are often associated with wetland habitats. Populations may vary annually and among locations, but the complete enumeration reported by Greenwood et al. (1985) is probably typical for agricultural areas interspersed with good wetland habitat. During late April, a known population of 23 adults (10 females, 13 males) in 1977 and 28 adults (20 females, 8 males) in 1978 inhabited a 31.4 km² area. Other population estimates from the prairie region determined by a variety of techniques include: 0.7–1.2/km² in Alberta (Bjorge et al. 1981), 1.9–3.1/km² in North Dakota (Upham 1967), and 0.4–1.4/km² in Iowa (Scott and Selko 1939).

Striped skunks are not active year around in northern environments and typically enter underground dens during November. Males emerge in January probably to search for estrous females that remain in winter dens until March (Mutch and Aleksiuk 1977; Gunson and Bjorge 1979; Schowalter and Gunson 1982). Males usually den alone, but communal dens may be occupied by two or more females and a solitary male (Gunson and Bjorge 1979; Anderson 1981).

Skunks are primarily nocturnal with peak activity levels one to two hours after sunset (Greenwood et al. 1985). During daylight hours, they use rest sites that may be underground or on the surface in dense cover (Storm 1972; Anderson 1981). The sites used as retreats may change daily. In Illinois, the number of consecutive days at a daytime resting site averaged 1.6 days for 43 skunks (Storm 1972). Movement patterns have been described for skunk populations over much of the prairie region (Bjorge et al. 1981; Anderson 1981; Sargeant et al. 1982; Rosatte and Gunson 1984; Greenwood et al. 1985). Home-range estimates based on radiotelemetry data typically range between 200–400 ha depending on the sex and age of the individual, the time interval monitored, season, and habitat. Adult males range over larger areas than do adult females, and juveniles typically disperse from their natal ranges between July and September. Adults also may disperse from established home ranges (Sargeant et al. 1982).

Skunks are habitat generalists. They thrive over a wide range of environmental conditions. Habitat use patterns have not been quantified within the prairie pothole region, but recent unpublished research suggests that they forage primarily in grassy cover in uplands or wet meadows (R. J. Greenwood and A. B. Sargeant, unpubl. data). Extensive use of grassy areas is common in other regions as well (Bailey 1971; Storm 1972). Skunks often retreat to lowland areas with dense cover during the day. Stands of emergent marsh vegetation may be used if the site is dry. Wetlands may also be used as sites for winter dens. In the Delta Marsh, Manitoba, striped skunks selected wet, low-lying areas for winter den sites in preference to a nearby drier, wooded ridge or adjacent dikes (Mutch 1977). Eight of 12 winter dens in the marsh were in stands of *Phragmites australis*. Despite the high water table, the flattened residual *Phragmites* and the covering soft snow provided excellent insulation. The unstable, sandy soil and greater snowpack associated with the wooded ridge apparently negated any positive benefits of the well-drained locations.

Skunks prey primarily on insects and small mammals, but during the spring and summer the eggs of ground nesting birds may become an important part of the diet (Verts 1967). In the prairie pothole region, skunks are believed to be a major predator on waterfowl nests (Stoudt 1971; Duebbert and Kantrud 1974; Duebbert and Lokemoen 1980). Nest depredation by skunks likely has the greatest impact on dabbling ducks that nest in upland cover. They probably encounter many waterfowl nests incidentally as they thoroughly investigate grasslands for insect prey (A. B. Sargeant, pers. commun.). Skunks may also destroy diving duck nests located over water, especially when drought conditions make them more accessible (Stoudt 1982).

White-Tailed Deer

One of the best-known and least documented facts is that white-tailed deer frequently use northern prairie wetlands for cover. Sparrowe and Springer (1970) monitored the movements of white-tailed deer in eastern South Dakota. Although use of wetlands by deer was not well quantified, it was apparent that marshes were often foci of deer activity, especially during fall and winter. The primary functions of dense cattail marshes were to provide thermal cover and refuge from hunters, but deer foraged on aspen (*Populus* spp.) and willows (*Salix* spp.) in some wetlands. Kucera (1976) found that deer in Delta Marsh, Manitoba, used wetlands more than wooded areas during winter, and related deer habitat preferences to snow thickness in five vegetation types. Marsh meadows were used most often, and deer foraged primarily on herbs (e.g., *Sonchus* spp., *Cirsium arvense*) associated with that habitat. The specific cover value of wetlands to deer in the prairie has not been measured, but deer usually bed in sites that offer the best shelter. During the harsh prairie winters, dense wetland cover may be especially critical to their survival. However, cover is less important when deer have an abundant supply of high-energy food (Moen 1968). The ameliorating effect of bedding in low-lying areas with dense vegetation cover can be approximated from energetic models (Moen 1973). During the spring and summer, the value of prairie wetlands to white-tailed deer is probably less than it is during fall and winter. Nonetheless, a small sample of females consistently used wetlands for fawning sites in central North Dakota (Harmoning 1976). Dispersed wetlands free of disturbance from agricultural activity may be especially important to fawn survival in the northern prairie region. The use of prairie wetlands by deer needs to be documented over a range of conditions.

DISCUSSION

From the preceding review, it is clear that wetlands can play an important role in the life cycles of many prairie mammals. Likewise mammals may markedly affect other components of northern prairie wetland ecosystems and the values humans extract from them. As the primary grazer in semipermanent marshes, muskrats directly affect vegetation structure. As a result, the pathways and rates of nutrient exchange may be altered. Small mammals, especially meadow voles, probably reach their greatest abundance in wetland meadows. Voles provide an important prey base for many carnivores; their cycle of abundance and scarcity is the proximate factor affecting life history patterns of other species. Mammalian carnivores throughout the prairie pothole region use wetlands as important habitats for obtaining food and shelter. As a result they have significant impacts on the production of other important wetland wildlife resources, such as waterfowl (Cowardin and Johnson 1979; Cowardin et al. 1985). Provision of optimal wildlife resource benefits from wetlands likely will demand innovative and diverse management methods (Sargeant and Arnold 1984). White-tailed deer may depend on wetlands for thermal cover to survive periods of extreme energetic stress that are common during the long winters. In some locations, wetlands are important fawning sites. Mammals clearly are important components of northern prairie wetland ecosystems and contribute to their ecologic function.

Wetland mammals also have important economic values although these have not been well quantified. For example, wetland mammals, as defined herein, are the major source of raw pelts entering the fur trade from the jurisdictions included in the prairie pothole region (Table 9.4). It is not possible to determine what proportion of the pelts sold within each jurisdiction was derived from the prairie pothole region because of differences in methods of recording fur sales. Nonetheless, the harvest of

TABLE 9.4. Estimated fur harvests of wetland mammals from principal jurisdictions of the prairie pothole region (1982–1984)

	Muskrat		Red fox[a]		Raccoon		Weasels[b]		Mink		Striped skunk	
	82/83	83/84	82/83	83/84	82/83	83/84	82/83	83/84	82/83	83/84	82/83	83/84
Alberta	81,985	98,819	3,464	2,527	49	31	10,827	15,828	9,585	4,549	62	19
Saskatchewan	106,836	218,881	15,123	17,562	2,856	3,876	6,650	12,981	10,581	18,134	4	35
Manitoba	168,047	235,980	14,055	10,586	4,090	3,081	5,991	5,212	9,910	7,314	69	0
Montana	56,776	35,480	9,887	6,087	10,170	4,731	692	244	4,293	2,595	1,029	4,999
North Dakota	68,328	52,701	26,660	29,451	11,056	12,631	208	28	4,387	3,309	377	181
Minnesota	570,000	865,000	60,000	63,000	141,000	157,000	2,000	3,000	57,000	58,000	34,000	36,000
South Dakota	48,273	61,967	37,733	26,152	27,201	26,157	568	406	6,811	9,151	17,727	11,530
Iowa	428,252	464,793	18,528	21,255	255,926	261,875	153	65	21,307	22,245	1,194	1,152

Source: Adapted from Linscombe and Setterthwaite, in press.
[a]Includes silver and cross foxes.
[b]Includes short-tailed, long-tailed, and least weasels.

furbearers from prairie wetlands contributes importantly to local economies. Recreation associated with the hunting and trapping of wetland mammals may also generate a substantial flow of dollars. Williamson and Doster (1981) estimated that the total annual flow of values from white-tailed deer in the United States was $8.22 billion in 1975. They estimated that a single deer was worth $1,657. While these estimates are undoubtedly high for the economies associated with deer in the prairies, they suggest that the economic value of the mammalian resource cannot be ignored. Wetland loss and degradation may affect the diverse ecologic and economic values emanating from wetland mammals.

The relationships between mammals and northern prairie wetlands need to be better understood. High priority should be placed on the following research:

1. Quantifying the effects of grazing by muskrats on vegetative structure and nutrient dynamics in prairie marshes. Conversely, what are the effects of vegetative food supply on muskrat energetics and populations?

2. Determining the dynamics of muskrat populations in pothole complexes. Of what importance are ephemeral and seasonal wetlands to muskrat population dynamics?

3. Determining the dynamics of *Microtus* populations in pothole complexes. Does the model of Smith et al. (1978) pertain to prairie wetland habitats?

4. Describing small mammal communities in wetlands throughout the prairie pothole region. How do small mammal communities vary among wetland types?

5. Determining the impacts of nest predators, such as raccoons, striped skunks, and Franklin's ground squirrels, on duck populations.

6. Describing the importance of wetlands to white-tailed deer in the prairie region. What types of wetlands provide optimum cover?

ACKNOWLEDGMENTS

This is a contribution of the Missouri Cooperative Fish and Wildlife Research Unit (University of Missouri-Columbia, Missouri Department of Conservation, U.S. Fish and Wildlife Service, and Wildlife Management Institute, cooperating), and the Missouri Agricultural Experiment Station Project 189, Journal Series No. 9975. I greatly appreciate the comments of T. W. Arnold, L. H. Fredrickson, R. J. Greenwood, and A. B. Sargeant on early drafts of the manuscript.

REFERENCES

Allen, S. H. 1984. Some aspects of reproductive performance in female red fox in North Dakota. J. Mammal. 65:246–55.

Anderson, P. 1981. Movements, activity patterns and denning habits of the striped skunk in the mixed-grass prairie. Master's thesis, Univ. Calgary, Calgary.

Arnold, T. W. 1986. The ecology of prairie mink during the waterfowl breeding season. Master's thesis, Univ. Mo., Columbia.

Bailey, T. N. 1971. Biology of striped skunks on a southwestern Lake Erie marsh. Amer. Midl. Nat. 85:196–207.

Bailey, V. 1926. A biological survey of North Dakota. N. Amer. Fauna 49.

Balser, D. S., H. H. Dill, and H. K. Nelson. 1968. Effect of predator reduction on waterfowl nesting success. J. Wildl. Manage. 32:669–82.

Barclay, M. R. 1984. Observations on the migration, ecology and behaviour of bats at Delta Marsh, Manitoba. Can. Field-Nat. 98:331–36.

Birney, E. C., W. E. Grant, and D. D. Baird. 1976. Importance of vegetative cover to cycles of *Microtus* populations. Ecol. 57:1043–51.

Bishop, R. A., R. D. Andrews, and J. R. Bridges. 1979. Marsh management and its relationship to vegetation, waterfowl, and muskrats. Proc. Iowa Acad. Sci. 86:50–56.

Bjorge, R. R., J. R. Gunson, and W. M. Samuel. 1981. Population characteristics and movements of striped skunks (*Mephitis mephitis*) in central Alberta. Can. Field-Nat. 95:149–55.

Choromanski-Norris, J. F. 1983. The ecology of the Franklin's ground squirrel in North Dakota. Master's thesis, Univ. Mo., Columbia.

Clark, R. J. 1975. A field study of the short-eared owl, *Asio flammeus* (Pontoppidan) in North America. Wildl. Monogr. 47.

Cooper, J. A. 1978. The history and breeding biology of the Canada geese of Marshy Point, Manitoba. Wildl. Monogr. 61.

Coues, E. 1897. New light on the early history of the greater northwest. The manuscript journals of Alexander Henry and of David Thompson. 1799–1814. Vol. 1: The Red River of the North. New York: Francis P. Harper.

Cowan, W. F. 1973. Ecology and life history of the raccoon (*Procyon lotor hirtus* Nelson and Goldman) in the northern part of its range. Ph.D. diss., Univ. N. Dak., Grand Forks.

Cowan, W. F., and J. R. Reilly. 1973. Summer and fall foods of mink on the J. Clark Salyer National Wildlife Refuge. Prairie Nat. 5:20–24.

Cowardin, L. M., and D. H. Johnson. 1979. Mathematics and mallard management. J. Wildl. Manage. 43:18–35.

Cowardin, L. M., D. S. Gilmer, and C. W. Shaiffer. 1985. Mallard recruitment in the agricultural environment of North Dakota. Wildl. Monogr. 92.

Danell, K. 1978. Food habits of the muskrat *Ondatra zibethica* (L.), in a Swedish lake. Ann. Zool. Fenn. 15:177–81.

Davis, C. B., and A. G. van der Valk. 1978. Litter decomposition in prairie glacial marshes. *In* Fresh-water wetlands: ecological processes and management potential, ed. R. E. Good et al., 99–113. New York: Academic Press.

Dorney, R. S. 1954. Ecology of marsh raccoons. J. Wildl. Manage. 18:217–25.

Douglass, R. J. 1976. Spatial interactions and microhabitat selections of two locally sympatric voles, *Microtus montanus* and *Microtus pennsylvanicus*. Ecol. 57:346–52.

Duebbert, H. F., and H. A. Kantrud. 1974. Upland duck nesting related to land use and predator reduction. J. Wildl. Manage. 38:257–65.

Duebbert, H. F., and J. T. Lokemoen. 1976. Duck nesting in fields of undisturbed grass-legume cover. J. Wildl. Manage. 40:39–49.

————. 1980. High duck nesting success in a predator-reduced environment. J. Wildl. Manage. 44:428–37.

Eberhardt, L. E. 1974. Food habits of prairie mink (*Mustela vison*) during the waterfowl breeding season. Master's thesis, Univ. Minn., St. Paul.

Eberhardt, L. E., and A. B. Sargeant. 1977. Mink predation on prairie marshes during the waterfowl breeding season. Proc. 1975 Predator symp. Missoula: Mont. For. Conserv. Exp. Stn.

Eberhardt, R. T. 1973. Some aspects of mink-waterfowl relationships on prairie wetlands. Prairie Nat. 5:17–19.

Errington, P. L. 1943. An analysis of mink predation upon muskrats in north central United States. Iowa Agric. Exp. Stn. Resour. Bull. 320:797–924.

————. 1948. Environmental control for increasing muskrat production. Trans. N. Amer. Wildl. Conf. 13:596–607.

————. 1963. Muskrat populations. Ames: Iowa State Univ. Press.

Errington, P. L., and W. J. Breckenridge. 1936. Food habits of marsh hawks in the glaciated prairie region of north-central United States. Amer. Midl. Nat. 7:831–48.

Errington, P. L., R. J. Siglin, and R. C. Clark. 1963. The decline of a muskrat population. J. Wildl. Manage. 27:1–8.

Fitzgerald, B. M. 1977. Weasel predation on a cyclic population of the montane vole (*Microtus montanus*) in California. J. Anim. Ecol. 46:367–97.

French, N. R., W. E. Grant, W. Grodzinski, and D. M. Swift. 1976. Small mammal energetics in grassland ecosystems. Ecol. Monogr. 46:201–20.

Fritzell, E. K. 1972. The effects of agricultural burning on nesting waterfowl. Master's thesis, South. Ill. Univ., Carbondale.

————. 1977. Dissolution of raccoon sibling bonds. J. Mammal. 58:427–28.

————. 1978a. Aspects of raccoon (*Procyon lotor*) social organization. Can. J. Zool. 56:260–71.

————. 1978b. Habitat use by prairie raccoons during the waterfowl breeding season. J. Wildl. Manage. 42:118–27.

————. 1978c. Reproduction of raccoons (*Procyon lotor*) in North Dakota. Amer. Midl. Nat. 100:253–56.

Fritzell, E. K., and R. J. Greenwood. 1984. Mortality of raccoons in North Dakota. Prairie Nat. 16:1–4.

Fritzell, E. K., and J. W. Matthews. 1975. A large raccoon litter. Prairie Nat. 7:87–88.

Gerell, R. 1969. Activity patterns of the mink, *Mustela vison* Schreber, in southern Sweden. Oikos 20:451–60.

————. 1970. Home ranges and movements of the mink *Mustela vison* Schreber in southern Sweden. Oikos 21:160–73.

Getz, L. L. 1961a. Factors influencing the local distribution of shrews. Amer. Midl. Nat. 65:67–88.

————. 1961b. Factors influencing the local distribution of *Microtus* and *Symaptomys*. Ecol. 42:110–19.

————. 1961c. Notes on the local distribution of *Peromyscus leucopus* and *Zapus hudsonius*. Amer. Midl. Nat. 83:455–61.

————. 1970. Habitat of the meadow vole, *Microtus pennsylvanicus,* during a population low. Amer. Midl. Nat. 83:455–61.

Grant, W. E., and E. C. Birney. 1979. Small mammal community structure in North American grasslands. J. Mammal. 60:23–36.

Greenwood, R. J. 1979. Relating residue in raccoon feces to food consumed. Amer. Midl. Nat. 102:191–93.

———. 1981. Foods of prairie raccoons during the waterfowl nesting season. J. Wildl. Manage. 45:754–60.

———. 1982. Nocturnal activity and foraging of prairie raccoons (*Procyon lotor*) in North Dakota. Amer. Midl. Nat. 107:238–43.

Greenwood, R. J., A. B. Sargeant, and D. H. Johnson. 1985. Evaluation of mark-recapture for estimating striped skunk (*Mephitis mephitis*) abundance. J. Wildl. Manage. 59:332–40.

Gunson, J. R., and R. R. Bjorge. 1979. Winter denning of the striped skunk in Alberta. Can. Field-Nat. 93:252–58.

Haggerty, S. M. 1968. The ecology of the Franklin's ground squirrel at Itasca State Park, Minnesota. Master's thesis, Univ. Minn., St. Paul.

Hamerstrom, F., F. N. Hamerstrom, and C. J. Burke. 1985. Effect of voles on mating systems in a central Wisconsin population of harriers. Wilson Bull. 97:332–46.

Harmoning, A. K. 1976. White-tailed deer dispersion and habitat utilization in central North Dakota. N. Dak. Game Fish Dept., P-R Project W-67-R-13, 14, and 15 Phase C Report 199-A.

Houston, C. S., and M. I. Houston. 1973. A history of raccoons in Saskatchewan. Blue Jay 31:103–4.

Johnson, D. H., and A. B. Sargeant. 1977. Impact of fox predation on the sex ratio of prairie mallards. U.S. Fish and Wildl. Serv. Res. Rep. 6.

Jones, J. K., Jr., D. M. Armstrong, R. S. Hoffmann, and C. Jones. 1983. Mammals of the Northern Great Plains. Lincoln: Univ. Nebr. Press.

Kaminski, R. M., and H. H. Prince. 1981. Dabbling ducks and aquatic macroinvertebrate responses to manipulated wetland habitat. J. Wildl. Manage. 45:1–15.

Kangas, P. C., and G. L. Hannan. 1985. Vegetation on muskrat mounds in a Michigan marsh. Amer. Midl. Nat. 113:393–96.

Kaufmann, J. H. 1982. Raccoon and allies. *In* Wild mammals of North America, ed. J. A. Chapman and G. A. Feldhammer, 567–85. Baltimore: The Johns Hopkins Univ. Press.

Keith, L. B. 1961. A study of waterfowl ecology on small impoundments in southeastern Alberta. Wildl. Monogr. 6.

Kiel, W. H., Jr., A. S. Hawkins, and N. G. Perret. 1972. Waterfowl habitat trends in the aspen parklands of Manitoba. Can. Wildl. Serv. Rep. Ser. 18.

Krebs, C. J., and J. H. Myers. 1974. Population cycles in small mammals. Adv. Ecol. Res. 8:267–399.

Kucera, E. 1976. Effects of winter conditions on the white-tailed deer of Delta Marsh, Manitoba. Can. J. Zool. 54:1307–13.

Lemen, C. A., and M. K. Clausen. 1984. The effects of mowing on the rodent community of a native tall grass prairie in eastern Nebraska. Prairie Nat. 16:5–10.

Lindell, J. R. 1971. Small mammal distribution in relation to marshland vegetation types in southeastern South Dakota. Master's thesis, Univ. S. Dak., Vermillion.

Linscombe, G., and A. J. Satterthwaite. 1987. Recent North American furbearer harvests. *In* Wild furbearer management and conservation in North America, ed. M. Novak et al. North Bay, Ontario: Ontario Trappers Association.

Linscombe, G., N. Kinler, and R. J. Aulerich. 1982. Mink. *In* Wild mammals of North America, ed. J. A. Chapman and G. A. Feldhammer, 629–43. Baltimore: The Johns Hopkins Univ. Press.

Lynch, G. M. 1971. Raccoons increasing in Manitoba. J. Mammal. 52:621–23.

_____. 1972. Effects of strychnine control on nest predators of dabbling ducks. J. Wildl. Manage. 36:436–40.

Lyon, M. W., Jr. 1932. Franklin's ground squirrel and its distribution in Indiana. Amer. Midl. Nat. 37:223–49.

MacArthur, R. A. 1978. Winter movements and home range of the muskrat. Can. Field-Nat. 92:345–49.

MacArthur, R. A., and M. Aleksiuk. 1979. Seasonal microenvironments of the muskrat (*Ondatra zibethicus*) in a northern marsh. J. Mammal. 60:146–54.

Marshall, W. H. 1936. A study of the winter activities of the mink. J. Mammal. 17:382–92.

Miller, H. W. 1971. Relationships of duck nesting success to land use in North and South Dakota. Proc. Int. Union Game Biol. Congr. 10:133–41.

Moen, A. N. 1968. Energy exchange of white-tailed deer, western Minnesota. Ecol. 49:676–82.

_____. 1973. Wildlife ecology. San Francisco: W. H. Freeman.

Murie, J. O. 1973. Population characteristics and phenology of a Franklin ground squirrel (*Spermophilus franklinii*) colony in Alberta, Canada. Amer. Midl. Nat. 90:334–40.

Murkin, H. R., R. M. Kaminski, and R. D. Titman. 1982. Responses by dabbling ducks and aquatic invertebrates to an experimentally manipulated cattail marsh. Can. J. Zool. 60:2324–32.

Mutch, G. R. P. 1977. Locations of winter dens utilized by striped skunks in Delta Marsh, Manitoba. Can. Field-Nat. 91:289–91.

Mutch, G. R. P., and M. Aleksiuk. 1977. Ecological aspects of winter dormancy in the striped skunk (*Mephitis mephitis*). Can. J. Zool. 55:607–15.

Nelson, J. W., and J. A. Kadlec. 1984. A conceptual approach to relating habitat structure and macroinvertebrate production in freshwater wetlands. Trans. N. Amer. Wildl. Nat. Resour. Conf. 49:262–70.

Pelikan, J. 1978. Mammals in the Reed swamp ecosystem. *In* Pond littoral ecosystems-structure and functioning: Ecological Studies 28, ed. D. Dykyjova and J. Kvet, 357–65. Berlin: Springer-Verlag.

Pelikan, J., J. Svoboda, and J. Kvet. 1970. On some relations between the production of *Typha latifolia* and a muskrat population. Zool. Listy 19:303–20.

Pendleton, G. W. 1984. Small mammals in prairie wetlands: Habitat use and the effects of wetland modifications. Master's thesis, S. Dak. State Univ., Brookings.

Perry, H. R., Jr. 1982. Muskrats. *In* Wild mammals of North America, ed. J. A. Chapman and G. A. Feldhammer, 282–325. Baltimore: The Johns Hopkins Univ. Press.

Polderboer, E. B., L. W. Kuhn, and G. O. Hendrickson. 1941. Winter and spring habits of weasels in central Iowa. J. Wildl. Manage. 5:115–19.

Risser, P. G., E. C. Birney, H. D. Blocker, S. W. May, W. J. Parton, and J. A.

Wiens. 1981. The true prairie ecosystem. US/IBP Synth. Ser. 16. Strouds-berg, Pa.: Hutchinson Ross Publ.

Ritchey, R. W., and R. Y. Edwards. 1956. Live trapping mink in British Columbia. J. Mammal. 37:114–16.

Rosatte, R. C., and J. R. Gunson. 1984. Dispersal and home range of striped skunks, *Mephitis mephitis,* in an area of population reduction in southern Alberta. Can. Field-Nat. 98:315–19.

Sargeant, A. B. 1972. Red fox spatial characteristics in relation to waterfowl predation. J. Wildl. Manage. 36:225–36.

———. 1978. Red fox prey demands and implications to prairie duck production. J. Wildl. Manage. 42:520–27.

———. 1982. A case history of a dynamic resource–the red fox. *In* Midwest furbearer management, ed. G. C. Sanderson, 121–37. Wichita: North Central Section, Central Mountains and Plains Section and Kansas Chapter of The Wildl. Soc.

Sargeant, A. B., and P. M. Arnold. 1984. Predator management for ducks on waterfowl production areas in the northern plains. Proc. Eleventh Vertebr. Pest Conf., Davis, Calif.

Sargeant, A. B., and L. E. Eberhardt. 1975. Death feigning by ducks in response to predation by red foxes (*Vulpes vulpes*). Amer. Midl. Nat. 94:108–19.

Sargeant, A. B., G. A. Swanson, and H. A. Doty. 1973. Selective predation by mink, *Mustela vison,* on waterfowl. Amer. Midl. Nat. 89:208–14.

Sargeant, A. B., W. K. Pfeifer, and S. H. Allen. 1975. A spring aerial census of red foxes in North Dakota. J. Wildl. Manage. 39:30–39.

Sargeant, A. B., R. J. Greenwood, J. L. Piehl, and W. B. Bicknell. 1982. Recurrence, mortality, and dispersal of prairie striped skunks, *Mephitis mephitis,* and implications to rabies epizootiology. Can. Field Nat. 96:312–16.

Sargeant, A. B., S. H. Allen, and R. T. Eberhardt. 1984. Red fox predation on breeding ducks in midcontinent North America. Wildl. Monogr. 89.

Schladweiler, J. L., and G. L. Storm. 1969. Den use by mink. J. Wildl. Manage. 33:1025–26.

Schneider, D. G., L. D. Mech, and J. R. Tester. 1971. Movements of female raccoons and their young as determined by radio-tracking. Anim. Behav. Monogr. 4:1–43.

Schowalter, D. B., and J. R. Gunson. 1982. Parameters of population and seasonal activity of striped skunks, *Mephitis mephitis,* in Alberta and Saskatchewan. Can. Field-Nat. 96:409–20.

Scott, T. G. 1943. Some food coactions of the northern plains red fox. Ecol. Monogr. 13:427–79.

———. 1947. Comparative analysis of red fox feeding trends on two central Iowa areas. Iowa Agric. Exp. Stn. Res. Bull. 354:427–87.

Scott, T. G., and L. F. Selko. 1939. A census of red foxes and striped skunks in Clay and Boone counties, Iowa. J. Wildl. Manage. 3:92–98.

Seabloom, R. W., and J. R. Beer. 1963. Observations of a muskrat population decline in North Dakota. Proc. N. Dak. Acad. Sci. 17:66–70.

Smith, L. M., and J. A. Kadlec. 1985. Fire and herbivory in a Great Salt Lake marsh. Ecol. 66:259–65.

Smith, M. H., M. N. Manlove, and J. Joule. 1978. Spatial and temporal dynamics of the genetic organization of small mammal populations. *In* Populations of small mammals under natural conditions, ed. D. P. Snyder, 99–113. Pittsburgh: Univ. Pittsburgh.

Sowls, L. K. 1948. The Franklin ground squirrel, *Citellus franklinii* (Sabine), and its relation to nesting ducks. J. Mammal. 29:113–37.

――――. 1949. Notes on the raccoon (*Procyon lotor hirtus*) in Manitoba. J. Mammal. 30:313–14.

Sparrowe, R. D., and P. F. Springer. 1970. Seasonal activity patterns of white-tailed deer in eastern South Dakota. J. Wildl. Manage. 34:420–31.

Spencer, A. W., and D. Pettus. 1966. Habitat preferences of five sympatric species of long-tailed shrews. Ecol. 47:677–83.

Stewart, R. E., and H. A. Kantrud. 1971. Classification of natural ponds and lakes in the glaciated prairie region. U.S. Fish and Wildl. Serv. Resour. Publ. 92.

Storm, G. L. 1972. Daytime retreats and movements of skunks on farmlands in Illinois. J. Wildl. Manage. 36:31–45.

Stoudt, J. H. 1971. Ecological factors affecting waterfowl production in the Saskatchewan parklands. U.S. Fish and Wildl. Serv. Resour. Publ. 99.

――――. 1982. Habitat use and productivity of canvasbacks in southwestern Manitoba. U.S. Fish and Wildl. Serv. Spec. Sci. Rep. Wildl. 248.

Sutton, R. W. 1964. Range extension of raccoon in Manitoba. J. Mammal. 45:311–12.

Tait, M. J., and C. J. Krebs. 1985. Population dynamics and cycles. *In* Biology of new world *Microtus,* ed. R. H. Tamarin, 567–620. Amer. Soc. Mammal. Spec. Publ. No. 8.

Teer, J. G. 1964. Predation by long-tailed weasels on eggs of blue-winged teal. J. Wildl. Manage. 28:404–6.

Trauger, D. L., and J. H. Stoudt. 1974. Looking out for the canvasback, part II. Ducks Unlimited 38:30–60.

United States Department of Interior 1979. Garrison Diversion Unit Biological Investigations: 1978 Annual Report. Bismarck, N. Dak.: USDI, Water and Power Resour. Serv.

――――. 1980. Garrison Diversion Unit Biological Investigations: 1979 Annual Report. Bismarck, N. Dak.: USDI, Water and Power Resour. Serv.

Upham, L. L. 1967. Density, dispersal, and dispersion of the striped skunk (*Mephitis mephitis*) in southeastern North Dakota. Master's thesis, N. Dak. State Univ., Fargo.

Urban, D. 1970. Raccoon populations, movement patterns and predation on a managed waterfowl marsh. J. Wildl. Manage. 34:372–82.

van der Valk, A. G., and C. B. Davis. 1978a. Primary production of prairie glacial marshes. *In* Fresh-water wetlands: ecological processes and management potential, ed. R. E. Good et al., 21–37. New York: Academic Press.

――――. 1978b. The role of seed banks in the vegetation dynamics of prairie glacial marshes. Ecol. 59:322–35.

Verts, B. J. 1967. The biology of the striped skunk. Urbana: Univ. Ill. Press.

Voight, D. R., and B. D. Earle. 1983. Avoidance of coyotes by red fox families. J. Wildl. Manage. 47:852–57.

Voights, D. K. 1976. Aquatic invertebrate abundance in relation to changing marsh vegetation. Amer. Midl. Nat. 95:312–22.

Waller, D. W. 1962. Feeding behavior of minks at some Iowa marshes. Master's thesis, Iowa State Univ., Ames.

Walley, W. J. 1972. Summer observation of the short-eared owl in the Red River Valley. Prairie Nat. 4:39–41.

Weller, M. W. 1979. Small mammal populations and experimental burning of

Dewey's Pasture, northwestern Iowa, 1970–74. Iowa State J. Res. 53:325–32.

Weller, M. W., and L. H. Fredrickson. 1973. Avian ecology of a managed glacial marsh. Living Bird 12:269–91.

Weller, M. W., and C. E. Spatcher. 1965. Role of habitat in the distribution and abundance of marsh birds. Iowa State Univ. Agric. Home Econ. Exp. Stn, Spec. Rep. No. 43. Ames.

Wilhelm, R. B., J. R. Choate, and J. K. Jones, Jr. 1981. Mammals of Lacreek National Wildlife Refuge, South Dakota. The Museum, Spec. Publ. 17. Lubbock: Texas Tech University.

Williamson, L. L., and G. L. Doster. 1981. Socio-economic aspects of white-tailed deer disease. *In* Diseases and parasites of white-tailed deer, ed. W. R. Davidson, 434–39. Tallahassee, Fla.: Tall Timbers Res. Stn.

Willner, G. R., G. A. Feldhammer, E. E. Zucker, and J. A. Chapman. 1980. *Ondatra zibethicus*. Mamm. Spec. 141.

Wrigley, R. E., J. E. Dubois, and H. W. R. Coupland. 1979. Habitat, abundance, and distribution of six species of shrews in Manitoba. J. Mammal. 60:505–20.

ABSTRACT

FATHEAD MINNOWS (*Pimephales promelas*) and/or brook sticklebacks (*Culaea inconstans*) are usually the only fishes that can tolerate the low dissolved oxygen concentrations found in wetlands less than 5 m deep in the prairie pothole and Nebraska sandhills regions. Based on data from Manitoba and Nebraska, about 10–20% of the wetlands, varying in maximum depth from 1 to 5 m, may support populations of these two species. Salinity and ion composition are important factors limiting fishes. Fathead minnows were collected in sulfate waters of 17,000 mg/l TDS in Saskatchewan and North Dakota but not in bicarbonate waters greater than 2,000 mg/l in Nebraska. The use of wetlands as seasonal rearing ponds to produce either fingerlings for stocking into other lakes or edible-sized fishes from stocked fingerlings has great potential. The maximum fish production was about 350 kg/ha in a six-month growing season for rainbow trout grown in a Manitoba wetland. In Manitoba, empirical approaches have been used to predict likelihood of summer- and winterkill of fishes, and management techniques are available to help control excessive algal blooms. Without management techniques to control mortality, yields are extremely variable and unpredictable.

KEY WORDS: fathead minnow, brook stickleback, salinity and fishes, fishes in northern prairie wetlands.

RAIRIE WETLANDS

INTRODUCTION

THE prairie pothole region and the sandhills region (see Winter, Chap. 2) contain thousands of wetlands and lakes that contain water throughout the year and thus have some potential for supporting fishes. These waters are sometimes referred to as prairie pothole ponds or lakes or lake marshes (see Murkin Chap. 11; Fritzell, Chap. 9) or, when waters are relatively high in dissolved solids, as alkaline, saline or salt lakes. While some of these bodies of water (generally those deeper than 5 m) support game fish populations, many others (generally those shallower than 5 m) tend to winterkill, making them marginal habitats for fishes.

In this chapter we look at the fishes that live in these shallower waters (maximum depths ranging from 1 to 5 m), which we will refer to as wetlands. Wetlands are eutrophic to hypertrophic (Barica 1980) and their surface areas vary widely from about 1 to 1000 ha (Table 10.1). In addition to summer- and winterkill, fish are further limited in wetlands by high salinities and by the fact that most wetlands lie in closed drainage basins, limiting fish dispersal.

Major anions and cations in waters exceeding 1,000 mg/l total dissolved solids vary from predominately magnesium/sodium-sulfate in Canadian provinces and the Dakotas (Barica 1975b; States Lakes Preservation Committee 1977) to sodium/potassium-bicarbonate in the Nebraska sandhills (McCarraher and Thomas 1968) (Table 10.2). While general trends in major ion composition from north to south are apparent, within a given area the major ion composition as well as the

J. J. PETERKA, Zoology Department, North Dakota State University, Fargo, North Dakota 58105.

TABLE 10.1. Characteristics of wetlands that may support fathead minnows and/or brook sticklebacks in Manitoba and Nebraska

	Manitoba[a]	Nebraska[b]
Max. depth (m) range	1.5–5[c]	1–4 (most 2m)
Area (ha) range	1–1,000[d]	1–930
Salinity (μmhos/cm at 25C)	400–6,500[e]	540–2,323[f]
Dominant algae	Blue-green	Blue-green
Chlorophyll-a (μg/l)	10–1,150[g]	. . .
Major cations/anions	Mg-Na/SO_4	Na-K/HCO_3
Water type, based on major anion	Sulfate	Bicarbonate

[a]From Lawler et al. 1974; Sunde and Barica 1975.
[b]From McCarraher 1962, 1977; McCarraher and Thomas 1968.
[c]Fewer than 1% of the lakes exceeded 4m maximum depth.
[d]97% of the lakes ranged from 1–8 ha.
[e]Most (two-thirds) lakes ranged from 1,000–3,000 μmhos/cm.
[f]Total dissolved solids (mg/l); these values are similar to water conductivity (μmhos/cm).
[g]Algal biomass exceeding 100 g/m³ (over 400 μg/l as chlorophyll-a) may cause total or partial summerkills of fish (Barica 1975).

salinity may vary considerably from wetland to wetland (Barica 1977; LaBaugh, Chap. 3). For example, Kelly's Slough in northeastern North Dakota has water of the sodium-chloride type (Burnham and Peterka 1975), and Driver and Peden (1977) report some wetlands in Saskatchewan with sodium-chloride waters.

Winters in the prairie pothole region are severe, with long periods of ice and snow cover. In northern parts of the region, wetlands remain frozen from five to six months each year, with maximum ice depths of 0.9 m in Manitoba (Barica 1979). In the sandhills of Nebraska, wetlands remain frozen for about four months, with maximum ice depths of 0.6 m (Schoenecker 1970).

TABLE 10.2. Percent composition of total dissolved solids (TDS) for wetland waters of 1,000–5,000 mg/l in Saskatchewan and Nebraska

	Saskatchewan lakes[a]	Nebraska lakes[b]
CO_3	0.7	21.5
HCO_3	6.4	52.8
SO_4	60.8	2.0
Ca	1.6	2.5
K	1.9	16.5
Mg	11.4	1.6
Na	9.0	26.6
Cl	2.3	5.3
TDS (mg/l)	5,188.0	1,429.0

[a]Rawson and Moore 1944; lakes Stoney and Last Mountain.
[b]McCarraher and Thomas 1968; 15 wetlands.

NATIVE FISHES

The two most common species found in wetlands in the prairie pothole region are the fathead minnow (*Pimephales promelas*) and brook stickleback (*Culaea inconstans*), which commonly occur together as the only fishes present in wetlands of the Dakotas and Saskatchewan (Held and Peterka 1974; Rawson and Moore 1944). Only the fathead minnow is native to wetlands in the Nebraska sandhills (McCarraher 1977). About 10 to 20% of wetlands in the Erickson-Elphinstone district in southwestern Manitoba have populations of fathead minnows and/or brook sticklebacks (Lawler et al. 1974). About 12% (240 of about 2,000 sandhills wetlands) have populations of fathead minnows (McCarraher and Thomas 1968). As some of these wetlands were deep enough to support other fishes, the percent of lakes restricted to only fathead minnows would be less than 12%. Other fishes, particularly northern pike (*Esox lucius*), may be present in wetlands for a few years following stocking by landowners.

Because even wetlands that have native populations of fathead minnows and sticklebacks in high-water years may lose all fishes in low-water years, there must be mechanisms for overland dispersal as most wetlands lie in closed basins. While there is no documentation of modes of dispersal, one likely natural mechanism is transfer of fish embryos and fry by aquatic birds. Undoubtedly, much transfer is done by humans; fathead minnows are especially valued as bait fishes.

CHARACTERISTICS FOR FISH SURVIVAL IN WETLANDS

Probable reasons for the success of fathead minnows and sticklebacks in wetlands include their tolerance to low dissolved oxygen, their high reproductive potential, and their tolerance to high concentrations of dissolved solids (salinity).

In laboratory and field experiments conducted in Wisconsin, fathead minnows appeared to tolerate lower dissolved oxygen concentrations than sticklebacks. Of three species tested (central mudminnow, [*Umbra limi*], fathead minnow, and brook stickleback), fatheads survived the longest (18 h) when confined in low-oxygen lake water (dissolved oxygen concentration of about 0.5 mg/l) without access to air bubbles (Klinger et al. 1982). Their tolerance to hypoxia is likely based on a metabolic system that can make greater use of anaerobic pathways than can systems of sticklebacks or mudminnows (Klinger et al. 1982).

Klinger et al. (1982) observed varied responses when dissolved oxygen concentrations were reduced. All three species tended to move upward in the water column, which brought fish closer to areas of available oxygen, both dissolved and gaseous. Although not documented in their studies, they suggest gaseous oxygen may be available to physostomous fathead minnows from air bubbles trapped beneath the ice. Bubbles near active muskrat dens may be especially important in not only providing sources of gaseous oxygen but in providing dissolved oxygen at their gas-water interfaces. Fathead minnows increased their swimming activity as dissolved oxygen decreased from 1.0 mg/l to 0.25 mg/l, but there was a decrease in activity for sticklebacks (Klinger et al. 1982). The increased swimming activity of fatheads may permit them to find microhabitats where dissolved oxygen are present. The pointed snouts of sticklebacks may permit them to utilize microlayers of dissolved oxygen at the ice-water interface, which, along with decreased activity and metabolic rates, may enable them to survive.

Studies in North Dakota have shown that when overwinter survival of fathead minnows was low, some minnows survived periods when we measured no dissolved oxygen and when hydrogen sulfide was present in late-winter water samples (Held 1971). It is likely that the minnows able to overwinter found microhabitats that had some dissolved oxygen. We noted spring seeps in several wetlands; these may be important in providing refuges where low concentrations of dissolved oxygen are present.

The few fatheads and brook sticklebacks surviving in the spring are able to rapidly build populations during the summer (Held 1971; Payer 1977; Moodie 1986). Both species have long spawning seasons and females may spawn several times. This fractional spawning results in a high fecundity, because a female can produce more eggs in a season than could be held in the coelomic cavity at one time. High fecundity is not typical among fishes that are nest builders and egg guarders, such as fathead minnows and sticklebacks. Fractional spawning is an important characteristic as it increases chances of a population surviving the short-term extremes in environmental conditions. In laboratory experiments, each pair of fathead minnows spawned from 16 to 26 times between May 22 to August 22 (Gale and Buynak 1982). The mean number of eggs spawned per female per season was 8,604 (range was 6,803–10,614). In a wetland in Manitoba, the estimated mean number of eggs spawned per female brook stickleback per season was 1,926 (Moodie 1986). The estimate is conservative (Moodie 1986) and was based on an average spawning of 214 eggs every 3 days for 28 days (mid-May to mid-July). On the average, a female brook stickleback produced 2.6 g of eggs per season, or 1.4 times its mean body weight of 1.91 g in May (prior to spawning). During the four-year study there was more than a fourfold variation in mean fecundity of sticklebacks, with fecundity inversely related to spring population density (Moodie 1986).

Spawning of fatheads begins in the spring when water temperatures reach 15.6°C and continues until temperatures drop in the fall to 15.6–18.4°C (Becker 1983). Spawning of brook sticklebacks coincides with fatheads; most nests were observed at water temperatures ranging from 15–19°C (Winn 1960). The spawning season for these two species in the prairie pothole region extends from mid-May to mid-August.

In North Dakota wetlands and the sandhills wetlands in Nebraska, fathead minnows achieved high populations even though they were commonly infested with the pleurocercoid of the cestode *Ligula intestinalis*. Fatheads with these large parasites had distended bodies and reduced gonads, which may reduce reproductive potential. McCarraher and Thomas (1968) reported 42% fewer eggs in infected female fatheads than in noninfected females, and high infestations of up to 88% in adult fatheads in Nebraska sandhills lakes. The parasites occurred in fatheads from five of eight wetlands sampled in North Dakota, with an incidence of infestation that ranged from 4.4 to 38.0% (Held and Peterka 1974).

Populations of only sticklebacks are unusual in wetlands, while populations of fatheads and fatheads/sticklebacks commonly occur in the prairie pothole region. Of eight North Dakota wetlands studied by Held and Peterka (1974) that contained fatheads, four had populations of sticklebacks. Sticklebacks were reported as the only fish species present in two wetlands in Manitoba (Moodie 1986). Sticklebacks apparently gained access to these wetlands via runoff water connections to a larger system that provided a source for sticklebacks following their periodic winterkill. Sticklebacks are normally associated with clear-water habitats and may be limited by lower tolerance to dissolved oxygen concentrations or perhaps to high turbidity than are fatheads.

The common occurrence of both fatheads and sticklebacks in wetlands in the prairie pothole region may be related to abundant food resources, which would reduce interspecific competition. The food habits of fatheads and brook sticklebacks in wetlands in North Dakota were similar. Crustaceans (cladocerans, copepods, and amphipods) comprised 94% by weight of food items found in 541 fathead stomachs and 95% by weight of food items found in 30 brook stickleback stomachs (Held and Peterka 1974).

INFLUENCE OF WATER SALINITY ON FISHES

Salinity is an important factor limiting fishes in these wetlands. Based largely on field observations, the upper tolerance limit to salinity varies not only with the species but with the major ions in the waters (Rawson and Moore 1944; Held and Peterka 1974; McCarraher 1971) (Table 10.3). Fathead minnows were collected in sulfate waters of

TABLE 10.3.   Upper tolerance limit of fishes to salinity (mg/l of TDS) in the prairie pothole and the Nebraska sandhills regions

	Location		
Species	Saskatchewan[a]	North Dakota	Nebraska[b]
Lake whitefish	2,000–15,000[c]		
Coregonus clupeaformis			
Common sucker	7,000–15,000[c]		
Catostomus commersoni			
Fathead minnow	17,000	12,000[d]	2,000
Pimephales promelas		18,000[f]	
		8,000[e]	
Yellow perch	8,000		
Perca flavescens			
Walleye	10,000–15,000[c]	3,000[e]	900
Stizostedion v. vitreum			
Northern pike	3,000–15,000[c]	3,000[e]	1,000
Esox lucius			
Brook stickleback	17,000	18,000[f]	
Culaea inconstans			
Ninespine stickleback	20,000		
Pungitius pungitius			

[a]From Rawson and Moore 1944; field observations from 60 lakes in Saskatchewan, most with magnesium-sulfate type water.

[b]McCarraher 1971; field observations from 13 lakes in Nebraska sandhills lakes with sodium-bicarbonate type of water.

[c]Upper limits in Quill lakes of central Saskatchewan; lakes with sodium-sulfate type water.

[d]From Held and Peterka 1974; field observations from 10 lakes in North Dakota with sodium-sulfate type water.

[e]From Burnham and Peterka 1975 and Mossier 1971; laboratory bioassays of hatching success.

[f]From Kelly's Slough North Dakota (Burnham and Peterka 1975), a lake with sodium-chloride type water.

12,000–17,000 mg/l in Saskatchewan and North Dakota, but not in bicarbonate waters greater than 2,000 mg/l in Nebraska (Table 10.3). Native fishes with the greatest tolerance to sulfate saline waters are sticklebacks (brook and ninespine) and fathead minnows; the upper tolerance is 20,000 mg/l (ninespine sticklebacks), with several species tolerating 15,000 mg/l (Table 10.3).

While it is difficult to assess the relative toxicities of various kinds of salts from reports in the literature, some general observations are available. Burnham and Peterka (1975) summarized their observations on the death of fathead minnow sac fry in water of 12,000 μmhos of the sodium-sulfate type and compared their findings with observations reported by other investigators. Burnham and Peterka found fry did not survive when (1) sulfates exceeded 8,000 mg/l (tolerance limits of fathead minnows were 7,500 mg/l in sulfate lakes in Saskatchewan) (Rawson and Moore 1944); (2) total alkalinity exceeded 1,000 mg/l (more than 2,000 mg/l caused a sharp decline in spawning success of fatheads in Nebraska saline lakes) (McCarraher and Thomas 1968); (3) potassium exceeded 300 mg/l (potassium averaged 236 mg/l [extreme of 500 mg/l] in 16 Nebraska lakes where fatheads survived for 6 or more months) (McCarraher and Thomas 1968); and (4) calcium levels were less than 7–10 mg/l (low calcium may increase toxicity of other substances) (McKee and Wolf 1963). High pHs of 9.2–9.3 were probably not at lethal limits as pHs as high as 9.4 (mean of 9.2) were observed in North Alkaline Lake, North Dakota, during ice-free periods 1969–1970 (Held 1971).

From field observations and laboratory tests, it appears adult fish tolerate higher salinities than sac fry (McCarraher and Thomas 1968; Burnham and Peterka 1975) (Table 10.3). Burnham and Peterka (1975) reported that sodium-sulfate type waters in North Dakota exceeding 7,000–8,000 μmhos may prevent successful reproduction of fathead minnows. Laboratory bioassays indicated that fry survive at 6,000 μmhos but not at 12,000 μmhos. Fathead minnow eggs spawned on floating boards placed in North Alkaline Lake, where lake water conductivity was 8,000 μmhos, lost their adhesiveness and were easily lost from the boards; all eggs removed to the laboratory died. Adult fatheads survived in North Alkaline Lake when winter conductivities were 16,000 μmhos, with successful reproduction in the spring and early summer when conductivities ranged from 6,000 to 7,000 μmhos.

FISH CULTURE IN WETLANDS

Despite problems of summer- and winterkill and high salinities, there has been considerable interest in the use of wetlands as seasonal rearing ponds to produce fingerlings for stocking into lakes or to produce edible-sized fishes from fish stocked as fingerlings (Lawler et al. 1974; Scidmore 1970). Ayles et al. (1976) reported 3,700 farmers in Manitoba, Saskatchewan, and Alberta harvested about one-half million rainbow trout in 1974. Trials in the late 1960s in these three provinces demonstrated that rainbow trout (*Salmo gairdneri*) stocked as fingerlings (3–4 g) in the spring reached harvestable sizes (200–300 g) in the fall (Sunde et al. 1970; Lawler et al. 1974). The advantage of wetlands for fish culture stems from the fact that they normally winterkill, which eliminates competition from other fishes. Further, they produce large populations of invertebrates used for food (Mathias et al. 1982). The most productive wetlands in terms of maximum standing crops of phytoplankton and benthos are those with salinities in the 1,000–3,000 μmhos range (Barica 1978; Rawson and Moore 1944). These are also salinities of wetlands used for most trout culture in Manitoba (Lawler et al. 1974).

In Manitoba experiments, lakes of 1–25 ha with maximum depths of 1–8 m were stocked with rainbow trout. Survival of stocked trout was highly variable; percent recoveries ranged 0–86% (Lawler et al. 1974). Most mortality of trout was attributed to summerkill. In North Dakota wetlands, high mortality of stocked trout resulted from summerkill and probably from bird predation, principally from double-crested cormorants (*Phalacrocroax auritus*) (Myers and Peterka 1976). Survival in three North Dakota wetlands with areas of 10.0–24.0 ha (mean depths of 1.0–1.7 m) was low the first month (May–June) after stocking, ranging 15–54%; high mortality may have been due to predation by birds, as dissolved oxygen and water temperatures were best for trout survival during those months. Ayles et al. (1976) attributed early (first 60 days following stocking) mortality of 60–90% of trout fingerlings stocked in Manitoba wetlands to predation by common terns (*Sterna hirundo*) and Forster's terns (*S. forsteri*).

To predict the likelihood of summerkill, Barica (1984) found a good correlation (r = 0.86) between maximum concentrations of ammonia during winter stagnation (February to early March) and phytoplankton biomass (chlorophyll-a) in the summer; the collapse of blue-green algae blooms triggers loss of dissolved oxygen. Attempts to find correlations between wetland morphometry (lake area, maximum and mean depth, lake volume, and drainage area) and chlorophyll-a concentrations (an index of wetland productivity) were unsuccessful (Barica 1978). Conductivity is not useful in predicting algal blooms except in a very general way; no algal blooms occurred in wetlands with conductivities exceeding 3,000 µmhos (Barica 1978). Although large blue-green algae blooms developed in some wetlands with conductivities ranging 300–3,000 µmhos, large blooms did not occur in others. In Manitoba wetlands used for trout culture, copper sulfate was used as an algacide to reduce blue-green algae blooms (Whitaker et al. 1978), and inorganic nitrogen fertilizers were added to encourage green rather than blue-green algae blooms (Barica et al. 1980).

To predict winterkill, a good correlation (r = 0.91) was found between mean depths of Manitoba wetlands and oxygen depletion rates (Barica 1984). Although this relationship provides an approximate estimate of the likelihood of winterkill, an exact method incorporates the initial dissolved oxygen storage of a wetland (on freeze-up) and the calculated rate of oxygen depletion as a function of mean depth, to estimate the time to reach total anoxia (Barica and Mathias 1979).

Attempts to predict salinity from wetland morphometry and elevation in Manitoba were unsuccessful (Barica 1978). Much of the variabil-

ity in salinity and ion composition of wetlands was attributed to complicated patterns of groundwater flow.

FISH PRODUCTION/YIELDS IN WETLANDS

Estimates of maximum fish production potential are scarce, as fish
survival in wetlands is usually reduced by environmental extremes and
possible predation from other animals. The highest yield of rainbow
trout from a Manitoba wetland (surface area of 3.2 ha and maximum
depth of 2.7 m) was 313 kg/ha wet weight (Lawler et al. 1974). Trout
were stocked (4,500/ha) as fingerlings (mean weight of 3 g) in the spring
and harvested (mean weight of 120 g) in November. Based on these
values and using exponential growth and mortality, production was
about 350 kg/ha; this must be close to a maximum value for production
of fish in these wetlands. Average annual yields of rainbow trout were
much less and varied from about 80 kg/ha in 1971 and 1972 to 30 kg/ha
in 1973 and 1974 (Lawler et al. 1974; Dr. Jack Mathias, pers. commun.);
average yields are based on about 20 wetlands each year. Recoveries of
stocked trout for 1970–1972 varied 0–86%, and averaged about 34%
for all lakes combined.

Payer (1977) estimated the production of fathead minnows in a
South Dakota wetland at 18 kg/ha from May to August (99% of the
production was from young-of-the-year). Payer acknowledged this value
was a low estimate of potential production and resulted from the drying
of the wetland (the wetland had a surface area and maximum depth of
16.2 ha and 0.74 m in the spring and by August had shrunk to 5.1 ha and
0.15 m), and inability to estimate the population for small individuals
(<35 mm total length). The minnows were able to expand their population from a brood stock density of 12/ha in the spring to 7,800/ha
young-of-the-year by August (biomass of 11 kg/ha). Maximum yields of
fathead minnows from two small farm dugouts in Manitoba (surface
areas of 0.09 and 0.11 ha) were 108 and 47 kg/ha, respectively; their
average weights were 1.3 and 3.0 g (Li and Ayles 1981).

Brook sticklebacks in a 9.8 ha wetland in Manitoba reached a maximum of 23,000 adults/ha (biomass of 27 kg/ha) in May 1982 (Moodie
1986), and a maximum of 80,290/ha (biomass of 80 kg/ha) in August
1976 (Tavarutmaneegul 1978); this latter estimate did not include young-
of-the-year fish.

The maximum yield of walleye fingerlings stocked in 12 farm dugouts in Manitoba was 36.4 kg/ha (mean was 7.6 kg/ha); the harvest was

variable and ranged 0–18% of fish stocked, with a mean of 4.8% (Li and Ayles 1981). At the time of harvest (112 growing days) walleyes averaged 16 g wet weight.

DISCUSSION

From this review, the success of fathead minnows and brook sticklebacks in wetlands in the northern prairie region is a function of their tolerance to low dissolved oxygen, high salinities, and high reproductive potential. Their energy demands would be expected to be particularly high just before and during the spawning season as their small sizes would preclude the storage of energy in body tissues needed to meet demands of reproduction. In the three-spined stickleback, *Gasterosteus aculeatus,* a species with a life history similar to the brook stickleback (Wootton 1973, 1984), the supply of food in the spring before spawning was important in determining the weight of the fish, which in turn was directly related to fecundity. Estimates by Wootton (1984) indicated that 5.4 g of food (wet weight) would be required to produce eggs for the spawning season for a female *G. aculeatus* weighing 1.0 g.

In addition to high fecundity associated with fractional spawning and an extended spawning season, fatheads and sticklebacks share several other life history characteristics that may help explain their success in wetlands. They are small and short lived (most live for one year and die after spawning). Males build nests and guard embryos (male sticklebacks guard young for a few days after hatching). Even some of the spawning behaviors associated with sticklebacks, such as leading behavior to the prospective spawning site, has recently been reported for fatheads (Cole and Smith 1987). Both species have small, oblique mouths; however, the large eyes, pointed snouts, and teeth on the jaws in sticklebacks indicate that marked differences in feeding ecology probably exist (Fig. 10.1). I found no studies that addressed interactions between these two species.

Wetlands are potentially useful as seasonal rearing ponds to produce either fingerlings for stocking into other lakes or edible-sized fishes from stocked fingerlings. Invertebrates provide abundant food and annual winterkills eliminate carryover of fishes that would prey on small fishes stocked each spring. Little is known about potential conflicts between fishes and waterfowl, although they may utilize similar invertebrate foods (Swanson and Nelson 1970).

While brook sticklebacks and fathead minnows may reach high densities in wetlands, tiger salamanders (*Ambystoma tigrinum*) may also

FIG. 10.1.   The fathead minnow (above) and the brook stickleback (below).

reach high densities. Larval tiger salamanders in a North Dakota wetland exceeded 5,000/ha (biomass of 180 kg wet weight/ha) in August (Weidenheft 1983). Salamanders normally occur in wetlands supporting sticklebacks and fatheads, as well as other wetlands where no fishes exist. Because of their large sizes (larval tiger salamanders in May in a North Dakota wetland averaged 160 g) and biomass, salamanders probably play an important role in wetland ecology. They, as well as brook sticklebacks and fathead minnows, deserve more attention in studies concerning the structure and function of northern prairie wetland communities.

ACKNOWLEDGMENTS

I thank Drs. Jack Mathias and Eric Moodie for providing unpublished data, and the North Dakota Water Resources Research Institute and the Department of Zoology, North Dakota State University, for providing funding for studies conducted in North Dakota.

REFERENCES

Ayles, G. B., J. G. I. Lark, J. Barica, and H. Kling. 1976. Seasonal mortality of rainbow trout (*Salmo gairdneri*) planted in small eutrophic lakes of central Canada. J. Fish. Res. Board Can. 33:647–55.

Barica, J. 1975a. Summerkill risk in prairie ponds and possibilities of its prediction. J. Fish. Res. Board Can. 32:1283–88.

———. 1975b. Geochemistry and nutrient regime of saline eutrophic lakes in the
Erickson-Elphinstone district of southwestern Manitoba. Fish. Mar. Serv.
Tech. Rep. No. 511.

———. 1977. Effect of freeze-up on major ion and nutrient content of a prairie
winterkill lake. J. Fish. Res. Board Can. 34:2210–15.

———. 1978. Variability in ionic composition and phytoplankton biomass of
saline eutrophic prairie lakes within a small geographic area. Arch. Hydrobiol. 81(3):304–26.

———. 1979. Some biological characteristics of plains aquatic ecosystems and
their effect on water quality. 1979 PARC Symp. Regina, Saskatchewan:
Can. Plains Cen.

———. 1980. Why hypertrophic ecosystems? In Hypertrophic Ecosystems, ed.
J. Barica and L. R. Muir, 9–11. The Hague: Dr. W. Junk Publ.

———. 1984. Empirical models for prediction of algae blooms and collapses,
winter oxygen depletion and a freeze-out effect in lakes: Summary and veri-
fication. Int. Ver. Theor. Angew. Limnol. 22:309–19.

Barica, J., and J. A. Mathias. 1979. Oxygen depletion and winterkill risk in
small prairie lakes under extended ice cover. J. Fish. Res. Board Can.
36:980–86.

Barica, J., H. Kling, and J. Gibson. 1980. Experimental manipulation of algae
bloom composition by nitrogen addition. Can. J. Fish. Aquat. Sci.
37(7):1175–83.

Becker, G. C. 1983. Fishes of Wisconsin. Madison: Univ. Wis. Press.

Burnham, B. L., and J. J. Peterka. 1975. Effects of saline water from North
Dakota lakes on survival of fathead minnow (Pimephales promelas) embryos and sac fry. J. Fish. Res. Board Can. 32:809–12.

Cole, K. C., and R. J. F. Smith. 1987. Male courting behaviour in the fathead
minnow, Pimephales promelas. Environ. Biol. Fishes. 18(3):235–39.

Driver, E. A., and D. G. Peden. 1977. The chemistry of surface water in prairie
ponds. Hydrobiol. 53(1):33–48.

Gale, W. F., and G. L. Buynak. 1982. Fecundity and spawning frequency of the
fathead minnow—a fractional spawner. Trans. Amer. Fish. Soc. 111:35–40.

Held, J. W. 1971. Some ecological aspects of the fathead minnows, Pimephales
promelas, in North Dakota saline lakes. Ph.D. diss., N. Dak. State Univ.,
Fargo.

Held, J. W., and J. J. Peterka. 1974. Age, growth, and food habits of the
fathead minnow, Pimephales promelas, in North Dakota saline lakes.
Trans. Amer. Fish. Soc. 103(4):743–56.

Klinger, S. A., J. J. Magnuson, and G. W. Gallepp. 1982. Survival mechanisms
of the central mudminnow (Umbra limi), fathead minnow (Pimephales promelas) and brook stickleback (Culaea inconstans) for low oxygen in winter.
Environ. Biol. Fishes 7(2):113–20.

Lawler, G. H., L. A. Sunde, and J. Whitaker. 1974. Trout production in prairie
ponds. J. Fish. Res. Board Can. 31:929–36.

Li, S., and G. B. Ayles. 1981. Preliminary experiments on growth, survival,
production and interspecific interactions of walleye (Stizostedion vitreum
vitreum) fingerlings in constructed earthern ponds in the Canadian Prairies.
Can. Tech. Rep. Fish. Aquat. Sci. 1041.

McCarraher, D. B. 1971. Survival of some freshwater fishes in the alkaline eutrophic waters of Nebraska. J. Fish. Res. Board Can. 28:1811–14.

————. 1977. Nebraska's sandhills lakes. Lincoln: Nebr. Game and Parks Comm.

McCarraher, D. B., and R. Thomas. 1968. Some ecological observations on the fathead minnow, *Pimephales promelas,* in the alkaline waters of Nebraska. Trans. Amer. Fish. Soc. 97(1):52–55.

McKee, J. W., and H. W. Wolf. 1963. Water quality criteria. The Resourc. Agency of Calif. State Water Quality Control Board Publ. No. 3-A.

Mathias, J. A., J. Martin, M. Yurkowski, J. G. I. Lark, M. Pabst, and J. L. Tabachek. 1982. Harvest and nutritional quality of *Gammarus lacustris* for trout culture. Trans. Amer. Fish. Soc. 111(1):83–89.

Moodie, G. E. E. 1986. The population biology of *Culaea inconstans,* the brook stickleback, in a small prairie lake. Can. J. Zool. 64:1709–17.

Myers, G. L., and J. J. Peterka. 1976. Survival and growth of rainbow trout (*Salmo gairdneri*) in four prairie lakes, North Dakota. J. Fish. Res. Board Can. 33:1192–95.

Payer, R. D. 1977. Estimate of production by a population of fathead minnows, *Pimephales promelas,* in a South Dakota prairie wetland. Master's thesis, S. Dak. State Univ., Brookings.

Rawson, D. S., and J. E. Moore. 1944. The saline lakes of Saskatchewan. Can. J. Res. 22:141–201.

Schoenecker, W. 1970. Management of winterkill lakes in the sandhill region of Nebraska. *In* A symposium on the management of midwestern winterkill lakes, ed. E. Schneberger, 53–56. Amer. Fish. Soc.

Scidmore, W. J. 1970. Using winterkill to advantage. *In* A symposium on the management of midwestern winterkill lakes, ed. E. Schneberger, 47–51. Amer. Fish. Soc.

State Lakes Preservation Committee. 1977. A plan for the classification, preservation, and restoration of lakes in northeastern South Dakota. Pierre, S. Dak.: South Dakota Legislature.

Sunde, L. A., J. Whitaker, and G. H. Lawler. 1970. Rainbow trout production in winterkill lakes. *In* A symposium on the management of winterkill lakes, 57–63. Amer. Fish. Soc. Spec. Publ.

Swanson, G. A., and H. K. Nelson. 1970. Potential influence of fish rearing programs on waterfowl breeding habitat. *In* A symposium on the management of winterkill lakes. Amer. Fish. Soc. Spec. Publ.

Tavarutmaneegul, P. 1978. Production of rainbow trout in small eutrophic lakes subject to periodic anoxia. Winnipeg: University of Manitoba.

Whitaker, J., J. Barica, H. Kling, and M. Buckley. 1978. Efficacy of copper sulfate in the suppression of *Aphanizomenon flos-aquae* blooms in prairie lakes. Environ. Pollut. 15:185–94.

Wiedenheft, W. D. 1983. Life history and secondary production of tiger salamanders (*Ambystoma tigrinum*) in prairie pothole lakes. Master's thesis, N. Dak. State Univ., Fargo.

Winn, H. E. 1960. Biology of the brook stickleback, *Eucalia inconstans.* Amer. Midl. Nat. 63(2):424–40.

Wootton, R. J. 1973. Fecundity of the three-spined stickleback (*Gasterosteus aculeatus* L.). J. Fish Biol. 5:683–88.

————. 1984. A functional biology of sticklebacks. Berkeley: Univ. Calif. Press.

HENRY R. MURKIN

11 THE BASIS FOR

ABSTRACT

FOOD CHAINS in prairie wetlands are complex, involving a diverse group of producers and consumers. The important factor limiting secondary production in any ecosystem is the net primary production of that system. The nutrient and energy resources of primary production are exploited by heterotrophic consumers through herbivory and detritivory. The vegetation of prairie wetlands changes with climatic conditions causing major fluctuations in both primary production and litter accumulation over time. Accurate estimates of total primary production are not possible at present due to a lack of information on belowground macrophyte production and algal productivity in wetland systems. These gaps in our understanding hamper detailed studies of wetland secondary production and food chains. High emergent primary production in prairie wetlands results in large quantities of litter entering the system. The processing of this litter by a variety of consumers is assumed to be the base of food chains associated with prairie wetlands. There have been, however, no detailed studies of detrital consumption and utilization by detritivores in prairie wetlands. A number of recent studies have reported that herbivory by birds and mammals on macrophytes may contribute significantly to the secondary production of these systems. Future research on grazing of algae by invertebrates is also required before the overall role of herbivory in prairie wetlands can be established in detail. Herbivory may be more important in these systems than previously thought, particularly during some stages of the wet-dry cycle.

KEY WORDS: aboveground production, algae, belowground production, detritivory, detritus, food chains, herbivory, invertebrates, life history, macrophytes, primary production, secondary production.

FOOD CHAINS IN PRAIRIE WETLANDS

INTRODUCTION

WHILE food chains in estuaries, coastal marshes, and associated marine areas have received considerable attention (Livingston and Loucks 1978; Hamilton and Macdonald 1979; Kennedy 1980; Pomeroy and Wiegert 1981; Boesch and Turner 1984), very little effort has been spent developing our understanding of food chains in northern prairie wetlands. Simple textbook models exist for some freshwater wetlands (Odum et al. 1984), however, food chains in these systems are complex, involving a wide array of consumers including bacteria, fungi, invertebrates, amphibians, reptiles, birds, and mammals (Clark 1978; Crow and Macdonald 1978). Because they fix carbon through photosynthesis and incorporate inorganic nutrients from the environment into organic forms, primary producers are the link between consumers and the resources of the system. As a result, the critical factor ultimately limiting secondary production is net primary production within the ecosystem.

In general, there are two basic avenues by which the nutrient and energy resources of primary production are made available to heterotrophic consumers. The first involves direct consumption of living plants by herbivores, and the second, the utilization of plant litter by various detritivores. The habitat provided by both living and dead plants is also important to the survival and reproduction of consumers within the system (Orth et al. 1984). The purpose of this chapter is to review our current knowledge of food chains in northern prairie wetlands and attempt to evaluate the relative importance of herbivory and detritivory to

HENRY R. MURKIN, Delta Waterfowl and Wetlands Research Station, R. R. 1, Portage la Prairie, Manitoba RIN 3A1.

overall secondary production in these systems. The complexity of food chain interactions in these wetlands, which themselves are extremely complex, both spatially and temporally, ensures that there is no simple answer to this objective.

COMPONENTS OF THE FOOD CHAINS IN WETLANDS

Study of food chain interactions in prairie wetlands is complicated by the characteristics of the consumers themselves. The temporal use patterns of consumers associated with these wetlands vary greatly (Sather and Smith 1984). Some consumers are completely dependent on wetlands for all of their annual requirements, whereas other species use wetlands for only some of their requirements. Some groups complete their entire life cycle within a single wetland. Others are present for only short periods in the life cycle or during the year. Still others travel from wetland type to wetland type. Those species that use wetlands throughout the year may be restricted to a particular habitat within the wetland or may use two or more habitats over the course of their life cycle. Attempting to determine the role wetlands play in the productivity of a species that occurs in the wetland for short periods during the day, the year, or maybe its entire life is certainly difficult, if not impossible.

Another major problem limiting work on food chain interactions and secondary production is the lack of information on the basic life history and ecology of the consumers present in the wetland (Murkin and Batt 1987). Although some information is available on waterfowl (Swanson and Duebbert, Chap. 8), fur-bearers (Fritzell, Chap. 9), and fish (Peterka, Chap. 10) use of these systems, data on many of the other groups is essentially nonexistent. Microbiological research involving bacteria, fungi, and other microconsumers in prairie wetlands is certainly lacking. A symposium addressing the use of freshwater wetlands by aquatic insects (Rosenberg and Danks 1987) concluded that very little is known about any of the insect families inhabiting these systems. Murkin and Batt (1987) suggest that secondary production work in freshwater wetlands is impossible at present because we lack basic life history information on most of the dominant invertebrate groups within these wetlands. This lack of background information requires compilation of species lists and basic life history information before food chain or production work can be attempted. Understanding wetland food chain interactions and secondary production also requires information on the trophic status of the species of interest. For many of the important consumers in the wetland ecosystem, such as invertebrates, this information is simply not available. These problems are complicated by the fact that some of the consumer groups for which we do have information may change their trophic status over the course of their life cycles (see Merritt and Cummins 1984). In addition, many wetland consumers are basically opportunistic omnivores eating whatever is available in the habitat (Montague et al. 1981; Smith et al. 1984).

PRIMARY PRODUCTION

Net primary production is normally high in wetlands (Richardson 1978), and can be very high in prairie glacial marshes at times (van der Valk and Davis 1978a). There are significant variations in macrophyte primary production within and among wetlands (Table 11.1) due to differences in climate, water levels, fertility, and so on (van der Valk and Davis 1980; Sather and Smith 1984). In prairie wetlands, there are also changes in primary production associated with wet-dry cycles (van der Valk and Davis 1978b; Kantrud et al. Chap. 5) (Table 11.2). A wet-dry cycle may take from 5 to 30 years to complete.

One aspect that is often overlooked during consideration of overall primary production within a wetland is belowground production by aquatic macrophytes. Emergent macrophytes, in particular, produce extensive systems of belowground roots and rhizomes that serve as stores for nutrients between growing seasons. These rhizomes are also the principal means of vegetative propagation for these species. Belowground macrophyte production is high in prairie marshes (Table 11.1). This belowground tissue represents a large pool of nutrients and energy that is usually ignored when considering wetland food chains. In temperate areas of North America, belowground biomass may be the only source of living plant material available to consumers during the winter.

Another area of neglect in the study of wetland production has been the contribution by algae to the overall primary production (see Crumpton, Chap. 6). Because algae do not have large standing crops at any point in time, they are usually considered unimportant to overall primary production. Hooper and Robinson (1976) and Shamess et al. (1985) have shown, however, that algae production in prairie wetlands can be quite high. Although standing algal biomass may be small, turnover rates are very high resulting in significant annual production (Table 11.1).

There are four important groups of algae in northern prairie wetlands: epiphyton, epipelon, phytoplankton, and metaphyton. Epiphytic algae grows on the surface of submersed plant material. In the Delta Marsh, a large northern prairie marsh in south-central Manitoba, the epiphytic algae belong to Chlorophyceae (green algae except Chara),

TABLE 11.1. Biomass estimates of the various primary producers in northern prairie marshes

Component	Annual production[a] (gC/m²/yr)	Reference
Emergent macrophytes		
Above ground		
Typha glauca	341–576	van der Valk and Davis (1978a)
	772–1075	van der Valk and Davis (1980)
	1351–1762	Neely and Davis (1985)
Scirpus validus	109–175	van der Valk and Davis (1978a)
	392–486	van der Valk and Davis (1980)
Scolochloa festucacea	135	Neckles (1984)
Sparganium eurycarpum	271–543	van der Valk and Davis (1980)
	637–1185	Neely and Davis (1985)
Below ground		
Typha glauca	525–649	van der Valk and Davis (1978a)
	1300–1779	Neely and Davis (1985)
Scirpus acutus	543–841	van der Valk and Davis (1978a)
Phragmites australis	504–704	van der Valk and Davis (1978a)
Sparganium eurycarpum	681–1123	Neely and Davis (1985)
Submersed macrophytes		
Several species combined	41–117	van der Valk and Davis (1978a)
Potamogeton pectinatus	5–112	Anderson (1978)
Algae		
Epiphytic on *Scirpus*	43.5	Hooper and Robinson (1976)
Epiphytic on *Typha*	22.9	Hooper and Robinson (1976)
Epiphytic on *Potamogeton*	11.8–48.5	Hooper and Robinson (1976)
Epipelon	100–300	Robinson, pers. comm.
Phytoplankton	5.6–77.6	Hosseini (1986)
(water depth = 50 cm)		
Metaphyton	8.8–69.0	Hosseini (1986)

[a]Biomass data has been converted to gC by assuming a 45% carbon content of plant tissue.

TABLE 11.2. Contribution of macrophytes and algae to overall primary production during the various stages of the wet-dry cycle of prairie wetlands

Vegetation	Drawdown	Regenerating	Degenerating	Lake marsh
Macrophytes				
Annuals	High	. . .	. . .	. . .
Emergents	Low	Moderate to high (increases as vegetative growth increases)	Moderate (decreases as marsh opens up)	Low to very low
Submersed	. . .	Low to moderate	Moderate to high (increases as marsh opens up)	Low to high (depends on amount of wind and wave action present)
Algal				
Phytoplankton	. . .	. . .	Low	Low
Epiphytes	. . .	Moderate to high (depends on amount of flooded substrate)	Moderate to high (depends on amount of flooded substrate)	Low to high (depends on submersed macrophyte development)
Epipelon	Low	Low to moderate (will decrease as marsh closes up)	Low to moderate (will increase as marsh opens up)	Low to high (depends on shading by submersed macrophytes)
Metaphyton	. . .	Low to moderate	Low to high	Low to moderate (depends on amounts of wind and wave action present)

Cyanophyceae (blue-green algae), and Bacillariophyceae (diatoms) (Hooper-Reid and Robinson 1978). Annual production values of epiphytes in the Delta Marsh are shown in Table 11.1.

Perhaps most important due to its contribution to overall wetland productivity, yet virtually unstudied, are the epipelic algae. These are the algae in the top few millimeters of the sediments within the wetland. The epipelic community in northern, shallow water bodies is dominated by Bacillariophyceae (diatoms) (Shamess et al. 1985). Preliminary work on the epipelon in wetlands shows that this community is very productive (Table 11.1).

Phytoplankton refers to the algal suspended in the water column. Although a large number of species are found within the phytoplanktonic community (Shamess et al. 1985), overall annual production in wetlands is thought to be low during all stages of the wet-dry cycle (Robinson, pers. comm.).

The most conspicuous algae community in wetlands with respect to standing crop is the metaphyton or flooding mats of filamentous algae. While techniques are still being developed to study the production of metaphyton in prairie wetlands (Hosseini 1986), initial estimates from work on the Delta Marsh indicate substantial primary production within the metaphyton community (Table 11.1).

The final producer group that has received even less attention than algae are the chemosynthetic bacteria. The importance of these organisms in freshwater wetland production and ecology is unknown.

DECOMPOSITION IN PRAIRIE WETLANDS

The high primary production in prairie wetlands ensures that a considerable amount of material enters the system as detritus. There are three components of the detritus pool in prairie wetlands: standing litter, fallen litter, and dissolved organic compounds that leach from both standing and fallen litter. Material enters the standing litter compartment with the death of the leaf and/or shoots (Davis and van der Valk 1978a). While a great deal of tissue enters the standing litter stage with senescence at the end of the growing season, leaf and shoot death occur throughout the growing season. Timing of shoot death varies greatly among the dominant emergent species. *Carex atherodes* shoots and leaves begin to die in the spring soon after new growth begins and continues throughout the growing season (Davis and van der Valk 1978a). In some of the bulrushes (*Scirpus* spp.), shoots begin to die in midsummer. For *Typha glauca,* Davis and van der Valk (1978a) report that 80% of the shoots alive during the periods of peak standing crops were killed by the first frosts of fall.

Litter decomposition involves three processes that take place simultaneously: (1) leaching of soluble substances occurs rapidly following death of the plant tissue and accounts for much of the weight loss during the early stages of decomposition; (2) mechanical fragmentation due to weathering or animal activities such as trampling, house building, and grazing; and (3) biological decay from the oxidation of detritus by bacteria, fungi, and other consumers (de la Cruz 1979).

In prairie marshes, litter is transferred from the standing litter compartment to fallen litter through fragmentation by wind, snow, and ice action (Davis and van der Valk 1978a). During periods of high muskrat populations, feeding and house building can cause living plant tissue to bypass the standing litter stage and directly enter the fallen litter compartment (Nelson 1982). While some leaching of nutrients takes place during the standing litter stage through rainfall and wave action, any soluble materials remaining in fallen litter are leached out soon after being submersed. Nutrients like sodium and potassium are loosely held within the plant tissue and are rapidly lost through leaching (Davis and van der Valk 1978b). Most nutrients other than calcium, iron, and aluminum show some leaching loss from standing litter.

Once within the fallen litter compartment, nitrogen may actually accumulate in the litter for the first few weeks. This increase can be attributed to the buildup in microbial populations (bacteria, fungi, diatoms, and various protozoa) on the litter (Polunin 1984; Rice and Hanson 1984) and direct absorption and complexing of nitrogen compounds by the litter particles (Lee et al. 1980). Evidence for increased microbial levels is the increased oxygen demand by decomposing plant tissues (Hargrave 1972). This nitrogen accumulation indicates that levels of nitrogen within the litter are too low to support microbial growth and reproduction; therefore, available nitrogen is extracted from the surrounding water (Melillo et al. 1984). Tissues rich in nitrogen are probably more suitable for microbial colonization than detritus with lower nitrogen levels (Davis and van der Valk 1978a). This would suggest that living tissue cut by animals such as muskrats and introduced directly into the fallen litter compartment would serve as excellent substrates for microbial activity (Nelson 1982).

As decomposition proceeds within the water, litter particle size becomes smaller due to further fragmentation caused by mechanical forces such as wave action and animal feeding activities. Various animals, primarily invertebrates, feed on detritus, fragmenting it into smaller particles. The resulting feces are again colonized by microbial populations (Turner and Ferrante 1979). As a result, there is a gradual decrease in detrital particle size and biomass over time. As the various organic compounds are digested through a series of consumers, the chemical structure of the detritus also becomes less complex (Polunin 1984).

As particle size is reduced, transport by water currents serves to alter the distribution of litter within the wetland (Nelson and Kadlec 1984). While the transport of detritus among salt marshes, estuaries, and adjacent marine areas has been suggested to have ecological implications with respect to overall estuarine secondary productivity (Nixon 1980; Gallagher et al. 1984), transport of detritus in freshwater wetlands has received very little attention. As litter particle size is reduced, it becomes more susceptible to transport in suspension by low velocity wind-induced currents (de la Cruz 1979). In lacustrine or riverine marshes, there may be a net export of litter from the wetland. This may be true for any wetland with an outlet through which water leaves the wetland. Many of the prairie potholes do not have an outlet; however, litter may be transported within the wetland through water currents (Nelson and Kadlec 1984). This results in detrital material being transported from areas of production to areas where there is little or no plant production.

As decomposition proceeds, the more refractory particulate and amorphous detritus become incorporated into the sediments (Wetzel 1984). The fate of this material in the sediments requires investigation. Another process requiring attention is the decomposition of the below-ground biomass. There have been no published studies on the decomposition of roots and rhizomes within the prairie wetland ecosystem.

HERBIVORY IN PRAIRIE MARSHES

Herbivores consume living plant tissue. Many researchers suggest that herbivory is relatively unimportant in wetlands and that only a small percentage of the overall primary production is consumed by herbivores (Gallagher and Pfeiffer 1977; Parsons and de la Cruz 1980; Simpson et al. 1983). There have, however, been few tests of this hypothesis (Pfeiffer and Wiegert 1981), nor has any attention been paid to the effects of herbivory on the various algal communities within freshwater wetlands. Herbivory obviously affects the energy and nutrients available to detrital food chains and ultimately the overall function of the wetland ecosystem (Smith and Kadlec 1985). Herbivores using wetlands range from the moose (*Alces alces*) feeding on submersed aquatic vegetation to micro-crustaceans filtering algae from the water column.

A number of cases have been documented where grazing has had a significant impact on the primary production within wetlands. Smith and Kadlec (1985) found that waterfowl and muskrats (*Ondatra zibethicus*) grazing in a Utah marsh reduced production and standing crops of *Typha latifolia, Scirpus lacustris,* and *S. maritimus* by 47.5, 25.4, and

8.9%, respectively. Because the exclosures used in this study did not exclude insects or small mammals, the overall effect of grazing may be higher than actually reported.

One of the dominant herbivores in freshwater wetlands is the muskrat (Fritzell, Chap. 9). Complete eat outs of wetland vegetation by muskrats have been documented many times (Errington et al. 1963; Weller and Spatcher 1965; Van Dyke 1972; Sipple 1979). Van der Valk and Davis (1978b) cite muskrats as one of the dominant factors reducing vegetation during the degenerating phase of the marsh vegetation cycle. McCabe (1982) showed that muskrats had a marked effect on vegetation densities and reproduction within a wetland in Utah through repeated grazing. Through selective feeding, muskrats can affect vegetation species composition within a wetland (Fuller et al. 1985) and, therefore, overall primary production rates within the wetland. During periods of optimal habitat conditions, muskrat population levels can increase very rapidly (Errington 1963). The normal phases of muskrat population development are low muskrat numbers, increasing population size as the food supply becomes established (regenerating marsh), overpopulation, range damage (degenerating marsh), and finally starvation (Lowery 1974). There is no doubt that during a muskrat eat out of a prairie marsh, herbivory is a dominant factor in the system's food chain (Perry 1982). Muskrats utilize the belowground portion of macrophytes as well as the aboveground material. Roots and rhizomes are the main food of muskrats during the winter (Dozier 1953). During eat outs, muskrats may dig to depths of 50 cm to uncover rhizomes (Lowery 1974). Besides vegetation directly consumed, muskrats use large quantities of plant material for building winter lodges, feeding huts, and feeding platforms. As a result, a great deal of uneaten plant material is introduced to the marsh through muskrat activity. This has definite implications for detritivores within the wetland. Green and growing shoots cut by muskrats for lodges and shelters have higher nutrient concentrations than dead leaves and stems that fall into the water following senescence and fragmentation (Nelson 1982). Muskrats tend to use the most available plant species for feeding and house building and, therefore, species utilized may vary among wetlands (Allen and Hoffman 1984). In the United States and Canada, cattails (*Typha* spp.) and bulrushes (*Scirpus* spp.) appear to be preferred foods and habitats (Willner et al. 1975). MacArthur and Aleksiuk (1979) found muskrat lodges in the Delta Marsh were usually constructed of cattails or bulrushes interspersed with pondweeds and bottom detritus. Not all plant species are capable of supporting equal populations of muskrats. In Manitoba, cattails can support approximately seven times as many muskrats as equivalent areas of bulrush

(Allen and Hoffman 1984). Carrying capacity near Mafeking, Manitoba, ranged from 7.4 muskrats/ha for *Carex* spp. to 64.2/ha for *Phragmites* (Butler 1940).

Among the other herbivorous mammals, many inhabitants of upland sites (such as hares and voles) make feeding forays into wetlands (Crow and Macdonald 1978). While small mammals are abundant in wetland areas, there has been no research reported on their productivity or their effect on overall wetland primary production. In terrestrial habitats, small mammals may have a major impact on annual primary production (Golley 1973). Working in Iowa, Weller (1981) reported higher densities of meadow voles (*Microtus pennsylvanicus*) and short-tailed shrews (*Blarina brevicauda*) in wet meadows along marshes than in drier upland sites. The effects of these high population levels on wetland primary production, particularly seed production, requires investigation.

Other important herbivores present in prairie freshwater wetlands are the waterfowl. One of the primary herbivores reported by Smith and Kadlec (1985) in their study on a Utah marsh was the Canada goose (*Branta canadensis*). The geese grazed on aboveground plant parts during spring and summer. Smith and Odum (1981) reported that snow geese (*Chen caerulescens*), feeding primarily on roots and rhizomes during winter, removed 58.1% of the available standing crop within a *Spartina* spp., *Distichlis spicata,* and *Scirpus* spp. marsh. Cargill and Jefferies (1984) documented that snow geese consumed approximately 80% of the net aboveground primary production within a *Puccinellia-Carex* marsh in northern Canada. An interesting sidelight to this study was that grazing by the geese actually increased the net aboveground primary production by about 30%. Waterfowl removed most of the aboveground biomass and 70% of viable seeds from the soil of coastal flats in the Netherlands affecting not only nutrient and energy dynamics of the area but also species composition of the vegetation surviving from year to year (Joenje 1985).

Feeding by mallards (*Anas platyrhynchos*) and blue-winged teal (*Anas discors*) completely eliminated sago pondweed (*Potamogeton pectinatus*) aboveground biomass from a shallow pond in the Delta Marsh (Wrubleski 1984). This removal of the pondweed had significant implications beyond the nutrient and energy considerations of the biomass removal. The elimination of the pondweed disrupted the major structural component of the open-water habitat, which in turn influenced the chironomid community structure of the pond. Removal of the pondweed eliminated the epiphytic chironomid species and appeared to benefit the larger, benthic dwelling species.

Invertebrates also feed on submersed and emergent vegetation in wetlands (Berg 1950; McDonald 1955; Skuhravy 1978), however, few large eat outs of emergent vegetation by invertebrates have been documented. Beule (1979) described the destruction of a large area of cattail in a waterfowl management area due to mining by the moth *Leucania scirpicola.* The actual amount of plant material consumed by the moth larvae was not recorded. Skuhravy (1978) noted that in a wetland in Czechoslovakia, one-third of the stems of *Phragmites* were damaged by insects. This resulted in a 10–20% loss of annual primary production. Smirnov (1961) reported a 0.4–7.0% loss of above ground macrophyte production to invertebrate herbivores in a shallow lake in the USSR. It appears that rather than consuming significant biomass within the wetland, invertebrate feeding causes only local damage to the plants involved. Simpson et al. (1979) also concluded that insect grazing on macrophytes in freshwater tidal marshes was minimal.

A major unstudied area of herbivory in wetlands has been the consumption of algae by primary consumers. Aquatic invertebrates are abundant in prairie wetlands, yet little is known about their feeding habits or trophic status. Cladocerans are abundant in the Delta Marsh (Murkin 1983) and other prairie wetlands. Porter (1977) reported that cladocerans and copepods feed primarily on phytoplankton in the water column. During periods of peak abundance, these crustaceans are potentially able to graze over 100% of the daily phytoplankton production (Smirnov 1961). Haney (1973), working in lakes, showed that cladocerans were responsible for 80% of the overall grazing activity by the zooplankton community. Porter (1977) found that cladocerans control both algal abundance and species composition by selectively grazing on the most palatable algal species present. To complicate matters, not all cladocerans feed exclusively on algae. Coveney et al. (1977) found that in an eutrophic lake, one species of Daphnia fed primarily on phytoplankton while another species fed almost exclusively on bacteria.

In many prairie wetlands, larva of the chironomidae (O. Diptera) are the most abundant invertebrate group present. Many of the species within this family are filter feeders that build tubes on plant material or in bottom sediments (Lamberti and Moore 1984). Planktonic algae and detritus are apparently their main food sources. It appears, however, that algae make up the majority of their diet during spring and summer when algal productivity is high. In addition, larvae inhabiting the littoral areas of lakes consume more algae than those in deeper profundal areas. Stomach contents of the chironomidae larva (*Procladuis nietus*) collected in the Delta Marsh contained primarily diatoms (Wrubleski, unpubl. data). Cattaneo (1983) reported that chironomid assemblages significantly reduced the biomass of lentic epiphytic algae.

Hunter (1980) found that the freshwater snails, *Lymnaea, Physa,* and *Helisoma,* all common inhabitants of prairie marshes, greatly reduced the standing crop of pond periphyton. Most of the evidence for invertebrates feeding on algae comes from studies other than wetlands. Before progress can be made toward understanding secondary production and food chains in prairie wetlands, further research into the trophic status of wetland invertebrates is urgently needed.

Vertebrates feeding on algae in wetlands has not been documented in any detail; however, American coots (*Fulica americana*), gadwalls (*Anas strepera*), and mallards (*A. platyrhynchos*) have been observed feeding on mats of metaphyton in the Delta Marsh (Murkin, pers. observ.). Dickman (1968) found that densities of filamentous green algae in a lake in British Columbia were controlled by the grazing activities of tadpoles (*Rana aurora*) within the lake.

DETRITIVORY IN PRAIRIE MARSHES

Although not very well documented in the literature, the "freshwater marshes are detritus-based systems" axiom is widely accepted by analogy with salt marshes. The idea is that the major trophic structure of the wetland ecosystem proceeds from plant detritus, to microorganisms, to a variety of invertebrate consumers, and then in some cases on to vertebrate predators (see Swanson and Duebbert, Chap. 8). This reasoning follows very closely the current theories on streams (Vannote et al. 1980) and salt marshes (Odum and Heald 1975). It appears aquatic macroinvertebrates are the key link in secondary production of these wetland systems. Few vertebrates in prairie wetlands have been described as detritivores, although bottom feeders such as carp are likely to ingest plant litter incidental to foods removed from the substrate. Bacteria, fungi, and other microorganisms are essentially the first-level consumers of dead plant material. However, the detritus and the associated microbes are normally considered to be the base of detrital food chains, with secondary production occurring at higher trophic levels (Darnell 1976).

Once dead plant material enters the fallen litter compartment as coarse particulate organic matter (CPOM), it is colonized by microorganisms, which increase its nutritive quality for secondary consumers. Detritivores may actually select litter with higher overall nutrient levels (Valiela and Rietsma 1984). The nutritive quality of the original litter may be of minor importance compared to the nutrients associated with the colonizing microorganisms (Ward and Cummins 1979; Findlay and Tenore 1982; Lawson et al. 1984). Motyka et al. (1985) found that colonized detritus was selected much more readily by aquatic detritivores than uncolonized litter. For many consumers, CPOM serves both as food and habitat. In prairie wetlands, CPOM normally enters the marsh as a pulse in spring; however, as mentioned earlier, there is also continuous input for many plant species throughout the year.

Cummins (1973) described the functional groups of invertebrates with respect to processing litter in streams. Nelson (1982) has shown that these concepts are useful in marshes as well. Shredders and grazers (or scrapers) are the first invertebrate groups to respond to CPOM and its associated microbial communities. An important shredder in prairie wetlands is the amphipod *Hyalella azteca* (Nelson 1982). De March (1981) describes *H. azteca* as primarily a detritivore; however, it will consume algae if they are available. Various snails are important grazers (scrapers) in prairie wetlands (see Pip 1978).

Early invading functional groups serve to reduce the particle size of the litter by their feeding activities. Some authors argue that detritivorous invertebrates do not actually digest detritus at all. They simply assimilate the microorganisms associated with the litter, then egest the dead plant material (in smaller particle sizes), which is then recolonized by decomposer microorganisms (Montague et al. 1981). As the litter particle size is reduced, this fine particulate organic matter (FPOM) becomes available to another set of consumers. Filter feeders remove the fine litter particles from the water column, while collectors gather FPOM from the substrate surfaces. The family Chironomidae in wetlands has representatives in both these functional groups. As the litter particle size is reduced through successive trophic functional groups, the residual material resistant to decomposition by micro-organisms and invertebrates is incorporated into the sediments of the wetland.

Another important detritus pool in aquatic environments is the dissolved organic molecules or complexes released during leaching or incomplete digestion by consumer organisms. Most research has focused on the large particulate detritus; however, the much smaller amorphous organic complexes and dissolved molecules may be more abundant in aquatic systems (Bowen 1984). Similar to particulate detritus, dissolved organic matter consists of a more labile fraction that is readily utilized by bacteria and a more refactory component that is utilized more slowly (Roman and Tenore 1984). Dissolved organic matter may be the primary food source for suspended bacteria, microflagellates, and protozoa within these environments (Linley and Newell 1984; Taylor et al. 1985). This consumption of dissolved nutrients by these microorganisms is an important mechanism in the transformation of dissolved nutrients into microbial biomass, which then can be utilized by higher consumers (Murray and Hodson 1985; Riemann 1985).

Unlike the few studies of herbivory with actual estimates of total

primary production consumed by primary consumers, there are no estimates of detrital consumption and utilization in wetlands. Because of
the vast amounts of plant litter observed in prairie wetlands and the
often high densities of assumed detritivores (i.e., the abundant invertebrate groups), it has been assumed that detritivory forms the base of the
food chains in these systems.

FOOD CHAINS AND THE VEGETATION CYCLE

The vegetation cycle of prairie marshes (see Kantrud et al., Chap. 5
for details) will certainly provide very different resources to secondary
consumers during each of the stages (Table 11.2). These changes in available resources would also result in changes in the roles of herbivory and
detritivory in food chains during the wet-dry cycle (Table 11.3).

During the drawdown stage, aquatic invertebrate and vertebrate
production is nonexistent. It appears that the terrestrial conditions
would be most suitable for terrestrial herbivores and detritivores. During
the first growing season of the drawdown, there would be little surface
litter present on the exposed mudflats, so basic food-chain support
would be herbivory on the primary production of the rapidly growing
mudflat annuals and perennials. If the drawdown persists for more than
one growing season, there will be some buildup of plant litter and the
potential of detritivore support within the terrestrial food chain.

With the return of standing water and the development of a regenerating marsh, there would be some potential for detritivore food-
chain support as the mudflat annual litter is submersed and decomposes.
The primary production by rapidly growing and expanding emergent
vegetation beds would provide potential for herbivore support. The
large surface areas provided by submersed mudflat annual litter and the
expanding macrophyte stands would also provide the potential for high
epiphytic algae production during these periods. Maximum algae growth
would occur on the flooded annual litter before the emergent vegetation
stands become too dense and cause shading of the water column. The
vast surface area provided by flooded annual plant litter for epiphytic
algae growth and invertebrate habitat may be one of the primary reasons
for the high overall productivity associated with newly flooded wetlands.
It appears that food chains in the regenerating marsh may be dominated
by the vast amounts of primary production during this stage of the
marsh cycle.

As the regenerating marsh shifts to the degenerating marsh stage,
the amount of living plant material in the wetland declines and the detritus added to the water column increases. Nelson (1982) suggests that the

TABLE 11.3. Contribution of herbivory and detritivory to food chains during the various phases of the wet-dry cycle of prairie wetlands

Function	Drawdown	Regenerating	Degenerating	Lake marsh
Herbivory				
Macrophytes	Low	Low	High	Low
Algae	...	Moderate	Moderate to high (depends on epiphyton)	Low to high
Detritivory	Low	Low to moderate	High	Low to moderate

litter added to the water by factors such as muskrats will be of high quality and further enhance detritivore production during these periods. This may imply a shift from primarily herbivore support of the food chains to detritivory; however, the surface area provided by the increased litter input to the water column may again increase algal production, particularly as the emergent vegetation stands thin out and light once again penetrates the water column. The nutrients leached from the newly submersed litter are also readily utilized by algal cells.

As the degenerating marsh opens to the lake marsh stage, both macrophyte primary production and litter production are at a minimum. The lake marsh characteristically consists of a shallow lake with a muddy bottom surrounded by a thin border of emergent vegetation. Some submersed vegetation persists in the open-water areas, however, the overall productivity of submersed plant species is lower than emergent vegetation (Table 11.1). The flocculent sediments consist of fine litter particles that are resistant to further decomposition. The emergents around the border of the lake would provide only minor amounts of living plant tissue and potential litter to the system. While normally considered unproductive, lake marshes often support large populations of Chironomidae larva. Murkin and Kadlec (1986) documented the highest densities of chironomid larva during the lake marsh stage of an artificially created wetland vegetation cycle. One possible source of food-chain support during this stage may be epipelic algae. This algae group prefers shallow, open pond situations with soft sediments and few macrophytes to shade the substrate. As shown earlier, epipelon may not have a large standing crop at any time; however, its rapid turnover rates result in relatively high levels of primary production over the course of a season. The epipelon may well be the main support of the available food chains during the lake marsh stage of the prairie wetland vegetation cycle.

CONCLUSIONS

There is no doubt that detritivory is an important component of the food chains in prairie wetlands. This review, however, suggests that herbivory is also a factor in wetland food chains, especially during some stages of the wet-dry cycle (Tables 11.2 and 11.3). I agree with Smith and Kadlec (1985) that grazing and herbivory require further investigation to establish their importance to overall wetland secondary production. Another area requiring attention is the role of algae in support of primary consumers. Algal contribution to overall wetland productivity may be much higher than presently anticipated. Even in salt marshes where detritus is generally considered to be the basis for the food chains of both the marsh and associated marine areas, algae are becoming recognized as important factors to the consumer production in these systems (Montague et al. 1981; Kitting 1984). Levinton et al. (1984) suggest that plant detritus contributes little to nutrition of secondary producers in a *Spartina* marsh, while microalgae form the bulk of foods used by consumers. The primary role of detritus in the secondary production and food chains of prairie wetlands may be to provide the habitat necessary for algae and invertebrate growth and reproduction.

ACKNOWLEDGMENTS

This chapter is Paper No. 21 of the Marsh Ecology Research Program, a joint project funded by Ducks Unlimited Canada and the Delta Waterfowl and Wetlands Research Station. I thank J. Kadlec, J. Nelson, and A. van der Valk for their comments on earlier drafts of the manuscript.

REFERENCES

Allen, A. W., and R. D. Hoffman. 1984. Habitat suitability index models: Muskrat. U.S. Fish and Wildl. Serv. FWS/OBS-82/10.46. Washington, D.C.: GPO.

Anderson, M. G. 1978. Distribution and production of sago pondweed *Potamogeton pectinatus* L. on a northern prairie marsh. Ecol. 59:154–60.

Berg, C. O. 1950. The biology of aquatic caterpillars which feed on *Potamogeton*. Trans. Amer. Microsc. Soc. 69:254–66.

Beule, J. D. 1979. Control and management of cattails in southeastern Wisconsin wetlands. Wis. Dept. Nat. Resour. Tech. Bull. 112. Madison.

Boesch, D. F., and R. E. Turner. 1984. Dependence of fishery species on salt marshes: The role of food and refuge. Estuaries 7:460–68.

Bowen, S. H. 1984. Evidence of a detritus food chain based on consumption of organic precipitates. Bull. Mar. Sci. 35:440–48.

Butler, L. 1940. A quantitative study of muskrat food. Can. Field-Nat. 54:37–40.

Cargill, S. M., and R. L. Jefferies. 1984. The effects of grazing by lesser snow geese on the vegetation of a sub-arctic salt marsh. J. Appl. Ecol. 21:669–86.

Cattaneo, A. 1983. Grazing on epiphytes. Limnol. Oceanogr. 28:124–32.

Clark, J. 1978. Freshwater wetlands: Habitats for aquatic invertebrates, amphibians, reptiles, and fish. *In* Wetland functions and values: The state of our understanding, ed. P. E. Greeson et al., 330–43. Minneapolis: Amer. Water Resour. Assoc.

Coveney, M. F., G. Cronberg, M. Enell, K. Larsson, and L. Olofsson. 1977. Phytoplankton, zooplankton and bacteria – standing crop and production relationships in an eutrophic lake. Oikos 29:5–21.

Crow, J. H., and K. B. Macdonald. 1978. Wetland values: Secondary production. *In* Wetland functions and values: The state of our understanding, ed. P. E. Greeson et al., 146–61. Minneapolis: Amer. Water Resour. Assoc.

Cummins, K. W. 1973. Trophic relations of aquatic insects. Annu. Rev. Entomol. 18:183–206.

Darnell, R. M. 1976. Organic detritus in relation to the estuarine ecosystem. *In* Estuaries, ed. G. H. Lauff, 376–82. Washington, D.C.: Amer. Assoc. Adv. Sci.

Davis, C. B., and A. G. van der Valk. 1978a. Litter decomposition in prairie glacial marshes. Freshwater wetlands: Ecological processes and management potential, ed. R. E. Good et al., 99–113. New York: Academic Press.

———. 1978b. The decomposition of standing and fallen litter of *Typha glauca* and *Scirpus fluviatilis*. Can. J. Bot. 56:662–75.

de la Cruz, A. A. 1979. Production and transport of detritus in wetlands. *In* Wetland functions and values: The state of our understanding, ed. P. E. Greeson et al., 162–74. Minneapolis: Amer. Water Resour. Assoc.

de March, B. G. E. 1981. *Hyalella azteca* (Saussure). *In* Manual for the culture of selected freshwater invertebrates, ed. S. G. Lawrence, 61–77. Can. Spec. Publ. Fish. Aquat. Sci. 54. Hull, Quebec: Can. Govt. Publ. Cen.

Dickman, M. 1968. The effect of grazing by tadpoles on the structure of a periphyton community. Ecol. 49:1188–90.

Dozier, H. L. 1953. Muskrat production and management. U.S. Fish and Wildl. Serv. Circ. 18. Washington, D.C.: GPO.

Errington, P. L. 1963. Muskrat populations. Ames: Iowa State Univ. Press.

Errington, P. L., R. J. Siglin, and R. C. Clark. 1963. The decline of a muskrat population. J. Wildl. Manage. 27:1–8.

Findlay, S., and K. Tenore. 1982. Nitrogen source for a detritivore: Detritus substrate versus associated microbes. Sci. 218:371–73.

Fuller, D. A., C. E. Sasser, W. B. Johnson, and J. G. Gosselink. 1985. The effects of herbivory on vegetation on islands in Atchafalaya Bay, Louisiana. Wetlands 4:105–14.

Gallagher, J. L., and W. J. Pfeiffer. 1977. Aquatic metabolism of the communities associated with attached dead shoots of salt marsh plants. Limnol. and Oceangr. 22:562–65.

Gallagher, J. L., H. V. Kirby, and K. W. Skirvin. 1984. Detritus processing and mineral cycling in seagrass (*Zostera*) litter in an Oregon salt marsh. Aquat. Bot. 20:97–108.

Golley, F. B. 1973. Impact of small mammals on primary production. *In* Ecological energetics of homeotherms, ed. J. A. Gessamen, 142–47. Utah State Univ. Monogr. Ser. 20. Logan: Utah State Univ. Press.

Hamilton, P., and K. B. Macdonald, ed. 1979. Estuarine and wetland processes. New York: Plenum Press.

Haney, J. F. 1973. An in situ examination of the grazing activities of natural zooplankton communities. Arch. Hydrobiol. 72:87–132.

Hargrave, B. T. 1972. Aerobic decomposition of sediment and detritus as a function of particle surface area and organic content. Limnol. Oceangr. 17:583–96.

Hooper, N. M., and G. G. C. Robinson. 1976. Primary production of epiphytic algae in a marsh pond. Can. J. Bot. 54:2810–15.

Hooper-Reid, N. M., and G. G. C. Robinson. 1978. Seasonal dynamics of epiphytic algal growth in a marsh pond: Productivity, standing crop and community composition. Can. J. Bot. 56:2434–40.

Hosseini, S. M. 1986. The effects of water level fluctuations on algal communities of freshwater marshes. Ph.D. diss., Iowa State Univ., Ames.

Hunter, R. O. 1980. Effects of grazing on the quantity and quality of freshwater Aufwuchs. Hydrobiol. 69:251–59.

Joenje, W. 1985. The significance of waterfowl grazing in the primary vegetation succession on embanked sandflats. Vegetatio 62:399–406.

Kennedy, V. S., ed. 1980. Estuarine perspectives. New York: Academic Press.

Kitting, C. L. 1984. Selectivity by dense populations of small invertebrates foraging among seagrass blade surfaces. Estuaries 7:276–88.

Lamberti, G. A., and J. W. Moore. 1984. Aquatic insects as primary consumers. *In* The ecology of aquatic insects. ed. V. H. Resh and D. M. Rosenberg, 164–75. New York: Praeger.

Lawson, D. L., M. J. Klug, and R. W. Merritt. 1984. The influence of the physical, chemical, and microbiological characteristics of decomposing leaves on the growth of the detritivore *Tipula abdominalis* (Diptera:Tipulidae). Can. J. Zool. 62:2339–43.

Lee, C., R. W. Howarth, and B. L. Howes. 1980. Sterols in decomposing *Spartina alterniflora* and the use of ergosterol in estimating the contribution of fungi to detrital nitrogen. Limnol. Oceanogr. 25:290–303.

Levinton, J. S., T. S. Bianchi, and S. Stuart. 1984. What is the role of particulate organic matter in benthic invertebrate nutrition? Bull. Mar. Sci. 35:270–82.

Linley, E. A. S., and R. C. Newell. 1984. Estimates of bacteria growth yields based on plant detritus. Bull. Mar. Sci. 35:409–25.

Livingston, R. J., and O. L. Loucks. 1978. Productivity, trophic interactions, and food-web relationships in wetlands and associated systems. *In* Wetland functions and values: The state of our understanding, ed. P. E. Greeson et al., 101–19. Minneapolis: Amer. Water Resour. Assoc.

Lowery, G. H., Jr. 1974. The mammals of Louisiana and its adjacent waters. Baton Rouge: La. State Univ. Press.

MacArthur, R. A., and M. Aleksiuk. 1979. Seasonal microenvironments of the muskrat (*Ondatra zibethicus*) in a northern marsh. J. Mammal. 60:146–54.

McCabe, T. R. 1982. Muskrat population levels and vegetation utilization: A basis for an index. Ph.D. diss., Utah State Univ., Logan.

McDonald, M. E. 1955. Cause and effects of a die-off of emergent vegetation. J. Wildl. Manage. 19:24–35.

Melillo, J. M., R. J. Naiman, T. D. Aber, and A. E. Linkins. 1984. Factors controlling mass loss and nitrogen dynamics of plant litter decaying in northern streams. Bull. Mar. Sci. 35:341–56.

Merritt, R. W., and K. W. Cummins. 1984. An introduction to the aquatic insects of North America. Dubuque, Iowa: Kendall/Hunt.

Montague, C. L., S. M. Bunker, E. B. Haines, M. L. Pace, and R. L. Wetzel. 1981. Aquatic macroconsumers. *In* The ecology of a salt marsh, ed. L. R. Pomeroy and R. G. Weigert, 69–85. New York: Springer-Verlag.

Motyka, G. L., R. W. Merritt, M. J. Klug, and J. R. Miller. 1985. Food-finding behavior of selected aquatic detritivores: Direct or indirect behavioral mechanism? Can. J. Zool. 63:1388–94.

Murkin, H. R. 1983. Responses by aquatic macroinvertebrates to prolonged flooding of marsh habitat. Ph.D. diss., Utah State Univ., Logan.

Murkin, H. R., and B. D. J. Batt. 1987. Interactions of vertebrates and invertebrates in peatlands and marshes. Mem. Entomol. Soc. Can. 140:15–30.

Murkin, H. R., and J. A. Kadlec. 1986. The response by benthic macroinverte-brates to prolonged flooding of marsh habitat. Can. J. Zool. 64:65–72.

Murray, R. E., and R. E. Hodson. 1985. Annual cycle of bacterial secondary production in five aquatic habitats of the Okefenokee Swamp ecosystem. Appl. Environ. Microbiol. 49:650–55.

Neckles, H. A. 1984. Plant and macroinvertebrate responses to water regime in a whitetop marsh. Master's thesis, Univ. Minn., Minneapolis.

Neely, R. K., and C. B. Davis. 1985. Nitrogen and phosphorus fertilization of *Sparganium eurycarpum* Engelm. and *Typha glauca* Godr. stands. I: Emergent plant production. Aquat. Bot. 22:347–61.

Nelson, J. W. 1982. Effects of varying detrital nutrient concentrations on ma-croinvertebrate abundance and biomas. Master's thesis, Utah State Univ., Logan.

Nelson, J. W., and J. A. Kadlec. 1984. A conceptual approach to relating habi-tat structure and macroinvertebrate production in freshwater wetlands. Trans. N. Amer. Wildl. Nat. Resourc. Conf. 49:262–70.

Nixon, S. W. 1980. Between coastal marshes and coastal waters—a review of twenty years of speculation and research in the role of salt marshes in estuarine productivity and water chemistry. *In* Estuarine and wetland proc-esses, ed. P. Hamilton and K. B. Macdonald, 437–525. New York: Plenum.

Odum, W. E., and E. J. Heald. 1975. The detritus based food web of an es-tuarine mangrove community. *In* Estuarine research, ed. L. E. Cronin, 265–86. New York: Academic Press.

Odum, W. E., T. J. Smith, III, J. K. Hoover, and C. C. McIvor. 1984. The ecology of tidal freshwater marshes of the United States east coast: A com-munity profile. U.S. Fish and Wildl. Serv. FWS/OBS-83/17, Washington, D. C.: GPO.

Orth, R. J., K. L. Heck, Jr., and J. van Montfrans. 1984. Faunal communities in seagrass beds: A review of the influence of plant structure and prey characteristics on predator-prey relationships. Estuaries 7:339–50.

Parsons, K. A., and A. A. de la Cruz. 1980. Energy flow and grazing behavior of conocephaline grasshoppers in a *Juncus reomerianus* marsh. Ecol. 61:1045–50.

Perry, H. R., Jr. 1982. Muskrats. *In* Wild mammals of North America: Biology, management, and economics, ed. J. A. Chapman and G. A. Feldhomer, 282–325. Baltimore: The Johns Hopkins Univ. Press.

Pfeiffer, W. J., and R. G. Wiegert. 1981. Grazers on *Spartina* and their preda-tors. *In* The ecology of a salt marsh, ed. L. R. Pomeroy and W. G. Wiegert, 87–112. New York: Springer-Verlag.

Pip, E. 1978. A survey of the ecology and composition of submerged aquatic snail-plant communities. Can. J. Zool. 56:2263–79.

Polunin, N. V. C. 1984. The decomposition of emergent macrophytes in fresh water. Adv. Ecol. Res. 14:115–66.

Pomeroy, L. R., and R. G. Wiegert, eds. 1981. The ecology of a salt marsh. Ecological studies 38. New York: Springer-Verlag.

Porter, K. G. 1977. The plant-animal interface in freshwater ecosystems. Amer. Sci. 65:159–70.

Rice, D. L., and R. B. Hanson. 1984. A kinetic model for detritus nitrogen: Role of the associated bacteria in nitrogen accumulation. Bull. Mar. Sci. 35:326–40.

Richardson, C. J. 1978. Primary productivity values in freshwater wetlands. *In* Wetland functions and values: The state of our understanding. ed. P. E. Greeson et al., 131–45. Minneapolis: Amer. Water Resour. Assoc.

Riemann, B. 1985. Potential importance of fish predation and zooplankton grazing on natural populations of freshwater bacteria. Appl. Environ. Microbiol. 50:187–93.

Roman, M. R., and K. R. Tenore. 1984. Detritus dynamics in aquatic systems: An overview. Bull. Mar. Sci. 35:257–60.

Rosenberg, D. M., and H. V. Danks. 1987. Conference on the aquatic insects of peatlands and marshes. Mem. Entomol. Soc. Can. 140.

Sather, J. H., and R. D. Smith. 1984. An overview of major wetland functions. U.S. Fish and Wildl. Serv. FWS/OBS-84/18. Washington, D.C.: GPO.

Shamess, J. J., G. G. C. Robinson, and L. G. Goldsborough. 1985. The structure and comparison of periphytic and planktonic algal communities in two eutrophic prairie lakes. Arch. Hydrobiol. 103:99–116.

Simpson, R. L., D. F. Whigham, and K. Brannegan. 1979. The mid-summer insect communities of freshwater tidal wetland macrophytes. Bull. N.J. Acad. Sci. 24:22–28.

Simpson, R. L., R. E. Good, M. A. Leck, and D. F. Whigham. 1983. The ecology of freshwater tidal wetlands. Biosci. 33:255–59.

Sipple, W. S. 1979. A review of the biology, ecology, and management of *Scirpus olneyi*. Vol. II: A synthesis of selected references. Md. Dept. Nat. Resour., Water Resour. Admin. Publ. No. 4. Cambridge, Md.

Skuhravy, V. 1978. Invertebrates: Destroyers of common reed. *In* Pond littoral ecosystems: Structure and functioning, ed. D. Dykyjova and J. Kvet, 376–87. New York: Springer-Verlag.

Smirnov, N. N. 1961. Consumption of emergent plants by insects. Verh. Internat. Ver. Limnol. 14:232–36.

Smith, L. M., and J. A. Kadlec. 1985. Fire and herbivory in a Great Salt Lake marsh. Ecol. 66:259–65.

Smith, S. M., J. G. Hoff, S. P. O'Neil, and M. P. Weinstein. 1984. Community and trophic organization of nekton utilizing shallow marsh habitats, York River, Virginia. Fish. Bull. 82:455–67.

Smith, T. J., III, and W. E. Odum. 1981. The effects of grazing by snow geese on coastal marshes. Ecol. 62:90–106.

Taylor, G. T., R. Iturriaga, and C. W. Sullivan. 1985. Interactions of bactivorous grazers and heterotrophic bacteria with dissolved organic matter. Mar. Ecol. Progr. Ser. 23:129–41.

Turner, J. T., and J. G. Ferrante. 1979. Zooplankton fecal pellets in aquatic ecosystems. Biosci. 29:670–77.

Valiela, I., and C. S. Rietsma. 1984. Nitrogen, phenolic acids, and other feeding cues for salt marsh detritivores. Oecologia 63:350–56.

van der Valk, A. G., and C. B. Davis. 1978a. Primary production of prairie glacial marshes. *In* Freshwater wetlands: Ecological processes and management potential, ed. R. E. Good et al., 21–37. New York: Academic Press.

_____. 1978b. The role of seed banks in the vegetation dynamics of prairie glacial marshes. Ecol. 59:322–35.

_____. 1980. The impact of a natural drawdown on the growth of four emergent species in a prairie glacial marsh. Aquat. Bot. 9:301–22.

Van Dyke, G. D. 1972. Aspects relating to emergent vegetation dynamics in a deep marsh, northcentral Iowa. Ph.D. diss., Iowa State Univ., Ames.

Vannote, R. L., G. W. Minshall, K. W. Cummins, J. R. Sedell, and C. E. Cushing. 1980. The river continuum concept. Can. J. Fish. Aquat. Sci. 37:130–37.

Ward, G. M., and K. W. Cummins. 1979. Effects of food quality on growth of a stream detritivore, *Paratendipes albimanus* (Meigen) (Diptera: Chironomidae). Ecol. 60:57–64.

Weller, M. W. 1981. Freshwater marshes: Ecology and wildlife management. Minneapolis: Univ. Minn. Press.

Weller, M. W., and C. E. Spatcher. 1965. Role of habitat in the distribution and abundance of marsh birds. Iowa Agric. Home Econ. Exp. Stn. Spec. Rep. 43. Ames.

Wetzel, R. G. 1984. Detrital dissolved and particulate organic carbon functions in aquatic ecosystems. Bull. Mar. Sci. 35:503–9.

Willner, G. R., J. A. Chapman, and J. R. Goldsberry. 1975. A study and review of muskrat food habits with special reference to Maryland. Publ. Wildl. Ecol. 2. Cambridge: Md. Wildl. Admin.

Wrubleski, D. A. 1984. Chironomid (Diptera:Chironomidae) species composition, emergence phenologies, and relative abundances in the Delta Marsh, Manitoba, Canada. Master's thesis, Univ. Manitoba, Winnipeg.

JEAN M. NOVACEK

12 THE WATER AN
OF TH

ABSTRACT

THIS CHAPTER attempts to consolidate the scattered literature on the Nebraska sandhills. An overview of the water and wetland resources of the sandhills is presented, with discussions on geology, hydrology, soils, limnology, and wetland vegetation. A brief synopsis of the fauna of the region is also included. The sandhills store a tremendous reserve of groundwater. The hydrology is not yet understood, but work is progressing in this area. The most economically important wetland type in the sandhills is the wet meadow, which produces high-quality prairie hay. Ironically, the wet meadow is in the most danger of development or degradation due to increased center-pivot irrigation sprinkler installation, especially in the eastern sandhills. Intensive irrigation development has caused much concern over groundwater depletion and subsequent wet meadow loss. Much research in Nebraska is currently addressing water resources and water policy issues.

KEY WORDS: Nebraska sandhills, water resources, wetlands, sandhills vegetation, hydrology, remote sensing, center-pivot irrigation.

WETLAND RESOURCES
NEBRASKA SANDHILLS

INTRODUCTION

THE sandhills region of Nebraska, the largest stabilized dune field in the Western Hemisphere, extends over approximately 51,800 km² of 15 north-central counties (Keech and Bentall 1971) (Fig. 12.1). Far from a desert, the sandhills region is entirely vegetated by mixed-grass prairie with numerous wetlands in many interdunal valleys. This rich, grass-covered dune sea stretches 427 km across from east to west and 209 km from north to south. The altitudes range from 670 m in the eastern part to 1310 m in the western part. Average dune heights range from 15 m above the valley floor in the eastern sandhills to more than 92 m in the western half.

The sandhills lie within a semiarid, cool climatic area with a mean annual temperature of 8.9°C and a range of −40.0°C to 43.3°C (Keech and Bentall 1971). The mean annual precipitation received in the eastern section is approximately 612 mm and in the western region approximately 383 mm, with the central portion averaging 510 mm over a 64-year period (Keech and Bentall 1971). About 80% of the precipitation is received during the months of April through September.

The Platte River at the southern boundary drains approximately three-fourths of the sandhills, while the Niobrara River drains the remainder at the northern edge. Several perennial streams, such as the North and Middle Loup rivers, Snake River, and Dismal River, originate in the dune field, in addition to many other smaller rivers and streams.

The sandhills region is an important agricultural resource to the state. The vegetated dunes provide excellent range and forage for beef cattle. Ranch-land agriculture forms the economic base for an estimated

JEAN M. NOVACEK, Star Route, Box 56, Bartlett, Nebraska 68622.

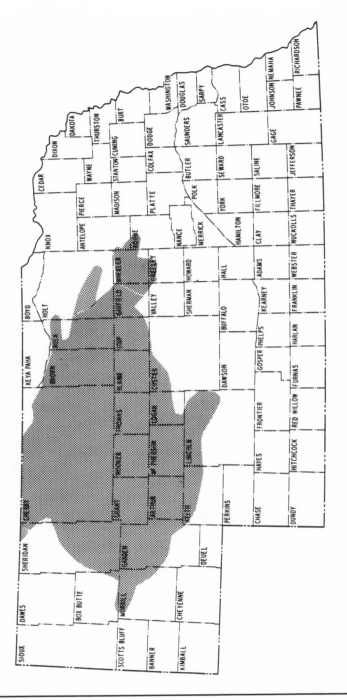

FIG. 12.1. The general area of the Nebraska sandhills shown within the context of the entire state. Scale is approximately 1 cm to 40 km.

34,000 people who are widely dispersed over this vast terrain (IANR Task Force 1983). Ranch sizes vary between 405 ha to 40,470–80,940 ha (IANR Task Force 1983). According to the 1981 cattle inventory, there were nearly 1.2 million head for the 15 county area (IANR Task Force 1983). On the average, at least 5.7 ha are required to support one animal-unit per year. The most common form of ranching is the cow-calf operation. In recent years, there has been an increase in irrigated crop production, but cattle ranching is still the dominant land-use.

Water is another extremely important resource that the sandhills harbor. It is currently estimated that the groundwater in storage under the sandhills is approximately 1.233×10^{12} m^3 (1 billion acre-feet) (Dreeszen 1984). This groundwater occupies the Ogallala Formation of the Tertiary Period plus some younger beds. Not only is this water a tremendously important resource to a great diversity of users in the state, but it also is the key to the abundance of plant and animal life in the sandhills. A great need exists for research addressing many aspects of the sandhills in all disciplines including hydrology, geology, geography, biology, and ecology. To be sure, as Dreeszen (1984) pointed out, the sandhills region is a "scientific frontier."

This chapter is intended as an overview of the water resources and wetlands of the Nebraska sandhills. An effort was made to review and cite as much of the pertinent literature as possible. What follows is a review of what is known about the geology, soils, hydrology, and groundwater quality of the area. Next, the limnology of sandhills lakes is discussed. Then, detailed information on sandhills wetlands is presented, including wetland classification and inventory, vegetation, and fauna. Finally, a brief outlook on sandhills wetlands is offered.

GEOLOGY

According to Swinehart (1984), the sandhills region is a high-latitude, low-energy dune sea. Large-scale dune formation occurred in the western and northwestern sandhills during the Hypsithermal Interval beginning about 7000 years before present (YBP) under a wind regime dominated by winds from the northwest (Warren 1976; Ahlbrandt and Fryberger 1980; Ahlbrandt et al. 1983; Swinehart 1984). Warren (1976) concluded that there were also important winds from the southwest at the time of large-scale dune formation and that these winds promoted the formation of lengthy linear dunes. Another episode of major dune activity that has been documented for the southeastern sandhills occurred between 3500–1500 YBP (Ahlbrandt et al. 1983). As recently as 600–250 YBP, drought conditions persisted long enough that the vegetative cover was effectively reduced such that aeolian movement of sand occurred a number of times (Ahlbrandt et al. 1983). There has been no documented evidence supporting dune activity before 10,000 YBP, and no verified connection between the formation of the sandhills and the formation of Pleistocene loess deposited in great quantities between 14,000–10,000 YBP (Swinehart 1984). In fact, in the southeastern section in Logan and Custer counties, dune sand has been found overlying the loess (Ahlbrandt and Fryberger 1980). Thus, the sandhills are a geologically young deposit.

According to Ahlbrandt and Fryberger (1980), there are no adequate textural and mineralogic data available to determine the source of the dune sands. One theory is that the sands came from the upper Tertiary Ogallala Formation in original or reworked form (Lugn 1935). Another source may have been from lower Pleistocene alluvial deposits according to Reed and Dreeszen (1965). Yet another source may have been from a widespread mantle deposit of unconsolidated fluviatile sediments along easterly-flowing paleorivers now buried by dune sands (Smith 1965). Warren (1976) suggested that large-scale dunes were derived from the winnowing of medium-sized fluvial sands.

Dune types found in the sandhills include small domes, barchan, barchanoid-ridge, transverse-ridge, parabolic, and blow-out dunes (Ahlbrandt and Fryberger 1980). Barchan, barchanoid-ridge, and transverse-ridge dunes are common throughout, with heights up to 92 m (Ahlbrandt and Fryberger 1980). Transverse-ridge dunes may range from a few kilometers to 16 km in length, their average width being about 1.2 km (Smith 1965). These large dunes may have slopes between 15–20° on the southern faces and between 5–10° on the northern flanks, with a microrelief on top on the order of 6 m (Smith 1965). The largest dunes are compound in form and are located in the central part, decreasing in size to the north and south. Large barchans are common at the margins, with parabolics and blow-outs common throughout (Ahlbrandt and Fryberger 1980). Since they are formed mostly in winter, blow-outs are typically located on the northwestern slopes of dunes. The dune formation is continually being modified by wind and water erosion and mass wasting. Ahlbrandt and Fryberger (1980) noted that the dunes north of the Niobrara River are much more heavily reworked than the dunes south of there.

The interdunal deposits are different from the upland dune sands in color, texture, thickness, internal structure, and organic matter content (Ahlbrandt and Fryberger 1980, 1981). Many of the interdunal valleys contain lakes, marshes, or wet meadows, and some may be interconnected by streams. Other interdunal valleys do not exhibit these phenomena and are locally called dry valleys.

Two major units of water-bearing strata underlie the dune sands: the Ogallala Group and the overlying Pliocene/Pleistocene age sands and gravels (Swinehart 1984). During the late Miocene or early Pliocene, about 6–10 million YBP, deposition of stream sediments, at first locally derived then later from the Rocky Mountains, occurred over a 4–6 million-year period forming the Ogallala Group (Diffendal et al. 1982). This water-bearing formation consists of consolidated and unconsolidated sediments of gravel or sand or silt and is highly variable in both composition and thickness (Diffendal et al. 1982). There are also some volcanic ash lentils present, in addition to caliche layers (Diffendal et al. 1982).

Atop the Ogallala Group are the quite coarse, stream-deposited Pliocene/Pleistocene sands and gravels, which are approximately 2–3.5-million-years old (Swinehart 1984). In the general area of the Dismal, Middle, and North Loup Rivers, the dune sands rest directly on this layer (Ahlbrandt et al. 1983). In the northern and northwestern sandhills, the dune sands generally rest directly overtop the Ogallala Group (Ahlbrandt et al. 1983).

SOILS

Sandhills soils fall predominantly into the soil order Entisol and into the Great Group Psamment (Dugan 1984). The notable characteristics of a typical sandhills profile include: an A Horizon usually less than 12 cm deep, no B Horizon, and fine to very fine sandy parent material (Lewis 1984). All soils are typically neutral in reaction, are low in organic matter, contain large quantities of magnesium and potassium with very little sodium, and are highly saturated with basic ions, especially calcium (Lewis 1984). The heavy minerals present include muscovite, biotite, and weatherable amphiboles and pyroxenes; the most common light mineral is quartz, which does not weather readily (Lewis 1984). The fine and very fine sands contain almost 30% potassium and/or plagioclase feldspars, which are weatherable minerals that release calcium and potassium ions (Lewis 1984).

In the central and eastern sandhills, the upland soils are of the Valentine series and the dry valley soils are of the Dunday series; in the extreme western sandhills, the Valent series compose the upland dune soils and the Daily series compose dry valley soils (Lewis 1984). The areal extent of the Valentine series is greater than all the combined areas of the other soil types found in the sandhills (Keech and Bentall 1971). Soils that are wet throughout the profile are classified as Aquents and Aquolls, which are subdivided into the following series based on topsoil thickness and calcium carbonate content: Gannett, Loup, Els, Tryon, Wildhorse, Hoffland, and Marlake (Lewis 1984). Soils that are occasionally wet are in the Aquic subgroup and are within either the Elsmere or Ipage series (Lewis 1984).

Dugan (1984) quantitatively evaluated the effects of five soil characteristics on the hydrologic responses of Nebraska soils, which were then grouped according to their similarities and mapped. Dugan determined that the three most important classification variables were average permeability of the 1.5 m soil profile, average maximum soil slope, and depth to the seasonal high water table. According to his data, the sandhills have an average soil permeability greater than 30.5 cm/hr, average maximum soil slopes ranging between 3–50%, and depth to seasonal high water table greater than 1.8 m for upland soils and less than 1.8 m for lowland soils. Dugan also computed the average permeability of the least permeable horizon and found that it ranged between 10–29 cm/hr, and he calculated the average available water capacity, which ranged between 0.18–0.23 cm/hr. Thus, the sandhills soils are quite permeable, allowing rapid infiltration and percolation of precipitation, but have low water-holding capacity.

Wind erosion is the major soil resource problem in the sandhills. Occurring when the vegetative cover is reduced or mechanically removed, wind erosion causes serious problems by loss of topsoil, damage by blowing sand, and deposition with subsequent smothering of range or crop plants. Wind erosion is especially common where the sod has been broken for irrigation development. There have been reported cases where fencerows and portions of range have been buried by sand, and where young corn plants have been damaged badly enough that irrigators have had to replant three or four times in one season (Nebr. NRC 1984). Control of wind erosion on irrigated fields is checked with crop residues and no-till or conservation tillage practices. Proper range management and grazing practices control erosion on range lands.

The Soil Conservation Service has devised a wind erosion hazard index, the product of the soil erodibility index and the climatic factor (Nebr. NRC 1984). A hazard index has been calculated for each general soil association in the sandhills. The lowest index value (<70) is found in the eastern sandhills along streams and wetlands and along the transition zone to the hardlands in the southeastern part (Nebr. NRC 1984). The maximum index in the eastern and central sandhills ranges between 90–100, which is also true where soils are of the Valentine series and the topography is variable (Nebr. NRC 1984). Due to a drier climate and a difference in soil types, the hazard index for the western sandhills is often greater than 170.

HYDROLOGY

The principal aquifer of the sandhills is composed of two geologic units, the younger Pliocene/Pleistocene sands and gravels and the older Ogallala Group sediments. The sand and gravel layer ranges in thickness from approximately 4.6 m to 42 m, with an average of 21.3 m (Nebr. NRC 1984). Predominant grain size is coarse sand to very fine gravel, with a range in size from fine sand to medium gravel (Nebr. NRC 1984). The hydraulic conductivity of these sands and gravels averages about 650–700 gal/dy/ft² (gpd/ft²); transmissivity is estimated between 10,000–100,000 gpd/ft (Nebr. NRC 1984). Porosity is estimated at 25–40% of the total volume, while specific yield is approximately 25% the total volume (Nebr. NRC 1984).

The Ogallala Group consists of much finer sediments, with texture ranges of clay-size to very fine gravel-size particles; however, the texture is variable, including fine to coarse sands, lightly cemented sands, silts, clayey silts, and siltstones (Nebr. NRC 1984). Thickness of these sediments is also quite variable, ranging from 61 m to greater than 122 m, with the average approximately 110 m (Nebr. NRC 1984). Because of this variability, hydraulic conductivity cannot be estimated.

Because of their ability to allow rapid infiltration of precipitation, the overlying dune sands are hydrogeologically significant since recharge of the groundwater reservoir is possible (Lawton 1984). It is estimated that the average annual precipitation received by the sandhills is 2.466×10^7 m³ (20 million acre-feet), of which about 25–50% becomes groundwater recharge according to Lawton (1984). The sandhills region is estimated to store over 1.233×10^{12} m³ (1 billion acre-feet), which is about half of the state's water supply (Dreeszen 1984). The saturated thickness of the principal aquifer ranges between 122–183 m; however, in corners of Cherry, Grant and Hooker counties, the saturated thickness is as much as 366 m (Lawton 1984).

Groundwater generally moves in an east-southeast direction in the sandhills, discharging into the North Platte, Niobrara, and Loup rivers or their tributaries, and locally discharging into lakes or wetlands (Dreeszen 1984). In Sheridan and Garden counties of the western sandhills, there is a groundwater mound, or high, as exhibited by a closed contour on the configuration of the water-table map of the state (CSD 1980). It is also interesting to note that Warren (1976) found that the dune floor exhibits a closed contour in this same region, closely coinciding with the groundwater high. On the eastern side of the high, groundwater moves toward the east, and groundwater moves to the west on the western side. It is thought that this groundwater mounding is due to renewed uplift of the Chadron Arch, which trends south-southeast through Sheridan, southeastern Cherry, northeastern Grant, and northwestern Hooker counties (Dreeszen 1984; Ginsberg 1984, 1985) (Fig. 12.2). The region west of the groundwater high is known as the closed basins region, which is characterized by poor surface drainage (Fig. 12.2). The closed basin area has only two surface outlets: Blue Creek at the southern boundary, which flows into the North Platte River, and Pine Creek at the northern boundary, which flows into the Niobrara River. There are numerous lakes and wetlands in the closed basins region, many of which are maintained by surface runoff rather than groundwater inflow (Keech and Bentall 1971). According to Keech and Bentall (1971), some of these lakes receive inflow with a suspension of fine-grained sediment from eastward-sloping tablelands to the west, which may have contributed to the formation of impermeable layers on lake bottoms. These lakes are often highly alkaline (McCarraher 1977). Another theory is that fine-grained evaporitic paleointerdunal deposits act as local permeability barriers (Bradley and Rainwater 1956).

Groundwater levels for Nebraska are summarized annually in a report sponsored by the Conservation and Survey Division (CSD) at the University of Nebraska-Lincoln (UNL) (Ellis and Pederson 1986). The natural equilibrium of Nebraska's groundwater system has been affected by many things, but the use of water for irrigation has caused the most significant fluctuations in groundwater levels. There are over 3,500 observation wells in the state, which are measured once in the spring to establish preirrigation levels and once in the fall to measure the effect of annual irrigation usage and to pinpoint problem areas. The groundwater level data are obtained from the fall measurements for documenting annual and long-term changes. The largest use of groundwater in recent years has been for irrigation purposes. By the end of 1985, a total of 70,985 irrigation wells had been registered in the state, which pumped the water used in irrigating almost 85% of the estimated 3 million ha of irrigated land. The estimated amount of water pumped in 1985 was 9.62 × 10^7 m^3 (7.8 million acre-feet). About 60% of the wells are located in 12 counties in the northeastern, southwestern, and central Platte valley parts of the state (Ellis and Pederson 1986).

Stock and domestic wells in the sandhills usually penetrate the Pliocene/Pleistocene sands and gravels, while the high-capacity irrigation wells tap the Ogallala Group (Nebr. NRC 1984). There were 296 new irrigation wells installed in the state in 1985, which was less than the average of 935 for the previous five years (Ellis and Pederson 1986). This was the first time in the last five decades that no Nebraska county had more than 20 new irrigation wells registered during the year (Ellis and Pederson 1986). This was probably due to decreasing farm prices and

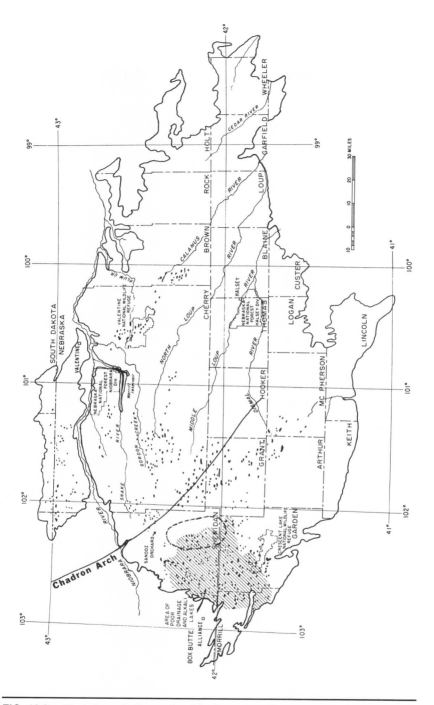

FIG. 12.2. Shaded area indicates closed basins region of the Nebraska sandhills, where there is typically no surface outflow. Black dots represent lakes of significant size. Approximate location of the Chadron Arch is shown by the southeast-trending line. Dashed line indicates approximate location of the groundwater high. Federally owned land within the sandhills is depicted. (*Adapted from Keech and Bentall 1971, with permission from the Conservation and Survey Division, Lincoln, Nebraska.*)

increasing costs of irrigation, plus a normal to above-normal amount of precipitation in 1978, 1979, and 1982–1984 (Ellis and Pederson 1986).

With the innovation of the center-pivot irrigation sprinkler system, the practice of irrigation moved from level lands to hilly terrain and sandy soils. Center-pivots allowed irrigation expansion into the sandhills only recently. Dreeszen (1984) stated that fewer than 150 wells had been registered by 1969, and he estimated that by 1984 there were just over 2,300 wells in the sandhills. Over half are located in the eastern sandhills counties of Brown, Rock, and Wheeler. The 1985 center-pivot inventory (Murray 1986) counted 398 pivots in Brown County, 487 in Rock County, and 533 in Wheeler County. Center-pivot system sizes vary from 20.2 to 202.4 ha, but most pivots irrigate about one quarter section, with the actual area averaging 53.8 ha (Murray 1986).

The Nebraska Natural Resources Commission (NRC) has been conducting a comprehensive water resources study in the eastern sandhills in Wheeler and Garfield counties. The study has found that farming utilizing irrigation has significantly increased through the 1970s, converting rangeland to cropland (Nebr. NRC 1984). In 1973 Garfield County had a total of 5 center-pivots and Wheeler County 73 (Nebr. NRC 1984). By 1985 Garfield County had increased to 86 pivots, and Wheeler County increased to 533 (Murray 1986). Wheeler County in particular has been rapidly developed, with a 3,414% increase in irrigated land between 1968–1980 (Nebr. NRC 1984). As a result of this intensified irrigation development, there have been some water supply problems. Some ranchers have reported the loss of stock and domestic wells, which they attribute to drawdowns from local irrigation pumping (Nebr. NRC 1984). Others have noted reduced production of wet meadow hay, either from drier conditions due to water-table declines, or from wetter conditions stemming from downslope runoff of excess irrigation water. If full development occurred, another problem could potentially be reduced stream flow. Some lands with excess water hazard have been developed, and, if drainage ditches have been constructed, problems such as flooding of hay meadows and wash-outs of county roads often occur downstream. I have personally witnessed such problems in Wheeler County.

Further study is continuing in order to more completely understand the hydrology and other water resource issues in the eastern Sandhills (Nebr. NRC 1984). Lawton (1986) has published data on the hydrogeology of water-quality monitoring transects in the eastern sandhills counties of Garfield, Wheeler, and Boone. The objectives of this study were to describe the hydrogeologic conditions, to establish baseline water chemistry data and pinpoint any existing water contamination, and to provide a network of monitoring wells for future water quality assessment. The results of the project allowed for the initial description of the hydrostratigraphy, groundwater flow conditions, and water chemistry of the area. However, even though general relationships were determined, specific predictions regarding the potential occurrence and fate of groundwater contaminants were not able to be made from existing data. Further sampling and data collection are planned to better assess the situation.

Lawton (1984) pointed out that the sandhills are a physiographic region with several hydrologic systems, with no definite boundaries. Five drainage basins make up the sandhills, all of which ultimately empty into the Missouri River: one-half lies within the Loup River drainage basin, one-fourth within the Niobrara River basin, and the remainder in the basins of the North Platte, Platte, and Elkhorn rivers.

Just a small percentage of stream flow in streams entirely within the sandhills is derived from surface runoff since most stream flow comes from the groundwater reservoir (Dreeszen 1984). Within the sandhills, stream flow rates are quite steady and discharge downstream increases greatly. This uniformity of flow is an indication of the regulating effects of the groundwater reservoir (Dreeszen 1984). Dreeszen (1984) pointed out that limited droughts, heavy rainfall events, and above-average wet seasons have scarcely any effects on the uniform stream flow rates. One-third of Nebraska's total average annual discharge from streams originates within the sandhills (Dreeszen 1984).

Lakes occur in the sandhills in three general areas: in the northeastern and extreme eastern part, along a southeast-trending line transecting parts of Sheridan, Cherry, Arthur, and McPherson counties, and in the closed basins region at the western edge. It is interesting to note that the Chadron Arch seems to have some geographic correlation with the central lake region (Fig. 12.2).

Ginsberg (1984, 1985) has suggested that three types of lakes exist in the sandhills: groundwater lakes, lakes in poor connection with the groundwater reservoir, and perched lakes with no groundwater connection. According to Ginsberg, groundwater lakes are fed by a local flow system where the water table is higher under the dunes than under the interdunal valley. Ginsberg indicated that there are variations of these lake-groundwater flow systems. One is where water flows into the lake from a local flow system while water leaves through the lake bottom near the middle and enters the groundwater reservoir. Another variation is a flow-through lake, which is a depression in the land surface extending below the water table, and in response to the slope of the saturated surface, groundwater flows in from the upgradient side and flows out the downgradient side (Hall 1976). Ginsberg (1984, 1985) speculated that a flow-though lake is often the middle lake in a string of lakes within an elongated interdunal valley. Lakes in poor connection with the groundwater have semipermeable bottom sediments. Ginsberg noted that these lakes often occur at different potential elevations than the local groundwater system. In Ginsberg's opinion, perched lakes have bottom sediments of quite low permeability and an unsaturated zone lies between the lake bottom and the water table. As a result, water levels in perched lakes are totally unrelated to water levels in the groundwater reservoir.

Ginsberg (1984, 1985) noted that lakes along and east of the Chadron Arch usually have some degree of hydraulic connection with the groundwater, are often fed by springs or seeps, and a few have surface outflow. These lakes tend to be only slightly alkaline. Lakes west of the arch are mostly highly alkaline, but the reason for this has not been determined. Ginsberg stated that some of the poorly connected and perched lakes do function as evaporitic basins, but some mechanism exists causing even some of the groundwater lakes to become alkaline. Ginsberg suggested that the chemical nature of the local strata through which the contributing groundwater passes may affect a lake's alkalinity.

Winter (Chap. 2) has emphasized that local groundwater flow systems most often have direct interaction with surface water bodies and that the configuration of the water table around a water body is important when determining seepage conditions. According to his data, where the water table slopes into a lake, groundwater discharge occurs, and where the water table slopes away from a lake, groundwater recharge occurs. Sites of groundwater discharge tend to be permanent water bodies that are relatively saline, and sites of groundwater recharge tend to be temporary and relatively fresh. Winter has indicated that, since constantly changing recharge conditions cause complex groundwater flow patterns, freshwater seeps or springs are often found discharging into saline lakes. He also noted that groundwater discharge contributed from local-flow systems and from regional flow systems can greatly vary between lakes, so the overall chemistries of the lakes also vary greatly.

According to LaBaugh (Chap. 3), lake water chemistry is affected by climatic or seasonal variations and groundwater. LaBaugh has noted that differences in concentration of major ions and salinity between adjacent water bodies are a function of the position of the wetland in the local groundwater flow system and may be related to the variability of the geologic and hydrologic setting of the wetland. He has stressed that interpretion of groundwater chemistry must be done separately from interpretation of lake water chemistry. Analysis of water from piezometers installed near a lake at Crescent Lake National Wildlife Refuge (CLNWR) in the western sandhills revealed that the well water was not at all similar to the groundwater moving into or out of the lake. La-

Baugh has found that the chemical composition of lakes can affect the chemistry of adjacent groundwater systems. Analyzing dissolved organic carbon values and other chemical constituents, LaBaugh discovered low values prevalent in areas of groundwater recharge and high values in areas of groundwater discharge. LaBaugh's studies demonstrate that water chemistry is an important tool in understanding the hydrology of wetlands.

Work on airborne thermal mapping of a flow-through lake in CLNWR using the Thermal Infrared Multispectral Scanner (TIMS) has recently been completed (Rundquist et al. 1985). This study looked at three different lakes and utilized thermal imagery to distinguish the relative temperature differences of lake surfaces. Rundquist et al. found that only one lake exhibited a strong flow-through signature, with cold water entering at the north end, mixing or slight warming evident in the middle, and the warmest water found at the south end. The water table is higher at the north end, and flowing springs have been noted here. Near the south end is the perennially flowing Blue Creek. These data confirm that the lake is a flow-through lake. Based upon the results of this study, contributions to regional hydrologic models may be possible, and sandhills lakes could be classified according to their thermal patterns. For other investigations utilizing TIMS data in the sandhills, see Queen et al. (1984) and Queen (1984).

Since 1981, Winter (Chap. 2) has been studying the relationship between groundwater and lakes in CLNWR. He has found that the configuration of the water table beneath the dunes varies depending upon dune topography and internal dune structure. If the topography between lakes is hummocky, groundwater recharge occurs at topographic lows causing water table mounds under the dunes, which prevent groundwater flow from a lake of higher elevation to one of lower elevation. If the dune between two lakes is sharply ridged, localized recharge does not occur, causing a water table trough between lakes. Winter has stated that lakes positioned along an elevational gradient and parallel to the principal direction of regional flow generally tend to have seepage from higher lakes to lower lakes.

During vegetational studies in the western sandhills, Harrison (n.d.) speculated that precipitation percolating through poorly vegetated, coarse-textured dune sands provides most of the water for local groundwater recharge. Significant recharge events do not usually occur during the growing season according to Harrison. He stated that only above-average precipitation amounts in winter or early spring provide sufficient moisture for recharge. Finer-textured dry valley soils with higher water-holding capacities support shallowly rooted grass species that efficiently absorb all available soil moisture. As such, Harrison concluded that no groundwater recharge occurs in these sites except in extremely wet years.

In efforts to learn more about sandhills lakes, monitoring their areal extent over time has been investigated. A report by Buckwalter (1983) describes the methods and results of the Sandhills Lake Monitoring Project. This project utilized 1973–1978 Landsat MSS imagery and visual interpretation techniques to measure the surface area of seven lakes in two test sites, one in the western part and one in the eastern. Results indicated that the western lakes steadily decreased in size from spring to fall. Since only two lakes were measured in the eastern region, no conclusive results were obtained. However, it was noted that one lake remained relatively stable and the other exhibited pronounced seasonal fluctuations probably related to precipitation events.

Another more recent project conducted by Lawson et al. (1985) utilized Landsat digital data for April to October 1979–1983 in order to monitor fluctuations in surface-water area of lakes in Valentine National Wildlife Refuge (VNWR) and CLNWR. Another objective of the study was to link the surface-water fluctuations with groundwater levels and precipitation data. Results indicated that using computer-compatible Landsat digital data is a more accurate technique than utilizing visual interpretation techniques for multitemporal measurements of lake fluctuations. However, the relationship between groundwater and precipitation could only be examined in a limited way due to missing ground-truth data. Correlation coefficients were computed, but no significant pattern emerged. Some water table wells were positively (but not significantly) correlated to all precipitation-lagged totals, and others were negatively correlated. This indicated to the authors that groundwater levels decreased at some wells with increased precipitation, while the reverse was true at others. In analyzing the relationship between precipitation and lake area, Lawson et al. found that larger lakes exhibit greater variation than do smaller lakes. Differences were also noted between lakes in VNWR and CLNWR. Lakes within CLNWR exhibit maxima in June and minima in October. Lakes within VNWR have marked dips in midseason. When examining the relationship of lake size and precipitation time, their data indicated that all lakes in CLNWR show highest correlation between lake size and the precipitation index for 45 days prior to lake measurement. No evidence of this relationship was found for lakes in VNWR, indicating the possibility of hydraulic connection with the groundwater. Since CLNWR is located within the closed basins region, the lakes may more directly respond to precipitation patterns.

In reviewing these recent papers (Buckwalter 1983; Ginsberg 1984, 1985; Lawson et al. 1985; Rundquist et al. 1985; Winter, Chap. 2) on sandhills lakes and their hydrological relationships, it is apparent that the authors more or less agree upon a few general patterns of the differences between lakes in the western sandhills and lakes in the eastern sandhills. Lakes in the western region appear to depend upon precipitation to a greater extent than lakes in the eastern region, which typically have some degree of connection with the groundwater reservoir. It follows, then, that lakes in the western part are more variable in areal extent than those in the eastern part. Finally, lakes in the western region tend to be more alkaline than lakes in the eastern region.

GROUNDWATER QUALITY

Since 1930 CSD-UNL in cooperation with the U.S. Geological Survey (USGS) Water Resources Division has been monitoring groundwater quality, analyzing a total of 17 physical, chemical, and biological parameters on a monthly basis, whereas heavy metals and pesticides are analyzed quarterly (Engberg and Spalding 1978; Nebr. NRC 1984). Groundwater used for municipal, domestic, livestock, irrigation, and industrial supplies is generally of good quality, with nitrate the constituent most likely to exceed health limits (Engberg and Spalding 1978). The major constituents of dissolved solids in Nebraska's groundwater, according to Engberg and Spalding (1978), are calcium, magnesium, sodium, potassium, bicarbonate, sulfate, chloride, and silica. Concentration of dissolved solids for the sandhills is less than 200 mg/l since most soluble material has already been leached from the porous sands (Engberg and Spalding 1978). Hardness of groundwater, reported as calcium carbonate, ranges between 0–60 mg/l in much of the central sandhills and ranges between 61–120 mg/l in the remainder of the region (Engberg and Spalding 1978). For a summary of other groundwater constituents in the sandhills, see Table 12.1.

Within the past 30 years, concentrations of nitrate (reported as N) in the groundwater have been a growing source of concern, especially in the Middle Platte River Basin and in a portion of Holt County in northeast Nebraska (Engberg 1967; Engberg and Spalding 1978; Nebr. NRC 1984). The primary source of nitrate in groundwater is fertilizer (Hergert 1984; Martin 1984). Hergert (1984) stated that nitrate losses from irrigated corn in the sandhills on Valentine sand range between 35–45 lb N/a/yr on unfertilized plots and over 90 lb N/a/yr on overfertilized plots. This demonstrates to Hergert that, even with the most careful fertilizer management, some nitrate will be lost to the groundwater reservoir. Hergert stressed the importance of site selection and spacing of center-pivot systems when planning to irrigate in the sandhills, because these

TABLE 12.1. Summary of groundwater constituents for the Nebraska sandhills

Dissolved solids	Hardness (CaCO₃)	Alkalinity[a]	Na⁺ & K⁺	SiO₂	NO₃[b]	SO₄²⁻	Cl⁻	F⁻	B[c]	Mn[c]	Se[c]	P[c]	Fe³⁺[c]
<200	0–120	<100	0–20	>50	<10	0–10	0–10	<0.3	<330	<50	0–10	>16	<100

Source: Adapted from Engberg and Spalding 1978.
Note: Concentrations are expressed as mg/l unless otherwise noted.
[a]Expressed as an equivalent amount of calcium carbonate.
[b]Nitrate concentrations too variable to generalize, but concentrations are increasing in all areas of Nebraska with increased agricultural development.
[c]Concentrations expressed in μg/l.

decisions ultimately affect the groundwater quality of the region. There has been a great deal of research done addressing this and other groundwater quality problems in the state. Some of this may be found in: Engberg (1967), Watts (1977), Hergert (1978, 1983, 1984), Junk et al. (1980), Spalding and Exner (1980), Hergert and Goeke (1981), Martin (1984), Nebr. NRC (1984), Adelman et al. (1985), and Lawton (1986).

LIMNOLOGY OF THE LAKES

The most extensive limnological investigation of sandhills lakes was conducted by McCarraher (1977), whose study spanned 18 years. All data presented in this section are based upon this work unless otherwise stated. McCarraher collected data from 1,640 lakes greater than 4 ha in size across the sandhills. Within the 1977 report, McCarraher has provided an extensive catalogue of sandhills lakes by county, including location, surface area, depth, alkalinity, drainage conditions, and fisheries information. Sandhills lakes are rather shallow, with an average depth of 0.98 m. The deepest lake is Blue Lake in Garden County with a depth of 4.2 m. For a brief summary of the general characteristics of lakes in the sandhills, see Table 12.2.

McCarraher also observed that lakes in the eastern two-thirds of the sandhills are generally dependent upon groundwater, most have surface drainage, and many have flowing springs or seeps that regulate lake levels and possibly provide dilution sources where alkalinity may be a problem. In the closed basins region where there is little surface drainage, many lakes are maintained by surface runoff rather than groundwater inflow, and many have impervious bottom sediments. These poorly drained lakes comprise about 94% of the strongly alkaline lakes found in the sandhills as a whole. McCarraher emphasized that all lakes in the sandhills are of the sodium and potassium-bicarbonate-carbonate-hydroxide types (See McCarraher 1971, 1972b.). Pointing out that few similar regions in the world contain such a large number of alkaline mineralized eutrophic lakes, McCarraher stressed that the sandhills is a "unique environmental ecosystem."

McCarraher (1959a) reported that 0.9–1.5 m of water evaporates annually from the lakes. Most lakes have a total dissolved solids content between 150–65,000 ppm (one lake had 448,000 ppm), and the dissolved salt content varies between 0.01–44.0% (McCarraher 1959a). For moderate to strongly alkaline lakes the cation dominance takes the following order: $Na^+ > K^+ > Mg^{2+} > Ca^{2+}$; anionic dominance for slightly to medium alkaline lakes is: $HCO_3^- > CO_3^{2-} > SO_4^{2-} > Cl^-$ (McCarraher 1977). The pH is another important factor and ranges between 7.8–10.8, with a mean of 9.4.

Wind action is the primary means of lake aeration. Dissolved oxygen content is inversely proportional to water temperature and decreases as alkalinity increases in lakes over 12,000 mg/l. No thermal stratification is evident in any lake, and water temperature fluctuates seasonally. Strongly alkaline lakes in Garden and Sheridan counties warm earlier in the spring and retain heat longer in the fall than less alkaline lakes. McCarraher has tabulated a chronolog of water quality data for lakes by county in his 1977 report.

McCarraher (1972b, 1977) estimated that there are between 2,000 and 2,400 intermittent, or playa, lakes (<0.25 ha) throughout the sandhills. Many of the larger, highly mineralized playas are located in the closed basins district. East of there are the less mineralized lakes where fluctuating groundwater is at the surface in interdunal valleys or depressions; these may also be fed by surface runoff. Approximately 60% of the playa lakes are alkaline eutrophic of the sodium bicarbonate type, and 40% range from strongly alkaline sodium-potassium hydroxide type to the sodium carbonate types. All playas have quite low concentrations of chlorides and sulfates. According to McCarraher, all of these characteristics set the playa lakes of Nebraska apart from the majority of playas in the American Southwest. In all lake types, maximum and minimum alkalinity concentration follows a seasonal pattern, with the greatest degree of fluctuation found in the moderately to strongly alkaline lakes.

SANDHILLS WETLANDS

Classification and Inventory

Based upon the Cowardin Classification System (Cowardin et al. 1979), the Nebraska sandhills wetlands fall within the Lacustrine and Palustrine systems, with a small percent in the Riverine system. Most wetlands along sandhills streams do not conform with their definition of Riverine systems. However, there are a few areas of aquatic communities that do conform (pers. obser.). In addition, seeps and springs are included in the Riverine system, and these are quite common along sandhills streams. Based upon personal observations, the wetland types present in the sandhills are enumerated in Table 12.3. A more comprehensive and accurate inventory is currently being completed by the U.S. Fish and Wildlife Service (USFWS) for the National Wetland Inventory in Nebraska in conjunction with the U.S. Environmental Protection Agency and the Nebraska Department of Environmental Control based

TABLE 12.2. Summary of lakes (>4 ha) within the sandhills counties based on the study of 1,640 lakes by McCarraher (1977)

County	Number of lakes	Surface area (ha)	Range of surface area (ha)	Mean depth (m)	Alkalinity	Range of TDS[a] (ppm)	pH
Arthur	30	1,520	7.3–647.8	0.8	Slight to moderate	158–1,400	7.9–9.5
Brown	17	1,034	8.0–250.0	0.9	Slight[b]	110–2,736	7.8–10.0
Box Butte	9	2,116	6.5–35.6	0.7	Medium to moderate	NA	NA
Cherry	408	10,650	1.0–920.0	1.1	Slight[c]	95–25,500	6.8–10.8
Garden	174[d]	5,368	4.0–393.0	0.8	Slight to strong	198–82,100	7.7–10.8
Grant	46[e]	1,451	4.0–151.0	1.0	Slight to medium	145–900	8.0–9.3
Holt	17	850	6.0–150.0	1.2	Slight	195–2,980	8.2–9.6
Logan	4	62	6.0–21.0	0.6	Slight	NA	NA
McPherson	18	246	4.0–78.0	0.8	Slight	148–3,200	8.2–8.9
Morrill	22	1,072	6.5–97.2	0.8	Moderate to strong	2,190–82,000	8.6–10.2
Rock	18	639	13.0–133.2	0.8	Slight	120–1,693	7.0–9.0
Sheridan	521[f]	6,622	5.7–362.3	0.7	Slight to strong	210–79,902	8.1–10.7
Wheeler	27	86	0.1–9.0	NA[g]	Slight	NA	NA

[a]Total dissolved solids.
[b]Four lakes are strongly alkaline.
[c]10 percent are medium to strongly alkaline.
[d]Estimate of 145 lakes <4 ha are present also, many of which are ephemeral and highly alkaline.
[e]Also 24 playa lakes present (<4 ha).
[f]Only 215 of these have permanent surface water >4 ha.
[g]Most have maximum depths of <1.2 m.

TABLE 12.3.   Types of sandhills wetlands based upon the Cowardin Classifica-
              tion System

Lacustrine system		
Subsystem	Class	Subclass
Limnetic	Unconsolidated bottom	
	Aquatic bed	Algal
		Rooted vascular
		Floating vascular
Littoral	Unconsolidated shore	
	Emergent wetland	Persistent
		Nonpersistent

Palustrine system	
Class	Subclass
Unconsolidated bottom	
Unconsolidated shore	
Aquatic bed	Algal
	Rooted vascular
	Floating vascular
Emergent wetland	Persistent
	Nonpersistent

Riverine system		
Subsystem	Class	Subclass
Lower perennial	Unconsolidated bottom	
	Unconsolidated shore	
	Aquatic bed	Algal
		Rooted vascular
		Floating vascular
	Emergent wetland	Nonpersistent

Source: Adapted from Cowardin et al. 1979.

upon data obtained from color-infrared aerial photography flown in 1982 (Boettcher 1984).

Rundquist (1983) discussed seven different wetland inventories that measured some aspect of sandhills wetlands. These included the Pre-1950 Survey and 1952–1953 Survey (U.S. Dept. Interior 1955a), 1954–1955 Survey (U.S. Dept. Interior 1955b), 1954–1960 Sandhill Lake Survey (McCarraher 1960a), 1962–1968 Wetland Survey (McMurtrey et al. 1972), 1974–1975 Wetland Inventory (Seevers et al. 1975), and the Lindbergh Project (Rundquist and Linden 1979) which led up to the 1979–1980 Wetland Inventory of the Northern Great Plains (Turner and Rundquist 1980). In the Turner and Rundquist (1980) and Rundquist et al. (1981) wetland inventories, the sandhills wetlands were classified into these categories: open water, marsh, riparian vegetation, and subirrigated meadow. Based upon the figures of Rundquist et al. (1981) for sandhills counties, the total areal extent of these wetlands were: 51,655.75 ha open water, 26,224.20 ha marsh, 9,272.60 ha riparian vegetation, 470,439.94 ha subirrigated meadow, and 557,591.53 ha overall total wetland area. In addition to these projects (Rundquist and Linden 1979; Turner and Rundquist 1980; Rundquist et al. 1981), further research evaluating and mapping sandhills wetlands utilizing remote sensing has been completed. (See Gilbert 1980; Gilbert et al. 1980; Linden 1984; Rundquist et al. in press.)

Vegetation

The flora of the sandhills was first extensively studied by Rydberg (1895). In 1893 Rydberg surveyed a portion of the central sandhills, but he did not visit the closed basins region. In his flora Rydberg presented a catalogue of species including notes on each species. Pool (1914) completed a more thorough study on sandhills vegetation. He divided the flora into formations that were subdivided into associations. Within his lowland formation category he included a "water-plant formation," "marsh formation" and "meadow formation." Pool's observations were astute and are still quite useful. McAtee (1941) compiled an extensive report on the wild-duck foods of the sandhills. This report was based upon the work of a UNL graduate student, Ray Thomson, who conducted research in 1915 on 44 lakes in Brown, Cherry and Garden counties. This report provides a listing of species by county by lake, along with general descriptions of the lakes, some notes on the vegetational distribution, and some notes on the value of plant species as waterfowl food. Tolstead (1942) conducted an intensive study on the vegetation of northern Cherry County in VNWR and Ft. Niobrara National Wildlife Refuge (FNNWR). He provided important information on microclimatological, environmental, and physical parameters, in addition to extensive data on vegetational communities. Tolstead also discussed the dominant species in detail and presented graphs illustrating root systems of several principal species. Other information on wetland vegetation may be found in Webber (1889, 1890), Kolstad (1966), Lindstrom (1968), Mahoney (1977), and Gilbert (1980).

The sandhills support a surprising variety of plant communities. The dominant vegetation is usually thought of as "sandhills prairie," which is a type of mixed-grass prairie including a large number of xerophytic psammophytes. However, since the water table is close to the surface in many interdunal valleys, there are sharp moisture gradients. As a result, there are obvious vegetational zones along the gradient, the composition of which depends upon depth to the water table and, in drier areas, upon soil texture (Rydberg 1895; Pool 1914; Frolik and Keim 1933; Tolstead 1942; Ehlers et al. 1952; Burzlaff 1962; Moore and Rhoades 1966; Brouse and Burzlaff 1968; Barnes and Harrison 1982; Barnes et al. 1984; Novacek 1986). Plants of the upland dune prairie are not in contact with the water table and are typically sand-binding species, in addition to several xerophytic Great Plains species. Blow-outs are stabilized by rhizomatous grasses, such as *Redfielda flexuosa, Muhlenbergia pungens,* and *Calamovilfa longifolia.* Upland dunes are dominated by *Andropogon hallii, Bouteloua hirsuta, Stipa comata,* and *Yucca glauca.* Dry valleys are also characterized by plants not in contact with the water table; these include *Andropogon scoparius, Bouteloua gracilis,* and *Panicum virgatum* (Novacek, unpubl. data).

A subirrigated meadow, or wet meadow, is a topographically broad, flat area where the water table is only a few decimeters below the land surface and where plants are in contact with the water table throughout the growing season. Depending upon the depth to the water table, wet meadows exhibit at least two vegetational communities (Tolstead 1942; Novacek 1986). Where the water is approximately 1 m below the surface, tall grasses typical of true prairie grow, such as *Andropogon gerardi* and *Sorghastrum nutans.* Where the water table ranges between 0.5 and 1.0 m below the surface, the characteristic graminoids are *Calamagrostis* spp., *Spartina* spp., *Juncus* spp., *Carex* spp., and many other members of the sedge family. In many wet meadows, ranchers have planted *Agrostis stolonifera* and *Phlelum pratense* in addition to several nonnative legumes (Novacek, unpubl. data).

Vegetational communities in wet meadows typically vary somewhat in areal extent (Tolstead 1942). Tolstead documented these changes during his four-year study, but he noticed no total loss of community. Sather (1958) mapped the cyclical climatic changes of vegetation during his four-year-study in VNWR. There is general agreement that the depth to the water table is an important factor in controlling vegetative structure in wet meadows (Frolik and Keim 1933; Tolstead 1942; Ehlers et al. 1952; Moore and Rhoades 1966; Brouse and Burzlaff 1968; Novacek 1986). All of these workers have also noted seasonal fluctuations in the water table. The highest level is normally found in early spring and the lowest level in early autumn. Periodical or cyclical fluctuations of the water table also occur (Tolstead 1942; Moore and Rhoades 1966). Tolstead (1942) stated that periodic fluctuations result from the cyclic occurrence of deficient or excessive precipitation. Tolstead also recorded daily fluctuations in the water table, which he attributed to extraction by plant roots from the capillary fringe above the water table and subsequent transpiration. Daily fluctuations are also related to daily local climatic conditions.

Other characteristics of wet meadows distinguish them from drier upland dune sites. Surface soil moisture of wet meadows is closely associated with water table levels (Moore and Rhoades 1966). Soil temperatures of wet meadows are cooler than soil temperatures of dunes (Tolstead 1942). Evaporation rates increase from wet meadows to upland dunes (Tolstead 1942). Higher humidity percentages are found in wet meadow vegetation than in dune vegetation (Tolstead 1942). Wet meadow soils are sandy enough that the water table does not affect oxygen content, unless there is a heavy precipitation event (Moore and Rhoades 1966). Not only does the depth to the water table affect vegetational productivity, but also these other favorable microclimatological factors create optimal growing conditions in wet meadows.

An extensive ecological study conducted on the algae of sandhills lakes was completed by Anderson and Walker (1920). Some species of algae were addressed in work done by Schnagl (1980). McCarraher (1977) presented a discussion and a table listing 71 algal genera collected from 34 sandhills lakes varying in water quality from slightly alkaline to strongly alkaline. In addition, he reproduced a list from an unpublished 1972 field collection of G. W. Prescott for three sandhills lakes.

Within the more alkaline sandhills lakes, the phytoplankton is composed almost exclusively of blue-green algae, including species of *Microcystis, Aphanizomenon,* and *Anabaena* (McCarraher 1977). Algal species of *Phormidium, Oscillatoria, Nostoc, Spirogyra, Coleochaete,* and *Chaetophora* are often found in emergent zones of many lakes (McCarraher 1977). Numerous algal blooms have been observed on strongly alkaline lakes, and, according to McCarraher (1977), the genera involved include *Oscillatoria, Spirulina,* and *Anthrospira.* In slight to medium alkaline lakes, the blooms consist of *Microcystis, Anabaena, Cladophora, Cosmarium,* and *Oscillatoria* (McCarraher 1977). McCarraher (1977) noted that diatom blooms periodically occur depending upon aeration and mineralization of nitrogen-containing organic matter. McCarraher also pointed out that the taxa and the ecology of algae within the sandhills is still poorly known due to the lack of systematic surveys.

Gibson (1976) utilized diatom fossils from sediment cores from three lakes in Sheridan County to determine the relative ages of the lakes. He found them to be quite young, ranging from 100 to 300 years old. Gibson also determined that the areas were probably marshes for several decades prior to becoming lakes. This is an interesting finding, and one that should be investigated by geologists, climatologists, or phytogeographers.

The Characeae of Nebraska has been extensively studied by Daily (1944) and Kiener (1944). (See also Daily and Kiener 1956.) Species of *Chara* are some of the most common submergent plants in sandhills lakes (McCarraher 1977). *Chara fragilis* is abundant in medium to moderately alkaline lakes, and *C. vulgaris* occurs in moderately to strongly alkaline lakes, where *C. verrucosa* may also be found according to McCarraher (1977). He stated that *C. coronata* is most often found in the intermittent playa lakes. Other species of *Chara* in sandhills wetlands include: *C. aspera, C. contraria, C. evoluta, C. excelsa,* and *C. kieneri* (McCarraher 1977). In Pool's water-plant formation, he singled out the Stonewort-Naiad association, composed of *Chara* spp., *Najas flexilis,* and *Zannichellia palustris* in shallow, quiet water above an open sandy bottom. Pool also noted that large numbers of various periphyton species were present, but did not indicate which species. Other vascular plants he noted occurring in this association were *Ruppia maritima* and *Eleocharis acicularis.* Pool additionally noted that some small lakes were completely dominated by species of *Chara.*

Recently much work on the bryophytes of Nebraska has been completed. Churchill (1976, 1977, 1982, 1985) has probably contributed the greatest amount toward understanding the moss flora. Spessard (1982) undertook a bryological survey of north-central Nebraska. Koch (1971) investigated the Pottiaceae of the state. Churchill and Redfearn (1977) reported on the Hepaticae and Anthrocerotae of the state. A county listing of the pteridophytes of Nebraska is included in Petrick-Ott (1975).

The hydrophytic communities of the sandhills vary depending upon the alkalinity of the waters. Most of the wetlands in the eastern two-thirds of the sandhills are only slightly alkaline, so they support a wide variety of plants. An abbreviated list of hydrophytic vascular plants of sandhills wetlands is included in Table 12.4.

The most common submergent vascular plant across the entire region is *Potamogeton pectinatus* (Novacek unpubl. data). McCarraher (1977) found this species present in 94% of the lakes he studied. McAtee (1941) indicated that this species is an extremely important duck food. McCarraher (1977) reported that *P. pectinatus,* along with *Ruppia maritima,* can withstand alkalinities up to 10,000 mg/l and a pH of 10.2.

The most common emergents throughout the sandhills are *Scirpus acutus* and *S. americanus;* while *Typha latifolia* and *Phragmites australis* are locally common (Novacek unpubl. data). McCarraher (1977) noted that *P. australis* is seldom found in lakes where alkalinity is greater than 15,000 mg/l, and *Typha latifolia* is not found where alkalinity exceeds 10,000 mg/l. *Zizania aquatica* had been reported as fairly common at the turn of the century (Rydberg 1895; Pool 1914; Anderson and Walker 1920; McAtee 1941) and has been known from seven sandhills counties. However, this species is now relatively rare, found mostly in slightly alkaline lakes and along sluggish streams in the eastern half (McCarraher 1977; Novacek unpubl. data).

The shoreline emergents able to withstand lakes with a pH of 10.5 and alkalinity values up to 10,000 mg/l are *Scirpus americanus* and *Distichlis spicata* var. *stricta* (McCarraher 1959a). These strongly alkaline lakes support no submergent vascular plants, but they do support

TABLE 12.4. List of common hydrophytic vascular plants found in the sandhills of Nebraska

Floating species
  Lemna minor
  Lemna perpusilla
  Lemna trisulca
  Spirodela polyrhiza
  Utricularia vulgaris
  Wolffia columbiana

Submergents
  Ceratophyllum demersum
  Myriophyllum spicatum var. *exalbescens*
  Najas flexilis
  Najas guadalupensis
  Potamogeton foliosus
  Potamogeton gramineus
  Potamogeton illinoensis
  Potamogeton natans
  Potamogeton nodosus
  Potamogeton pectinatus
  Potamogeton pusillus
  Potamogeton richardsonii
  Potamogeton zosteriformis
  Ranunculus aquatilis
  Ranunculus longirostris
  Ruppia maritima
  Zannichellia palustris

Semiaquatic species[b]
  Bidens cernua
  Bidens coronata
  Bidens frondosa
  Carex comosa
  Carex hystericina
  Carex lanuginosa
  Carex vulpinoidea
  Cyperus aristatus
  Cyperus strigosus
  Eleocharis acicularis
  Eleocharis erythropoda
  Eleocharis macrostachya
  Eupatorium maculatum
  Glyceria grandis
  Helenium autumnale
  Juncus nodosus
  Juncus torreyi
  Lobelia siphilitica
  Lycopus asper
  Lythrum dacotanum
  Phalaris arundinacea
  Rumex maritima
  Scutellaria galericulata
  Sparganium eurycarpum
  Spartina pectinata
  Triglochin maritima
  Verbena hastata

Emergents[a]
  Alisma plantago-aquatica
  Asclepias incarnata
  Beckmannia syzigachne
  Campanula aparinoides
  Carex stipata
  Cicuta maculata
  Echinochloa muricata
  Eupatorium perfoliatum
  Helianthus nuttallii
  Leersia oryzoides
  Leptochloa fascicularis
  Lycopus americanus
  Lysimachia thyrsiflora
  Mimulus glabratus
  Phragmites australis
  Polygonum amphibium
  Polygonum coccineum
  Polygonum lapathifolium
  Sagittaria cuneata
  Sagittaria latifolia
  Scirpus acutus
  Scirpus americanus
  Scirpus fluviatilis
  Scirpus validus
  Scutellaria lateriflora
  Thelypteris palustris
  Typha latifolia

Subirrigated meadow species
  Agalinis tenuifolia
  Agrostis stolonifera
  Calamagrostis canadensis
  Calamagrostis inexpansa
  Carex brevior
  Carex meadii
  Carex nebraskensis
  Carex praegracilis
  Carex sartwellii
  Carex scoparia
  Carex stricta
  Crepis runcinata[c]
  Cyperus rivularis
  Cyperus strigosus
  Distichlis spicata var. *stricta*
  Eleocharis erythropoda
  Fimbristylis puberula var. *interior*
  Galium trifidum
  Hemicarpha micrantha
  Hypoxis hirsuta
  Juncus balticus
  Juncus dudleyi
  Juncus interior
  Juncus torreyi
  Lobelia spicata
  Lythrum dacotanum
  Plantago eriopoda[c]
  Spartina gracilis[c]
  Spartina pectinata
  Sphenopholis obtusata
  Spiranthes magnicamporum

Source: Adapted from Novacek, unpublished data.
[a]Some of these species may also be categorized as semiaquatics.
[b]Some of these species may also be found in subirrigated meadows.
[c]Found only in the closed basins region.

phytoplankton composed mostly of blue-green algae (McCarraher 1970). *Distichlis* is quite common in the closed basins region, but it is not usually found along lakes that are slightly alkaline (Novacek unpubl. data).

The most common shrubby species of sandhills wetlands are *Amorpha fruticosa* and *Salix exigua* (Novacek unpubl. data). Other thicket-forming species include *Salix petiolaris, S. rigida,* and *Cornus stolonifera.* Of the few trees found along sandhills wetlands, *Populus deltoides* and *Salix amygdaloides* predominate. *Celtis occidentalis, Fraxinus pennsylvanica, Ulmus americana,* and *Acer negundo* may be found associated with some lakes and streams (Novacek, unpubl. data).

Another type of wetland peculiar to the sandhills occurs where a blow-out intersects the water table. The blow-outs are predominantly caused by cattle trampling and often occur near fence lines. Pool (1914) called these "blow-out ponds." A few aquatic species colonize these areas, which often become completely dominated by *Eleocharis acicularis* (Novacek unpubl. data). An additional wetland type is formed by windmill tank overflows that are characterized by typical palustrine vegetation. At times aquatic vegetation will colonize the windmill tanks themselves, in which case *Ceratophyllum demersum* is often the most common (Novacek unpubl. data).

Fisheries

A multiauthored special issue of the *NEBRASKAland Magazine* (Bouc 1987) deals with the fish, fisheries, and aquatic resource issues of Nebraska. This is an impressive and informative collection of articles in full color. An identification key is also included. Descriptions of Nebraska's fishes, photographs, distribution maps, and a list of uncommon species may also be found in Morris et al. (1972). In his report on sandhills lakes, McCarraher (1977) extensively addresses fisheries and fish species distribution, in addition to presenting ecological data relating to sport fishery for Hackberry Lake in CLNWR and Hudson Lake in Cherry County.

According to McCarraher (1959a), there are 19 species of freshwater fish inhabiting lakes of the sandhills. At the time of his 1959 report, he noted that approximately 58% of the lakes were supportive of fish life, 33% were nonsupportive, and 9% were borderline. He pointed to bicarbonate alkalinity as the limiting factor. All species disappear from lakes with bicarbonate values exceeding 900 mg/l except the fathead minnow, which tolerates up to 1,500 mg/l (McCarraher 1959a, 1962, 1969, 1971, 1977; McCarraher and Thomas 1968).

For other reports on fishes in sandhills lakes, see Bennet and Pedley (1931), McCarraher (1959b, 1959c, 1960b, 1962, 1969), McCarraher and

Gregory (1970) and McCarraher and Thomas (1968). Problems in fisheries management have been addressed by McCarraher (1969, 1971, 1977) and by Shoenecker (1971). Of the 1,640 lakes investigated by Mc-Carraher (1969), only 22% had no problems with fish winterkill. McCarraher noted that lake bottom types were directly related to winterkill conditions. Lakes with silt basins or soft muck with abundant aquatic vegetation often experienced winterkill, because as plants decompose in ice-capped shallow lakes, CO_2 concentrations may build up to toxic levels. McCarraher pointed out that, due to excessive blue-green algal blooms, some lakes have experienced summer fish kill. The decomposition of blue-green algae deprives the system of dissolved oxygen and may also release hydroxylamine and hydrogen sulfide, both highly toxic substances. He indicated that there have been reports of cattle deaths or illness due to drinking waters contaminated with algal toxicants. Since most lakes are either too shallow or too high in alkalinity, McCarraher stated that only about 14% of the sandhills lakes he studied are suitable for sport fishery.

No fish species are indigenous to the 2,500 closed basins region wetlands (Brennan pers. comm.). Since settlement, however, many species have been introduced to the larger, deeper lakes. Major sport fishes of the sandhills are northern pike, largemouth bass, bluegill, and yellow perch (McCarraher 1977). According to Brennan (pers. comm.), several fish are native to sandhills rivers, including northern pike, red horse sucker, channel catfish, perch, and species of dace and minnow. A brief list of fishes present in the sandhills is included in Table 12.5.

Invertebrates

The abundance of zooplankton in sandhills lakes depends upon the seasonal thermal regime and the seasonal variation in dissolved oxygen (McCarraher 1977). The most widely distributed zooplankter in the sandhills is *Cyclops bicuspidatus* (McCarraher 1977). Large numbers of

TABLE 12.5. Fish species present in the sandhills

Cyprinus carpio	*Micropterus salmoides*
(Carp)	(Largemouth bass)
Esox americanus vermiculatus	*Notemigonus crysoleucas*
(Grass pickerel)	(Golden shiner)
Esox lucius	*Perca flavescens*
(Northern pike)	(Yellow perch)
Ictalurus melas	*Pimephales promelas*
(Black bullhead)	(Fathead minnow)
Lepomis cyanellus	*Pomoxis nigromaculatus*
(Green sunfish)	(Black crappie)
Lepomis macrochirus	*Stizostedion vitreum*
(Bluegill)	(Walleye)

Source: Adapted from McCarraher 1977.

rotifers are present in most lakes, especially the more alkaline ones, with *Brachionus plicitilis* being the most widely distributed (McCarraher 1977). The amphipod, *Hyallela azteca,* is found in only 18% of sandhills lakes according to McCarraher (1977). Distribution data from selected lakes by county are presented in McCarraher (1977). This report also contains data on the occurrence of gastropods in relation to selected water quality parameters and an extensive table of the distribution of phyllopods with water quality data. Further work on copepods may be found in Holland (1980). For a summary of the invertebrates within sandhills wetlands, see Table 12.6.

TABLE 12.6.   Summary of invertebrates from sandhills wetlands

Phyllum Arthropoda	
Class Crustacea	

Subclass Branchipoda	
Anostracans	Conchostracans
Artemia salina	*Cyzicus mexicanus*
Branchinecta campestris	Notostracans
Branchinecta lindahli	*Lepidurus couesii*
Branchinecta mackini	
Chirocephalopsis bundyi	Subclass Copepoda
Eubranchipus ornatus	Calanoid Copepods
Streptocephalus seali	*Diaptomus clavipes*
Cladocerans	*Diaptomus nevadensis*
Alona sp.	*Diaptomus sicilis*
Bosmina coregoni	*Diaptomus siciloides*
Ceriodaphnia sp.	Cyclopoid Copepods
Chydorus sp.	*Cyclops bicuspidatus*
Daphnia galeata	Harpacticoid Copepods
Daphnia magna	*Canthocamptus* sp.
Daphnia pulex	
Daphnia similis	Subclass Malacostraca
Moina sp.	Amphipods
Pleuroxus denticulatus	*Hyallela azteca*
Simocephalus sp.	

Phyllum Aschelminthes	
Class Rotifera	

Rotifers
Asplanchna spp.
Brachionus spp.
Filinia spp.
Hexarthra sp.
Keratella spp.
Notholca squamula
Platyias polyacanthus
Synchaeta pectinata

Phyllum Mollusca	
Class Gasteropoda	

Gastropods
Gyraulus sp.
Helisoma sp.
Lymnaea sp.
Physa sp.
Promenetus sp.

Source: Adapted from McCarraher 1977.

McCarraher (1970) conducted ecological studies on the distribution of fairy shrimp from 246 sites in 74 lakes, both temporary and permanent, across the sandhills. He discovered five new records for the state, including *Artemia salina*. The dominant environmental factor in relation to distribution was water mineralization, with sodium and potassium compounds predominating. Water quality data for lakes where *A. salina* has been collected indicate quite high concentrations of carbonate, bicarbonate, hydroxide, and potassium ions, pH ranges of 10.0–10.6, and total dissolved solids between 26,622–135,640 ppm. McCarraher also noted that copepods (*Diaptomus* spp.) and cladocerans (*Bosmina* spp. and *Daphnia* spp.) occurred in most lakes where fairy shrimp were found. Large numbers of fly (*Ephydra*) larvae and adults were also found associated with the alkaline lakes. Earlier work by McCarraher (1959b) reported on the relationship of phyllopods with young northern pike in Cherry County.

Amphibians and Reptiles

The most recent work on the herpetofauna of Nebraska has been conducted by Lynch (1985), who presented an annotated catalogue with distribution maps. Another still useful resource work was compiled by Hudson (1942). Distribution studies of leopard frogs have been conducted by Kruse (1978) and Lynch (1978). Numerous studies on the sandhills lizard populations have been completed by Ballinger et al. (1979), Jones and Droge (1980), Ballinger et al. (1981), Droge et al. (1982), and Ballinger and Jones (1985). The amphibian and reptile species list for the sandhills is presented in Table 12.7, which includes those inhabiting uplands and wetlands.

The tiger salamander is one of the most common amphibians in sandhills wetlands. According to Lynch (1985), this species is widely distributed in the state. McCarraher (1977) has noted that the tiger salamander occurs throughout the sandhills in lakes devoid of fish, where they will dominate the vertebrate fauna. According to Brennan, CLNWR manager (pers. comm.), the bullsnake is a major wetland predator on amphibians, small mammals, and bird nests. Studies conducted at CLNWR have shown that their prey species range from eggs of small shorebirds to young muskrats.

Mammals

An excellent resource work on the distribution and taxonomy of the mammals of Nebraska was compiled by Jones (1964) based upon his research of nearly 18 years. Jones discussed the environment and factors that influence the distribution and speciation of mammals in the state. The taxonomic treatment is detailed and precise. Distribution maps are included for all but the rarest species. Jones also addressed introduced

TABLE 12.7. The amphibians and reptiles of the Nebraska sandhills

Salamanders	Turtles
Ambystoma tigrinum	*Chelydra serpentina*
(Tiger salamander)	(Snapping turtle)
	Chrysemys picta
Frogs and toads	(Painted turtle)
Acris crepitans	*Emydoidea blandingii*
(Northern cricket frog)	(Blanding's turtle)
Bufo cognatus	*Kinosternon flavescens*
(Great Plains toad)	(Yellow mud turtle)
Bufo woodhousii	*Terrapene ornata*
(Rocky Mountain toad)	(Ornate box turtle)
Pseudacris triseriata	*Trionyx spiniferus*
(Western striped chorus frog)	(Spiny softshell)
Rana catesbeiana	
(Bull frog)	Snakes
Rana pipiens	*Coluber constrictor*
(Northern leopard frog)	(Green or blue racer)
Spea bombifrons	*Crotalus viridis*
(Plains spadefoot toad)	(Prairie rattlesnake)
	Heterodon nasicus
Lizards	(Western hognose snake)
Cnemidophorus sexlineatus	*Lampropeltis triangulum*
(Six-lined racerunner)	(Milk snake)
Eumeces multivirgatus	*Nerodia sipedon*
(Many-lined skink)	(Northern watersnake)
Holbrookia maculata	*Pituophis catenifer*
(Lesser earless lizard)	(Bull snake)
Sceloporus undulatus	*Thamnophis radix*
(Northern prairie lizard)	(Plains gartersnake)
	Thamnophis sirtalis
	(Red-sided gartersnake)

Source: Adapted from Lynch 1985.

mammals, species of unverified occurrence within the state, and type localities.

The wildlife resources of Nebraska have been summarized by the Nebraska Game and Parks Commission (1972), emphasizing game species. This inventory discusses major species or species groups, their ranges, distribution, and density. Data are presented in tables, maps, appendices, and narrative.

Wolfe (1984) noted that extensive change occurred in the sandhills after settlement during the mid-1800s. Large ungulate populations declined severely due to their use as survival food by settlers. The American bison was never common in the region and had disappeared totally by the 1880s. Elk were also not abundant, found largely in drainage basins, and they disappeared by the 1860s. Mule deer and white-tailed deer were common, but were hunted out by the early 1900s. Mule deer are found on uplands most often, and white-tail are associated with bottomlands. Deer were completely protected from 1907 to 1945 when limited hunting was allowed, and today deer are common in the region once again. Typically associated with short-grass prairie, pronghorn antelope were not common in the sandhills and were extirpated by the 1900s. According to Wolfe, beginning in the 1930s antelope began recovering in the panhandle region of Nebraska and extended their range into the western sandhills. Also during the period 1958–1962, more than 1,000 pronghorn were transplanted to 20 sites within the sandhills, and since 1964, hunting has been allowed.

Carnivores present include coyote, badger, swift fox, mink, long-tailed weasel, least weasel, striped skunk, and raccoon (Brennan pers. comm.; Wolfe 1984). Wolfe (1984) noted that the badger is a particularly important predator upon the plains pocket gopher, which is quite common throughout the sandhills. A major food source of the coyote is the meadow jumping mouse, which is common around sandhills wetlands. Muskrat is also a preferred food of the coyote according to Fichter et al. (1955) and Sather (1958). Sather (1958) stated that mink is a major predator on muskrat, and he suspected that badger and raccoon also occasionally prey upon them.

Black-tailed prairie dogs are not common in the region due to the sandy soils, although Wolfe (1984) indicated that a recent survey of 7 counties showed approximately 148 dog towns extending over about 1,498 ha. Both the white-tailed and black-tailed jackrabbit occur in the sandhills, and the eastern cottontail is common (USFWS 1981a). Numerous small rodents inhabit the region, including meadow vole, prairie vole, plains pocket gopher, plains pocket mouse, silky pocket mouse, hispid pocket mouse, western harvest mouse, deer mouse, northern grasshopper mouse, and Ord's kangaroo rat (Jones 1964). Table 12.8 presents some of the mammals associated with sandhills wetlands and wet meadows.

TABLE 12.8. Abbreviated list of mammal species associated with sandhills wetlands and wet meadows

Castor canadensis	*Mustela vison*
(Beaver)	(Mink)
Cryptotis parva	*Ondatra zibethica*
(Least shrew)	(Muskrat)
Mephitis mephitis	*Procyon lotor*
(Striped skunk)	(Raccoon)
Microtus ochrogaster	*Reithrodontomys megalotis*
(Prairie vole)	(Western harvest mouse)
Microtus pennsylvanicus	*Sorex cinereus*
(Meadow vole)	(Masked shrew)
Mustela frenata	*Zapus hudsonius*
(Long-tailed weasel)	(Meadow jumping mouse)

Source: Adapted from Jones 1964.

Birds

Several notable species of birds occur on sandhills uplands. The most conspicuous, perhaps, is the long-billed curlew, which is a nesting species in the western half. The curlew is most often seen near wet meadow sites. Two other conspicuous birds are the upland sandpiper and the black-billed magpie. Numerous passerines also utilize the upland prairies, including species of sparrows, larks, and buntings. In my opinion, the three most common passerines throughout the sandhills are the horned lark, western meadowlark, and grasshopper sparrow. In the extreme western part, the lark bunting is frequent. In most wet meadows, the bobolink may be found. Mourning doves are common nesters throughout. Upland game birds include the ring-necked pheasant, greater prairie chicken, and sharp-tailed grouse. Pheasants are found where there is a mix of bottomland vegetation, grassland, and croplands (Wolfe 1984). Greater prairie chickens are associated with wet meadows in the eastern sandhills. The annual harvest of prairie chickens in Nebraska is approximately 23,000 birds (Wolfe 1984). The sharp-tailed grouse is perhaps the most sought-after game bird, with annual harvests ranging between 40,000–70,000 birds (Wolfe 1984). These birds are found primarily on upland sandhills prairie.

The sandhills wetlands are significant areas in Nebraska as well as the northern plains for waterfowl production. Many species are present, but the most numerous primary nesters are the mallard, blue-winged teal, pin-tail, and northern shoveler (Wolfe 1984). The dominant upland nesting duck throughout the sandhills is the blue-winged teal, and one of the most common over-the-water nesters is the ruddy duck (Brennan pers. comm.). The most common nesting ducks at CLNWR are mallard, blue-winged teal, and ruddy duck (USFWS 1981c). The most common nesting ducks at VNWR are blue-winged teal, mallard, and gadwall (USFWS 1981b). The giant Canada goose has been reintroduced into the sandhills and now comprises a breeding population (Wolfe 1984). The trumpeter swan has been reported as a rare nester at VNWR and CLNWR (USFWS 1981b, 1981c).

One of the most important species of midcontinent waterfowl is the mallard. In a recent article about mallards, Gabig (1985) stated that Nebraska generally accounts for approximately 2% of the mallard breeding population in the northern central flyway. Gabig estimated that nearly 40,000 breeding birds utilize Nebraska's wetlands. According to Brennan (pers. comm.), nest success of the mallard in the sandhills averages around 10%. In a three-year study at CLNWR, nest success ranged between 5–10% (Brennan pers. comm.).

Nebraska is an important migratory stopover and wintering ground for many ducks. Mallards comprise about 25% of all ducks that migrate through the state (Gabig 1985). According to Gabig (1985), almost 90% of the ducks, or more than 300,000 individuals, overwintering in Nebraska are mallards, and, of these, nearly 80% are drakes. The annual mallard harvest from 1961 to 1980 averaged 55–56% of the total duck harvest, and drakes comprise approximately 85% of the mallard harvest (Gabig 1985).

Much research effort is concentrated on the mallard currently, and much concern over loss of wetland habitat has been generated. Gabig (1985) pointed out that only 10% of the original wetlands in the Rainwater Basin in southeastern Nebraska remains because this area is intensively farmed. The sandhills wetlands, on the other hand, are relatively secure since the predominant agricultural land-use is cattle ranching, and ranchers realize the importance of wetlands and wet meadows to their economic well-being. Haying and grazing may remove much of the vegetative cover, but improved management practices have allowed the vegetation to remain intact and in good condition over the years. In most cases, wetlands and wet meadows are not extensively grazed since hay is the primary crop removed from these areas.

According to Wolfe (1984), around 80 species of aquatic birds have been reported from the sandhills. The white pelican is a common summer resident and migrant. Larger nesting species include great blue heron, black-crowned night heron, double-crested cormorant, American bittern, willet, killdeer, and Wilson's phalarope. A striking bird of the western sandhills is the American avocet, which utilizes the fauna of the strongly alkaline lakes as a high protein food source for its young (McCarraher 1977). Species that typically nest on mats of floating vegetation or near shoreline include the eared grebe, western grebe, pied-billed grebe, Forster's tern, black tern, American coot, Virginia rail, and sora.

A total of 275 bird species utilize CLNWR in some manner; 93 of these are nesting species (USFWS 1981c; Brennan pers. comm.). VNWR is utilized by 235 species, 95 of which are nesting birds (USFWS 1981b). FNNWR is used by 201 species, 74 of which nest there (USFWS 1975). A list of nesting species that utilize wetlands or wet meadows in these National Wildlife Refuges is presented in Table 12.9.

SANDHILLS WETLANDS OUTLOOK

Sandhills wetlands are important to wildlife, waterfowl, and other aquatic birds, plant life, and people. They offer recreational opportunities, are aesthetically pleasing, and provide water for livestock in some

TABLE 12.9. Nesting bird species associated with wetlands of the National Wildlife Refuges within the Nebraska sandhills

Species	CLNWR[a] Spring	CLNWR[a] Summer	VNWR[b] Spring	VNWR[b] Summer	FNNWR[c] Spring	FNNWR[c] Summer
Eared grebe	c	c	u	c	⋯	⋯
Western grebe	c	c	u	c	⋯	⋯
Pied-billed grebe	c	c	u	c	⋯	⋯
Double-crested cormorant	c	c	u	a	⋯	⋯
Great blue heron	c	u	⋯	⋯	⋯	⋯
Black-crowned night heron	c	c	⋯	o	⋯	⋯
American bittern	c	c	u	c	⋯	⋯
Trumpeter swan	r	r	u	r	⋯	⋯
Canada goose	c	c	u	u	⋯	c
Mallard	a	c	a	a	c	c
Gadwall	c	c	a	c	c	c
Pintail	c	c	c	c	c	u
Green-winged teal	c	u	⋯	⋯	⋯	⋯
Blue-winged teal	a	a	a	a	c	c
Cinnamon teal	r	r	⋯	⋯	⋯	⋯
American wigeon	u	u	c	u	⋯	⋯
Northern shoveler	a	c	a	c	c	c
Wood duck*	r	r	⋯	⋯	⋯	⋯
Redhead	c	u	c	u	c	u
Canvasback	c	u	c	o	⋯	⋯
Lesser scaup	c	u	⋯	⋯	⋯	⋯
Ruddy duck	c	c	c	c	⋯	⋯
Northern harrier	c	u	u	u	⋯	⋯
Greater prairie chicken	⋯	⋯	u	u	u	u
Virginia rail	c	⋯	c	c	⋯	⋯

Source: U.S. Fish and Wildlife Service 1975, 1981b, 1981c.
Notes: Breeding season abundance is noted by a (abundant), c (common), u (uncommon), r (rare), o (occasional). An asterisk (*) indicates a suspected, but not yet documented, nester.
[a]Crescent Lake National Wildlife Refuge, Garden County.
[b]Valentine National Wildlife Refuge, Cherry County.
[c]Ft. Niobrara National Wildlife Refuge, Cherry County. Only a small percent of the refuge is wetland, thus few birds associated with wetlands are present.
[d]Documented for the first time in Nebraska in 1985 at CLNWR (Brennan, pers. comm.).

TABLE 12.9. *(continued)*

Species	CLNWR[a]		VNWR[b]		FNNWR[c]	
	Spring	Summer	Spring	Summer	Spring	Summer
Sora	c	c	c	c	..	..
American coot	c	c	a	a	..	..
Killdeer	a	c	c	c	c	c
Common snipe	u	r	..	..	..	..
Long-billed curlew	c	c	..	..	c	c
Upland sandpiper	c	c	c	c	c	c
Spotted sandpiper	u	u	..	..	..	..
Willet	u	u	u	u	..	..
American avocet	c	c	r	r	..	..
Black-necked stilt[d]	r	r	..	..	..	..
Wilson's phalarope	a	c	a	c	..	..
Forster's tern	c	c	c	c	..	..
Black tern	c	c	a	a	..	..
Franklin's gull	u	u	..	..	..	..
Belted kingfisher	..	..	o	o	u	u
Tree swallow	r	r	o	o	u	..
Rough-winged swallow*	u	u	..	..	..	..
Barn swallow	a	a	a	a	c	c
Cliff swallow	u	r	..	..	c	c
Marsh wren	a	a	a	a	..	..
Bell's vireo	r	r	o	o	..	..
Yellow warbler	u	u	c	c	c	c
Common yellowthroat	a	a	o	o	c	c
Bobolink	c	c	o	o	..	..
Eastern meadowlark	c	c	c	c	u	u
Yellow-headed blackbird	a	a	c	c	..	u
Red-winged blackbird	a	a	a	a	c	c
Swamp sparrow	u	u	..	o	c	..
Song sparrow	..	..	o	o	..	..

375

areas. The wet meadow is the single most important wetland in the sandhills, however, as an economic resource to local ranchers. Native hay harvested from wet meadows provides important winter forage for livestock and is sometimes sold as a cash crop (Nebr. NRC 1984). Ehlers et al. (1952) stated that an individual ranch's efficiency is determined by the ratio of summer grazing to winter forage. Brouse and Burzlaff (1968) pointed out that many ranchers scale the size of their herd to available winter hay supply.

Ironically, the wetland most threatened by drainage or development is the wet meadow (Christian 1983; Nebr. NRC 1984). Increased center-pivot irrigation development is a major source of concern, especially in the eastern sandhills. Some pivots are placed in the meadows themselves; however, most concern is directed toward possible wet meadow loss due to lowering of the water table, which would then affect the productivity of the meadows (Novacek 1986). Christian (1982) stated that the wet meadows in Dundy County in the southwestern Nebraska sand plains have been almost completely eliminated due to center-pivot development. Water level declines and irrigation impacts are important issues in the state, and work is underway assessing the situation (Nebr. NRC 1981, 1984). Other work directed toward this includes Lawson et al. (1985), Hoesel (1973), Huntoon (1974), Heimes and Luckey (1980).

Christian (1982) attempted to monitor wet meadow loss utilizing remote sensing techniques. He found Landsat MSS data too general since resolution is not fine enough to accurately assess vegetational community borders. In addition, since Landsat passes over a given area every 18 days and there is no guarantee of cloud-free days, the system is temporally unreliable. Christian suggested that aerial color-infrared photography could be a viable alternative for monitoring large areas. Flights can be scheduled around inclement weather and can coincide with field work. There are still some problems, however, since range conditions vary across the region, haying times differ, climatic factors vary, and the water table fluctuates.

Within the sandhills it is typical to see a recovery of the water table in the fall after the heavy irrigation season (Johnson and Pederson 1984). This is not the case in the sand plains region adjacent to the eastern sandhills in Holt County. According to Johnson and Pederson (1984), in 1966 when measurement of the water-table level began, the estimated preirrigation development water-table level near O'Neill was 10.7 m below the land surface. By 1982 the water table had declined to its lowest recorded depth, almost 16.5 m below the surface. In 1983 a slow rise in water-table levels began and continued to rise slightly until the summer of 1985. By the fall of 1985, water-level declines of 1.5 m or more from estimated predevelopment levels were recorded in a total area of about 15,200 ha (Ellis and Pederson 1986). Other nearby locales had experienced a 1.5–4.8 m fall in the water table, with the largest decline, 6.5 m, occurring northwest of O'Neill (Ellis and Pederson 1986). The reported net water-level change for 1985 in the O'Neill area since 1966 was approximately −3.0 m (Ellis and Pederson 1986). Johnson and Pederson (1984) stated that in most years of normal or below-normal precipitation, groundwater withdrawals for irrigation purposes is heavy enough in the O'Neill area to cause net water-level declines. In years with above-normal precipitation and below-normal irrigation pumpage, greater groundwater recharge may occur, but not, however, to the point of returning to predevelopment levels.

There is concern that the same type of water-level declines may occur in the eastern sandhills. If the water table were to permanently decline under wet meadows, it is suspected that hay yields would be affected. Most likely, yields would be drastically reduced causing severe economic hardships to area ranchers who depend upon this hay for winter feed. An intensive investigation of the relationship between wet meadow species net primary productivity and depth to the water table and other microclimatic factors is currently underway in the eastern sandhills in Wheeler County by the author. It is anticipated that a model to predict the direction of future changes in productivity in response to changes in the water table can be developed. The data generated will provide useful input to water policy decision-making processes in the state of Nebraska.

The sandhills of Nebraska remain a relatively unknown region scientifically. The biology and ecology of sandhills wetlands have been little studied, and much research in these areas is needed. The major thrust of current study is toward water resources usage and management. As Winter (Chap. 2) and LaBaugh (1986) have pointed out, it is important to establish and monitor long-term research sites to intensively investigate wetlands of the northern prairie region. Winter has suggested that type localities be designated, and all aspects of these sites be studied. Since the hydrology is beginning to be understood and the instrumentation is in place, in addition to ongoing remote sensing research by the University of Nebraska-Lincoln, CLNWR is an excellent site for a type locality within the closed basins region. In the central sandhills, VNWR would be a representative site, and another long-term research site should be established in the eastern sandhills, possibly in Wheeler or Garfield County. Such intensive, multidisciplinary studies across an east-west transect within the sandhills would be extremely valuable for all aspects of wetland and water resource issues.

ACKNOWLEDGMENTS

I would like to thank the many people who contributed information, observations, and other important input to the preparation of this
review. Thanks goes especially to Kevin Brennan, refuge manager of
CLNWR; Donald Rundquist, UNL Remote Sensing Center; and Donald
Farrar, Department of Botany at Iowa State University. I am indebted to
the Nebraska Natural Resources Commission and to the Center for
Rural Affairs Small Farm Resources Project for funding my research on
eastern sandhills wet meadows. I am deeply grateful to my husband,
Wayne Thunker, for his patience and support during the preparation of
this manuscript. My warmest thanks goes to all of the friendly and
cooperative sandhillers who have allowed me access to their land.

REFERENCES

Adelman, D. D., W. J. Schroeder, R. J. Smaus, and G. P. Wallin. 1985. Over-
view of nitrate in Nebraska's ground water. Trans. Nebr. Acad. Sci. 13:75–
81.
Ahlbrandt, T. S., and S. G. Fryberger. 1980. Eolian deposits in the Nebraska
Sandhills. U.S. Geol. Surv. Prof. Paper 1120:1–24.
_____. 1981. Sedimentary features and significance of interdune deposits. Soc.
Econ. Paleontol. Mineral. Spec. Publ. No. 31:292–314.
Ahlbrandt, T. S., J. B. Swinehart, and D. G. Maroney. 1983. The dynamic
Holocene dune fields of the Great Plains and Rocky Mountain Basins,
U.S.A. In Eolian sediments and processes, ed. M. E. Brookfield and T. S.
Ahlbrandt, 379–406. Amsterdam: Elsevier.
Anderson, E. N., and E. R. Walker. 1920. An ecological study of the algae of
some Sandhills lakes. Amer. Microsc. Soc. Trans. 39:51–85.
Ballinger, R. E., and S. M. Jones. 1985. Ecological disturbance in a Sandhills
prairie: Impact and importance to the lizard community on Arapaho Prairie
in western Nebraska. Prairie Nat. 17(2):91–100.
Ballinger, R. E., J. D. Lynch, and P. H. Cole. 1979. Disturbance and natural
history of amphibians and reptiles in western Nebraska with ecological
notes on the herpetiles of Arapaho Prairie. Prairie Nat. 11:65–74.
Ballinger, R. E., D. L. Droge, and S. M. Jones. 1981. Reproduction in a Nebraska Sandhills population of the northern prairie lizard *Sceloporus undulatus garmani*. Amer. Midl. Nat. 106:157–64.
Barnes, P. W., and A. T. Harrison. 1982. Species distribution and community
organization in a Nebraska Sandhills mixed prairie as influenced by plant/
soil-water relationships. Oecologia 52:192–201.
Barnes, P. W., A. T. Harrison, and S. P. Heinisch. 1984. Vegetation patterns in
relation to topography and edaphic variation in Nebraska Sandhills prairie.
Prairie Nat. 16(4):145–58.
Bennet, G. W., and H. Pedley. 1931. Report on investigations in the Cherry
County lakes. Lincoln, Nebr.: Game, For. Parks Comm.

Boettcher, M. 1984. National Wetland Inventory in Nebraska Sandhills. Remote Sensing Cen. Map Inform. Cen. Newsl. Lincoln: Conserv. Surv. Div., Univ. Nebr.

Bouc, K. 1987. The fish book. NEBRASKAland 65(1):1–132.

Bradley, E., and F. H. Rainwater. 1956. Geology and groundwater resources of the upper Niobrara River basin, Nebraska and Wyoming. U.S. Geol. Surv. Water Supply Paper 1368:1–70.

Brennan, K. J. 1985. Letter to author from Crescent Lake National Wildlife Refuge manager, Ellsworth, Nebraska.

Brouse, E. M., and D. F. Burzlaff. 1968. Fertilizers and legumes on subirrigated meadows. Univ. Nebr. Agric. Exp. Stn. Bull. 501.

Buckwalter, D. W. 1983. Monitoring Nebraska's Sandhills lakes. Conserv. Surv. Div. Resour. Rep. No. 10. Lincoln: Univ. Nebr.

Burzlaff, D. F. 1962. A soil and vegetation inventory and analysis of three Nebraska Sandhills range sites. Univ. Nebr. Agric. Exp. Stn. Res. Bull. 206.

Christian, D. R., Jr. 1982. Monitoring subirrigated meadow loss in the Nebraska Sandhills using remote sensing techniques and theory. Univ. Nebr.-Omaha Remote Sensing Appl. Lab. Unpublished Res. Rep.

Churchill, S. P. 1976. Contributions toward a moss flora of Nebraska. Bryologist 79:241–42.

_____. 1977. Contributions toward a moss flora of Nebraska II. Bryologist 80:160–62.

_____. 1982. Mosses of the Great Plains. VI: The Niobrara Basin of Nebraska. Trans. Kans. Acad. Sci. 85:1–12.

_____. 1985. Mosses of the Great Plains. X: The Niobrara Valley Preserve and adjacent areas in Nebraska. Trans. Nebr. Acad. Sci. 13:13–19.

Churchill, S. P., and P. L. Redfearn, Jr. 1977. The Hepaticae and Anthrocerotae of Nebraska. Bryologist 80:640–45.

Conservation and Survey Division. 1980. Configuration of the water table, Nebraska – spring 1979 (map). Lincoln: Univ. Nebr.

Cowardin, L. M., V. Carter, F. C. Golet, and E. T. LaRoe. 1979. Classification of wetlands and deepwater habitats of the United States. U.S. Fish and Wildl. Serv., Biol. Serv. Prog. FWS/OBS-79/31.

Daily, F. K. 1944. The Characeae of Nebraska. Butler Univ. Bot. Stud. 6:149–71.

Daily, F. K., and W. Kiener. 1956. The Characeae of Nebraska – additions and changes. Butler Univ. Bot. Stud. 13(1):36–46.

Diffendal, R. F., Jr., P. K. Pabian, and J. R. Thomasson. 1982. Geologic history of Ash Hollow Park, Nebraska. Conserv. Surv. Div. Educ. Circ. 5.

Dreeszen, V. H. 1984. Overview of Nebraska and the Sandhills. In The Sandhills of Nebraska – yesterday, today and tomorrow, 1–15. Nebr. Water Resour. Cent. 1984 Water Resour. Sem. Ser. Lincoln: Univ. Nebr.

Droge, D. L., S. M. Jones, and R. E. Ballinger. 1982. Reproduction of Holbrookia maculata in western Nebraska. Copeia 1982:356–62.

Dugan, J. T. 1984. Hydrologic characteristics of Nebraska soils. U.S. Geol. Surv. Water Supply Paper 2222.

Ehlers, P. G., G. Viehmeyer, R. Ramig, and E. M. Brouse. 1952. Fertilization and improvement of native subirrigated meadows in Nebraska. Univ. Nebr. Agric. Exp. Stn. Circ. 92.

Ellis, M. J., and D. T. Pederson. 1986. Groundwater levels in Nebraska, 1985. Conserv. Surv. Div. Water Surv. Paper 61. Lincoln: Univ. Nebr.

Engberg, R. A. 1967. The nitrate hazard in well water, with special reference to Holt County, Nebraska. Conserv. Surv. Div. Water Surv. Paper 21. Lincoln: Univ. Nebr.

Engberg, R. A., and R. F. Spalding. 1978. Groundwater quality atlas of Nebraska. Conserv. Surv. Div. Resour. Atlas No. 3. Lincoln: Univ. Nebr.

Fichter, E. H., G. Schildman, and J. H. Sather. 1955. Some feeding patterns of coyotes in Nebraska. Ecol. Monogr. 25:1–37.

Frolik, A. L., and F. D. Keim. 1933. Native vegetation in the prairie hay district of north-central Nebraska. Ecol. 14(3):298–305.

Gabig, P. J. 1985. Mallards—past and prospects. NEBRASKAland 63(10):18–33.

Gibson, J. C. 1976. Diatoms in Nebraska's Sandhills lakes. Crescent Lake Nat. Wildl. Refuge Unpubl. Res. Rep.

Gilbert, M. C. 1980. A technique for evaluating Nebraska Sandhills wetlands. Master's thesis, Univ. Nebr., Omaha.

Gilbert, M. C., M. W. Freel, and A. J. Bieber. 1980. Remote sensing and field evaluation of wetlands in the Sandhills of Nebraska. U.S. Army Corps of Eng., Omaha Div. Unpubl. Rep.

Ginsberg, M. H. 1984. Physical characteristics of the Sandhills: Hydrology. In The Sandhills of Nebraska—yesterday, today and tomorrow, 37–43. Nebr. Water Resour. Cent. 1984 Water Resour. Sem. Ser. Lincoln: Univ. Nebr.

_____. 1985. Nebraska's Sandhills lakes: a hydrogeologic overview. Water Resour. Bull. 21:573–78.

Hall, F. R. 1976. Relationships between small water bodies and groundwater. In Advances in groundwater hydrology, ed. Z. A. Saleem, 248–61. Amer. Water Resour. Assoc.

Harrison, A. T. n.d. Measurement of actual transpiration of native grass stands as a component of Nebraska Sandhills groundwater hydrology. Nebr. Water Resour. Cent. Proj. Completion Rep. A-066-NEB. Lincoln: Univ. Nebr.

Heimes, F. J., and R. R. Luckey. 1980. Evaluating methods for determining water use in the High Plains in parts of Colorado, Kansas, Nebraska, New Mexico, Oklahoma, South Dakota, Texas and Wyoming. U.S. Geol. Surv. Water Resour. Invest., Denver.

Hergert, G. W. 1978. Nitrogen losses from sprinkler-applied nitrogen fertilizer. Nebraska Water Resour. Cent. Proj. Completion Rep. A-045-NEB. Lincoln: Univ. Nebr.

_____. 1983. Distribution of mineral nitrogen under native range and cultivated fields in the Nebraska Sandhills. Sandhills Agric. Lab., North Platte Stn., 8th Progr. Rep., 1982–1983. Lincoln: Univ. Nebr.

_____. 1984. Possible changes in the Sandhills: Ground and surface water quality and other environmental impacts. In The Sandhills of Nebraska—yesterday, today and tomorrow, 121–27. Nebr. Water Resour. Cent. 1984 Water Resour. Sem. Ser. Lincoln: Univ. Nebr.

Hergert, G. W., and J. W. Goeke. 1981. Distribution of mineral nitrogen under native range and cultivated fields in the Nebraska Sandhills. Sandhills Agric. Lab., North Platte Stn., 7th Progr. Rep. 1980–1981. Lincoln: Univ. Nebr.

Hoesel, S. F. 1973. The impact of center-pivot irrigation on the Sandhills of Nebraska: Brown County, a case study. Master's thesis, Univ. Nebr., Omaha.

Holland, R. S. 1980. Carotenoid pigmentation of two calanoid copepods from

Goose Lake, Nebraska. Master's thesis, Univ. Nebr., Lincoln.

Hudson, G. E. 1942. The amphibians and reptiles of Nebraska. Conserv. Surv. Div. Conserv. Bull. 24.

Huntoon, P. W. 1974. Predicted water level declines for alternative groundwater developments in the Upper Big Blue River Basin, Nebraska. Conserv. Surv. Div. Resour. Rep. No. 6. Lincoln: Univ. Nebr.

Institute of Agriculture and Natural Resources (IANR) Task Force. 1983. IANR Task Force Report. Lincoln: Univ. Nebr.

Johnson, M. S., and D. T. Pederson. 1984. Groundwater levels in Nebraska: 1983. Conserv. Surv. Div. Water Surv. Paper No. 57. Lincoln: Univ. Nebr.

Jones, J. K., Jr. 1964. Distribution and taxonomy of mammals of Nebraska. Univ. Kans. Publ., Mus. Nat. Hist. 16(1):1–356.

Jones, S. M., and D. L. Droge. 1980. Home range size and spatial distribution of two sympatric lizard species (*Sceleropus undulatus, Holbrookia maculata*) in the Sandhills of Nebraska. Herpetol. 36:127–32.

Junk, G. A., R. F. Spalding, and J. J. Richard. 1980. Areal, vertical and temporal differences in groundwater chemistry. II: Organic constituents. J. Environ. Qual. 9(3):479–83.

Keech, C. F., and R. Bentall. 1971. Dunes on the plains: The Sandhills region of Nebraska. Conserv. Surv. Div. Resour. Rep. No. 4. Lincoln: Univ. Nebr.

Kiener, W. 1944. Notes on the distribution and bio-ecology of the Characeae in Nebraska. Butler Univ. Bot. Stud. 6:131–48.

Koch, R. G. 1971. The Pottiaceae of Nebraska. Bryologist 74:206–7.

Kolstad, O. A. 1966. The genus *Carex* of the High Plains and associated woodlands in Kansas, Nebraska, South and North Dakota. Ph.D. diss., Univ. Kans., Lawrence.

Kruse, K. C. 1978. Causal factors limiting the distribution of leopard frogs in eastern Nebraska. Ph.D. diss., Univ. Nebr., Lincoln.

LaBaugh, J. W. 1986. Wetland ecosystem studies from a hydrologic perspective. Water Resour. Bull. 22(1):1–10.

Lawson, M. P., D. C. Rundquist, R. C. Balling, Jr., R. S. Cerveny, and L. P. Queen. 1985. Variability in the surface area of Sandhills lakes and its relationship to precipitation and groundwater level. Dept. Geogr. Occas. Papers No. 7. Lincoln: Univ. Nebr.

Lawton, D. R. 1984. Physical characteristics of the Sandhills: Groundwater hydrogeology and stream hydrology. *In* The Sandhills of Nebraska—yesterday, today and tomorrow, 44–55. Nebr. Water Resour. Cent. 1984 Water Resour. Sem. Ser. Lincoln: Univ. Nebr.

————. 1986. Hydrogeology of water-quality monitoring transects in an irrigated area of the eastern Sandhills, Nebraska. Conserv. Surv. Div. Water Surv. Paper No. 60. Lincoln: Univ. Nebr.

Lewis, D. T. 1984. Characteristics of the soils in the Sandhills region of Nebraska. *In* The Sandhills of Nebraska—Yesterday, today and tomorrow, 62–73. Lincoln: Nebr. Water Resour. Center.

Linden, J. S. 1984. A remote sensing analysis of selected wetlands within the Nebraska Sandhills region. Master's thesis, Univ. Nebr., Omaha.

Lindstrom, L. E. 1968. The aquatic and marsh plants of the Great Plains of central North America. Ph.D. diss., Kans. State Univ., Manhattan.

Lugn, A. L. 1935. The Pleistocene geology of Nebraska. Nebr. Geol. Surv. Bull. 10, 2d Ser.

Lynch, J. D. 1978. The distribution of leopard frogs (*Rana blairi and Rana pipiens*) in Nebraska. J. Herpetol. 12:157–62.

_____. 1985. Annotated checklist of the amphibians and reptiles of Nebraska. Trans. Nebr. Acad. Sci. 13:33–57.

Mahoney, D. L. 1977. Species richness and diversity of aquatic vascular plants in Nebraska with special reference to water chemistry parameters. Master's thesis, Univ. Nebr., Lincoln.

Martin, D. L. 1984. Possible changes in the Sandhills: Ground and surface water quality and other environmental impacts. *In* The Sandhills of Nebraska — yesterday, today and tomorrow, 109–20. Nebr. Water Resour. Cent. 1984 Water Resour. Sem. Ser. Lincoln: Univ. Nebr.

McAtee, W. L. 1941. Wild duck foods of the Sandhills region of Nebraska. USDA Bull. No. 794. Washington, D.C.: GPO.

McCarraher, D. B. 1959a. Limnology of sulfate-bicarbonate lakes in Nebraska. Nebr. Game, For. Parks Comm. Unpubl. Abstr. Lincoln.

_____. 1959b. Phyllopod shrimp populations of the Big Alkalai Lake drainage, Nebraska, and their relationship to young pike (*Esox lucius*). Amer. Midl. Nat. 61(2):509–10.

_____. 1959c. The northern pike-bluegill combination in north-central Nebraska farm ponds. Prog. Fish. Cult. 21(4):188–89.

_____. 1960a. Sandhills Lake Survey. Nebr. Game, For. Parks Comm., Job Completion Report. Lincoln.

_____. 1960b. Pike hybrids (*Esox lucius* x *Esox vermiculatus*) in a Sandhills lake, Nebraska. Trans. Amer. Fish. Soc. 89(1):82–83.

_____. 1962. Northern pike (*Esox lucius*) in alkaline lakes of Nebraska. Trans. Amer. Fish. Soc. 91(3):326–29.

_____. 1969. The Nebraska Sandhills lakes: Their characteristics and fisheries management problems. Nebr. Game, For. Parks Comm. Unpubl. Rep. Lincoln.

_____. 1970. Some ecological relations of fairy shrimp in alkaline habitats of Nebraska. Amer. Midl. Nat. 84(1):59–68.

_____. 1971. Survival of some freshwater fishes in the alkaline eutrophic waters of Nebraska. J. Fish. Res. Board Can. 28:1811–14.

_____. 1972a. A preliminary bibliography and lake index of inland mineral waters of the world. U.N. Fish. Circ. 146. Rome: FAO.

_____. 1972b. The small playa lakes of Nebraska: Their ecology, fisheries and biological potential. Playa Lakes Symp. Trans. Internat. Cent. for Arid and Semi-Arid Land Stud. Lubbock: Texas Tech. Univ.

_____. 1977. Nebraska's Sandhill lakes. Nebr. Game Parks Comm. Lincoln.

McCarraher, D. B., and R. W. Gregory. 1970. The current status and distribution of Sacremento perch, *Archoplites interruptus,* in North America. Trans. Amer. Fish. Soc. 99:700–07.

McCarraher, D. B., and R. E. Thomas. 1968. Some ecological observations on the fathead minnow, *Pimephales promelas,* in the alkaline waters of Nebraska. Trans. Amer. Fish. Soc. 97(1):52–55.

_____. 1972. Ecological significance of vegetation to northern pike, *Esox lucius,* spawning. Trans. Amer. Fish. Soc. 101(3):560–63.

McMurtrey, M. D., R. Craig, and G. Schildman. 1972. Survey of habitat. Nebr. Wetlands Surv. Lincoln: Nebr. Game Parks Comm.

Moore, A. W., and H. F. Rhoades. 1966. Soil conditions and root distribution in two wet meadows of the Nebraska Sandhills. Agron. J. 58:563–66.

Morris, J., L. Morris, and L. Witt. 1972. The fishes of Nebraska. Lincoln: Nebr. Game Parks Comm.

Murray, G. L. 1986. Center-pivot irrigation systems in Nebraska, 1985 (map). Lincoln: Remote Sensing Cent., Conserv. Surv. Div., Univ. Nebr.

Nash, K. G. 1978. Geochemistry of selected closed basin lakes in Sheridan County, Nebraska. Master's thesis, Univ. Nebr., Lincoln.

Nebraska Game and Parks Commission. 1972. The Nebraska fish and wildlife plan: Vol. I: Nebraska wildlife resources inventory. Lincoln, Nebr.: Nebr. Game Parks Commission.

Nebraska Natural Resources Commission (NRC). 1981. Sandhills area study decision document. State Water Plan. Rev. Process. Lincoln.

———. 1984. Progress report on the Sandhills area study. State Water Plan. Rev. Process. Lincoln.

Novacek, J. M. 1986. Native hay production along a depth to water table gradient in eastern Sandhills wet meadows, Wheeler county, Nebraska. Nebr. Nat. Resour. Comm. 1985 Final Rep. Lincoln.

Petrick-Ott, A. J. 1975. A county checklist of the ferns and fern allies of Kansas, Nebraska, South Dakota and North Dakota. Rhodora 77:478–511.

Pool, R. J. 1914. A study of the vegetation of the Sand Hills of Nebraska. Univ. Minn. Bot. Stud. 4(3):190–312.

Queen, L. P. 1984. The NASA "TIMS" activity in Nebraska. Remote Sensing Cent. Map Inform. Cen. Newsl. Lincoln: Conserv. Surv. Div. Univ. Nebr.

Queen, L. P., D. C. Rundquist, P. J. Budde, and M. S. Kuzila. 1984. A TIMS thermal-infrared analysis of selected landscape parameters: The Nebraska Sandhills. Proc. Internat. Symp. Remote Sensing Environ. Environ. Res. Inst. Mich.

Reed, E. C., and V. H. Dreeszen. 1965. Revision of the classification of the Pleistocene deposits of Nebraska. Nebr. Geol. Surv. Bull. 23.

Rundquist, D. C. 1983. Wetland inventories of Nebraska's Sandhills. Nebr. Remote Sensing Cent. Conserv. Surv. Div. Resour. Rep. No. 9. Lincoln: Univ. Nebr.

Rundquist, D. C., and J. S. Linden. 1979. Toward a digital classification of wetlands in the Nebraska Sandhills region: A test of Landsat MSS data. Final report. New York: Charles A. Lindbergh Fund, Inc.

Rundquist, D. C., S. A. Samson, and D. E. Bussom. 1981. Wetland atlas of the Omaha District, Missouri River District. U.S. Army Corps of Engineers Contract No. DACW-80-C-0220.

Rundquist, D. C., G. L. Murray, and L. P. Queen. 1985. Airborne thermal mapping of a "flow-through" lake in the Nebraska Sandhills. Water Resour. Bull. 21(6):989–94.

Rundquist, D. C., J. R. Jensen, and L. P. Queen. (In press) Comparative infrared signatures from inland wetland canopies. Paper presented at the Annu. Meet. Assoc. Amer. Geogr., Detroit, Mich., April, 1985.

Rydberg, P. A. 1895. Flora of the Sand Hills of Nebraska. Contrib. U.S. Nat. Herb. 3(3):133–203.

Sather, J. H. 1958. Biology of the Great Plains muskrat in Nebraska. Wildl. Monogr. No. 2.

Schnagl, J. A. 1980. Seasonal variations in water chemistry and primary productivity in four alkaline lakes in the Sandhills of western Nebraska. Master's thesis, Univ. Nebr., Lincoln.

Seevers, P. M., R. M. Peterson, D. J. Mahoney, D. G. Maroney, and D. C. Rundquist. 1975. An inventory of Nebraska wetlands with the use of imagery from the Earth Resources Technology Satellite. Proc. 4th Annu. Remote Sensing of Earth Resour. Conf., Univ. Tenn. Space Inst.

Shoenecker, W. 1971. Management of winterkill lakes in the Sandhills region of Nebraska. Symp. Manage. Winterkill Lakes, North-Central Div. Amer. Fish. Soc. Misc. Publ.

Smith, H. T. U. 1965. Dune morphology and chronology in central and western Nebraska. J. Geol. 73(4):557–78.

Spalding, R. F., and M. E. Exner. 1980. Areal, vertical and temporal differences in groundwater chemistry. I: Inorganic constituents. J. Environ. Qual. 9(3):466–79.

Spessard, L. L. 1982. A bryological survey of north-central Nebraska. Trans. Nebr. Acad. Sci. 10:17–20.

Swinehart, J. B. 1984. Physical characteristics of the Sandhills: Geology. *In* The Sandhills of Nebraska — yesterday, today and tomorrow, 32–36. Nebr. Water Resour. Cent. 1984 Water Resour. Sem. Ser. Lincoln: Univ. Nebr.

Tolstead, W. L. 1942. Vegetation of the northern part of Cherry County, Nebraska. Ecol. Monogr. 12(3):255–92.

Turner, J. K., and D. C. Rundquist. 1980. Wetlands inventory of the Omaha District, Missouri River District. U.S. Army Corps of Engineers Contract No. DACW-45-79-C-0019.

United States Department of Interior. 1955a. Wetlands inventory of Nebraska. U.S. Fish and Wildl. Serv., Office River Basin Stud. Billings, Mont.

———. 1955b. Permanent water inventory of Nebraska. U.S. Fish and Wildl. Serv., Office of River Basin Stud. Billings, Mont.

United States Fish and Wildlife Service. 1975. Birds of Fort Niobrara National Wildlife Refuge. Washington, D.C.: Dept. Inter./GPO.

———. 1981a. Crescent Lake. Washington, D.C.: Dept. Inter./GPO.

———. 1981b. Birds of Valentine National Wildlife Refuge. Washington, D.C.: Dept. Inter./GPO.

———. 1981c. Birds of Crescent Lake National Wildlife Refuge. Washington, D.C.: Dept. Inter./GPO.

Warren, A. 1976. Morphology and sediments of the Nebraska Sandhills in relation to Pleistocene winds and the development of aeolian bedforms. J. Geol. 84:685–700.

Watts, D. G. 1977. Nitrogen loss from soil and its relationship to irrigation management. Nebr. Water Resour. Cent. Completion Rep. Proj. B-024-NEB. Lincoln: Univ. Nebr.

Webber, H. J. 1889. The flora of central Nebraska. Amer. Nat. 23:633–36.

———. 1890. The flora of central Nebraska. Amer. Nat. 24:76–78.

Wolfe, C. 1984. Physical characteristics of the Sandhills: Wetlands, fisheries and wildlife. *In* The Sandhills of Nebraska — yesterday, today and tomorrow, 54–61. Nebr. Water Resour. Cent. 1984 Water Resour. Sem. Ser. Lincoln: Univ. Nebr.

INDEX

This index covers material cited in the text, the tables, and the figures of *Northern Prairie Wetlands.* Text material is cited in roman type. Tabular material is cited in **boldface** type. Material appearing in figures is cited in *italics.*

Actitis macularia, **374–75**
Aechmophorus occidentalis, 373, **374–75**
Agalinis tenuifolia, **365**
Agelaius phoenicius, **374–75**
Agricultural disturbances, 30, 157–62; and the composition of aquatic beds and floating vegetation, **151**; and the composition of emergent vegetation, **148**, **149**; and waterfowl populations, 222–23, 257–58. *See also* Burning; Drainage; Grazing; Sediment
Agricultural management practices to reduce erosion and runoff, 103, 106
Agricultural runoff. *See* Surface runoff
Agropyron intermedium, 254
Agropyron repens, **148**
Agropyron smithii, 254
Agrostis stolonifera, **154–55**, **365**
Aix sponsa, 207, **374–75**
Alberta, southern: duck populations, 216, **217**, 218, 219, **219**, **220**; fur harvest, **293**
Alces alces, 270, 324
Algae: blooms, 81, 194, 196, 197, 310, 363, 367; community structure, 189–92; and dissolved nutrients, 81; grazing by invertebrates, 327; population dynamics, 195–98;

populations and vegetation cycles, 194–95; primary production, 193–96, **194**, **320**, **321**, **331**; species of Nebraska sandhills, 363, 366–67
Alisma gramineum, **146**, **156–57**
Alisma plantago-aquatica, **146**, **156–57**, **365**
Alopecurus aequalis, **146**, **156–57**
Aluminum, leaching from litter, 323
Ambystoma tigrinum. See Tiger salamander
American avocet, 373, **374–75**
American bison, 370
American bittern, 373, **374–75**
American coot, 373, **374–75**; and algae, 328; predation, 256, 289
American crow, 255
American white pelican, 373
American wigeon, 206, 211, **211**, 212, **212**, 213, *213*, **215**, 216, 217, 221, 223, **233**, 239–40, 244, 248, **250**, 251, **253**, **374–75**
Ammodramus savannarum, 372
Ammonia, 108, 111–12, 310; in rivers and streams, **100**; in sediments and surface water, 113–14; in subsurface drainage, **99**; in surface runoff, **97–98**; volatilization, 111, 122
Amorpha fruticosa, 366